More than a dozen pretenders appeared in Russia in the early seventeenth century, during the period of civil strife and foreign invasion known as the Time of Troubles. The most successful of these was the First False Dimitry, who occupied the throne in 1605–6; he was followed by Second and Third False Dimitrys and by various other impostors.

Maureen Perrie traces the careers of these pretenders and offers explanations of their success. She argues that support for the false tsars and tsareviches was influenced not only by the ingenious tales they told to justify their claims, but also by religious-miraculous notions of Christ-like rulers risen from the dead, and by 'popular monarchist' views of the true tsar as the scourge of the boyars. Her conclusion draws comparisons and contrasts between the Russian pretenders and royal impostors who appeared elsewhere in early modern Europe.

Pretenders and popular monarchism
in early modern Russia

Pretenders and popular monarchism in early modern Russia

The false tsars of the Time of Troubles

Maureen Perrie

Centre for Russian and East European Studies
University of Birmingham

CAMBRIDGE
UNIVERSITY PRESS

Published by the Press Syndicate of the University of Cambridge
The Pitt Building, Trumpington Street, Cambridge CB2 1RP
40 West 20th Street, New York, NY 10011-4211, USA
10 Stamford Road, Oakleigh, Melbourne 3166, Australia

First published 1995

Printed in Great Britain at the University Press, Cambridge

A catalogue record for this book is available from the British Library

Library of Congress cataloguing in publication data

Perrie, Maureen, 1946–
    Pretenders and popular monarchism in early modern Russia: the false tsars of
the Time of Troubles/Maureen Perrie
        p.   cm.
    Includes bibliographical references.
    ISBN 0 521 47274 1
    1. Russia – History – Time of Troubles, 1598–1613. 2. Russia – Kings and
rulers – Succession. I. Title.
DK111.P36 1995
947′.045 – dc20 94-48442 CIP

ISBN 0 521 47274 1 hardback

wv

Contents

Illustrations

Preface

My interest in the pretenders of the Time of Troubles dates back more than twenty years, although my work on the topic has been somewhat intermittent. My approach to the subject has undergone considerable modification over the course of time. In the 1970s, inspired by notions of pretenders as 'social bandits' and their followers as 'primitive rebels', I was drawn to the Time of Troubles by Soviet works that depicted the period as a 'peasant war' whose participants were guided by 'popular socio-utopian legends about returning royal deliverers'. Preliminary research, however, indicated that these concepts could not be supported by the evidence. Discouraged, I moved off to work in other fields, returning to the Time of Troubles only when my study of the folklore about Ivan the Terrible suggested potentially more fruitful approaches to pretence. The thinking behind the present volume has been influenced by semiotic interpretations of cultural history, by the concept of *mentalité*, and by studies of symbolism and ritual in popular culture – although an inherent tendency to scepticism and empiricism has, I hope, saved me from some of the more self-indulgent excesses of 'theory'.

Over the years in which this book has been in the making I have accumulated a number of debts. Some of the material was first presented to seminars at the universities of Birmingham, East Anglia, Glasgow and London, and I am most grateful to participants for their comments. The Study Group on Eighteenth-Century Russia has provided a welcoming and discerning audience for papers that strictly lay outside its chronological remit. British scholars working on pre-Petrine Russian history form a small and select group: Paul Dukes, Lindsey Hughes, John Klier, Philip Longworth, Denis Shaw and R. E. F. Smith have at various times and in various ways provided much valued support and encouragement. Among Russian historians, I have benefited from discussions in Moscow with L. V. Danilova, the late V. B. Kobrin, V. D. Nazarov, A. A. Preobrazhenskii and A. L. Yurganov. R. G. Skrynnikov of St Petersburg University has provided encouragement over a long period of time. Fellow members of the Centre for Russian and East European Studies at Birmingham have displayed surprising tolerance towards a colleague whose interests seemed to be drifting ever further away from their own more contemporary concerns. Some have even pretended to believe my protestations about the 'relevance' of my work to the post-Soviet period, when Russia, in her new Time of Troubles, was beset with false prophets, if not (yet) with false tsars.

Research for the book has been conducted in Birmingham, in the Alexander Baykov and Main University Libraries; in London, in the British Library and in the library of the School of Slavonic and East European Studies (SSEES); in Moscow, in what was then the Lenin Library; and in what was then Leningrad, in the Saltykov-Shchedrin State Public Library and the Library of the Academy of Sciences (BAN). I am grateful to the staffs of all these libraries for their efforts on my behalf; and especially to Jenny Brine of the Baykov Library for her assistance at a time when I was particularly dependent on the lifeline of Inter-Library Loans.

Research visits to Russia have been funded by the University of Birmingham and by the British Council. In the later stages of work on the book I benefited from the exchange agreement, initiated by the historians at SSEES, between the English 'consortium' universities and the Institutes of History of the Academy of Sciences in Moscow.

Finally I should like to thank my husband Bill for his patience, tolerance and support. As for our sons, Martin and Alan: the publication of this volume should finally convince them that 'writing a book' was not just a euphemism for listening to Radio Three in the study, and avoiding tiresome domestic chores.

Note on transliteration, names and dates

Transliteration from Russian follows the simplified form of the British Standard (BS 2979–1958). Some first names have been anglicised (e.g. Michael, Peter); Dimitry has been preferred to the more correct Dmitrii or Dimitrii. Personal names and placenames from Belorussian and Ukrainian areas that formed part of the Polish-Lithuanian Commonwealth in the early seventeenth century have posed a particular problem: they are mostly given in transliterated Russified form. Even with Polish names, I have not been entirely consistent: Marina Mniszech is preferred to the more correct Maryna Mniszchówna. I apologise for any offence to national sentiment that may be caused by such hybrid usages, which have been adopted purely in the interests of convenience and simplification.

Dates are given according to the Old Style (Julian) calendar, which was nine days behind the Western (Gregorian) calendar in the sixteenth century, and ten days behind in the seventeenth. Occasionally, when citing sources that used the Western calendar, I have provided both dates. The Russian calendar in this period numbered years from the creation (5509 BC), and the year began on 1 September. Dates in the form '1605/6' (where the month is unknown) refer to the Russian year 7114, i.e. the period from 1 September 1605 to 31 August 1606.

Chronology of events

1533–84	**Reign of Ivan IV ('the Terrible')**
1547	Ivan's coronation as first tsar
1552	Conquest of Kazan'
1557	Conquest of Astrakhan'
1558–83	Livonian War
1565–72	*oprichnina*
1571	Burning of Moscow by Crimean Tatars
1581	Death of Tsarevich Ivan Ivanovich
1584–98	**Reign of Fedor Ivanovich**
1591	Death of Tsarevich Dimitry of Uglich
1598–1605	**Reign of Boris Godunov**
1601–3	Famine
1603	Khlopko uprising
1603	Appearance of First False Dimitry at Brahin
1604–5	Invasion of Russia by First False Dimitry
1605	13 April: death of Boris Godunov; accession of Fedor Borisovich
	1 June: rising in Moscow against Godunovs
	21 July: coronation of First False Dimitry
1605–6	**Reign of First False Dimitry**
1606	April: appearance of Tsarevich Peter-Ileika on Volga
	8 May: Dimitry's marriage to Marina Mniszech
	17 May: murder of First False Dimitry
	19 May: election of Shuiskii as tsar
	1 June: Shuiskii's coronation
1606–10	**Reign of Vasilii Shuiskii**
1606–7	Bolotnikov revolt
1606	summer: appearance of Tsarevich Ivan Augustus in Astrakhan'
	November: arrival of Tsarevich Peter-Ileika at Putivl'
	November–December: siege of Moscow by Pashkov and Bolotnikov
1607	January: arrival of Tsarevich Peter ('the Bear') in Orsha

	June: appearance of Second False Dimitry in Starodub
	June–October: siege of Tula
	10 October: surrender of Bolotnikov and Tsarevich Peter at Tula
	November: Tsarevich Fedor comes to Dimitry's camp at Bryansk
1608	24 April: Dimitry denounces cossack 'tsareviches'
	June: Dimitry's arrival at Tushino
	September: Marina acknowledges Dimitry at Tushino
1609	February: military agreement between Shuiskii and Sweden
	September: Poles besiege Smolensk
	December: Dimitry flees from Tushino to Kaluga
1610	24 June: Żółkiewski defeats Dimitry Shuiskii at Klushino
	17 July: deposition of Vasilii Shuiskii
	August: Muscovites swear allegiance to Władysław
	September: Poles occupy Moscow
	11 December: murder of Dimitry at Kaluga
1611	March: first national liberation army besieges Moscow
	March: Third False Dimitry arrives in Ivangorod
	July: Swedes occupy Novgorod
1612	July: Zarutskii flees from Moscow encampments
	August: second national liberation army, under Minin and Pozharskii, arrives at Moscow
	November: liberation of Moscow
1613	February: election of Michael Romanov as tsar
1613–45	**Reign of Michael Romanov**
1613	autumn: Zarutskii arrives in Astrakhan' with Marina and Tsarevich Ivan Dimitrievich
1614	12 May: Zarutskii flees from Astrakhan'
1617	Treaty of Stolbovo with Sweden
1618	Treaty of Deulino with Poland
1634	Peace of Polyanovka with Poland
1645–76	**Reign of Aleksei**
1669–71	Razin rebellion
1676–82	**Reign of Fedor Alekseevich**
1682–1725	**Reign of Peter I ('the Great')**
1761–2	**Reign of Peter III**
1762–96	**Reign of Catherine II ('the Great')**
1773–4	Pugachev revolt

Glossary of Russian terms

ataman	Cossack chieftain; the elected leader of a cossack band.
boyar (Russian *boyarin*, pl. *boyare*)	In the narrow sense, the highest rank of member of the tsar's boyar duma (*boyarskaya duma*) or council. More broadly, a member of those aristocratic clans whose senior representatives were eligible for appointment to boyar status.
dvor	'Court': more specifically, after the abolition of the *oprichnina* (q.v.), the government of the tsar's personal domain.
dvoryanin (pl. *dvoryane*)	Nobleman (literally, 'courtier'); a military servitor of higher rank than a *syn boyarskii* (q.v.).
d'yak	'Secretary': a leading official in the bureaucracy.
gramota	An official document or charter; a proclamation.
izvet	Communication, petition.
kholop	Slave, bondsman.
murza	Tatar nobleman.
narod	The ('common') people: a category comprising peasants, slaves, cossacks and artisans.
okol'nichii	'Lord-in-waiting': a member of the boyar council, holding the court rank below boyar.
oprichnina	In 1565–72, the divison of the realm that was directly under the tsar's control (cf. *zemshchina*). By extension, the tsar's bodyguard (*oprichniki*), and the reign of terror that they implemented.
raskat	A form of execution in which the victim was thrown from the top of a tower.
ras[s]triga, ros[s]triga	Unfrocked monk.
samozvanchestvo (*samozvanstvo*)	Pretence, imposture: the 'pretender phenomenon'. Cf. *samozvanets* (pl. *samozvantsy*), a pretender, impostor.
skomorokh	Minstrel, popular entertainer.

strelets (pl. *strel'tsy*)	Musketeer.
syn boyarskii (pl. *deti boyarskie*)	Literally, 'boyar's son': the most junior rank among the service nobility.
tsar (Russian *tsar'*)	From 1547, the official title of the Russian ruler (previously grand prince). Cf. tsaritsa (tsar's wife); tsarevich (tsar's son); tsarevna (tsar's daughter).
ukraina	A region of Russia to the south-west of Moscow, including the towns of Tula and Orel. Not to be confused with Ukraine, then part of Poland-Lithuania.
verst (Russian *versta*)	Unit of length: 0.663 mile; 1.067 km.
voevoda	(1) A general, military commander; (2) a town or city governor.
vor	State (political) criminal; 'rogue', scoundrel. Cf. *vorenok* (dim.), 'little rogue'.
yurta	Cossack settlement.
zemshchina	The 'land': in the reign of Ivan IV, the territory that was governed by the boyar duma, rather than by the *oprichnina* or *dvor* (q.v.).

Abbreviations

AAE	*Akty, sobrannye v bibliotekakh i arkhivakh Rossiiskoi imperii Arkheograficheskoyu ekspeditsieyu*
AI	*Akty Istoricheskie*
ChIOIDR	*Chteniya v Imperatorskom Obshchestve Istorii i Drevnostei Rossiiskikh pri Moskovskom Universitete*
PL	*Pskovskie letopisi*
PLDR	*Pamyatniki literatury Drevnei Rusi*
PSRL	*Polnoe sobranie russkikh letopisei*
RIB	*Russkaya Istoricheskaya Biblioteka, izdavaemaya Imperatorskoyu Arkheograficheskoyu Kommissieyu*
SGGiD	*Sobranie Gosudarstvennykh Gramot i Dogovorov, khranyashchikhsya v Gosudarstvennoi Kollegii Inostrannykh Del*
SIRIO	*Sbornik Imperatorskogo Russkogo Istoricheskogo Obshchestva*
VIB	*Vosstanie I. Bolotnikova*
ZhMNP	*Zhurnal Ministerstva Narodnogo Prosveshcheniya*

Introduction

More than a dozen impostors, all claiming to be long-lost tsars or tsareviches, appeared in Russia in the early seventeenth century, in the period of civil strife that is generally known as the 'Time of Troubles' (*smutnoe vremya*). The Troubles were sparked off by the invasion of Russia in 1604 by the First False Dimitry, a pretender proclaiming himself to be the youngest son of Tsar Ivan the Terrible (1533–84). Tsarevich Dimitry of Uglich had died in 1591, in mysterious circumstances; seven years later, the old dynasty of the Muscovite rulers came to an end, with the death of Dimitry's elder half-brother, Tsar Fedor Ivanovich. The throne passed to Boris Godunov, Tsar Fedor's brother-in-law, who was widely believed to have plotted against the heirs of Ivan the Terrible in order to gain power for himself. Godunov had been tsar for five years when the pretender appeared in Poland. 'Dimitry' defeated Boris's armies, succeeded in obtaining the throne, and occupied it for almost a year. The overthrow and murder of the pretender in May 1606 led to a further period of civil war and foreign invasion, in which there appeared not only new false Dimitrys, but also various other 'tsareviches' who professed themselves to be descendants of Tsar Ivan. Order was restored only in 1613, when a new dynasty was established with the election of Michael Romanov as tsar.

Pretence was not an exclusively Russian phenomenon.[1] Royal imposture, indeed, may be regarded as an occupational hazard of any hereditary monarchical system. Ancient history provides the examples of the Pseudo-Smerdis of Persia and the False Agrippa of Rome;[2] the medieval period offers

---

[1] The phenomenon of pretence or royal imposture is known in Russian as *samozvanstvo* or *samozvanchestvo*. A pretender (*samozvanets*) is literally a 'self-styled' (*samozvannyi*) tsar or tsarevich, that is, someone who has falsely adopted a royal title and identity. *Samozvanets* is therefore a narrower term than the English word 'pretender', which can be used for any claimant to a throne (the broader Russian equivalent is *pretendent*). 'Impostor' is perhaps the more correct translation, but I shall follow established custom and practice in using 'pretender' along with 'impostor' as English equivalents of *samozvanets*.

[2] Bercé, *Le roi caché*, pp. 369–70. This book provides a useful overview of pretenders and the popular political ideas associated with them.

the False Count Baldwin of Flanders and the False Emperor Frederick II.[3]
The closest parallels and the most immediate precedents for the Russian pretenders of the Time of Troubles, however, can be found in early modern
Europe. England had known the impostors Lambert Simnel and Perkin Warbeck in the late fifteenth century;[4] and in the last decades of the sixteenth
century a number of royal pretenders appeared in Moldavia,[5] as well as a
series of False Don Sebastians in Portugal.[6] Nor was pretence purely a pre-
modern phenomenon: about forty claimants to the identity of Louis XVII
were to appear in the early nineteenth century.[7]

In spite of these precedents and parallels elsewhere, however, royal imposture has long been considered to have had especial significance in Russia.[8]
It has particularly attracted the attention of historians because it was associated with major popular uprisings in the seventeenth and eighteenth centuries:
not only those of the Time of Troubles, but also the Pugachev rising of
1773–4 and (to a lesser extent) the revolt of Sten'ka Razin in 1669–71. Two
generalising essays about pretence by pre-revolutionary Russian historians,
written almost a century apart, linked the phenomenon with revolts in which
cossacks sought to take advantage of the credulity and gullibility of the
uneducated peasant masses in order to rouse them to rebel under the banner
of a 'true tsar'.[9] A number of more recent scholars have associated pretence
with 'popular monarchism', the naive faith in the benevolence of the tsar
towards the common people (*narod*) that was believed to be particularly
characteristic of the Russian peasantry.[10] My own interest in *samozvanchestvo*, indeed, sprang from a concern with the evolution of popular monarchism in Russia, in its various forms, from the sixteenth to the twentieth
centuries.[11] Yet not all Russian pretenders were themselves recruited from
the ranks of the *narod*, nor were their supporters drawn exclusively from the
lower classes. A number of pretenders were confidence tricksters, political
opportunists or adventurers; others were pathetic deluded individuals. Many
had no popular support, or only a handful of followers.[12] And popular monarchism itself could assume forms other than pretence, such as rebellion 'in

[3] Cohn, *The Pursuit of the Millennium*, pp. 90–93, 113–15.
[4] Gairdner, *History of the Life and Reign of Richard the Third*; Gairdner, *Henry the Seventh*;
Pollard, ed., *The Reign of Henry VII*; Alexander, *The First of the Tudors*.
[5] Mokhov, *Ocherki*; *Istoricheskie svyazi*, vol. 1.
[6] D'Antas, *Les faux Don Sébastien*; Brooks, *A King for Portugal*; Bercé, *Le roi caché*, ch. 1.
[7] Bercé, *Le roi caché*, pp. 328–39.
[8] Solov'ev, 'Zametki o samozvantsakh', p. 265; Klyuchevskii, *Sochineniya*, vol. 3, p. 27; Chistov, *Russkie narodnye*, p. 29; Troitskii, 'Samozvantsy', p. 134; Longworth, 'The Pretender
Phenomenon', p. 61; Uspenskii, 'Tsar' i samozvanets', p. 201.
[9] [Shcherbatov], *Kratkaya povest'*; Solov'ev, 'Zametki o samozvantsakh'.
[10] Field, *Rebels*, pp. 1–26.
[11] Perrie, *The Image of Ivan the Terrible*, pp. 1–4.
[12] Troitskii, 'Samozvantsy'; Longworth, 'The Pretender Phenomenon'.

the name of the tsar' – directed against his evil counsellors – and the idealis-
ation of individual rulers of the past as 'good tsars'. Thus the precise relationship of pretence to popular monarchism has to be established empirically for
each individual occurrence of the phenomenon.

Of all the Russian pretenders of the seventeenth century, the best known
is the First False Dimitry. His adventures captured the imagination of contemporaries well beyond the frontiers of Russia, and literary treatments of his
story were popular throughout Europe long before Pushkin's verse drama
served as the basis for Musorgskii's opera, *Boris Godunov*.[13] Nineteenth-
century historians were fascinated by the question of the pretender's true
identity, and some were intrigued by the possibility that he might really have
been the son of Ivan the Terrible.[14] By the end of the nineteenth century, the
proliferation of popular literature about the First False Dimitry had somewhat
discredited the topic of pretence in the Time of Troubles as a 'serious' subject
for historical study. S. F. Platonov, the author of what is still the most influential account of the period, referred somewhat prissily to the 'arbitrary conjectures and speculative hypotheses' of popular historians, and insisted that
for the purposes of his own scholarly analysis there was 'not the slightest
necessity to dwell on the question of the identity of the first Pretender'.[15] For
Platonov, pretence was simply a political device employed by various warring
social groups whose struggle for power in the Time of Troubles derived from
a deep-rooted crisis in sixteenth-century Muscovy.

In the Soviet period the designation of the early seventeenth century as a
'Time of Troubles' was abandoned in favour of the notion of a 'peasant war',
and the historiography was dominated by sterile debates about how best to
fit the events of the period into a conceptual framework derived from the
inappropriate model of Germany in 1525.[16] I. I. Smirnov's study of the Bolotnikov revolt of 1606–7 depicted that episode alone as the 'first peasant war'
in Russia,[17] and this became the orthodox position. After Stalin's death, however, some Soviet historians contended that the entire sequence of events
from 1603 to 1614 constituted a 'peasant war'.[18] Pretenders were of interest
to Soviet historians if – like Pugachev – they could be identified as leaders
of peasant wars. But the pretenders of the early seventeenth century did not

[13] Brody, *The Demetrius Legend*; Emerson, *Boris Godunov*.
[14] See especially Kostomarov, *Kto byl pervyi Lzhedimitrii?*; Pierling, *Rome et Démétrius*;
Bestuzhev-Ryumin, *Pis'ma*; Suvorin, *O Dimitrii Samozvantse*; Waliszewski, *La crise révolutionnaire*; Barbour, *Dimitry*.
[15] Platonov, *Ocherki*, p. 189; p. 447, n. 71.
[16] See, in particular, the debate in the journal *Voprosy Istorii* in 1958–61: Zimin, 'Nekotorye
voprosy'; Smirnov, 'O nekotorykh voprosakh'; 'O nekotorykh spornykh voprosakh'; Koretskii, 'Iz istorii krest'yanskoi voiny'; Ovchinnikov, 'Nekotorye voprosy'; Sklyar, 'O nachal'nom
etape'; 'O krest'yanskoi voine'.
[17] Smirnov, *Vosstanie Bolotnikova*.
[18] Zimin, 'Nekotorye voprosy'; Makovskii, *Pervaya krest'yanskaya voina*.

easily lend themselves to such a categorisation. In the early Soviet period M. N. Pokrovskii and his disciples had attempted to present the First and Second False Dimitrys as cossack or peasant tsars, but the revival of Russian nationalism under Stalin encouraged scholars to view these pretenders as puppets of the 'feudal Polish interventionists'.[19] Only Bolotnikov's ally, the cossack 'Tsarevich Peter', was regarded as the leader of an anti-feudal uprising.[20] In the post-Stalin period, however, revisionists such as A. A. Zimin argued that although pretenders such as the First False Dimitry were themselves 'political adventurers', they were able to acquire widespread popular support from peasants and slaves.[21]

In discussing the 'ideology' of 'peasant wars', Soviet historians of the older generation were required to base themselves on Stalin's comment of 1931 that leaders of popular rebellions in Russia, such as Razin and Pugachev, were 'tsarists', who 'acted against the landowners, but for "the good tsar" '. Stalin identified Bolotnikov, along with Razin and Pugachev, as the leader of a peasant uprising against 'feudal oppression';[22] and in his monograph on the Bolotnikov rising I. I. Smirnov linked pretence with peasant monarchism: 'the tsarist psychology of the peasantry created the social base for "*samozvanstvo*", because in this the peasant faith in the "good tsar" found its expression'.[23] The slogan of the 'good tsar', Smirnov observed somewhat cryptically, constituted a 'peculiar peasant utopia'.[24]

An interesting development of this approach to the phenomenon of pretence was provided, after Stalin's death, in an influential book by the Soviet folklorist K. V. Chistov. Chistov was primarily concerned not with pretenders but with popular myths. He placed *samozvanchestvo* in the context of 'popular socio-utopian legends' in which tsars or tsareviches were removed from power because their courtiers feared that they planned to liberate the people from oppression. The peasants however believed that these ousted rulers would return one day to implement the reforms that had been thwarted by the 'traitor-boyars'. Pretenders, according to Chistov, attracted popular support because they were seen as the embodiments of these longed-for royal 'deliverers', and pretence constituted 'one of the most curious ideological and political manifestations of the feudal crisis and one of the most specific and persistent forms of anti-feudal protest'.[25]

---

[19] For a review of Soviet historiography of the period, see Skrynnikov, *Sotsial'no-politicheskaya bor'ba*, pp. 6–9.

[20] Troitskii, 'Samozvantsy', pp. 134–8.

[21] Zimin, 'Nekotorye voprosy', p. 99.

[22] Stalin, 'Beseda', p. 113.

[23] Smirnov, *Vosstanie Bolotnikova*, p. 29.

[24] *Ibid.*, p. 506.

[25] Chistov, *Russkie narodnye*, p. 29. For a critical review of Chistov's views, based on evidence relating to the Time of Troubles, see Perrie, ' "Popular Socio-Utopian Legends" '.

The most recent work by a Russian historian on the early seventeenth century is a series of volumes by the prolific R. G. Skrynnikov.[26] In his first publications on this period Skrynnikov presented the events as an anti-feudal peasant war that constituted a form of popular protest against the process of enserfment. In line with this approach, Skrynnikov not only reproduced Smirnov's view that faith in the 'good tsar' was a 'peculiar peasant utopia', but he also endorsed Chistov's views about 'popular socio-utopian legends', and saw pretenders as leaders of anti-feudal peasant movements.[27] In his most recent works, however, Skrynnikov has abandoned these interpretations. He now rejects the appropriateness of the concept of a 'peasant war' even for the Bolotnikov rising of 1606–7, and views the Time of Troubles as a civil war caused not only by the enserfment of the peasantry, but also by a crisis within the system of land allocation to the nobility. Skrynnikov continues to regard pretence as an expression of a 'social utopia or myth about a kindly tsar-deliverer', but he now argues that this myth, together with faith in the 'good tsar', was characteristic not only of the peasants but also of many other social groups.[28]

Rather a different approach to the phenomenon of pretence has been taken by the distinguished Russian scholar B. A. Uspenskii, in a brief but stimulating essay on *samozvanchestvo* that places it in the broader context of the political philosophy of Muscovite Russia and its religious culture. The process of the sacralisation of the monarchy in the sixteenth century, in Uspenskii's view, reflected the notion that true tsars were chosen by God alone. When the natural hereditary order of succession was broken, the new elected ruler was seen by some as a false tsar; and the accession of such a usurper – or 'pretender on the throne' – provoked the appearance of other pretenders, all claiming to be the true tsar. Uspenskii's approach is of particular interest because – in contrast to other Soviet scholars – he considers pretence from the perspectives of both 'high' and popular culture, and his semiotic outlook illuminates many aspects of contemporary reactions to the appearance of pretenders.[29]

The present study too endeavours to place pretence in the broad context of the mentality of the age, and to examine both popular and 'official' atti-

---

[26] Skrynnikov has produced a bewildering number of works on the period, some of a scholarly nature and others of a more popular character. Many of them overlap considerably in their content. His more scholarly works, which cover events to 1607, are: *Sotsial'no-politicheskaya bor'ba*; *Rossiya v nachale XVII v.* (a revised version of the previous work); and *Smuta v Rossii*. His 'popular-scientific' works are: *Boris Godunov* (available in an English translation with the same title); *Minin i Pozharskii* (available in an English version as *The Time of Troubles*); and *Samozvantsy*.

[27] See, for example, Skrynnikov, *Sotsial'no-politicheskaya bor'ba*, pp. 97–100, 324–6.

[28] Skrynnikov, *Rossiya v nachale XVII v.*, pp. 79–80, 249–51; Skrynnikov, *Smuta v Rossii*, pp. 246–53.

[29] Uspenskii, 'Tsar' i samozvanets'.

tudes towards the phenomenon. The book is not primarily designed as a history of the Time of Troubles, but it inevitably deals with the main political and military events of the period as background to the appearance and activities of the pretenders.[30] The main focus, however, is on the *samozvantsy* themselves, and on the ways in which they were perceived both by their supporters and by their opponents. Because of this emphasis, attention has been paid not just to major historical actors such as the first two False Dimitrys, but also to the minor pretenders and to the theatres of the civil war where they were active – the Volga basin, and the towns of north-west Russia.

The book comprises four main sections. The Prologue, entitled 'Tsarevich Dimitry and Boris Godunov', deals with events from the death of Ivan the Terrible in 1584 to the Khlopko rising of 1603, as background to the appearance of the first pretender in Lithuania. Part 1 is devoted to the career of the First False Dimitry, while Part 2 covers the period of the Bolotnikov rising of 1606–7. Part 3 is concerned with the later stages of the Troubles, to 1614. Two chapters in this section deal with the career of the Second False Dimitry, while the final chapter is devoted to the Third False Dimitry and to the fate of 'Tsarevich' Ivan Dimitrievich, the son of the Second False Dimitry. A brief Epilogue discusses later pretenders in early modern Russia, focussing on the period between the end of the Time of Troubles and the accession of Peter the Great. The Conclusion attempts to place the Russian impostors of the Time of Troubles in a wider context, comparing them with pretenders elsewhere in early modern Europe. It also discusses how and why *samozvantsy* succeeded in attracting so much support in the early seventeenth century, and tries to establish the precise relationship of pretence to 'popular monarchism' in this period.

---

[30] For general coverage of the period in English, see Platonov, *Boris Godunov*, together with Platonov, *The Time of Troubles*; and Skrynnikov, *Boris Godunov*, together with Skrynnikov, *The Time of Troubles*. There is a useful short treatment in Crummey, *The Formation of Muscovy*, ch. 8.

Prologue Tsarevich Dimitry and Boris Godunov

The end of a dynasty

Ivan the Terrible and the politics of succession

The death of Tsar Fedor Ivanovich in 1598 brought to an end the old dynasty of Muscovite grand princes and tsars that traced its origins to the semi-legendary figure of Ryurik the Viking, the ninth-century Prince of Novgorod (see Figure 1). The expiry of the dynasty can only partly be attributed to declining fertility in the royal house: the nature of Muscovite court politics also influenced the outcome.

Until the fifteenth century, succession in the grand-princely family had been collateral: it could pass to younger brothers and cousins before being transferred to the next generation. The ambiguities in this system had led to a dynastic war after the death of Vasilii I in 1425; thereafter, linear succession from father to son became the norm, and the grand princes of Moscow took pains to eliminate collateral heirs. They imprisoned or exiled their uncles and brothers, and restricted their marriages. The resulting erosion of the collateral lines contributed to the end of the dynasty.

Succession by primogeniture in the royal house, it has been suggested, was favoured by the boyar clans, that group of elite families whose members were eligible for appointment as royal counsellors.[1] The boyars derived their influence at court from their marriage links with the grand prince, and linear succession enabled them to plan their marriage strategies around a stable dynasty with an established principle of succession. As long as the dynasty survived, the boyars competed for the tsar's favour; the end of the dynasty meant that they were faced with the prospect of competing for the throne itself. Marriage relationships with the royal house were to prove crucial to the outcome of that competition.

---

[1] Kollmann, *Kinship and Politics*, pp. 123–8, 155–9. See also Keenan, 'Muscovite Political Folkways', pp. 136–45.

7

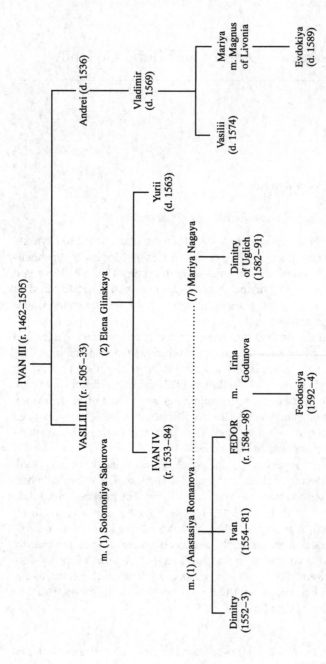

Figure 1 The Muscovite royal house in the sixteenth century (simplified form).
Note Reigning grand princes and tsars are given in capitals

The marital history of Tsar Fedor's father, Ivan the Terrible, had been complex.[2] Ivan's first marriage, to Anastasiya Romanova (Anastasiya Romanovna Zakharina-Yur'eva), ended with Anastasiya's death in 1560. Four of the six children of this union died in infancy, including Dimitry, the firstborn son. The other two sons reached adulthood: Ivan and Fedor, born in 1554 and 1557 respectively. The tsar's second marriage, to the Kabardinian princess Mariya Temryukovna, produced a son who died in childhood. After Mariya's death in 1569 Ivan married for a third time, but the bride, Marfa Sobakina, died soon after the wedding. The Orthodox Church permitted only three marriages, but the tsar claimed that his union with Sobakina was unconsummated because of her illness, and he successfully petitioned the church council to permit him to marry again. This fourth marriage, to Anna Koltovskaya, was shortlived, however, and Anna was forced to take the veil.

Ivan married again in 1575, but this bride too – Anna Vasil'chikova – was despatched to a convent shortly afterwards. His next alliance, to the widow Vasilisa Melent'eva, lasted for about a year, and appears to have ended with Vasilisa's natural death. The tsar's seventh wife, Mariya Nagaya, survived her husband. Ivan's last three marriages were entered into against the rules of the church and their legality was therefore in doubt, although the tsar and his brides did go through a form of wedding ceremony.[3]

Ivan's marriage to Mariya Nagaya took place in 1580.[3] The English agent Jerome Horsey describes Mariya as 'a very beautiful young maiden of a noble house and great family'.[4] Although we must take Horsey's judgement of Mariya's beauty on trust, his assessment of her pedigree requires some qualification. The Nagois belonged to the higher ranks of the service nobility rather than to the old titled aristocracy. Mariya's father and grandfather held the rank of lord-in-waiting (*okol'nichii*), and at the time of her marriage to the tsar the most powerful member of the Nagoi clan at court was Mariya's uncle, Afanasii Fedorovich, who had been ambassador to the Crimea from 1563 to 1573. On his return to Moscow Afanasii Nagoi soon became a state councillor (*dumnyi dvoryanin*), and an influential courtier.[5] Ivan's betrothal to Afanasii's niece continued an established pattern of marriage to relatives of his current favourites: Marfa Sobakina had been the protégée of the notorious *oprichnik* Malyuta Skuratov, and Anna Vasil'chikova was a kinswoman of the boyar Vasilii Umnoi-Kolychev.[6]

[2] For details of Ivan's wives and children, see Skrynnikov, *Ivan Groznyi*, pp. 206–14; Skrynnikov, *Tsarstvo terrora*, *passim*; Zimin, *V kanun*, *passim*; Kaiser, 'Symbol and Ritual', pp. 249–50.

[3] Skrynnikov, *Rossiya posle oprichniny*, p. 67.

[4] Berry and Crummey, eds., *Rude and Barbarous Kingdom*, p. 286.

[5] Skrynnikov, *Rossiya posle oprichniny*, pp. 11, 29, 100; Zimin, *V kanun*, p. 19.

[6] Skrynnikov, *Rossiya posle oprichniny*, p. 99.

At the time of Ivan's marriage to Mariya, the question of the succession did not seem to be an urgent one. The tsar had two adult sons by his first wife. Both were married, but childless. Since they were still young, however, their childlessness could not be considered to pose any major threat to the continuation of the dynasty. Barren or otherwise unwanted wives could be despatched to nunneries. This had been the fate of Solomoniya Saburova, the first wife of Ivan's father, Grand Prince Vasilii III. Tsar Ivan's fourth and fifth wives, Anna Koltovskaya and Anna Vasil'chikova, had been sent to convents, as had the first two wives of Tsarevich Ivan Ivanovich. And Tsar Ivan himself, as we have seen, openly flouted the church's rules which limited the number of permitted marriages to three.

In November 1581 the situation was altered dramatically by the death of the tsar's elder son. Ivan Ivanovich died as the result of a blow inflicted by his father, during an argument in which the tsar also struck the tsarevich's pregnant wife, Elena Sheremeteva, causing her to miscarry.[7] Tsar Ivan was overcome by remorse as a result of his son's death. Apart from the personal tragedy, the dynastic implications were considerable. Tsarevich Ivan was undoubtedly the stronger and more capable of Ivan's sons. With his death, the succession passed to Fedor, the younger son, who was physically and mentally feeble. Fedor's childlessness now acquired much greater political significance. The Dutch merchant Isaac Massa asserts that Tsar Ivan tried to persuade Fedor to divorce his wife Irina,[8] but there is no contemporary evidence to support this claim.[9] Any attempt to make Fedor renounce Irina would have undermined the position at court of her kinsmen, the Godunovs: Irina's ambitious brother, Boris, would have been particularly opposed to such a move.

Dynastic considerations were very much to the fore in the last years of Ivan's life. In the spring of 1582 the tsar sent his ambassador Fedor Pisemskii to England to negotiate a marriage between Ivan and Lady Mary Hastings, a distant kinswoman of Queen Elizabeth. These negotiations were unsuccessful. The English understandably regarded Ivan's existing marriage to Mariya Nagaya as an obstacle, and although Pisemskii was instructed to explain that Ivan was willing to divorce his Russian wife in favour of a foreign bride, the envoy was embarrassed when news of the birth of Tsarevich Dimitry was received at the English court during his mission. 'When you left [home],' Sir Thomas Randolph informed the Russian envoy in January 1583, 'your sovereign had one son, but now a second son has been born to him.' Pisem-

---

[7] Sources differ as to the cause of the fateful quarrel between Ivan and his heir. See Skrynnikov, *Rossiya posle oprichniny*, pp. 91–2; Zimin, *V kanun*, pp. 90–93.

[8] Massa, *A Short History*, p. 24.

[9] Massa's evidence is accepted by Skrynnikov (*Rossiya posle oprichniny*, pp. 106–7) but rejected by Zimin (*V kanun*, p. 106).

skii dismissed the news as a slanderous rumour put about by opponents of the Anglo-Russian alliance, but the negotiations concerning Mary Hastings were doomed.[10]

The tsar continued to yearn for an English wife, however. Discussions concerning other possible brides took place in the course of Sir Jerome Bowes' embassy to Russia in 1583–4, but the question was unresolved at the time of Ivan's death in March 1584. Jerome Horsey alleges that Ivan was so anxious for an English bride that he could have been persuaded to designate any children she might bear him as his heirs,[11] but Horsey undoubtedly exaggerates the threat which the proposed marriage presented to Fedor's chances of succession. Certainly during Pisemskii's negotiations in England in 1582–3 it was made clear to Queen Elizabeth that Fedor 'and his children' would succeed, while any sons that Mary Hastings bore to the tsar would be granted appanages (*udely*) 'as befits their royal rank'.[12] But Ivan's negotiations with Bowes were surrounded with great secrecy, and it is quite possible that the Godunovs were anxious about Ivan's intentions. Horsey alleges that their fears about the prospective English marriage led Boris Godunov and Bogdan Bel'skii, Ivan's closest favourite in the last year of his life, to hasten the tsar's death.[13]

The only alternative heir to Fedor was the infant Tsarevich Dimitry, Ivan's son by Mariya Nagaya. On the night of Tsar Ivan's death, according to the chronicler, Boris Godunov 'and his sympathisers' arrested and imprisoned the Nagois on a charge of treason.[14] Two months later, on 24 May, a week before Fedor's coronation, Tsarevich Dimitry, with his mother and some of his Nagoi relatives, was sent to live in the town of Uglich, on the upper Volga, which had been allocated to him as an appanage principality (*udel*).[15] Other members of the Nagoi clan, including Mariya's uncle, Afanasii, were imprisoned in various towns on the lower Volga.[16] This was not untypical Muscovite treatment of a lateral heir; but it is possible that these measures were taken in response to a real – rather than a potential – attempt by the Nagois and their allies to secure the succession for Dimitry instead of Fedor. Foreign observers, including the Polish ambassador, Leo Sapieha, allege that Bogdan Bel'skii – whom Sapieha describes as the 'guardian' of the younger

---

[10] Likhachev, ed., *Puteshestviya russkikh poslov*, pp. 152–3, 401–2. Likhachev suggests that the news of Dimitry's birth was brought to London by the Polish magnate Albrecht Laski. Dimitry was born on 19 October 1582.

[11] Berry and Crummey, eds., *Rude and Barbarous Kingdom*, pp. 303–4.

[12] Likhachev, ed., *Puteshestviya russkikh poslov*, p. 151.

[13] Berry and Crummey, eds., *Rude and Barbarous Kingdom*, pp. 304–6; Purchas, *Purchas his Pilgrimage*, pp. 983–4.

[14] *PSRL*, vol. 14, p. 35, para. 6.

[15] Yakovleva, 'K istorii moskovskikh volnenii'.

[16] *RIB*, vol. 13, p. 715; cf. *PSRL*, vol. 32, p. 195.

tsarevich – led an unsuccessful attempt to gain the throne for Dimitry.[17] Russian sources do not specifically allege that Bel'skii planned to put Dimitry on the throne, but the *New Chronicle* states that rioters in the capital accused Bel'skii and his accomplices of murdering Tsar Ivan and plotting against Tsar Fedor and the boyars. After these riots, Bel'skii was exiled to the Volga town of Nizhnii Novgorod.[18]

Boris Godunov and Tsarevich Dimitry

Boris Godunov's prompt action had secured the succession for Fedor, and the exile of Afanasii Nagoi and Bogdan Bel'skii strengthened the position of the new tsar's brother-in-law. In view of Fedor's mental incapacity, Ivan had appointed a regency council to rule in his son's name. Boris initially shared his influence over Fedor with three other regents: Nikita Romanovich Zakharin-Yur'ev, Prince I. F. Mstislavskii and Prince I. P. Shuiskii.[19] The council of regents comprised representative figures from the major interest groups at court in the last years of Ivan's reign. Nikita Romanovich, like Boris Godunov, owed his place to his kinship with the new tsar: he was the brother of Fedor's mother, Anastasiya (see Figure 2). Both the Romanovs and the Godunovs belonged to non-titled boyar families that had risen to prominence in Ivan's reign. Mstislavskii and Shuiskii, by contrast, were leading members of old princely clans. Tsar Ivan's conflicts with his boyars had led to the splitting of the realm in 1565 into two parts, the *zemshchina*, ruled by the boyar council, and the *oprichnina*, under the tsar's direct control. After the abolition of the *oprichnina* in 1572 the division of the elite continued, the tsar's personal 'court' (*dvor*) coexisting with the boyar duma of the *zemshchina*. Some historians have depicted the *zemshchina* as the power base of the old aristocracy, while the *oprichnina* and later the *dvor* represented the new service nobility. But Ivan's policies were complex and contradictory, and both of the administrative divisions were socially heterogeneous. Of the four members of the regency council, Prince Ivan Mstislavskii and Nikita Romanovich were *zemshchina* boyars, while Prince I. P. Shuiskii and Boris Godunov served in the *dvor*.[20]

---

[17] Bestuzhev-Ryumin, 'Obzor sobytii', p. 51.

[18] *PSRL*, vol. 14, p. 35, para. 9.

[19] I am not persuaded by R. G. Skrynnikov's argument that, contrary to the evidence of some contemporaries, Boris was not included in the regency council because the old tsar wanted Fedor to divorce the childless Irina Godunova: Skrynnikov, *Rossiya nakanune*, pp. 11–12. For an effective counter-argument, see Zimin, *V kanun*, pp. 106–8. Some sources also name Bogdan Bel'skii as a member of the regency council: Zimin, *V kanun*, pp. 106–8.

[20] Pavlov, *Gosudarev dvor*, pp. 3–29.

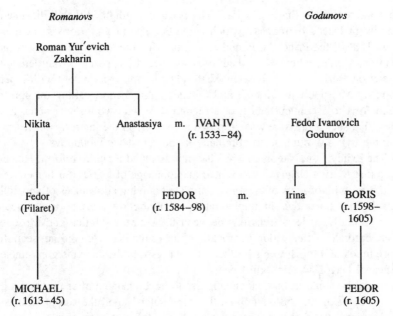

Figure 2 Marriage alliances of the Romanov and Godunov clans with the old dynasty

The first years of Fedor's reign witnessed a steady growth in Boris's power.[21] Nikita Romanovich fell ill in the summer of 1584, and died in the following year, leaving Boris as the protector of his sons. At the end of 1584 Peter Golovin, the state treasurer and a supporter of Mstislavskii, was disgraced and exiled for alleged malpractice. Soon afterwards Prince Mstislavskii himself was banished. These developments left the Shuiskiis as the Godunovs' main rivals for power.

As long as Tsaritsa Irina remained childless, Boris's position was still insecure, since the possibility remained that Fedor might be prevailed upon to divorce her. In 1585 Boris had attempted to ensure the continuation of Fedor's line by importing from England a doctor and midwife skilled in gynaecological matters. Irina had suffered a number of miscarriages, and it was hoped that Western medical expertise might enable her to carry a pregnancy to its full term. There was opposition at court, however, to the entrusting of such delicate matters to foreigners, and the midwife was allowed

[21] For the court politics of this period see, for example, Skrynnikov, *Rossiya nakanune*, pp. 9–73; Zimin, *V kanun*, pp. 104–52; Pavlov, *Gosudarev dvor*, pp. 29–43.

to come no further than Vologda.[22] The episode highlighted the political sensitivity of Irina's barrenness, which could be exploited by Boris's enemies.

In 1586–7 the Princes I. P. and A. I. Shuiskii were accused of treason and sent into exile, where they died soon afterwards, apparently murdered in secret on Boris's orders. It seems that their 'treason' was linked with a petition by Metropolitan Dionisii and others to Tsar Fedor, calling on him to send Irina to a convent and take a second wife who would bear sons. It is clear that such a measure was proposed not simply in the interests of preserving the dynasty, but also to eliminate the power of the Godunovs.

The exile of the Nagois in 1584 had not assumed a punitive form. Horsey says that Mariya Nagaya was granted the appanage of Uglich for herself and Dimitry, 'with officers of all sortes appointed, having allowances of apparell, jewels, diet, horse &c., in ample maner, belonging to the estate of a princesse'.[23] Initially, at least, relations between the courts at Uglich and Moscow were cordial.[24] After Fedor's coronation, the young tsarevich did not seem to pose much of a threat to his brother's power, especially since his great-uncle, Afanasii Nagoi, was in exile.

Boris's attitude to the Nagois appears to have changed after the 'treason' of the Shuiskiis in 1586. At about this time Peter Nagoi, the son of Afanasii Fedorovich, was forced to enter a monastery:[25] this punishment may indicate the Nagois' complicity in the plot against Boris Godunov.[26] According to Horsey, Boris complained to him in 1586 of 'practices between the empress' mother to Tsarevich Dmitrii her kindred and some other the princes joined with him in commission by the old emperor's will' – apparently a reference to the Shuiskiis.[27]

By the late 1580s it was forbidden to pray for Dimitry in churches, on the grounds that he was not legitimate, because his mother had been Tsar Ivan's seventh wife. The English diplomat Giles Fletcher wrote that 'this charge was given to the priests by the emperor himself by procurement of the Godunovs, who make him believe that it is a good policy to turn away the liking of the people from the next successor'.[28] Boris's campaign against Dimitry may have included the dissemination of rumours about the boy's evil personality. Fletcher describes the tsarevich as a bloodthirsty child, whose temperament resembled that of his father:

---

[22] Berry and Crummey, eds., *Rude and Barbarous Kingdom*, p. 319; Hamel, *England and Russia*, pp. 233–6; cf. Skrynnikov, *Rossiya nakanune*, pp. 34–5.

[23] Hakluyt, *Voyages*, vol. 2, p. 270.

[24] Platonov, *Ocherki*, p. 148; Yakovleva, 'K istorii moskovskikh volnenii'.

[25] *AI*, vol. 1, no. 225, pp. 427–8.

[26] Skrynnikov, *Rossiya nakanune*, p. 61.

[27] Berry and Crummey, eds., *Rude and Barbarous Kingdom*, pp. 321–2.

[28] *Ibid.*, p. 228.

That he is natural son to Ivan Vasil'evich the Russe people warrant it by the father's quality that beginneth to appear already in his tender years. He is delighted (they say) to see sheep and other cattle killed and look on their throats while they are bleeding (which commonly children are afraid to behold), and to beat geese and hens with a staff till he see them lie dead.[29]

The German mercenary Conrad Bussow also states that Dimitry had inherited his father's cruelty, but the example that Bussow cites is rather more politically significant than Fletcher's. Bussow relates that the tsarevich, while playing with his young friends in the snow, ordered them to build snowmen to represent the leading courtiers of his brother, Tsar Fedor. When the snowmen were built, the tsarevich began to cut off their heads, arms and legs, or to run them through with his sword, crying out that this was how he would treat the princes and boyars when he became tsar. The first snowman whose head was cut off represented Boris Godunov.[30]

It is not improbable that the Nagois harboured resentment against Boris and communicated this to the tsarevich. The report of the official inquiry into Dimitry's death contains allegations about the hostility of the Nagois towards the court at Moscow, and implies that they were concerned about ensuring Dimitry's succession. According to some witnesses, Michael Bityagovskii, the crown official at Uglich, had accused the Nagois of keeping wizards and witches to harm the tsar and the empress. Bityagovskii's widow alleged that the wizard (*vedun*) Andryusha Mochalov had been asked by Michael Nagoi to foretell how long Tsar Fedor and Tsaritsa Irina would live. The investigators took these accusations seriously, and gave orders that Mochalov was to be brought to Moscow in chains.[31]

But if the Nagois were accused of trying to harm Tsar Fedor by supernatural means, Boris Godunov was said to have plotted to use human agents against Tsarevich Dimitry. Various sources describe attempts on Dimitry's life, and hint strongly that Boris was behind them. These allegations relate to the late 1580s: that is, to the period after the exile of the Shuiskiis. Jerome Horsey notes that 'some secret practice by the discontented nobility to supplant the protector and all his designs and greatness' was followed by an attempt to poison Dimitry and his Nagoi relatives.[32] Giles Fletcher also alleges that attempts to kill Dimitry were made by 'some that aspire to the

---

[29] *Ibid.*, pp. 128–9.
[30] Bussov, *Moskovskaya khronika*, p. 80. The same story can be found in Petrei, *Istoriya*, p. 170. Massa (*A Short History*, p. 30) states that the tsarevich complained that Boris had usurped Fedor's power, and sees this as a sign of the boy's intelligence. Palitsyn (*Skazanie*, pp. 101–2), the only Russian source to mention Dimitry's hatred of Boris, says that the tsarevich often spoke and acted childishly and foolishly against his brother's favourites, including Boris.
[31] Klein, ed., *Delo rozysknoe*, pp. 32, 35, 40, 42.
[32] Berry and Crummey, eds., *Rude and Barbarous Kingdom*, p. 330. Horsey describes Boris as 'lord protector' for Fedor: *ibid.*, p. 307.

succession if this emperor die without any issue', adding the circumstantial detail that 'the nurse that tasted before him of certain meat (as I have heard) died presently'.[33] Fletcher's allegation, which was recorded before Dimitry's death in 1591, adds greater credibility to the account of an attempt to poison Dimitry in the Russian chronicle,[34] which has been dismissed as legendary by some commentators.[35]

The *New Chronicle*, compiled at the court of Patriarch Filaret in 1630, provides the most detailed account of Boris's alleged plot to murder Dimitry. After the failure of his attempt to poison the tsarevich, the chronicler asserts, Boris consulted his kinsmen and his friend Andrei Kleshnin. Eventually Kleshnin found an official, the *d'yak* (secretary) Michael Bityagovskii, who was willing to murder Dimitry. Boris sent Bityagovskii to Uglich with his son Danilo and his nephew Nikita Kachalov. When they arrived at Uglich, the chronicle continues, they began to take charge of everything. Mariya Nagaya suspected their evil intentions towards the tsarevich, and kept a close watch on his movements. Then the Bityagovskiis sought the assistance of Dimitry's governess (*mamka*), Vasilisa Volokhova, and her son Osip, in order to gain access to the tsarevich and kill him on 15 May 1591.[36]

Although it has seemed improbable to some historians that Boris should have plotted so openly against the tsarevich, some independent sources corroborate the chronicle account. There is evidence that Michael Bityagovskii was sent to Uglich only a short time before Dimitry's death, probably in 1590.[37] And the report of the commission of inquiry confirms the chronicler's statement that Bityagovskii's high-handed actions antagonised the Nagois. One witness stated that Michael Nagoi, the tsaritsa's brother, quarrelled with Michael Bityagovskii because the latter refused to give him more money than he was allowed by the royal treasury.[38] Other witnesses spoke of disagreements between Michael Bityagovskii and Michael Nagoi over the *posokha*, a levy of men to perform labour-service for the state.[39]

It seems fairly clear that Boris Godunov had a motive for getting rid of Tsarevich Dimitry. In order to establish this, it is not necessary to believe

---

[33] *Ibid.*, p. 128. Contemporaries considered Fletcher's allegations to be directed against Boris, cf. 'The Merchants' Protest' in Fletcher, *Of the Russe Commonwealth*, ed. Pipes, Appendix C, p. 62.

[34] *PSRL*, vol. 14, p. 40, para. 25; cf. *RIB*, vol. 13, pp. 7, 765–6.

[35] Tyumenev, 'Peresmotr izvestii', p. 351.

[36] *PSRL*, vol. 14, pp. 40–1, para. 25. In the chronicle Vasilisa Volokhova is called Mariya, and her son Osip is called Danilka. The information that Nikita Kachalov was Mikhail Bityagovskii's nephew comes from the 'Povest' 1606g.' (*RIB*, vol. 13, p. 7). The commission's report refers to Osip Volokhov as Nikita Kachalov's brother-in-law (*shurin*): Klein, ed., *Delo rozysknoe*, p. 32. Thus those accused of Dimitry's murder were linked by family ties.

[37] Zimin, 'Smert' tsarevicha Dimitriya', p. 106; Zimin, *V kanun*, pp. 172–3.

[38] Klein, ed., *Delo rozysknoe*, p. 14.

[39] *Ibid.*, pp. 2, 35, 39.

that the Nagois were involved in plots against Boris in the 1580s, although it is probable, and understandable, that the exiles at Uglich should have felt hostile and resentful towards the Godunovs. All of Boris's actions at this period appear to have been directed towards the elimination of rivals to his power, and his victims included other members of the old dynasty who were in the line of succession. In 1585 the widowed Queen Mariya, the daughter of Tsar Ivan's cousin, Prince Vladimir Staritskii, was persuaded to return to Russia from Livonia, where she had been living since the death of her husband, King Magnus. She and her daughter were put into a convent, where the girl soon died, 'of no natural disease', according to Giles Fletcher.[40] Tsarevich Dimitry and his Nagoi relatives posed the greatest threat to Godunov since, as long as Fedor and Irina remained childless, Dimitry was the heir presumptive to the throne. In spite of Boris's attempts to prove that Dimitry was illegitimate and thus excluded from the succession, the very fact that he was appanage prince of Uglich was evidence enough that his father had regarded him as legitimate: Uglich was the traditional domain of the younger sons or brothers of the grand princes of Moscow.

It was of course still possible that Tsar Fedor might produce an heir. Irina Godunova was to give birth to a daughter in 1592. But this does not deprive Boris of a motive for wanting to eliminate Dimitry in 1591, when Fedor had no child. If Tsar Fedor had died suddenly, Dimitry would have succeeded to the throne, and the influence of the Godunov clan at court would have been replaced by that of the Nagois. But Dimitry's death meant that, if Fedor were to die without issue, the possibility of the succession lay open for Boris, through Irina, as the events of 1598 were to demonstrate.

Death at Uglich

At mid-day on 15 May 1591 the bell of the Cathedral of the Transfiguration rang out in Uglich. The tsarevich's relatives ran to his palace, and found him dying of a throat wound. Dimitry's mother, Mariya Nagaya, and her brother Michael immediately alleged that the young prince had been murdered by Osip Volokhov, Nikita Kachalov and Danilo Bityagovskii. The townspeople of Uglich came running up, thinking that the sounding of the alarm bell signalled an outbreak of fire in the citadel. On being told that Dimitry had been murdered, they killed the three alleged assassins, together with the secretary Michael Bityagovskii, who attempted to prevent the lynching of his son and his friends. Several servants and associates of the Bityagovskiis were also killed in the course of the riot which ensued.

---

[40] Berry and Crummey, eds., *Rude and Barbarous Kingdom*, pp. 129, cf. 315–17. Mariya's daughter Evdokiya died in 1589: Skrynnikov, *Rossiya nakanune*, p. 61.

Four days later, on 19 May, a commission of enquiry arrived at Uglich from Moscow to investigate the death of Tsarevich Dimitry. This commission consisted of three men: the boyar Prince Vasilii Ivanovich Shuiskii, the *okol'-nichii* Andrei Petrovich Kleshnin and the *d'yak* Elizar' Vyluzgin. Metropolitan Gelasii, the bishop of Krutitsa, also accompanied them, to conduct the burial service for the tsarevich. After several days spent questioning the inhabitants of Uglich, the commission reported to the tsar and the Patriarch in Moscow that Dimitry had accidentally killed himself in the course of an epileptic fit, and that his Nagoi relatives were guilty of treason in inciting the riot which had led to the deaths of the Bityagovskiis and others.[41]

Controversy has raged for centuries concerning the real cause of the death of Dimitry of Uglich. The evidence of contemporary sources is inconclusive. The report of the commission of enquiry is regarded by some historians as trustworthy and reliable; others consider it to be highly tendentious, compiled to protect Boris Godunov from the charge of organising Dimitry's murder. Certainly there are many suspicious features in the report. It does not include the evidence of several important witnesses, including Tsaritsa Mariya herself. As for the witnesses whose testimony is included, the questions which were put to them often appear loaded, and some of the answers are curiously stereotyped. On the other hand, the document is full of circumstantial detail concerning the events at Uglich, and it is unlikely that the entire report was simply fabricated by the commission, as some contemporaries suggested.[42]

Sources which present the alternative version, that Dimitry was murdered on the orders of Boris Godunov, date mainly from the seventeenth century. Some historians have rejected these later sources as biased, and stress the length of time which had elapsed between Dimitry's death and the writing of these accounts. But their arguments overlook the fact that it was politically unthinkable that Dimitry's death could have been depicted as murder in Russia in the lifetime of Boris Godunov. The narrative literary accounts are certainly full of inconsistencies and improbabilities, and it is unlikely that any of them is accurate in all its detail. But on balance the hypothesis that Dimitry was murdered appears more probable than the official contemporary version that his death was accidental.[43]

The allegation that the tsarevich was murdered was made by the Nagois immediately after his death, as the report of the commission of enquiry makes

[41] These facts are common to the contemporary report of the commission of enquiry and to the account in the seventeenth-century *New Chronicle*.

[42] E.g. *RIB*, vol. 13, pp. 782–3.

[43] For a discussion of the sources and historiography, see Perrie, 'Jerome Horsey's Account'. R. G. Skrynnikov is a staunch advocate of the reliability of the commission's report. See, for example, his 'Boris Godunov i tsarevich Dmitrii', and *Rossiya nakanune*, pp. 74–85. A. A. Zimin, by contrast, tended to give greater credence to the chronicle version: Zimin, 'Smert' tsarevicha Dimitriya'; Zimin, *V kanun*, pp. 153–82.

clear. Michael Nagoi, the tsaritsa's brother, told the investigators that Dimitry had been killed by Osip Volokhov, Nikita Kachalov and Danilo Bityagov-skii.[44] According to other witnesses, the tsaritsa also accused these three youths.[45] And a large number of the townspeople of Uglich were so convinced of the truth of the Nagois' accusations that they attacked and killed the presumed murderers.

Within a few days, the accusation that Dimitry's death was murder had spread beyond Uglich. Jerome Horsey, who was residing at Yaroslavl', reported in a letter to Lord Burghley of 10 June 1591 that on 19 May

a most unfortunate chaunce befell the yonge prince of ix yers adge, sone unto the old Emperor and brother unto this; was cruelly and trecherously murdered; his throte cutt in the presence of his dere mother the Emperis; with other suche lycke most prodigious matter which I dare not wryt of, beinge not so tedious as odious and daungerous.[46]

From Horsey's later memoirs, it appears that he heard this version of the tsarevich's death from Afanasii Nagoi, the tsaritsa's uncle, who was living in exile in Yaroslavl'. Afanasii Nagoi had roused Horsey in the middle of the night, to tell him that

the Charowich Demetrius is dead, his throate was cut about the sixt hour by the Deaks Sonne one of his Pages: confessed upon the Racke, by Boris his setting on: and the Empresse poysoned, and upon point of death, her haire, nayles and skinne fall off; helpe, helpe with some good thing for the passion of God.[47]

The most authoritative Russian source to describe the events at Uglich as murder is the *New Chronicle*. This account was compiled after Dimitry's canonisation as a saint, and it incorporates many pious literary embellishments that reflect the tsarevich's later status as a holy martyr. For example, the chronicler compares Boris Godunov to the 'accursed Svyatopolk', the son of Prince Vladimir of Kiev, who had murdered his younger brothers Boris and Gleb in order to secure his right of succession to the principality.[48] (The canonisation of Boris and Gleb as political martyrs served as a model for Dimitry's subsequent elevation to sainthood.)[49] And Michael Bityagovskii's

[44] Klein, ed., *Delo rozysknoe*, p. 3.

[45] *Ibid.*, pp. 9–10, 17.

[46] Bond, ed., *Russia*, p. 365; 19 May was probably the date on which Horsey heard of Dimitry's death, which occurred on the 15th.

[47] Purchas, *Purchas his Pilgrimage*, p. 991. For a comparison of this version of Horsey's account with that in his 'Travels', see Perrie, 'Jerome Horsey's Account'. The 'Deaks Sonne' was Danilko, the son of the *d'yak* Mikhail Bityagovskii.

[48] *PSRL*, vol. 14, p. 40, para. 25.

[49] On the canonisation of princes in early Russia for secular political reasons, see Cherniavsky, *Tsar and People*, ch. 1.

willingness to serve as Boris's agent in the killing of Dimitry – 'his sovereign, the innocent lamb' – is compared to Judas Iscariot's betrayal of Christ for thirty pieces of silver.[50] Nevertheless, the chronicle account of Dimitry's death is detailed and circumstantial, and is probably based on testimony from contemporaries who were close to the events of 1591.

According to the *New Chronicle*, on 15 May the tsarevich's governess, Vasilisa Volokhova, took Dimitry down to the courtyard, accompanied by his nurse, while his mother remained upstairs in her room. In the courtyard Volokhova's son Osip, pretending to admire the tsarevich's necklace, cut his throat with a knife, but failed to kill him. Osip Volokhov then fled from the scene, while his accomplices Danilo Bityagovskii and Nikita Kachalov attacked the nurse in an attempt to prevent her cries from rousing the palace. Bityagovskii and Kachalov finished off the tsarevich, and fled in their turn when the tsaritsa appeared and broke into a lament for her son. Meanwhile the sexton, realising what had happened, tolled the bell to summon help. When Dimitry's kinsmen and the townspeople of Uglich arrived at the scene, they found the tsarevich's body in the courtyard, with his mother and nurse lying beside him as if they too were dead. Overcome with grief, the townspeople stoned to death not only the murderers, but also Michael Bityagovskii and his wife and their accomplices, twenty victims in all.[51]

The chronicle goes on to describe the cover-up operation which Boris instituted. A messenger was sent from Uglich to Tsar Fedor, to tell him that his brother had been killed 'by his slaves'. The envoy was however intercepted by Boris, who rewrote his letter to inform Fedor that Dimitry had cut his own throat in the course of an epileptic fit, as a result of the negligence of the Nagois. Prince Vasilii Shuiskii, Andrei Kleshnin and others were then sent to Uglich to investigate the affair and to bring the Nagois back with them to Moscow. After burying Dimitry at Uglich, Shuiskii began to interrogate the townspeople, asking them 'how he had killed himself through the negligence of the Nagois. But they all said unanimously – monks and priests, men and women, old and young – that he had been killed by his slaves, and by Michael Bityagovskii, on the orders of Boris Godunov and his advisers.'[52] Prince Vasilii returned to Moscow and told Tsar Fedor that his brother had died by his own hand. Boris had the Nagois tortured in order to make them agree with the commission's verdict, but they still insisted that Dimitry had been murdered. Boris then forced Tsaritsa Mariya to take the veil, and despatched her to a remote convent at Beloozero; the other Nagois were imprisoned and exiled. The inhabitants of Uglich were also punished for their actions: some

---

[50] *PSRL*, vol. 14, pp. 40–1, para. 25.

[51] *Ibid.*, pp. 41–2, para. 25. According to the report of the commission, Bityagovskii's wife survived.

[52] *Ibid.*, p. 42, para. 25.

were executed, others were imprisoned, or had their tongues cut out. Many were exiled to Siberia, where they founded the town of Pelym. Volokhova and the assassins' widows, by contrast, were rewarded with money and land.[53]

The allegation that Boris was responsible for Dimitry's death remained current in the capital and elsewhere. Foreign observers reported rumours that fires that broke out in Moscow on 24 May 1591 had been caused by Godunov, in order to distract attention from Dimitry's death; similar accusations were later made in Russian literary sources of the seventeenth century.[54] In June the Crimean khan Kazy-Girei invaded, and came close to the outskirts of Moscow before he was repulsed. Many 'simple people' in the southern frontier districts (*ukraina*), through which the Tatars passed *en route* for Moscow, believed that Boris Godunov had invited them to invade, fearing popular wrath for the death of Dimitry. Investigators were sent from Moscow to the *ukraina* towns to hunt down the disseminators of this rumour. As a consequence, the chronicle tells us: 'many people died from torture, and others were executed, and tongues were cut out, and some died in prisons. And because of this many places became deserted.'[55]

After 1591 memories of Dimitry of Uglich appear to have faded. The birth of a daughter to Fedor and Irina in 1592 seemed to have resolved the dynastic question, but the child, Feodosiya, died two years later. Boris's position, however, remained strong, since there was clearly no question of Tsar Fedor divorcing a wife who had borne him a child. Rumours had blamed Boris for Feodosiya's death,[56] but he had scant motive to murder the tsarevna, since his position as 'protector' was doubly secure if Fedor had an heir. Nor is it likely that Boris was responsible for Fedor's death in 1598, as rumour alleged.[57] As long as Fedor lived, Boris's role as regent was guaranteed; Fedor's death, by contrast, would lead to a succession crisis, in which Boris would have to fight to obtain the crown.

Tsar Fedor Ivanovich died on the night of 6 January 1598. He was succeeded by his widow, but after a week Irina entered the Novodevichii Convent and took the veil as the nun Alexandra. On 17 February her brother Boris Godunov was elected tsar by a specially convened Assembly of the Land. According to contemporary accounts, his most serious rival had been Tsar Fedor's cousin, Fedor Nikitich Romanov. A Lithuanian spy reported that Tsar Fedor had on his death-bed expressed the view that Fedor Nikitich

---

[53] *Ibid.*, p. 42, para. 26.
[54] Zimin, 'Smert' tsarevicha Dimitriya', pp. 107–9; Perrie, 'Jerome Horsey's Account', pp. 42–4.
[55] *PSRL*, vol. 14, p. 44, para. 32.
[56] Bussov, *Moskovskaya khronika*, p. 80.
[57] Berry and Crummey, eds., *Rude and Barbarous Kingdom*, p. 361; Zimin, *V kanun*, pp. 213–14.

stood the better chance of election, since Boris's origins were too humble.[58] But Godunov managed the election with great skill, appearing reluctant to aspire to the throne, and agreeing to accept it only under pressure from delegations of loyal subjects. In contrast to the assertions of previous historians that the bulk of the old aristocracy opposed Boris's election, A. P. Pavlov has recently argued that Godunov's opponents were relatively small in number, comprising primarily the Romanovs and their kinsmen, and Bogdan Bel'skii. Boris had the support of the great majority of the boyars, and his victory reflected his predominance in the government since the late 1580s.[59]

On the eve of the Troubles

Russia and her neighbours

When Boris came to the throne in 1598 he could justifiably feel that Russia, under his rule as 'protector' for Tsar Fedor, had recovered well from the damage inflicted on the country by the reign of Ivan the Terrible. In foreign affairs, in particular, the situation seemed stable and secure.[60]

Muscovy's main rival in the west was the Polish–Lithuanian Commonwealth (*Rzeczpospolita*, literally 'Republic'), formed by the Union of Lublin in 1569. The *Rzeczpospolita* had a single Diet (the *Sejm*) that elected the king, but Poland and Lithuania each retained a separate administrative system. The Commonwealth constituted a large and powerful state in east and central Europe, incorporating much of present-day Belorussia (Belarus) and Ukraine. Unlike the Baltic Lithuanians and the West Slav Poles, who were predominantly Catholic, the Belorussians and Ukrainians (or Ruthenians) were, like the Russians, East Slav in language and ethnicity, and Orthodox in religion. After the Lublin Union, the upper classes of the eastern lands became increasingly Polonised, and the influence of the counter-reformation led to the spread of Catholicism. The Orthodox were divided by the Brest Union of 1596 that created the Uniate Church: Orthodox in ritual, but owing allegiance to the Pope. Religious tolerance remained, however, and not only Catholics, Ortho-

---

[58] Prochaska, ed., *Archiwum domu Sapiehów*, vol. 1, p. 177.

[59] Pavlov, *Gosudarev dvor*, pp. 50–60.

[60] The following brief review of foreign policy in the reigns of Tsar Fedor and Boris Godunov is largely based on secondary sources. In addition to the works of the major nineteenth-century historians Karamzin and Solov'ev, I have consulted: Skrynnikov, *Rossiya nakanune*; Skrynnikov, *Sotsial'no-politicheskaya bor'ba*; Skrynnikov, *Rossiya v nachale XVII v.*. Accounts available in English include Grey, *Boris Godunov*; Platonov, *Boris Godunov*; Skrynnikov, *Boris Godunov*, 1982; Crummey, *The Formation of Muscovy*, ch. 8. For the broader European context, see Elliott, *Europe Divided*, and Parker, *Europe in Crisis*.

Map 1 Russia and her neighbours at the beginning of the seventeenth century

dox and Uniates but also Protestants and Jews were free to practise their religion in the *Rzeczpospolita*.[61]

In the disastrous Livonian War (1558–83), Ivan the Terrible had hoped to acquire for Russia a firm foothold on the Baltic by conquering the lands ruled by the Teutonic Order of Knights (Estonia, Livonia and Courland). This attempt at Russian expansion provoked a reaction not only from Poland-Lithuania, but also from Sweden, and Ivan was eventually obliged to relinquish his gains. In the Truce of Yam Zapol'skii in 1582, Russia ceded Livonia to Poland. On Ivan's death in 1584, King Stephen Bathory refused to ratify the truce, but the danger of renewed war with the *Rzeczpospolita* was averted by the death of Bathory himself in December 1586. Tsar Fedor was a candidate in the ensuing election for the vacant Polish throne, but the successful contestant was Sigismund Vasa, the son of King John III of Sweden. In 1591 Sigismund ratified a fifteen-year truce which the Poles had agreed with Moscow during the inter-regnum. This assuaged to some extent the Russians' fears that Sigismund's election to the Polish throne might presage the political union of Muscovy's two chief enemies on the Baltic. And indeed, although Sigismund succeeded to the Swedish throne on his father's death in 1592, his devout Catholicism was to prove an obstacle to his acceptance by his Protestant Swedish subjects.

By the terms of the three-year truce concluded between Russia and Sweden on the River Plyussa in August 1583, the Swedes retained their conquests in Estonia, including the port of Narva, as well as Ivangorod and some other Russian towns on the Baltic that they had acquired during the Livonian War. In 1585 the truce was extended for four years, but on its expiry, in 1590, the Russians resumed hostilities. Muscovite troops recaptured Ivangorod, but failed to take Narva. Clashes between Russia and Sweden continued, and by the terms of the Peace of Tyavzin, concluded in 1595, Moscow regained her Russian towns. Narva, however, remained under Swedish control.[62]

After Godunov's election as tsar, peace had to be renegotiated with Poland. In 1600 an embassy led by the Lithuanian chancellor Leo Sapieha arrived in Moscow, and a twenty-year peace was agreed in 1601. King Sigismund's position at this time was weak. His Protestant Swedish lands had rebelled against him in 1597, and in 1599 he was deposed by the Swedish estates. His uncle, Duke Charles, became ruler of Sweden and was crowned king, as Charles IX, in 1604 (see Figure 3). The rift between Poland and Sweden was to dominate Baltic politics in the ensuing decades. The opening years

---

[61] The history of Poland–Lithuania in the second half of the sixteenth century is covered in chapters 16–21 of the *Cambridge History of Poland (to 1696)*, and in Davies, *God's Playground*, vol. 1, especially chs. 12–14.

[62] For conflicts in the Baltic in the late sixteenth and early seventeenth centuries, see Oakley, *War and Peace*, chs. 1–4.

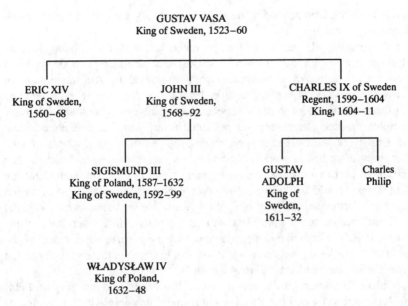

Figure 3 The House of Vasa in Sweden and Poland during the Time of Troubles.

of the seventeenth century witnessed a conflict between Sigismund and Charles over Livonia, from which Russia remained aloof.

After the Russian conquest of the Tatar khanates of Kazan' and Astrakhan' on the Volga in the 1550s, the main threat to Muscovy in the south came from the Crimean Tatars, who were clients of the Turkish sultan. The burning of Moscow by Devlet-Girei, the Crimean khan, in 1571, during the Livonian War, had revealed the dangers for Russia of simultaneous warfare on her southern and western frontiers. The Crimean Tatars invaded again in 1591, under Kazy-Girei, in collusion with the Swedes, but they were repulsed on the outskirts of Moscow. In the summer of 1598 Boris led an army to Serpukhov, on the River Oka south of Moscow, to counter a rumoured invasion from the Crimea, but the Tatars did not appear.

After the ending of the Livonian War the Russians had been able to devote more attention to the fortification of their southern frontiers. A network of fortress towns was constructed in the basin of the rivers Don and Donets and their tributaries, as a defence against Tatar raids. Livny and Voronezh were completed in 1585, and after Kazy-Girei's incursion of 1591 further construction work led to the founding of Elets in 1592; of Oskol, Kursk and Belgorod in 1596; and of Valuiki and Tsarev-Borisov in 1599 – the latter named in honour of Godunov's accession to the throne. These defences served to deter raids from the Crimea, and relations between the tsar and the khan remained generally peaceful.

The process of Russian expansion created a need to populate the new frontier towns with military servitors. On the southern steppes, the ranks of the petty nobility (*deti boyarskie*) were expanded by the recruitment of cossacks, and also of various fugitives from the centre, leading to the creation in these districts of a military service class of heterogeneous and relatively humble origins. The absence of peasants in any significant numbers meant that many of these frontier servicemen received only small grants of land that they often had to work themselves with their own labour. From the late sixteenth century onwards, the government decreed that state ploughlands on the steppe should be cultivated by compulsory labour in order to provision the new fortresses, and this obligation (*gosudareva desyatinnaya pashnya*) fell not only on the peasants but also on the petty military servitors. In the view of R.G. Skrynnikov, the grievances of these small servicemen of the southern frontier districts comprised a major element in the social discontent that fuelled the civil war of 1604 onwards.[63]

The establishment of the new towns on the steppe frontier, or 'wild field' (*dikoe pole*), provided the Russian government not only with a new line of defence against the Tatars, but also with a means of controlling the waves of fugitive peasants and slaves from the centre who had fled to the south to escape the economic devastation caused by the Livonian War. These migrants swelled the ranks of the free cossacks on the Russian borderlands.

By the end of the sixteenth century all the main river basins of Eastern Europe had their bands or 'hosts' of cossacks, free cavalrymen recruited from the neighbouring Slav peasant population, with an admixture of Tatars and other indigenous nomadic peoples of the steppes.[64] In the *Rzeczpospolita*, the most important group of cossacks were the Zaporozhians of Ukraine, who lived on the lower reaches of the River Dnieper, 'beyond the rapids'. In Russia, cossacks dwelt on the Don and its tributary the Donets; and also on the Rivers Terek, Volga and Yaik, which flowed into the Caspian Sea. The cossack settlements lay beyond the fortified frontier of Russia, and their inhabitants lived by fishing, piracy and fighting, often as mercenary soldiers. They regarded themselves as free to choose whether or not to serve in the tsar's armies, but with the creation of the new frontier towns a number of previously free cossacks permanently entered Russian state service.

Conflicts between the free cossacks and the Russian government were particularly acute on the Volga, where cossack piracy disrupted Muscovy's trade

---

[63] Skrynnikov, *Rossiya v nachale XVII v.*, pp. 20–7, 112–15.

[64] For discussion of the cossacks in the second half of the sixteenth century, see Skrynnikov, *Sibirskaya ekspeditsiya Ermaka*, ch. 3; Longworth, *The Cossacks*, ch. 1.

and diplomatic links with Persia. Downriver from Kazan' the Russians had established a number of fortified ports – Samara, Saratov and Tsaritsyn – to protect their communications with Astrakhan' and to exert surveillance over the indigenous nomadic peoples of the Volga basin, such as the Bashkirs and the Nogai Tatars. Punitive expeditions launched against the river pirates from these new fortresses drove many Volga cossacks further afield, to the Yaik, the Don and the Terek, in the hope of enjoying greater freedom. After Boris's accession to the throne, however, and especially after the construction of the southerly fortress of Tsarev-Borisov in 1599, the government endeavoured to exert more control over the Don cossacks, forbidding them to trade in the Russian frontier fortresses, and imprisoning those who did venture into towns.[65]

The conquest of Kazan' and Astrakhan' had provided the Russians with access not only to the Caspian Sea and to Persia, but also to the North Caucasus. Russian cossacks were to be found in the mountains above the River Terek as early as the 1550s. The Kabardinian khan sought the support of the Russians against the Turks (an alliance that was cemented by Tsar Ivan's marriage in 1561 to the Kabardinian princess Mariya Temryukovna), and in 1567 the Russians established a fortress on the River Terek. Later a new fort was constructed at the mouth of the Terek, in order to protect Russian communications with Kabarda and with Orthodox Georgia, which sought Russian aid against Turkey and against the Moslem prince (Shevkal) of Tarki in Daghestan. In 1593 Russian troops established a fort on the River Koisu, but failed to obtain a foothold in Tarki itself. A second attempt to capture Tarki in 1604 ended in the defeat and massacre of a Russian army by the Shevkal and his Turkish allies.

The end of the Livonian War had also led to Russian eastward expansion beyond the Urals, into Siberia.[66] Towards the end of the reign of Ivan the Terrible, the Stroganov merchants of Sol' Vychegodsk, on the River Vychegda, hired the cossack *ataman* Ermak to defend their expanding trading interests against raids by the Siberian Tatars. The cossacks advanced eastward and defeated the Siberian khan Kuchum, but Ermak himself was killed in a Tatar counter-attack in 1584. From 1586, however, new attempts were made to establish a Russian presence in Siberia. Forts were constructed in 1586 at Tyumen' on the River Tura and at Tobol'sk on the Irtysh, and subsequently a further chain of forts was built along the River Ob, culminating in the founding of Tomsk in 1604. Their new subject peoples in Siberia provided the Russians with valuable tribute in the form of furs.

---

[65] Stanislavskii, *Grazhdanskaya voina*, pp. 17–20.
[66] For a detailed account of Ermak's pioneering activity in Siberia, see Skrynnikov, *Sibirskaya ekspeditsiya Ermaka*.

Tsar Boris

Boris at first moved cautiously to establish his power. Immediately after his election he pursued a conciliatory policy towards his erstwhile opponents. On the day of Godunov's coronation, Alexander Nikitich Romanov was made a boyar, and his brother Michael received the rank of *okol'nichii*. Bogdan Bel'skii, who was first cousin to Boris's wife, the new Tsaritsa Mariya Grigor'evna, also became an *okol'nichii*.[67] Within a couple of years, however, Bel'skii and the Romanovs were in disgrace. In 1599 Bel'skii was entrusted with the construction of the new fortress of Tsarev-Borisov on the Donets. Soon it was reported that Bel'skii had been rash enough to boast that while Boris was tsar in Moscow, he – Bel'skii – was tsar in Borisov. Godunov chose to interpret this as treason. Bel'skii was summoned back to Moscow, and subjected to humiliating punishment: a Scottish officer named Gabriel was ordered to remove Bel'skii's luxuriant beard by pulling it out in handfuls. The self-styled tsar of Tsarev-Borisov was then sent into exile, and all his property was confiscated.[68]

In 1600 Boris turned his attention to the Romanovs. Alexander Nikitich was accused of plotting to poison the tsar, and his brothers Fedor, Ivan, Michael and Vasilii were also implicated. Fedor Nikitich, the eldest brother and head of the clan, was forced to become a monk – which deprived him of the possibility of ever acceding to the throne – and he was incarcerated, under the name of Filaret, in the Antoniev Siiskii monastery in the north of Russia. His wife and children, together with the rest of the clan, were imprisoned in remote localities. Other kinsmen of the Romanovs, including the boyar Prince Boris Kambulatovich Cherkasskii, were also subjected to exile and imprisonment. Alexander, Michael and Vasilii Romanov soon died in exile, as did Prince Boris Cherkasskii. In 1602, however, some of the survivors, including Ivan Nikitich Romanov, were pardoned and allowed to return to Moscow; but Fedor-Filaret remained in exile.[69] Boris's victims may also have included the Shuiskiis, who, according to Margeret, were 'exiled several times'.[70] Russian sources state that Prince Ivan Ivanovich Shuiskii was denounced for sorcery and was deprived of his rank as boyar, but do not provide evidence of any systematic persecution of the clan.[71]

It is impossible to tell whether there really were any conspiracies against Boris at this time. R.G. Skrynnikov suggests that Godunov was responding to genuine plots by the boyars, who aimed to prevent Boris's son Fedor from

---

[67] Zimin, *V kanun*, p. 232; Pavlov, *Gosudarev dvor*, pp. 64–5.
[68] Bussov, *Moskovskaya khronika*, pp. 92–3; Skrynnikov, *Sotsial'no-politicheskaya bor'ba*, pp. 18–20, 27–8.
[69] Skrynnikov, *Sotsial'no-politicheskaya bor'ba*, pp. 21–6, 28–34.
[70] Margeret, *The Russian Empire*, p. 60.
[71] Pavlov, *Gosudarev dvor*, pp. 76–7.

succeeding to the throne, should the tsar succumb to an illness that afflicted him in 1600.[72] But the evidence for this is slight, and it seems more probable that Boris was simply taking his revenge on those who had opposed his election in 1598.[73]

According to foreign observers, Boris fabricated cases against his boyar victims by encouraging their slaves to denounce them as traitors. Isaac Massa asserts that Boris had members of leading families falsely denounced, then secretly persecuted them.[74] And the French mercenary Jacques Margeret states that 'if a servant came to accuse his master, however falsely, with the hope of freeing himself, he was rewarded by Boris. Then the master or one of his principal servants would be tortured to make him confess to that which he had never done, or seen, or heard.'[75] The Russian chronicler confirms Margeret's assertion that Boris offered generous rewards to slaves who denounced their masters. Prince Fedor Shestunov's slave Voika served as an example, when he publicly accused Prince Fedor of treason and was rewarded with money, an estate and the rank of *syn boyarskii*. Other slaves followed suit, and were similarly rewarded: while slaves who refused to testify against their masters were tortured, imprisoned and killed.[76] In inciting slaves to denounce their masters as traitors, in order to further his own political interests, Boris was reviving a notorious practice of Ivan the Terrible's reign, which he himself had earlier used against the Shuiskiis in 1586.[77]

Slaves were no doubt particularly willing to denounce their owners in cases where they had suffered at their hands: revenge for harsh treatment could thus be legitimised as the deserved punishment of traitors, while the accusers enjoyed rewards for their loyal service to the tsar. These campaigns of political denunciation – encouraged by Tsars Ivan and Boris for reasons of their own – may have helped to reinforce a popular stereotype of the boyars as traitors to the tsar as well as exploiters of their social inferiors. This was an important component of the 'popular monarchism' that was in process of formation in late sixteenth-century Russia.[78] Ivan's persecution of the boyars in the *oprichnina* period had created the impression that he sought to eliminate abuses of their powers; and this contributed to the development of an image of the tsar as the protector of the ordinary people against mistreatment by the magnates. Ivan the Terrible had shamelessly manipulated public opinion in order to create his image as a 'good tsar'; and Boris too may have hoped to capitalise on popular hostility to the boyars in order to gain support

---

[72] Skrynnikov, *Sotsial'no-politicheskaya bor'ba*, pp. 24–6.
[73] Pavlov, *Gosudarev dvor*, pp. 73–6.
[74] Massa, *A Short History*, p. 44.
[75] Margeret, *The Russian Empire*, p. 60.
[76] *PSRL*, vol. 14, p. 52, para. 70.
[77] *Ibid.*, pp. 36–7, para. 13.
[78] Perrie, 'The Popular Image of Ivan the Terrible'; Perrie, *The Image of Ivan the Terrible*.

for himself. But, as subsequent events were to demonstrate, popular monarchism was a double-edged weapon, and Godunov ran the risk of being himself perceived as a 'traitor-boyar' who had usurped the throne.

Soon, in addition to the problem of conspiracies, real or imaginary, Boris was faced with a natural calamity. At the beginning of the seventeenth century Russia was afflicted by a severe famine that was to last for three years.[79] The summer of 1601 was unusually cold and wet, and the autumn frosts arrived early, ruining the harvest. In the spring of 1602, severe frost destroyed the winter-sown grain, and the crops failed again. And although growing conditions were more favourable in 1603, the peasants did not have sufficient seedcorn to produce a decent crop. Grain prices soared, in spite of an attempt by the government to prevent speculation.[80] According to the harrowing accounts of contemporaries, Russians were reduced to eating cats and dogs, and even to cannibalism. Villages were deserted by their starving inhabitants, and corpses littered the roads leading to the towns and cities which were the centres of famine-relief operations organised by the government. The population of the capital was swollen by fugitives from the hungry provinces, attracted by the prospect of generous relief provision. But the state's resources were inadequate for the scale of the disaster. Starvation was accompanied by disease, and as many as 120,000 deaths were recorded in Moscow alone.[81]

Boris's programme of famine-relief consisted not only in the distribution of state reserves of grain and money, but also in measures to increase the mobility of the unfree categories of the population. A gradual process of enserfment in the second half of the sixteenth century had eroded the traditional right of peasants to leave their landlords in the autumn, on St George's Day.[82] In November 1601, however, Boris restored this right to certain categories of peasants, and the concession was repeated in November 1602.[83]

---

[79] Smirnov, *Vosstanie Bolotnikova*, pp. 63–5; Koretskii, *Formirovanie krepostnogo prava*, pp. 117–48; Skrynnikov, *Rossiya v nachale XVII v.*, pp. 38–44.

[80] *Zakonodatel'nye akty*, no. 49, pp. 67–9.

[81] For contemporary eyewitness accounts of the famine, see *PSRL*, vol. 14, p. 56, para. 76; Palitsyn, *Skazanie*, pp. 105–6; *VIB*, pp. 49–50; Bussov, *Moskovskaya khronika*, pp. 97–8; Margeret, *The Russian Empire*, pp. 58–9; Massa, *A Short History*, pp. 51–4.

[82] The precise character of the process of enserfment in the 1580s and 1590s is still the subject of considerable scholarly debate. See, for example, Smith, *The Enserfment*, pp. 23, 98; Hellie, *Enserfment and Military Change*, pp. 96–106; Koretskii, *Zakreposhchenie krest'yan*, ch. 2; Koretskii, *Formirovanie krepostnogo prava*, chs. 1–2; Skrynnikov, *Rossiya nakanune*, ch. 12.

[83] *Zakonodatel'nye akty*, nos. 50–1, pp. 70–1. For discussion of this legislation, see Smirnov, *Vosstanie Bolotnikova*, pp. 65–6; Koretskii, *Formirovanie krepostnogo prava*, ch. 4; Skrynnikov, *Rossiya v nachale XVII v.*, pp. 45–50.

In addition to the peasantry, Muscovite Russia had various categories of slaves.[84] Former freemen who sold themselves into slavery as a result of endebtedness (*kabal'nye kholopy*) often served their masters as household servants or as agricultural labourers. Others, who might themselves have been impoverished nobles, comprised a category of 'military slaves', professional soldiers who formed part of their masters' armed retinues and accompanied them on campaign when they had to render military service to the crown. Legislation enacted in 1597 prevented slaves from freeing themselves by paying off their debts; they were obliged to serve until the death of their masters.[85] In August 1603, however, Boris issued a decree liberating slaves whose masters had dismissed them from their service in the course of the famine and had left them to fend for themselves.[86] The monastic chronicler Avraamii Palitsyn explains that during the famine some noblemen had freed their slaves; but others had simply driven them out without manumission documents, thereby preventing them from entering the service of new masters. These former bondsmen joined the ranks of the destitute slaves of boyars who had been disgraced in the opening years of Boris's reign. Some were able to survive as independent artisans, but many died of hunger. The military bondsmen, however, migrated to the south-western frontier, where they engaged in 'great sin', 20,000 of them later joining forces with the cossacks (*starye vory*) in the Bolotnikov revolt of 1606–7.[87]

In 1602–3 there was widespread unrest in central Russia. According to Isaac Massa, in September 1603 many boyars' bondslaves joined forces to attack and plunder travellers, and made the roads to Poland and Livonia impassable.[88] This was the 'banditry' which the *New Chronicle* describes as being led by a certain Khlopa or Khlopko – a nickname derived from *kholop*, the Russian word for slave. In the famine years the bandits operated not only in the wilds, but also close to the capital. Boris sent his commander Ivan Basmanov against them, and Basmanov's troops engaged in open battle with Khlopko's men near Moscow. Basmanov was killed in the battle, but the bandits were routed and fled to the south-west borderlands (*ukraina*), with the tsar's forces in hot pursuit.[89] According to Massa, Basmanov's troops were ambushed by the bandits, who were subsequently captured and hanged

---

[84] For discussion of slavery, see Hellie, *Slavery in Russia*; Paneyakh, *Kholopstvo*; Skrynnikov, *Rossiya nakanune*, ch. 9.

[85] *Zakonodatel'nye akty*, no. 47, pp. 64–6.

[86] *Ibid.*, no. 52, pp. 71–2.

[87] Palitsyn, *Skazanie*, pp. 106–8.

[88] Massa, *A Short History*, p. 65. The Dutch original is *lyfeygene knechte*; the Russian translation as *kholopy* (slaves) is probably more correct than 'serfs' in Edward Orchard's English version: Massa, 'Kratkoe povestvovanie', p. 96.

[89] *PSRL*, vol. 14, p. 58, para. 84.

by government forces.[90] Khlopko himself was amongst those taken prisoner, having been severely wounded in the battle outside Moscow.[91]

Russian historians writing in the Soviet period tended to present the Khlopko rising as an anti-feudal struggle of slaves and peasants which was either a 'precursor' of the Peasant War or the first stage of that war.[92] R. G. Skrynnikov, however, has recently argued that there is no evidence that peasants participated in the rising, and he speculates that those slaves who resorted to banditry in the famine years were not agricultural labourers, but rather the former military bondsmen described by Palitsyn. Their predatory actions, far from constituting part of an anti-feudal peasant war, actually added to the suffering of the famine-stricken peasants and the urban poor.[93]

It is doubtful whether the events of the famine years can be seen as a part of the Time of Troubles. By 1604 the effects of the famine had largely been overcome, and social unrest in central Russia, at least, had subsided. The famine did however leave a legacy in the form of the destitute military bondsmen who drifted to the south-west frontier, where they were subsequently to provide eager recruits for the army of the First False Dimitry and later for Bolotnikov. If Skrynnikov is correct in his surmise that these men had earlier participated in the banditry that plagued central Russia in 1602–3, then there may well have been an element of continuity between the Khlopko rising and the Time of Troubles. But it was the appearance of 'Tsarevich Dimitry' on the border, and his incursion into the Seversk lands, that was to mark the real beginning of the civil war in Russia.

---

[90] Massa, *A Short History*, p. 65.

[91] *PSRL*, vol. 14, p. 58, para. 84.

[92] For the view that the events of 1602–3 were the 'precursor' of the Peasant War (i.e. of the Bolotnikov revolt of 1606–7), see Smirnov, *Vosstanie Bolotnikova*, pp. 71–83. A. A. Zimin was the main advocate of the rival interpretation, that the Khlopko rising was the first stage in a more protracted Peasant War that lasted from 1602 to 1614: Zimin, 'Nekotorye voprosy', pp. 98–9.

[93] Skrynnikov, *Rossiya v nachale XVII v.*, pp. 69–72; Skrynnikov, *Smuta v Rossii*, pp. 249–50; Skrynnikov, 'The Civil War in Russia', pp. 62–3. Skrynnikov's views on this episode – as on many others – have undergone considerable modification in recent years. In his biography of Boris Godunov he wrote as follows about the events of 1603: 'Official sources tried to discredit the actions of the lower classes by describing them as "banditry", but in reality a peasant war was emerging (*nazrevala*) in Russia' (Skrynnikov, *Boris Godunov*, 1978, p. 153).

Part 1

The First False Dimitry

1   The fugitive monk

Rumours of a pretender

The first mention of a False Dimitry occurred within a month of the death of Tsar Fedor Ivanovich. On 5/15 February 1598, at the height of the election campaign, Andrzej Sapieha, the commandant of the Lithuanian frontier town of Orsha, sent a curious report to Krzysztof Radziwiłł, the governor of Vilnius, about events across the Russian border. Sapieha reported rumours that a letter had been sent to the city of Smolensk in the name of Dimitry, stating that he had succeeded to the throne; it seemed that he had been in hiding until the time was right for him to appear. The boyars in Moscow had investigated the story, and had been assured by a member of the Nagoi clan that Dimitry of Uglich was dead, murdered on the orders of Boris Godunov. But Boris had a friend who greatly resembled the dead tsarevich, and he hoped to have this man made tsar if he himself were not elected. In the course of the boyars' investigation, Boris was accused not only of having murdered Dimitry, but also of having poisoned Tsar Fedor in order to obtain the throne for himself. During the quarrel, Fedor Nikitich Romanov had attempted to stab Boris Godunov to death.[1]

Sapieha's sensational report was based on information supplied by a spy whom he had sent across the frontier into Russia, and confirmed by a Russian merchant who had come to Orsha from Smolensk.[2] Its contents are very improbable, and it is difficult to draw any firm conclusions from it.[3] We do not know whether a letter in Dimitry's name really did appear in Smolensk, or whether this was just a rumour. No other source refers to the existence of a pretender at this early date; and it is of course highly unlikely that Boris should have groomed a false Dimitry as his own puppet. The suggestion that he had done so was undoubtedly put about by his opponents in order to

---

[1] Prochaska, ed., *Archiwum domu Sapiehów*, vol. 1, pp. 177–9. For Russian translations of this letter, see Ptashitskii, 'Perepiska litovskogo kantslera', pp. 209–11; and 'Iz L'vovskogo arkhiva', pp. 340–3.

[2] Prochaska, ed., *Archiwum domu Sapiehów*, vol. 1, pp. 177, 179.

[3] For discussion of Sapieha's report, see Platonov, *Ocherki*, pp. 178–80; Golubtsov, ' "Izmena" smol'nyan', pp. 221–31; Zimin, *V kanun*, pp. 216–17.

discredit him. Not only did the rumour depict Boris as the patron of a pretender; but by implying that he wanted to rule through an impostor, it also highlighted the weakness of his claim to the throne in his own right. Nevertheless, Sapieha's report provides evidence that the idea of a False Dimitry had been formulated and put into circulation in 1598. The seed had been broadcast: it remained to be seen where it would take root, and what fruit it would bear.

According to Jacques Margeret, Dimitry's name resurfaced two years later. Boris's persecutions of 1600 onwards, Margeret argues, were inspired by the circulation of rumours that Dimitry was still alive.[4] The historian S. F. Platonov, noting that the disgrace of the Romanovs in 1600 coincided with the appearance of these rumours about Dimitry, suggested that Boris might have suspected them of setting up a pretender.[5] K. V. Chistov, however, has argued that the rumours of 1600 constituted evidence not of a plot by the Romanovs and other boyars, but of the formation of a 'popular socio-utopian legend' about Dimitry as a 'returning tsar-deliverer' who had escaped death at the hands of the villainous traitor Boris Godunov. This 'legend' about Dimitry, Chistov asserted, 'was not the fruit of an individual's devising, but arose naturally, and was devised by the collective consciousness of the peasant, cossack and urban masses'.[6] In the view of R. G. Skrynnikov, too, Margeret's evidence indicates that rumours about Dimitry were circulating widely among the ordinary people in 1600, possibly inspired by Boris's serious illness in that year, which revived concern for the succession.[7]

According to Chistov and Skrynnikov, therefore, reports that Dimitry was alive had become widespread among the masses by 1600. They both face some difficulty in explaining why, if this were so, there is no evidence that such rumours played any part in the Khlopko rising of 1603. Chistov's explanation is that at that time 'the legend had not yet acquired the necessary . . . social colouration': in other words, there were no expectations at this stage that Dimitry's return would lead to social improvements for the ordinary people. It was not until 1604, in the aftermath of the famine, according to Chistov, that the rumours that the tsarevich was still alive were transformed into a fully formed 'socio-utopian legend, capable of uniting the masses in a particular struggle'.[8] The emergence of the 'socio-utopian legend' was 'accompanied' by the appearance of a pretender.[9] Skrynnikov agrees with Chistov that it took some time before the 'legend' of Dimitry acquired a

[4] Margeret, *The Russian Empire*, pp. 60–1.
[5] Platonov, *Ocherki*, pp. 186–7.
[6] Chistov, *Russkie narodnye*, pp. 40–1.
[7] Skrynnikov, *Rossiya v nachale XVII v.*, pp. 81–2.
[8] Chistov, *Russkie narodnye*, p. 41.
[9] *Ibid.*, p. 42.

'social colouration' and became a force capable of uniting the actions of the lower orders. This was why the insurgent followers of Khlopko did not make use of Dimitry's name in 1603. Like Chistov, Skrynnikov implies that the appearance of the First False Dimitry was somehow inspired by a socio-utopian legend: 'Popular rumours and expectations,' he writes, 'created the soil for the appearance of a pretender.'[10]

There is however no clear evidence that the belief that Dimitry was alive was widespread among the Russian people before the pretender's invasion in 1604. If Margeret is correct that rumours about Dimitry were current in 1600 (and no other source dates them so early), it seems likely that they reflected the first stages of the activity of the pretender himself, rather than the formation of a 'popular socio-utopian legend' about Tsarevich Dimitry of Uglich.

The man who called himself Dimitry

In 1603 a young man appeared on the estate of Prince Adam Vishnevetskii (Wiśniowiecki) at Brahin in Lithuania, claiming to be Tsarevich Dimitry of Uglich, the youngest son of Ivan the Terrible.

Conrad Bussow provides a colourful account of Dimitry's revelation of his royal identity. According to Bussow, the pretender obtained employment as a valet in Prince Adam's service. One day, when the young man was attending him in his bath, Vishnevetskii lost his temper with him and boxed him on the ears. The servant burst into tears at this humiliation, and cried out, 'If only you knew who I really am!' When Vishnevetskii demanded an explanation, the youth launched into an account of his escape from death at the hands of Boris's assassins, and showed Prince Adam a golden cross, richly bejewelled, which, he said, had been given to him at his christening by his godfather Prince Ivan Mstislavskii. Vishnevetskii was immediately convinced of the young man's royal origin, and ordered his servants to bring him clothing fit for a prince.[11]

The Russian chronicle provides an equally dramatic account of how the young man, who had obtained employment as a servant in Prince Adam's house, revealed his 'true' identity. Pretending to be fatally ill, he took to his bed and in a bare whisper asked for a priest to be sent to hear his confession. He begged the priest to give him an honourable burial, befitting a tsar's son. He was too ill, he said, to tell his full story, but under his bed he had a document which would explain everything. When he was dead, the priest should read it secretly, but not tell anyone what it contained, for this was

[10] Skrynnikov, *Rossiya v nachale XVII v.*, p. 82.
[11] Bussov, *Moskovskaya khronika*, pp. 94–5.

God's will. The priest, however, told Prince Adam the story, and Vishnevetskii appeared at his servant's sickbed to interrogate him personally. The youth made an apparent effort to conceal the manuscript, but Prince Adam seized it by force and read it. According to the chronicler, this piece of paper, which the youth had written himself, described how Dimitry had escaped death at the hands of Boris's assassins: the son of a priest at Uglich had been killed in his stead, while the real tsarevich had been saved by some boyars and by the Shchelkalovs, officials who had been entrusted by Tsar Ivan with his care.[12]

These accounts of the pretender's revelation of his identity are likely to be fanciful and legendary. Certainly Prince Adam himself did not provide any such dramatic details. In a letter dated 7 October 1603, Vishnevetskii informed the Polish chancellor, Jan Zamoyski, that a man had arrived at his house claiming to be the son of Tsar Ivan, and hoping that the king would help him to regain his father's throne. Vishnevetskii had had initial doubts about his visitor's story, but more than twenty Muscovites had subsequently recognised him as the tsarevich, and he thought it worth informing Zamoyski about him.[13] Zamoyski was sceptical and non-committal. He wrote back suggesting that Prince Adam notify King Sigismund directly about Dimitry, as a possible preliminary to sending the pretender in person either to the king or to Zamoyski himself, to enable them to form their own judgement of his claim.[14] It was in response to this request that Vishnevetskii sent Sigismund an account of Dimitry's biography which was subsequently forwarded to the Vatican on 8 November by the papal nuncio in Craców, Claudio Rangoni.[15]

This report purportedly conveyed the pretender's own account of himself. Rangoni told the Vatican that Vishnevetskii had only lent his pen to his guest, and that its substance had emanated exclusively from the hero of the tale.[16] The story began with some historical background about Ivan the Terrible, his wives and sons. It then proceeded to the reign of Fedor, and described how Boris Godunov had plotted to obtain the throne for himself. Having gained power by killing his fellow regents, Boris conspired against Dimitry's life. He assigned the tsarevich tutors of his own choosing, whom he hoped to use as his agents to poison him. One of these tutors, however, warned Dimitry of Boris's intentions. His attempt to kill him by poison having been thwarted, Boris next hired assassins to cut Dimitry's throat while he was asleep in bed at night. The tutor, however, again intervened. He substituted

[12] *PSRL*, vol. 14, p. 60, para. 86.
[13] Sobieski, *Szkice Historyczne*, pp. 81–2. For a Russian translation, see Pirling, 'Nazvannyi Dimitrii i Adam Vishnevetskii', pp. 125–6.
[14] Zholkevskii, *Zapiski*, pril. no. 3, cols. 7–10 (misdated Feb.–Apr. 1604: cf. Skrynnikov, *Sotsial'no-politicheskaya bor'ba*, p. 150, n. 4).
[15] Pirling, 'Nazvannyi Dimitrii i Adam Vishnevetskii', p. 126.
[16] Pirling, *La Russie et le Saint-Siège*, vol. 3, p. 42.

another boy, a relative of the tsarevich, of a similar age, who was killed in his stead while the tutor helped Dimitry to escape. Soon after this the tutor fell gravely ill, but before he died he entrusted the tsarevich to the care of a faithful friend, a nobleman, who brought the boy up. When this protector in turn was about to die, he advised Dimitry to enter a monastery. The tsarevich became a monk, and wandered from one monastery to another. One day a fellow monk recognised him as Dimitry, 'because of his way of walking and heroic manners'. Fearing danger, he fled to Poland. He stayed secretly with the Duke of Ostrog (Prince Vasilii Ostrozhskii, the governor of Kiev) and with Lord Gabriel Hoyski; then he eventually came to Prince Vishnevetskii's house, and there declared himself to be the Prince of Moscow.[17]

To a modern scholar, this account of the pretender's biography is of course highly unconvincing. As the Jesuit historian Pierling has shown, the report contains some accurate, detailed and little known information, together with much which is inaccurate and highly improbable. Some of the details of the riot at Uglich which followed the discovery of the body suggest that the author may have been familiar with the events of 1591 (although he suggests that the murder took place at night). The least convincing part of the report is the section which describes Dimitry's escape from Uglich and his subsequent life: Dimitry's two protectors are not named, and their premature deaths meant that no witnesses could be produced to vouch for the young man's story.[18] These weaknesses in the pretender's own attempt to demonstrate that he was Dimitry of Uglich have convinced most historians that, whoever else he may have been, he was certainly not the youngest son of Ivan the Terrible.[19]

In spite of the improbabilities of the young man's story, Adam Vishnevetskii was willing to accept him as Tsarevich Dimitry. It was probably not accidental that the pretender turned up on Prince Adam's estate and found support for his story there. Adam Vishnevetskii had his own reasons for acknowledging a pretender to the Russian throne. The Vishnevetskii family, a clan of powerful and independent Ukrainian magnates, had a history of involvement in such adventures. A famous ancestor of Prince Adam's, Dimi-

---

[17] Nowakowski, ed., *Źródła do dziejów Polski*, vol. 2, pp. 65–70. This is a Latin translation of the Polish original, wrongly dated 1606. Pierling established the correct date by discovering that this text is virtually identical to the report which Rangoni forwarded to the Vatican with a letter dated 8 November 1603: Pierling, *La Russie et le Saint-Siège*, vol. 3, pp. 42, 399. See also the Italian version incorporated into Rangoni's letter of 2 July 1605 to Pope Paul V: *ibid.*, pp. 431–4.

[18] Pierling, *La Russie et le Saint-Siège*, vol. 3, pp. 401–5; Pirling, *Iz smutnogo vremeni*, pp. 2–12. See also the evaluation of the pretender's story by Skrynnikov: *Samozvantsy*, pp. 35–6.

[19] Even historians such as A. S. Suvorin, K. Waliszewski, S. D. Sheremetev and P. L. Barbour, who argue that the pretender was the real tsarevich, base their conclusions not on Adam Vishnevetskii's report to King Sigismund, but on Jerome Horsey's account of the events of May 1591. See Perrie, 'Jerome Horsey's Account', pp. 36–8.

try Vishnevetskii, had supported a Moldavian pretender in the sixteenth century,[20] and the Vishnevetskiis were also linked by marriage with Jeremy Mogila, the Polish candidate who gained the Moldavian throne in 1595.[21] The pretender may well have known of these encouraging precedents. The Vishnevetskiis, moreover, could claim a distant kinship by marriage with the old Muscovite dynasty. A sister of Ivan IV's grandmother, Anna Glinskaya, had married a Vishnevetskii prince.[22] Recognition by the Vishnevetskiis therefore had a particular significance for Ivan's supposed son.[23] But the most immediate motive for Vishnevetskii's acceptance of Dimitry was his land dispute with Boris Godunov. Prince Adam's estates on the left bank of the River Dnieper included territory which was contested between Russia and Lithuania. Two towns on the border which were claimed by Vishnevetskii had been burned by the Russians in 1603, and Prince Adam would undoubtedly have welcomed a pretext for a war of revenge against Muscovy.[24]

On receiving Vishnevetskii's report, King Sigismund requested him to bring the pretender to Craców.[25] But before Prince Adam could obey, Dimitry left Brahin and entrusted himself to the patronage of Prince Adam's cousin, Prince Constantine Vishnevetskii, and to Prince Constantine's father-in-law, Jerzy Mniszech, the Palatine of Sandomierz, whose family seat was at Sambor in Poland. It is not entirely clear why the pretender made this move. Bussow relates that when Boris heard that a supposed Dimitry was at Brahin, he sent envoys to Prince Adam Vishnevetskii to offer him certain Russian towns and fortresses, and a large sum of money, if he would hand the impostor over to him. Vishnevetskii refused, interpreting Boris's action as evidence of the pretender's authenticity. Fearing that the tsar might try to kidnap Dimitry, he moved him further from the border, to his ancestral castle of Vishnevets. When Boris offered a greater reward, and sent assassins to kill Dimitry, Prince Adam moved him even deeper into the heartland of Poland, to the Mniszechs' estate at Sambor.[26] R. G. Skrynnikov, however, suggests that the pretender himself quickly became disenchanted with Prince Adam's ability to help him, and turned his attention instead to Polish families with influence at court. Unlike his cousin Prince Adam, who was Orthodox, Prince Con-

---

[20] Sobieski, *Szkice Historyczne*, pp. 51–2, 75; Pirling, 'Nazvannyi Dimitrii i Adam Vishnevetskii', p. 124; Golobutskii, *Zaporozhskoe kazachestvo*, p. 83; Mokhov, *Ocherki*, pp. 44–5.
[21] Golobutskii, *Zaporozhskoe kazachestvo*, pp. 133–5.
[22] Tikhomirov, 'Samozvanshchina', 1964, p. 21; Tikhomirov, 'Samozvanshchina', 1969, p. 118.
[23] Skrynnikov, *Sotsial'no-politicheskaya bor'ba*, p. 115.
[24] Pierling, *La Russie et le Saint-Siège*, vol. 3, pp. 46–7; Sobieski, *Szkice Historyczne*, pp. 68–79; Pirling, 'Nazvannyi Dimitrii i Adam Vishnevetskii', p. 124; Barbour, *Dimitry*, pp. 7–8; Skrynnikov, *Sotsial'no-politicheskaya bor'ba*, pp. 113–15.
[25] Pierling, *La Russie et le Saint-Siège*, vol. 3, p. 41.
[26] Bussov, *Moskovskaya khronika*, pp. 95–6.

stantine Vishnevetskii was a Catholic, and had powerful contacts in Poland.[27]

While he was still on Prince Adam's estate at Brahin, the pretender and his patron had tried to recruit support both from the Zaporozhian and from the Don cossacks, but met with little success. The Zaporozhians apparently suspected, with good reason, that Dimitry would be unable to pay them; the Don cossacks were more responsive, but their envoys were arrested at the frontier. Attempts to establish contacts with the Crimean Tatars were also unsuccessful.[28] Dimitry's new patrons, on the other hand, offered him the opportunity of obtaining Polish troops.

From this point onwards, Dimitry's pretence became an issue of high-level international politics. Jerzy Mniszech belonged to a Polish faction who favoured the renewal of war with Russia, and for whom the appearance in Poland of a pretender to the Russian throne provided a convenient pretext for action. Mniszech offered Dimitry military aid in return for the promise of territorial gains at the expense of Russia. Their agreement was cemented by the pretender's betrothal to Mniszech's daughter Marina, and by his secret adoption of Roman Catholicism.

In March 1604 Jerzy Mniszech took Dimitry to Cracόw, where he had an audience with the king. Sigismund III was an ardent champion of the counter-reformation, and the prospect of the conversion of Orthodox Russia sorely tempted him to forget the peace he had recently concluded with Boris. There was strong opposition in the Polish Senate, however, to an adventure in support of Dimitry, and Sigismund was able to offer only semi-official encouragement to Mniszech's undertaking. The attitudes towards Dimitry of the rival factions in the *Sejm* were largely predetermined by their views on Polish foreign policy, but both sides made use of their assessments of the pretender's account of himself in order to justify their positions.

The Polish chancellor, Jan Zamoyski, who was particularly opposed to a Russian war, had been cautious about the pretender from the outset. In his reply to Adam Vishnevetskii's letter of 7 October 1603, Zamoyski had written: 'As for the Muscovite staying with Your Lordship, who calls himself the son of the Muscovite Prince Ivan Vasil'evich, then very often such matters turn out to be true, but often also to be inventions.'[29] Later, at a session of the *Sejm* on 1 February 1605, Zamoyski compared Dimitry's story to 'a comedy by Plautus or Terence'. Was it likely, he asked, that someone else could have been killed in the tsarevich's stead, as the pretender claimed? What sort of plotter did not check to make sure that the assassin he had hired

---

[27] Skrynnikov, *Sotsial'no-politicheskaya bor'ba*, p. 157; cf. Pierling, *La Russie et le Saint-Siège*, vol. 3, p. 55; Pirling, 'Nazvannyi Dimitrii i Adam Vishnevetskii', p. 127.

[28] Skrynnikov, *Sotsial'no-politicheskaya bor'ba*, pp. 152–5.

[29] Zholkevskii, *Zapiski*, pril. no. 3, col. 9.

had killed the right person?[30] Vishnevetskii's account had also met with a sceptical response in the Vatican. Pope Clement VIII wrote in the margin of Rangoni's despatch: 'Sara un altro Re di Portogallo resuscitato' – a reference to the false Don Sebastians of the 1590s.[31] In Poland, the bishop of Płock, in a letter to the king dated 6 March 1604, expressing his scepticism about various themes in the pretender's story, also compared Dimitry to the Portuguese pretenders, and to those of Moldavia.[32]

In spite of these doubters, however, Sigismund himself and many of his courtiers, as well as princes of the Catholic Church such as Claudio Rangoni and the veteran Jesuit Antonio Possevino, gave every appearance of taking Dimitry's story seriously. It seized the imagination of contemporaries, and various literary versions soon began to circulate in Europe.[33] Ironically, K. V. Chistov regards these foreign accounts as valuable evidence of the content of the 'popular socio-utopian legend' about Dimitry in the form in which it was circulating among contemporary Russians.[34] Chistov does not seem to realise that most of these versions of Dimitry's story are based on Adam Vishnevetskii's report to the king, and therefore reflect the account of himself that the pretender offered in Lithuania, rather than rumours current among the Russian masses.

Dimitry's Polish adherents claimed that their support for the pretender was based not only on his account of his escape from death, but also on the testimony of witnesses who identified him as Tsarevich Dimitry. In his letter to Jan Zamoyski of 7 October 1603, Adam Vishnevetskii had referred to the 'more than twenty Muscovites' whose recognition of Dimitry at Brahin had convinced him of the young man's authenticity.[35] Subsequently, further 'witnesses' were found to 'recognise' the tsarevich. In a circular letter to the senators of February 1604, in which he summarised Vishnevetskii's report on Dimitry of the previous November, King Sigismund described the testimony of a certain Livonian who had served the tsarevich and had been present at the time of his death. This Livonian had gone to see the pretender, and had identified him as Dimitry on the basis of conversations with him, and from familiar distinguishing marks on his body.[36] Rangoni reported fuller details to Rome: a Livonian who had been taken prisoner by the Russians in his childhood had recognised the pretender as Tsarevich Dimitry, recalling

---

[30] *RIB*, vol. 1, col. 16.

[31] Pierling, *La Russie et le Saint-Siège*, vol. 3, p. 41.

[32] *Ibid.*, pp. 64–5.

[33] For references to many of these sources, see Perrie, ' "Popular Socio-Utopian Legends" ', p. 230.

[34] Chistov, *Russkie narodnye*, pp. 43–4.

[35] Sobieski, *Szkice Historyczne*, p. 81.

[36] Sigismund's letters to Jan Zamoyski, 15 Feb. 1604, in Zholkevskii, *Zapiski*, pril. no. 2, cols. 7–8; and to Christopher Zenovich, 18 Feb. 1604, in Ptashitskii, 'Despoty Zenovichi', pp. 135–6.

that the young tsarevich had had a wart beside his nose, and one arm longer than the other – features which could be discerned also on the pretender.[37] It was apparently to this man that Jerzy Mniszech referred when he was interrogated by the Russian boyars after the pretender's death in 1606. Mniszech described the testimony of one Petrovskii, a servant of the Lithuanian chancellor, Leo Sapieha. Petrovskii claimed to have previously served Tsarevich Dimitry at Uglich, and recognised the young man who was staying with Prince Constantine Vishnevetskii as his former master, because of certain marks on his body.[38] The Russian authorities subsequently informed the Poles that Petrovskii had never been anywhere near Uglich. He was Petrusha, a former slave of the Russian *syn boyarskii* Istoma Mikhnev, who had escaped from his master when the latter was in Vilnius on a diplomatic mission, and who had then been taken into service by Leo Sapieha.[39]

Further witnesses to the pretender's identity were soon found. Jerzy Mniszech informed the boyars that when the pretender was staying with him at Sambor one of his servants had recognised the pretender as the true heir to the Russian throne. This servant, who had been captured by the Russians at Pskov during the Livonian War, and had been taken to Russia as a prisoner, claimed to have known Tsarevich Dimitry as a child. Mniszech also reported that a number of Muscovites had come to Craców and had identified the pretender as the tsarevich in front of the king and the senators.[40] The fugitive Russian monk Varlaam claimed in 1606 that Dimitry had been 'recognised' in the king's presence not only by 'Istoma Mikhnev's man Petrushka', but also by five brothers Khripunov, by a guide named Ivashko Shvar, and by some tradesmen from Kiev.[41] Later, when Tsar Vasilii Shuiskii's government reproached the Poles for accepting the pretender on the basis simply of the dubious evidence of Petrovskii and of Mniszech's servant, the Polish envoys to Moscow insisted that many other Russians had also acknowledged him as the true tsarevich.[42]

After his audience with the king in Craców, Dimitry returned with Mniszech to Sambor, and spent the summer gathering military support. Sigismund turned a blind eye to the private army that Mniszech was recruiting in the vicinity of Lwów. At the end of August, Dimitry left Sambor and began his march towards Moscow.

---

[37] Pierling, *La Russie et le Saint-Siège*, vol. 3, pp. 49–50, 434–5; Pierling, *Rome et Démétrius*, p. 176.

[38] *SGGiD*, vol. 2, no. 139, p. 294.

[39] *SIRIO*, vol. 137, p. 264. For further details, see Golubtsov, ' "Izmena" smol'nyan', pp. 241–2.

[40] *SGGiD*, vol. 2, no. 139, pp. 294–5.

[41] *AAE*, vol. 2, no. 64, p. 143. Two Khripunovs, Osip and Kiril, are mentioned in the 'Skazanie . . . o Rastrige', p. 10.

[42] *SIRIO*, vol. 137, pp. 565–6.

Plate 1 Inscription in the book presented by Prince Vasilii Ostrozhskii to
the monks Grigorii, Varlaam and Misail in 1602

Grisha Otrep'ev

Who was the First False Dimitry? Boris Godunov's government accused him
of being the renegade monk Grigorii (Grisha, Grishka) Otrep'ev, and this view
has generally predominated in subsequent scholarship.[43] The Russians were
apparently confident that they had identified the pretender by the summer of
1604, when Boris sent Grisha Otrep'ev's uncle, Smirnoi Otrep'ev, to Craców,
with secret instructions to inspect the self-styled Dimitry and denounce him.
The Poles, however, would not allow Smirnoi to see the pretender.[44]

---

[43] Historians who accept the view that the pretender was Grisha Otrep'ev include Karamzin,
Solov'ev and Skrynnikov. Others believe that Dimitry was an impostor, but do not consider
him to have been Otrep'ev. A range of alternative theories has been put forward concerning
his identity. The nineteenth-century historian Kostomarov argues that he was the son of a
petty Russian nobleman who fled to Poland–Lithuania in the reign of Ivan IV and had obtained
an estate there: Kostomarov, *Smutnoe vremya*, p. 642. Ilovaiskii believes that he was a petty
service nobleman from West Russia: Ilovaiskii, *Smutnoe vremya*, p. 328. According to the
French historian Prosper Mérimée, he was a Ukrainian cossack: Mérimée, *Episode*, pp. 301–
5. A contemporary Polish source reported that after Dimitry's arrival in Moscow he was said
to be the son of the Polish king (*Królewicz Polski*): Aleksandrenko, comp., 'Materialy', pp.
438, 539. The German mercenary Conrad Bussow claimed that he was an illegitimate son of
Stephen Bathory: Bussow, *Moskovskaya khronika*, p. 93, cf. Hirschberg, *Dymitr Samozwaniec*,
pp. 280–2. Isaac Massa reports that some Russians said he was 'a Pole sent by the machinations of the Jesuits into Muscovy': Massa, *A Short History*, p. 147. Jerome Horsey asserts
that he was 'son to a priest that carried aqua-vitae to sell about the country': Berry and
Crummey, eds., *Rude and Barbarous Kingdom*, p. 364. None of these hypotheses amounts
to anything more than speculation. Equally unconvincing are the views of those historians
(Sheremetev, Suvorin, Waliszewski, Barbour) who share the view of contemporaries such as
Jacques Margeret that the pretender really was Tsarevich Dimitry of Uglich. There is also a
fourth category of agnostic historians, including Platonov and Klyuchevskii, who believe that
the truth about the pretender's identity is impossible to determine on the basis of existing
evidence. For a discussion of the sources and historiography relating to the pretender's identity, see Ilovaiskii, *Smutnoe vremya*, pp. 324–7. See also Graham, 'A Note', pp. 357–60.

[44] Pierling, *La Russie et le Saint-Siège*, vol. 3, pp. 93–6.

In September 1604 Boris sent another envoy, Postnik Ogarev, to Poland with a letter to King Sigismund which depicted the pretender as Yushka (Yurii) Bogdanovich Otrep'ev, a good-for-nothing young nobleman who had been forced to take monastic vows because of his bad behaviour: 'in his wickedness he refused to obey his father, fell into heresy and delinquency, stole, gambled, caroused and frequently ran away from his father'.[45] After his tonsure, Yushka had become the monk Grisha. He had been a deacon in the Miracles monastery in the Moscow Kremlin, and subsequently served as a scribe at the court of Patriarch Iov. But he did not abandon his evil ways, and was sentenced by the Holy Synod to life imprisonment in the Beloozero monastery. To avoid this fate, he had fled from Moscow with the priest Varlaam and the chorister Misail Povadin. Grisha had gone to Kiev, where he had lived in the Pecherskii monastery. Thereafter he travelled to Ostrog and to the Vishnevetskiis at Brahin, where he had declared himself to be Tsarevich Dimitry of Uglich.[46]

Patriarch Iov's *gramota* (proclamation) of 14 January 1605 added some further details of Grisha's adventures, citing the evidence of three witnesses who had been Otrep'ev's companions on his journey to Lithuania, or who had encountered him there. The monk Pimen, from the Dneprov monastery, had told the Holy Synod that he had met Grisha, Varlaam and Misail at the Spasskii monastery at Novgorod Seversk and had guided them across the frontier into Lithuania.[47] Venedikt, from the great monastery of the Trinity and St Sergius, near Moscow, had met Grisha in Kiev at the Pecherskii and Nikol'skii monasteries, and with Prince Vasilii Ostrozhskii. Then Grisha had joined the Lutherans, and had begun to associate with the Zaporozhian cossacks. Venedikt had denounced him to the abbot (*igumen*) of the Pecherskii monastery, who had sent Venedikt with some of his monks and servants to apprehend him. But Grisha, learning of the search party, had sought refuge with Prince Adam Vishnevetskii, where he had begun to call himself Tsarevich Dimitry.[48] Stefan the icon-painter, a townsman from Yaroslavl', confirmed much of Venedikt's evidence. He had seen Grisha in Kiev as a deacon in the Pecherskii and Nikol'skii monasteries, and with Prince Vasilii Ostrozhskii; and Grisha had also come to his icon-stall in monastic dress, accompanied by Zaporozhian cossacks. Then Grisha had gone to Prince Adam Vishnevetskii and had begun to call himself Tsarevich Dimitry.[49]

The testimony of the monk Venedikt, that Grisha had consorted with 'Lutherans' (Protestants) after leaving Kiev, is consistent with the statement

---

[45] *SIRIO*, vol. 137, p. 176.
[46] *Ibid.*, pp. 176–7.
[47] *AAE*, vol. 2, no. 28, p. 79. Varlaam was later to state that the fugitives had been guided across the frontier from Novgorod Seversk by a certain Ivashka Semenov. See below, p. 47.
[48] *Ibid.*
[49] *Ibid.*

in Adam Vishnevetskii's report to the king that the pretender had stayed with Lord Gabriel Hoyski. Hoyski's residence at Hoszcza, near Ostrog, was a centre of Arianism (the doctrine of radical Protestant sectarians also known as Unitarians, Anti-trinitarians or Socinians). Hoyski was an ardent proselytiser for his faith, and had established a school at Hoszcza at which the pretender might have studied.[50] Venedikt's evidence indicates that Grisha had joined the Zaporozhian cossacks after his association with the 'Lutherans', although the testimony of Stefan the icon-painter suggests that Otrep'ev's links with the Zaporozhians began while he was still serving as a monk in Kiev. R. G. Skrynnikov speculates that Grisha may have established his contacts with the cossacks through the Arians, who had a number of adherents in Zaporozh'e.[51]

An important piece of evidence that helps to establish the pretender's identity as Grisha is the petition (izvet) addressed to Tsar Vasilii Shuiskii in 1606 by the monk Varlaam Yatskii who had accompanied Otrep'ev from Moscow to Lithuania in 1602.[52] Some pre-revolutionary historians were sceptical about the authenticity of this document,[53] but the work of Soviet scholars suggests that it is more reliable than its critics had thought.[54] Varlaam had been named by the Russian government as a companion and accomplice of Grisha during his flight from Moscow, and in his petition the monk was anxious to demonstrate his innocence in the entire affair. Varlaam insisted that he had known nothing of Otrep'ev's claim to be Tsarevich Dimitry until after they had parted company in Lithuania. Subsequently, when he learned that Grisha was calling himself Dimitry, Varlaam had gone to Craców and told the king that the supposed tsarevich was the monk Grigorii Otrep'ev who had accompanied him to Kiev from Moscow. The king and senators did not believe him, but sent him to Sambor, where the pretender was staying with Jerzy Mniszech. When Varlaam arrived at Sambor, the pretender

[50] See Pirling, Istoricheskie stat'i i zametki, pp. 148–60.
[51] Skrynnikov, Sotsial'no-politicheskaya bor'ba, pp. 111–12.
[52] AAE, vol. 2, no. 64, pp. 141–4; also in 'Inoe skazanie', RIB, vol. 13, cols. 18–25.
[53] Solov'ev accepted the izvet as a reliable source: Solov'ev, Istoriya Rossii, vol. 4, n. 65, pp. 697–9. But it was dismissed as a propagandistic fabrication by Kostomarov and Platonov: Kostomarov, Kto byl pervyi Lzhedimitrii?, pp. 20–4; Kostomarov, Smutnoe vremya, pp. 274–9; Platonov, Drevnerusskie skazaniya, pp. 12–14. See also Ilovaiskii, Smutnoe vremya, pp. 334–6.
[54] E. Kusheva argues that the original version of the izvet is the unpublished 'Academy' copy, and that the versions published in AAE, vol. 2 and in RIB, vol. 13 are later literary reworkings, incorporating the texts of the pretender's proclamations of 1604 and 1605: Kusheva, 'Iz istorii', pp. 39–58. I. A. Golubtsov reached similar conclusions independently at about the same time: Golubtsov, ' "Izmena" smol'nyan', pp. 243–51. Golubtsov also notes (ibid., p. 250) that the catalogue of the Russian Foreign Office of 1626 contains a reference to the interrogation of the elder Varlaam Yatskii in the year 113 (1604/5) (should be 114 or 115) about his relationship with Grishka. Their findings have been accepted by R. G. Skrynnikov: Sotsial'no-politicheskaya bor'ba, pp. 101–6.

ordered him to be stripped of his monastic attire, beaten and tortured. Dimitry alleged that Varlaam and his companion, the *syn boyarskii* Yakov Pykhachev, had been sent by Boris Godunov to kill him. Pykhachev was executed, denouncing Dimitry to the last as Grisha Otrep'ev;[55] Varlaam was put in irons and imprisoned. He was still languishing in the Sambor dungeon when Dimitry set off on his campaign on 15 August 1604.[56] After five months, somewhat to his surprise, he was freed by Mniszech's wife and her daughter Marina.[57] He went to the Pecherskii monastery in Kiev, and from there returned to Russia.[58]

According to Varlaam's petition, on the Monday of the second week in Lent in 1602 he had happened to meet a young monk on the Varvarka, a street near St Basil's Cathedral in central Moscow. The youth introduced himself as Grigorii Otrep'ev, a deacon of the Miracles monastery in the Kremlin. In spite of his elevated position as assistant to Patriarch Iov, the young man wished to renounce the worldly glory and wealth of the capital and planned to leave Moscow for a distant monastery in Chernigov. Varlaam had told him that the Chernigov monastery would be too small for someone who had experienced life in Moscow; Grigorii had then proposed a visit to the Pecherskii monastery in Kiev, as the first stage in a pilgrimage to Jerusalem, and suggested that Varlaam might like to accompany him. Varlaam objected that the Pecherskii monastery was in hostile Lithuanian territory, but his companion informed him that a peace treaty had recently been signed between Poland and Russia, and the border could now be crossed freely. Varlaam's patriotic scruples having thus been assuaged, they agreed to meet next day on the Icon-Painters' Row, near Red Square.[59]

When Varlaam turned up at the appointed place and time, he found Grigorii with another companion, the monk Misail Povadin, whom Varlaam already knew, having encountered him at the home of Prince Ivan Ivanovich Shuiskii (I. I. Shuiskii, who was in disgrace under Boris Godunov, was the brother of the future Tsar Vasilii). They headed south-west via Bolkhov and Karachev to Novgorod Seversk, where they obtained the services of a guide, Ivashko Semenov, who took them to Starodub, and thence across the Lithuan-

---

[55] Pierling notes that Varlaam's petition is the only Russian source to report that Pykhachev was executed at Sambor, a fact which is confirmed by a letter from Jerzy Mniszech to Rangoni of 18 September 1604. In Pierling's eyes, this confirms the reliability of Varlaam's evidence: Pierling, *Rome et Démétrius*, pp. 53, 201–2; Pierling, *La Russie et le Saint-Siège*, vol. 3, p. 415; Pirling, *Iz smutnogo vremeni*, pp. 24–5. See also Skrynnikov, *Sotsial'no-politicheskaya bor'ba*, p. 170.

[56] *AAE*, vol. 2, no. 64, pp. 143–4.

[57] Skrynnikov suggests that the reason for Varlaam's release was the defeat of Dimitry's army at Dobrynichi and Jerzy Mniszech's departure from the pretender's camp: *Sotsial'no-politicheskaya bor'ba*, p. 102.

[58] *AAE*, vol. 2, no. 64, p. 144.

[59] *Ibid.*, pp. 141–2.

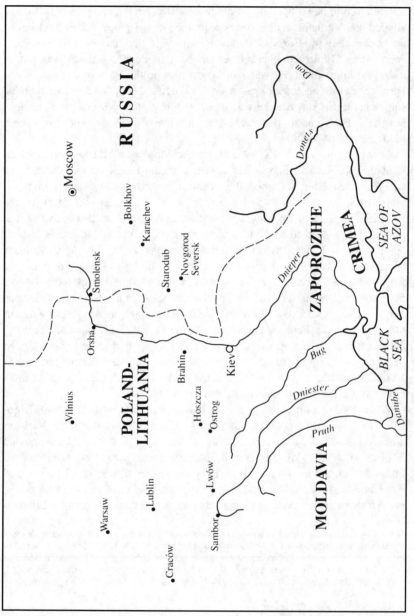

Map 2 Russia and Poland–Lithuania, showing places visited by the First False Dimitry in 1602–4

ian border. In Kiev they were received hospitably at the Pecherskii monastery by the Archimandrite Elisei. After three weeks, however, Grigorii announced that he wished to leave monastic life and enter the service of Prince Vasilii Ostrozhskii. This had angered Varlaam, who demanded that the archimandrite oblige Grisha to remain in the monastery and carry out his vow concerning the pilgrimage to Jerusalem. Elisei and his monks, however, had pointed out to Varlaam that there was freedom of conscience in Lithuania. But when Varlaam asked to be allowed to remain in the Pecherskii monastery, Elisei had insisted that the Russian visitors all leave together. Varlaam and Misail then accompanied Grigorii to Ostrog, where they spent the summer at Prince Vasilii's family seat.[60]

There is independent evidence that Varlaam, Misail and Grigorii were in Ostrog in the summer of 1602. In 1851 a book was discovered in the library of the Zagorovskii monastery in Volynia province. It was printed in Ostrog in 1594 and bore the inscription:

In the year from the creation of the world 7110, in the month of August on the fourteenth day [1602], this book of Basil the Great was given to us, Grigorii, and his brethren Varlaam and Misail, by Konstantin Konstantinovich, called Vasilii in holy baptism, by God's grace Illustrious Prince of Ostrog and governor of Kiev.

Below the name Grigorii the words 'tsarevich of Muscovy' had been inserted, apparently in the same handwriting (see Plate 1).[61] This does not in itself prove that Grigorii was the First False Dimitry, but it does serve to corroborate Varlaam's assertion (and that of other Russian sources) that he and Misail Povadin, together with the monk Grisha Otrep'ev, had obtained the patronage of Prince Vasilii Ostrozhskii in the summer of 1602.

Up to and including their sojourn at Ostrog, the paths of Varlaam and Grigorii had coincided, but in autumn 1602 Prince Vasilii sent Varlaam and Misail to the Trinity monastery at nearby Derman, while Grigorii went to Pan Hoyski at Hoszcza.[62] Varlaam's information about Grigorii's subsequent adventures was thus obtained at second hand. At Hoszcza, he learned, Grigorii had discarded his monastic attire and become a layman. He had also begun to study Latin and Polish there, and to take an interest in Lutheranism. Outraged by this news of the young man's apostasy, Varlaam had gone to Prince Vasilii at Ostrog and begged him to return Grigorii to his monastic status

---

[60] *Ibid.*, p. 142.
[61] Dobrotvorskii, 'Svedenie', pp. 57–8, and reproduction of the inscription, facing p. 72; Dobrotvorskii, 'Kto byl pervyi Lzhedimitrii?', pp. 96, 10.
[62] *AAE*, vol. 2, no. 64, p. 142. In a letter of 2 March 1604 to King Sigismund, Janusz, the son of Prince Vasilii Ostrozhskii, states that the pretender had spent some time at his father's monastery at Derman before going to the 'Anabaptists' (Arians): Aleksandrenko, comp., 'Materialy', p. 427.

and send him to join his former companions at the Derman monastery. Prince Vasilii, however, had reminded Varlaam that there was religious freedom in Lithuania.[63] Grigorii spent the winter at Hoszcza, but disappeared after Easter (presumably to visit the Zaporozhian cossacks, although Varlaam does not mention this episode). He next turned up at Brahin, where he told Prince Adam Vishnevetskii that he was Tsarevich Dimitry Ivanovich of Uglich.[64]

Pierling was the first scholar to note that there is a significant correspondence between the content of Varlaam's *izvet* and the account of the pretender's biography that Vishnevetskii sent to King Sigismund. According to Vishnevetskii's report, the pretender had stayed secretly in Lithuania with Prince Ostrozhskii and with Pan Gabriel Hoyski before revealing himself to Prince Adam at Brahin.[65] And according to Varlaam, Grigorii Otrep'ev had lived at Ostrog with Prince Vasilii Ostrozhskii, and at Hoszcza with Pan Hoyski, before going to Brahin.[66] This demonstrates conclusively, according to Pierling, that Dimitry was Grisha Otrep'ev. There is no evidence that Varlaam, writing in 1606, knew of Vishnevetskii's report of 1603, and hence there is no possibility that the later source was influenced by the earlier one.[67] This argument has also been endorsed by R. G. Skrynnikov,[68] and it seems generally persuasive. The correspondence between the routes of Grisha Otrep'ev and of the pretender provides a strong circumstantial case for the identification of the First False Dimitry as Grisha Otrep'ev.

The 'pretender intrigue': conspiracy theories

If the pretender was indeed Grisha Otrep'ev, was he acting alone, or did he have influential patrons who devised his pretence?[69] The answers that historians have offered to this question are often related to their broader interpretations of the Time of Troubles. S. F. Platonov, for example, argued that the career of the First False Dimitry belonged to the first, 'dynastic' phase of the Troubles, when various factions of courtiers competed for the

---

[63] *AAE*, vol. 2, no. 64, pp. 142–3.

[64] *Ibid.*, p. 143.

[65] Nowakowski, ed., *Źródła*, vol. 2, p. 70.

[66] *AAE*, vol. 2, no. 64, pp. 142–3.

[67] Pierling, *La Russie et le Saint-Siège*, vol. 3, pp. 414–15; Pirling, *Iz smutnogo vremeni*, pp. 24–6.

[68] Skrynnikov, *Sotsial'no-politicheskaya bor'ba*, pp. 105–6.

[69] Some contemporary commentators and subsequent historians who believe that Dimitry was not Grisha Otrep'ev have argued that the pretence was masterminded in Poland by the Jesuits, who planned to use the pretender as the instrument for the conversion of Russia to Catholicism (see, for example, Shaum, 'Tragoedia Demetrio-Moscovitica', p. 8; Bitsyn, 'Pravda o Lzhedimitrii') or by noble Polish–Lithuanian families such as the Vishnevetskiis, Mniszechs and Sapiehas, who supported the pretender in the *Rzeczpospolita* (Ilovaiskii, *Smutnoe vremya*, pp. 1–10, 259–61, 328).

throne. Boris's aristocratic opponents, in Platonov's view, were responsible for setting up the pretender as a weapon to unseat him, and their actions reflected long-standing divisions within the Muscovite elites.[70] K. V. Chistov rejected Platonov's interpretation, and viewed the pretender as the embodiment of a 'popular socio-utopian legend' about Tsarevich Dimitry that reflected the aspirations of the peasant and cossack masses. For Chistov, the appearance of the First False Dimitry was associated primarily with the introduction of serfdom in the late sixteenth century, which gave rise to an anti-feudal peasant war.[71] In R. G. Skrynnikov's most recent interpretation, the 'civil war' of the early seventeenth century is caused both by divisions within the nobility and by the process of enserfment:[72] accordingly, both boyar plots and popular utopian legends, as we shall see, play their part in the creation of his First False Dimitry.

The idea that the pretender was set up by the boyars was first put forward by contemporaries. According to Conrad Bussow, when Boris Godunov heard of the surrender of Putivl' to the pretender in 1604, he accused the boyars of preparing the False Dimitry in order to encompass his overthrow – 'in which he was not mistaken', Bussow adds.[73] The Romanovs are the clan most frequently mentioned by those historians who accept this view.

A number of sources link Otrep'ev with the Romanovs. In November 1604 Boris's government informed the Emperor Rudolph II in Vienna that Grisha had been a slave of Michael Romanov, who had dismissed him from his service because of his bad behaviour.[74] Patriarch Iov's *gramota* of 14 January 1605 stated that Otrep'ev had lived at the Romanovs' court, had been guilty of (political) crimes (*zavorovavsya*) and had become a monk in order to avoid the death penalty.[75] Subsequently Vasilii Shuiskii added further details, telling the Poles that Grisha had been a slave of the sons of Nikita Romanovich, and also of Prince Boris Cherkasskii.[76] A later chronicler states that Grisha had frequented the court of Prince Boris Cherkasskii, and had become a monk because of Boris's persecution of the Romanovs and Cherkasskiis.[77] It was this last piece of evidence, in particular, that led Platonov to suggest, albeit somewhat tentatively, that the pretence was set up by the Romanovs

---

[70] Platonov, *Ocherki*, pp. 186–90, 224–5. S. M. Solov'ev had also concluded that the pretender was most probably set up by Boris's boyar opponents: Solov'ev, *Istoriya Rossii*, vol. 4, pp. 405–6.

[71] Chistov, *Russkie narodnye*, pp. 27–30, 33–46.

[72] See, for example, Skrynnikov, *Rossiya v nachale XVII v.*, pp. 249–51; Skrynnikov, *Smuta v Rossii*, pp. 3–8; Skrynnikov, 'The Civil War in Russia', pp. 70–4.

[73] Bussow, *Moskovskaya khronika*, p. 100.

[74] Archival source, cited by Skrynnikov, *Rossiya v nachale XVII v.*, p. 83. This Michael Romanov was a younger brother of Fedor Nikitich: *ibid.*, p. 84.

[75] *AAE*, vol. 2, no. 28, p. 78.

[76] *SIRIO*, vol. 137, pp. 247, 319, 367.

[77] 'Skazanie . . . o Rastrige', pp. 3–4.

and their kinsmen.[78] R. G. Skrynnikov in his early works on the Time of Troubles appeared to endorse this view.[79] But in a later work Skrynnikov argues that the Romanovs had no more reason to set up a pretender in 1600 than had Boris Godunov in 1598.[80] The author now asserts that Grisha Otrep'ev might have obtained his political views from the Romanovs, but there is no firm evidence that his patrons played a direct part in devising his pretence.[81] Skrynnikov still concludes, however, that Grisha was tonsured in 1600, that is, in the year of the disgrace of the Romanovs, thereby confirming the chronicler's assertion that Grisha's forcible monasticisation was linked with Boris's persecution of that clan. It seems more likely, however, that Otrep'ev became a monk some years earlier than this.[82] Certainly, if he was shriven only in 1600, his monastic career must indeed have been a meteoric one.[83]

The 'pretender intrigue', in Skrynnikov's revised view, originated not in the Romanovs' mansion, but within the walls of the Miracles monastery in the Moscow Kremlin.[84] In his book on the 'socio-political struggle' in early seventeenth-century Russia, Skrynnikov suggested that the mastermind of Grisha's pretence was the monk Varlaam. Varlaam, like other monks in the Kremlin monastery, Skrynnikov speculated, was an opponent of Boris Godunov, and sought to make use of popular utopian ideas about Tsarevich Dimitry in order to organise a 'political intrigue' against Boris.[85] In the revised version of this book, published in 1988, Skrynnikov suggested that Varlaam was acting as the agent of Prince Ivan Shuiskii and other boyar opponents of Boris Godunov.[86] In his semi-popular biography of Grisha Otrep'ev, the author developed this hypothesis further. Before coming to Moscow, he surmised, Varlaam had travelled widely through Russia, picking up all sorts of gossip in the course of his wanderings: 'Being a sharp-witted person, Varlaam was apparently the first to appreciate the significance of the rumours flooding the country about the miraculous escape of Dimitry, the legitimate heir.'[87] It is not surprising, Skrynnikov continued, that a 'pretender intrigue'

[78] Platonov, *Ocherki*, pp. 186–7.
[79] Skrynnikov, *Boris Godunov*, 1978, pp. 159–61.
[80] Skrynnikov, *Rossiya v nachale XVII v.*, p. 82.
[81] Skrynnikov, *Sotsial'no-politicheskaya bor'ba*, p. 106; Skrynnikov, *Rossiya v nachale XVII v.*, pp. 96–7.
[82] Skrynnikov, *Rossiya v nachale XVII v.*, pp. 85–7. Many sources which Skrynnikov cites, but chooses not to accept, suggest that Grisha was shriven before 1600. The date of 1600 is derived from the 'Skazanie . . . o Rastrige' which, as Skrynnikov himself admits, is a late and often unreliable source.
[83] *Ibid.*, pp. 86–91.
[84] Skrynnikov, *Sotsial'no-politicheskaya bor'ba*, p. 106; Skrynnikov, *Rossiya v nachale XVII v.*, p. 97.
[85] Skrynnikov, *Sotsial'no-politicheskaya bor'ba*, pp. 107–9.
[86] Skrynnikov, *Rossiya v nachale XVII v.*, p. 99.
[87] Skrynnikov, *Samozvantsy*, p. 40.

should have been devised by the itinerant clergy: 'The monks knew the mood of the people, and at the same time they had entrée to the boyars' mansions.' Varlaam's petition revealed that he had met Misail Povadin at the house of Prince Ivan Shuiskii, and Skrynnikov conjectured that Shuiskii and other disaffected boyars instigated the pretence in the hope of unseating Boris: 'the magnates hostile to Boris were prepared to use any means to get rid of the elected dynasty. The monks were an appropriate instrument in their hands.'[88]

Skrynnikov's complex scenario – of an intrigue involving popular socio-utopian legends, Kremlin monks and boyar clans such as the Shuiskiis – is extremely unconvincing. In the first place, as we have already noted, there is no evidence that rumours about Dimitry were widespread amongst the masses at this date. Nor is it likely that any member of the Shuiskii family would have been willing to toy with the idea of a pretence. The Shuiskiis, like the Romanovs, had valid claims to the throne in their own right which they could put forward in the event of Boris's death, and neither clan had any real interest in creating a false Dimitry. The Princes V. I. and D. I. Shuiskii were to fight loyally for Boris against the pretender in 1604–5.[89] And far from benefiting from his victory, they barely escaped with their lives when Dimitry came to the throne.

Let us now consider Skrynnikov's hypothesis that Varlaam played a major part in the 'intrigue'. The idea that Grisha's pretence was aided and abetted by an older monk is not new: it was put forward by some contemporaries, and endorsed by the nineteenth-century historian Karamzin.[90] According to the Swede Petrei, for example, Grisha's parents had put their headstrong son into a monastery as a youth, in order for him to receive a disciplined upbringing. There 'a certain crafty monk', ill disposed towards Boris, had the idea of transforming Otrep'ev into the tsarevich. He familiarised Grisha with the chronicles and with events from Russian history, and when the young man proved an apt pupil the two fled together to Lithuania, where the older monk continued to coach Grisha in his role of Dimitry. When Otrep'ev had learned his lesson, the two parted: Grisha went to Prince Adam Vishnevetskii, to whom he revealed himself as the tsarevich, while his companion went to the Russian cossacks, and rallied them to Dimitry's cause.[91]

In the 1920s the historian I. A. Golubtsov suggested that this unnamed monk who taught Grisha his part may have been none other than Varlaam.[92] Golubtsov was anxious to refute Platonov's hypothesis that the boyars had devised the idea of setting up a pretender against Boris, and he argued per-

[88] *Ibid.*
[89] Pavlov, *Gosudarev dvor*, p. 78.
[90] Karamzin, *Istoriya*, vol. 3, t.XI, col. 73.
[91] Petrei, *Istoriya*, pp. 186–8, 194–5, 242.
[92] Golubtsov, ' "Izmena" smol'nyan', p. 247.

suasively that this view underestimated the boyars' level of political consciousness.[93] In place of Platonov's speculation about a boyar conspiracy,
Golubtsov suggested that the Poles, and especially the Sapiehas, played an
important part in creating the pretender. Golubtsov produced a complex and
circumstantial chain of events linking Varlaam with the Smolensk district
and hence with Poland–Lithuania and the Sapieha family.[94] This part of
Golubtsov's hypothesis is extremely far-fetched and unconvincing, but his
suggestion that Varlaam was Grisha Otrep'ev's mentor appears to have influenced R. G. Skrynnikov. What basis is there for such a view?

It certainly seems improbable that Varlaam learned of Otrep'ev's claim to
be Tsarevich Dimitry only after Grisha had parted from his erstwhile travelling companions at Ostrog, as the monk affirmed in his *izvet*. As we have
already noted, Varlaam's petition is a self-serving document, and it offers a
very tendentious account of his relationship with Otrep'ev. It is unlikely that
Varlaam made Grisha's acquaintance accidentally on a Moscow street, as he
claimed to have done.[95] In his *izvet*, Varlaam stated that he belonged to the
Pafnut'ev monastery at Borovsk;[96] Patriarch Iov's *gramota* of 14 January
1605, however, described both Varlaam and Misail as monks of the Miracles
monastery,[97] and hence as colleagues of Grigorii and of Iov himself.

According to the *New Chronicle*, Grisha had declared himself to be Tsarevich Dimitry while he was still a deacon in the Miracles monastery. He had
asked a lot of questions about the death of Tsarevich Dimitry and, apparently
joking, he told his fellow monks that one day he 'would be tsar in Moscow'.
The brothers laughed at him, but Iona, the Metropolitan of Rostov, denounced
him to Boris as a vessel of Satan, and the tsar ordered him to be sent to
Solovki under a heavy guard. Grisha, however, was forewarned, and fled
from Moscow.[98] It thus seems entirely probable that Varlaam, in spite of his
protestations of ignorance, was aware of Grisha's pretence from the outset.
But it is not necessary to accept that it was Varlaam who suggested his role
to Grisha, let alone that they were both part of a broader conspiracy involving
either Polish families such as the Sapiehas (as Golubtsov suggests) or Russian
boyars including the Shuiskiis (as in Skrynnikov's hypothesis). If Varlaam
had indeed organised the 'intrigue', why did the pretender throw him into
prison at Sambor? Skrynnikov can only offer the feeble suggestion that 'Varlaam knew too much about Otrep'ev and his true origin, and the latter decided
to rid himself of his mentor.'[99]

[93] *Ibid.*, pp. 231–2.
[94] *Ibid.*, pp. 238–9, 242–3, 251.
[95] *Ibid.*, p. 247; Skrynnikov, *Sotsial'no-politicheskaya bor'ba*, p. 109.
[96] *AAE*, vol. 2, no. 64, p. 141.
[97] *Ibid.*, no. 28, p. 78.
[98] *PSRL*, vol. 14, p. 59, para. 85.
[99] Skrynnikov, *Sotsial'no-politicheskaya bor'ba*, p. 170.

It seems much more satisfactory to abandon all these complex theories of conspiracy and intrigue, and to conclude that Grisha acted on his own initiative. The Otrep'ev family had links with Uglich, and Grisha's interest in the death of Tsarevich Dimitry could have been influenced by local oral traditions about the events of 1591.[100] Later, as a deacon in the Miracles monastery in the Moscow Kremlin, and scribe at the Patriarch's court, he would have had access to the sort of information about the family life of Tsar Ivan, and about the Uglich affair, that was reflected in the tale he related to Prince Adam Vishnevetskii.

While recognising that Grisha would have been able to learn many details about Dimitry of Uglich, R. G. Skrynnikov nevertheless dismisses the possibility that Otrep'ev might have been acting independently:

In view of the traditional system of thinking that predominated in the middle ages, it is difficult to imagine that a monk accepted into a monastery in the capital 'because of his poverty and orphanhood' would himself have dared to put forward his pretensions to the royal crown. Most likely he was acting at the suggestion of people who remained in the shadows.[101]

All of the evidence that we have about Grisha Otrep'ev, however, suggests that he was a young man reacting against the 'traditional system of thinking that predominated in the middle ages'. His youthful rebellion against his father had been punished by forcible monasticisation. As a monk, he displayed exceptional talents, and was rewarded with rapid promotion. But he was still dissatisfied; and his alienation may have assumed the form of religious dissent.

A number of sources describe Otrep'ev as a heretic or magician. Boris Godunov's government told the Poles in September 1604 that Grisha's interest in heretical ideas had begun before his tonsure, and that after he had become a monk he had continued to practise heresy and black magic and the summoning of unclean spirits.[102] In 1606 Vasilii Shuiskii's envoys to Poland reported that Dimitry had fallen into heresy while he served at the Patriarch's court.[103] And in Petrei's account, the 'crafty monk' who acted as Grisha's mentor in his Russian monastery 'taught him many scoundrelly tricks, because he was a black magician, skilled and capable of all manner of things, and Grishka had a great understanding and sympathy for such matters'.[104]

---

[100] Golubtsov, ' "Izmena" smol'nyan', p. 239; Skrynnikov, *Sotsial'no-politicheskaya bor'ba*, p. 107.
[101] Skrynnikov, *Sotsial'no-politicheskaya bor'ba*, p. 108.
[102] *SIRIO*, vol. 137, pp. 176–7.
[103] *Ibid.*, p. 248.
[104] Petrei, *Istoriya*, p. 186.

Some historians have assumed that these allegations of heresy and black magic were levelled against Otrep'ev purely to discredit him;[105] and it may well be the case that contemporaries regarded his pretence as sufficient evidence in itself that he was a magician. As Boris Uspenskii has pointed out, *samozvanchestvo* was perceived in Old Russian culture as a form of 'anti-behaviour', characteristic of sorcerers or heretics.[106] Official denunciations of Grisha Otrep'ev as an impostor suggested that he acquired the identity of Tsarevich Dimitry by magical means. The Patriarch's *gramota* of 14 January 1605, for example, associated Grisha's assumption of Dimitry's name with heresy and sorcery as well as with treason:

and in Lithuania he renounced the [Orthodox] Christian faith and scorned the clerical life, discarded his monastic garb and inclined to the Latin heresy, fell into black magic and sorcery, and at the summons of the Devil, and in accordance with the designs of the Lithuanian King Sigismund and the Lithuanian people, that renegade unfrocked monk began falsely to call himself by the name of Tsarevich Dimitry of Uglich.[107]

Otrep'ev's adoption of the identity of Dimitry of Uglich was thus evidently seen by Russian contemporaries as evidence that he was an instrument of Satan. But we should not discount the possibility that the accusations of heresy and necromancy that were levelled against him had a basis in reality.[108] Grisha clearly felt constrained by his Russian Orthodox background and upbringing, and it is not at all unlikely that even before he fled from Moscow he may have dabbled in black magic as well as in 'heretical' forms of Christianity. There is little evidence of the survival into the second half of the sixteenth century of the Orthodox heretics, such as the 'Judaisers', who were

---

[105] Skrynnikov, *Rossiya v nachale XVII v.*, pp. 83, 91–2.

[106] Uspenskii, 'Tsar' i samozvanets', pp. 214–17. The association of imposture with magic and 'heresy' in early modern Europe was not unique to Russian culture. In sixteenth-century France, Arnaud du Tilh was suspected of acquiring the identity of Martin Guerre through necromancy, and it is likely that he and Bertrande de Rols were interested in Protestantism: Davis, *The Return of Martin Guerre*, pp. 43, 48–50, 60, 84, 86, 92, 103, 109, 118.

[107] *AAE*, vol. 2, no. 28, pp. 78–9. In contrast to the earlier assertions of Boris's envoys to Poland, the Patriarch here alleges that Otrep'ev's interest in heresy and necromancy began only after he had left Russia.

[108] Uspenskii himself leaves this possibility open: 'For our purposes here it is sufficient to note that pretenders were *perceived* as sorcerers, in as much as they were seen as self-appointed, travesty tsars. The question arises as to how far anti-behavior was inherent in these pretenders and how far it was attributed to them by public opinion. It must be supposed that this was a question of the degree of self-awareness of the pretender, which varied in each actual case. As we have already said, many pretenders undoubtedly believed that they were genuine tsars, yet among them there were also some adventurers who were perfectly well aware of the unlawfulness of their claims. *A priori* it must be assumed that anti-behavior was in the main characteristic of the pretenders in the second category, i.e. those who perceived themselves as mummers.' Uspenskii, 'Tsar' i samozvanets', p. 229, n. 50. Cited in David Budgen's translation (Uspenskij, 'Tsar and Pretender', p. 291, n. 109).

persecuted in the late fifteenth century.[109] Protestantism and Catholicism, however, were brought to Moscow in the sixteenth century by Western visitors; and forms of magic, such as soothsaying and astrology, were practised at the courts of Ivan the Terrible and Boris Godunov.[110] The pretender's subsequent interest in Arianism, and his opportunistic conversion to Roman Catholicism, are indicative of his lack of commitment to the Orthodox faith. Otrep'ev's heterodox religious views may therefore have provided an impetus for his actions; an estrangement from Orthodoxy was undoubtedly a psychological and spiritual prerequisite for any would-be *samozvanets* who was a deliberate impostor.

It is difficult to speculate further about Grisha's motivation.[111] Various possibilities suggest themselves. It may be that the youth suffered some kind of identity crisis as a result of his monasticisation. The young nobleman Yurii Bogdanovich Otrep'ev had already undergone an enforced change of name and *persona* when he was obliged to become the deacon Grigorii: the role of Dimitry of Uglich, by contrast, was an identity that he could choose for himself. Otrep'ev was of an age with the murdered tsarevich, and the rumours of 1598 about the false Dimitry supposedly groomed by Boris may have suggested his possible new role. It certainly seems likely that Grisha, as a former retainer of the Romanovs, nurtured a political hostility towards Boris Godunov, and he may have welcomed the prospect of serving as an agent of divine retribution against the usurper. Alternatively, there may have been some episode in Yurii Otrep'ev's past that led him to suspect that he was not his parents' child, and he may have persuaded himself that he really was the tsarevich.

It is quite possible, therefore, that the idea of calling himself Tsarevich Dimitry originated with Grisha himself, when he was a monk in the Miracles monastery. His earliest actions seem to confirm the hypothesis that he was acting alone. The pretender does not seem to have had any clear ideas about where or how to obtain support. His initial claim to be Tsarevich Dimitry, rashly made within the walls of the Kremlin, had almost ended in disaster, when he was mocked by his fellow monks and denounced for treason. After his enforced flight from Moscow, he was more circumspect about his royal identity, at least until he had left Russian soil. The *New Chronicle* relates that when Otrep'ev and his companions departed from Novgorod Seversk, prior to crossing the border into Lithuania, Grisha left a note for the archi-

---

[109] On heresy in mid-sixteenth-century Muscovy, see Bushkovitch, *Religion and Society*, pp. 26–7.

[110] Berry and Crummey, eds., *Rude and Barbarous Kingdom*, pp. 279, 304–6, 362. On the importation of Western 'magical' texts and practitioners into Russia, see Ryan, 'The *Secreta Secretorum*' and Ryan, 'Aristotle and Pseudo-Aristotle'.

[111] For a general discussion of the psychology of royal impostors, see Bercé, *Le roi caché*, ch. 7.

mandrite of the Spasskii monastery who had provided them with horses and a guide for their onward journey. This note, which the archimandrite found in his cell after the visitors' departure, read, 'I am Tsarevich Dimitry, the son of Tsar Ivan; and when I sit on my father's throne in Moscow, I shall reward you for providing me a refuge in your cloister.'[112]

Some sources suggest that once he was in Lithuania, Grisha made at least two attempts to obtain recognition as Tsarevich Dimitry before his appearance at Brahin. According to a Russian source, when he was at the Pecherskii monastery in Kiev Grigorii pretended to be ill, and revealed to the abbot, apparently *in extremis*, that he was a tsarevich in disguise, hiding from Boris.[113] It seems, too, that Grisha had made an unsuccessful bid to gain support for his pretence from Prince Vasilii Ostrozhskii. The Jesuits reported rumours that Grigorii had turned for help to Prince Vasilii, but Ostrozhskii had ordered his haiduks to throw him out.[114]

Otrep'ev's first unsuccessful attempts to gain support for his pretence bear all the hallmarks of a naive and opportunistic individual undertaking. It was only at Brahin, when he acquired his first influential patron, that Grisha was drawn into the web of vested interests that were to influence his further actions. By the time he left Sambor in August 1604, the pretender had been taken over not only by the Mniszechs and their friends, but also by the Polish Jesuits.

[112] *PSRL*, vol. 14, pp. 59–60, para. 85.
[113] Belokurov, ed., *Razryadnye zapisi*, p. 1.
[114] Pierling, *La Russie et le Saint-Siège*, vol. 3, p. 45.

2 The campaign for the crown

The invasion of Russia

The pretender's chosen route for his march on Moscow approached the Russian capital from the south-west, crossing the frontier near Kiev. In contrast to the more northerly road, which was barred by the well-fortified border town of Smolensk, this route passed through the smaller towns of the Seversk district, and was conveniently close to the territory of the Zaporozhian and Don cossacks, from whom the pretender still hoped to obtain backing. More importantly, Dimitry's path to Moscow took him through that south-west frontier region where the discontent of the service class was greatest, and where fugitive military bondsmen from the centre had gathered in significant numbers during the famine years. The pretender was careful to prepare the ground in advance, sending agents ahead of him to distribute proclamations and appeals to his Russian subjects.[1]

At the time when Dimitry's army was preparing to cross the Lithuanian frontier into Russia, it comprised about 2,500 men, about half of whom were Ukrainian cossacks.[2] These cossacks were mostly servitors of the Polish crown; the Zaporozhians declined to play a part, and a large detachment of them went off to fight the Turks on the Black Sea instead.[3] The number of Russians in Dimitry's army at this time was relatively small: only about 200 men, most of whom were apparently from the lower classes rather than the nobility. The handful of nobles included a certain Ivan Poroshin, and the brothers Khripunov who had 'recognised' Dimitry in Craców.[4]

Before Dimitry crossed the Russian border, he received new envoys from the Don cossacks, restating their willingness to serve the tsarevich 'as their natural sovereign'.[5] They brought with them a captured Russian nobleman, Peter Khrushchov, who had been sent to the Don by Boris Godunov to gain the cossacks' support against the pretender. On his arrival in Dimitry's camp,

[1] *SIRIO*, vol. 137, pp. 248, 260.
[2] Nazarov, 'K istorii nachal'nogo perioda', p. 185.
[3] Skrynnikov, *Sotsial'no-politicheskaya bor'ba*, pp. 231–2.
[4] *Ibid.*, p. 169.
[5] *SGGiD*, vol. 2, no. 81, p. 173.

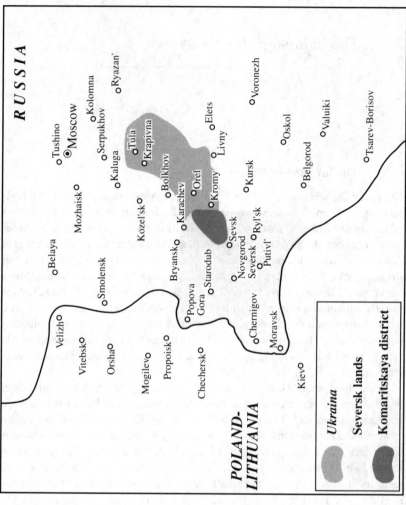

Map 3 The towns of south-west Russia. This map shows the region most affected by the campaign of the First False Dimitry in 1604–5, the Bolotnikov revolt of 1606–7 and the campaign of the Second False Dimitry in 1607–8

Khrushchov gave the latter a tremendous propaganda coup, by immediately 'recognising' him as the true tsarevich because of his supposed facial similarity to Ivan IV. Dimitry graciously pardoned Khrushchov, and interrogated him closely about the situation in Russia. The information which Khrushchov provided was extremely gratifying. He told Dimitry that the propaganda campaign waged by his agents had been very effective in the border regions, especially in the town of Putivl', where the people, on reading his missives, had expressed 'great love for the tsarevich'. In addition, one of Boris's commanders, Peter Sheremetev, whom Khrushchov had met on his journey to the Don, had expressed his reluctance to fight against Dimitry, saying, 'it is difficult to fight against one's natural sovereign'.[6]

Khrushchov also reported on the reaction at the court in Moscow to the news of Dimitry's appearance in Lithuania. Tsar Boris was in poor health, and had not gone out for several weeks; he dragged one leg, which appeared to be paralysed. He had ordered the execution of two of his noblemen, Vasilii Smirnov and Men'shoi Bulgakov, whose servants had denounced them for drinking the health of Tsarevich Dimitry at a private banquet. Mariya Nagaya, the mother of Dimitry of Uglich, had been brought to Moscow and was held under close guard in the Novodevichii convent: Boris and the Patriarch had both interrogated her closely. Finally, Khrushchov reported that Boris's sister Irina, the widow of Tsar Fedor, had suddenly died in her convent. There were rumours that Boris had killed her for refusing to acknowledge his right, and that of his son, to the throne. Dimitry was alive, she had said, and he was the true heir.[7]

Undoubtedly Khrushchov told Dimitry what he thought the latter wanted to hear; there may have been little truth in some of his assertions, but it is not impossible that Khrushchov was accurately repeating rumours which had gained currency in Russia since the news of Dimitry's presence in Poland had spread across the border. There is no reason to believe that Khrushchov's testimony was invented by Mniszech's aides, as Skrynnikov suggests, although it undoubtedly contributed to the pretender's propaganda effort.[8] Dimitry could have genuine grounds for optimism, when he crossed the Russian frontier, concerning the likely success of his adventure.

On 13 October 1604 Dimitry's troops crossed the River Dnieper and entered Russian territory.[9] The first Russian border fortress, Moravsk (Monastyrevskii Ostrog), surrendered without a struggle to the cossack vanguard of Dimitry's army, the insurgent inhabitants sending Boris's com-

[6] *Ibid.*, pp. 173–5.
[7] *Ibid.*, pp. 176–8.
[8] Skrynnikov, *Sotsial'no-politicheskaya bor'ba*, pp. 171–2.
[9] For a detailed narrative of the initial stages of Dimitry's campaign, see Skrynnikov, *Sotsial'no-politicheskaya bor'ba*, pp. 174–216.

manders as prisoners to the tsarevich. In Chernigov, the townspeople recognised the pretender, but the governor, Prince I. A. Tatev, and some of his lieutenants, at first attempted to resist. After the surrender of the fortress, one of these officers, N. S. Vorontsov-Vel'yaminov, refused to acknowledge the pretender, and was executed on his orders. Prince Tatev and the other captive commanders were quick to swear the oath of loyalty to their 'true' sovereign.

Dimitry's army then laid siege to Novgorod Seversk, which was well fortified by Godunov's general P. F. Basmanov. The pretender's attempt to take the fortress by storm was repulsed, causing a crisis of confidence in Dimitry's camp. Morale was raised, however, by news of the surrender of Putivl', the most important town in the area. Here, as elsewhere, the fortress garrison, as well as the townspeople, went over voluntarily to the pretender. The more easterly Russian towns of Ryl'sk and Kursk soon followed the example of the Seversk towns. The pretender gained the support, too, of the peasants of the prosperous Komaritskaya district, and of the rural districts of Kromy and Okolenki.

On 18 December Boris's general, Prince F. I. Mstislavskii reached Novgorod Seversk and attempted to raise the siege. In a battle on 21 December Mstislavskii was wounded and his troops were obliged to retreat. Novgorod Seversk continued to hold out against the besiegers, however, and on 1 January Dimitry's Polish troops mutinied, angered by the pretender's failure to pay them. On 2 January the majority of the mercenaries deserted the tsarevich's camp. Mniszech himself found urgent reasons to return to Poland. By this time, however, Dimitry's army included several thousand Zaporozhian and Don cossacks. Undaunted by the departure of the Polish mercenaries, Dimitry pressed on towards the heartland of Russia, occupying Sevsk without opposition. On 21 January 1605, however, he again encountered Mstislavskii's army, and suffered a severe defeat at Dobrynichi. After this battle the Zaporozhian cossacks deserted Dimitry's camp. The pretender himself fled first to Ryl'sk and then to Putivl', where the local inhabitants persuaded him to stay and set up his new headquarters.

After his victory at Dobrynichi, Mstislavskii imposed harsh repressions on his Russian prisoners, and on the peasant population of the Komaritskaya district that had supported the pretender. But Boris's generals were unable to follow up their success by recapturing the towns which had gone over to the pretender. Godunov's army under the command of Mstislavskii concentrated all its efforts on the siege of Kromy, a small but strategically placed fortress which was held for Dimitry by the Don cossack *ataman* Korela. Having failed to take it by storm, the government forces settled down for a long siege. The defenders dug themselves well in, and their ability to hold out was enhanced when supplies and reinforcements managed to get through from Putivl'.

Meanwhile the rising in Dimitry's favour spread further, to the southern steppe fortresses. Oskol, Valuiki, Tsarev-Borisov, Voronezh and Belgorod all acknowledged Dimitry in January and February 1605, followed shortly afterwards by Elets and Livny. The population of these fortresses consisted almost entirely of petty military servitors, such as cossacks and *strel'tsy*. There were very few urban tradespeople, and the surrounding districts contained hardly any peasants. This demonstrates that Dimitry's support came not only from the rural and urban lower classes, but also from the military service class. Only a handful of servicemen in the southern fortresses refused to acknowledge the pretender.

By claiming to be the true tsarevich, Dimitry was able to denounce the local representatives of Boris's government – the military governors of the frontier towns – as traitors to be overthrown by the faithful subjects of the rightful heir. But Dimitry's appeal was not based on any overt incitement of class struggle. Nobles, and even Boris's governors and commanders, were spared, and accepted into the pretender's army, if they acknowledged him as the true tsar. Some were even given positions of authority: G. B. Dolgorukii and Ya. Zmeev, Boris's *voevody* at Kursk, were appointed by Dimitry as *voevody* at Ryl'sk.[10] This suggests that Dimitry based his appeal primarily on his claim to be the 'true' tsar, rather than on specific appeals to class or sectional interests. The only proclamation of Dimitry's which survives from this period, dated November 1604, is addressed to all social groups in the conventional descending hierarchical order. It makes vague promises of rewards and honours for those who recognise and serve him, and expresses his desire that 'all Orthodox Christians' should live in 'peace and quiet and prosperity'.[11]

The social composition of Dimitry's support in the autumn and winter of 1604/5 was therefore much more complex than the Soviet formula of an anti-feudal peasant war implied. In the debate about the 'first peasant war' in the journal *Voprosy Istorii* in 1958–61, A. A. Zimin and his supporters argued that the pretender's campaign for the throne involved a mass popular uprising of peasants and slaves, under the banner of the 'good tsar' Dimitry.[12] I. I. Smirnov, however, continued to assert the older Soviet view that Dimitry was merely a puppet of Polish interventionists.[13] R. G. Skrynnikov rejects the views of both sides in this debate. He argues, on the one hand, that after the battle of Dobrynichi the role of Polish intervention forces in Dimitry's

[10] *Ibid.*, p. 188.
[11] *AAE*, vol. 2, no. 26, p. 76.
[12] Zimin, 'Nekotorye voprosy', p. 99; Ovchinnikov, 'Nekotorye voprosy', pp. 82–3; Skylar, 'O nachal'nom etape', pp. 91–9; 'O krest'yanskoi voine', pp. 111–15.
[13] Smirnov, 'O nekotorykh voprosakh', p. 117.

army was negligible.[14] On the other hand, Dimitry's Russian supporters were mainly urban rather than rural, and the participation of so many military servicemen meant that the movement he led could not be regarded as 'anti-feudal'.[15] In relation to the 'ideology' of the movement, however, Skrynnikov still uses the old Stalinist formula about popular faith in the 'good tsar', amplified by K. V. Chistov's theory about 'popular socio-utopian legends about the returning tsar-deliverer'.[16]

According to Chistov, the extensive popular support that the pretender attracted on the south-west frontier demonstrated the potency of the 'socio-utopian legend' about Dimitry: 'thousands of people in these regions knew the legend, believed in the advent of the tsarevich-deliverer, awaited him and linked with him their cherished social aspirations'. They viewed Dimitry as 'the realisation of the legend with which were linked extreme hopes, evoked by despair'.[17] Chistov may be correct that the population of the frontier region saw Dimitry as a potential liberator from the oppression they had suffered in Boris's reign, although there is no evidence that the pretender promised to abolish slavery or serfdom. But, contrary to the Soviet scholar's assertions, Dimitry's proclamations did not contain any detailed account of his escape from death and subsequent adventures.[18] Thus we have no evidence that the inhabitants of the frontier districts were familiar with the details of the pretender's story that had been spread among his supporters in Poland, nor that their willingness to accept him as the true tsarevich was based on their acceptance of this story as proof of his identity and authenticity.

Dimitry's proclamations to his Russian subjects, issued after he had invaded Muscovy, describe his escape from death in predominantly religious terms. In his circular proclamation (*okruzhnaya gramota*) of November 1604, for example, he states that he had been saved from Boris's assassins 'by God's will, shielded by His strong right hand ... God in His mercy did not wish [Boris's] wicked design to be implemented, and God covered Me, your true-born Sovereign, with His invisible hand and preserved Me for many

---

[14] Skrynnikov, *Sotsial'no-politicheskaya bor'ba*, p. 203.

[15] *Ibid.*, p. 325.

[16] *Ibid.*, pp. 175, 182. In the revised version of this book, Skrynnikov qualified his previous acceptance of I. I. Smirnov's assertion that the slogan of the 'good tsar' was 'a peculiar peasant utopia': not only the peasants, but also the military service class, Skrynnikov now argues, believed in the 'good tsar': compare Skrynnikov, *Sotsial'no-politicheskaya bor'ba*, pp. 98–9 with Skrynnikov, *Rossiya v nachale XVII v.*, pp. 79–81.

[17] Chistov, *Russkie narodnye*, p. 42.

[18] The text of Dimitry's supposed letter to Boris, which Chistov cites to suport his argument (*Russkie narodnye*, p. 40), appears to be a Polish literary composition, based on Prince Adam Vishnevetskii's report to the king, rather than an authentic proclamation issued to the pretender's Russian subjects. Kostomarov dismisses it as a 'pure invention' (*Kto byl pervyi Lzhedimitrii?*, pp. 36–7). An extract from this text was published in Kognowicki, *Życia Sapiehów*, vol. 2, pp. 81–2. For the full text in Russian translation, see Kostomarov, *Smutnoe vremya*, pp. 84–6.

years in His providence (*v sudbakh svoikh*)'.[19] The emphasis in these proclamations on divine rather than human agency, and on the role of God's providence in saving the tsarevich, implies a miraculous element in his reappearance.
And it seems that popular Russian belief in Dimitry was based not so much on
a secular 'socio-utopian legend' as on a religious-miraculous outlook.

There is little evidence of the popular response within Russia to the spread
of news of Dimitry's appearance in Lithuania. But the evidence that we do
have is very instructive. In a letter to Dimitry of 15/25 November 1603, the
Don cossacks had addressed him as their 'sovereign tsarevich, granted by the
will and blessing of God, risen like Lazarus from the dead'.[20] Here the idea
of Dimitry's miraculous 'resurrection' is clearly expressed. And at the end
of 1604, when the Komaritskaya district was rising up in support of the
pretender, it was reported that in Smolensk the townspeople were whispering
that 'if Tsarevich Dimitry is risen (*vospryal*), we cannot oppose him'.[21]

There is indirect evidence in Boris Godunov's official propaganda of the
existence of rumours of Dimitry's 'resurrection'. In a letter to King Sigismund of September 1604, Boris denounced the pretender as the renegade
monk Grisha Otrep'ev, but added, 'Even if this rogue is Prince Dimitry of
Uglich *risen from the dead*, he is [the son] of a seventh unlawful wife.'[22] The
comment was presumably intended to be ironic, but it not only undermined
Godunov's previous insistence that the pretender was Grisha Otrep'ev, but
also implied that it was possible for Tsarevich Dimitry to have risen from
the grave.

Apparently to counter such ideas of Dimitry's resurrection, Patriarch Iov
in his *gramota* of 14 January 1605 stressed that Dimitry of Uglich was dead
and buried, and could not rise from the grave before the Last Judgement and
the general resurrection.[23] Viewed in conjunction with the evidence that the
Don cossacks considered Dimitry to have risen like Lazarus from the grave,
this suggests that any 'legend' of Tsarevich Dimitry within Russia at this
time was based on the idea of his miraculous return from the dead, rather
than the more mundane scenario of his rescue by his doctor or teacher.
I. A. Golubtsov has speculated that notions about the 'miraculous escape, or
even *resurrection* of the tsarevich' might have gained currency amongst the
petty nobility, the townspeople and the monastic clergy of the western border-

---

[19] *AAE*, vol. 2, no. 26, p. 76. Cf. also no. 34, p. 89; no. 37, pp. 92–3.
[20] Aleksandrenko, comp., 'Materialy', p. 413. This letter survives only in a corrupt Polish translation: see Skrynnikov, *Sotsial'no-politicheskaya bor'ba*, pp. 153–4.
[21] Golubtsov, ' "Izmena" smol'nyan', p. 233.
[22] *SIRIO*, vol. 137, p. 178 (my emphasis). Dimitry was denied the title of tsarevich because of
his presumed illegitimacy. Boris could not of course acknowledge that Dimitry claimed to
have escaped assassination at Uglich, since the official view was that the boy had died
accidentally.
[23] *AAE*, vol. 2, no. 28, p. 78.

lands.[24] The monks in particular, he suggests, being accustomed to the idea of miracles, could easily 'accommodate the idea of a tsarevich resurrected or miraculously saved from death'.[25]

The imagery used by the pretender's supporters may also be interpreted as a poetic metaphor for death and rebirth or resurrection. When Dimitry crossed the Russian frontier in October 1604, he was greeted as the 'bright sun' (*krasnoe solnyshko*), and when he entered the fortress of Moravsk, the inhabitants cried out, 'Our sun is rising; it has long been set; Dimitry Ivanovich is restored to us.'[26] This image associated Dimitry not only with Ivan the Terrible and with Prince Vladimir of Kiev, who are compared to the sun in Russian folklore, but also with the depiction of Christ in liturgical texts as 'the sun of righteousness'.[27]

Popular support for the pretender therefore assumed the form of a quasi-religious messianic or millenarian movement in which Dimitry was viewed as the true tsarevich, miraculously risen, Christ-like, from the grave.[28] Some of his adherents had a quite fanatical belief in him, and were prepared to suffer martyrdom for his sake. According to Massa, the tortures and executions that Boris's troops inflicted on the people of the Komaritskaya district were counter-productive, since: 'the more the executioners went about tormenting the inhabitants, the more these persisted in recognising Dmitry as their legitimate master. No suffering could induce them to deny him. They remained staunch and unshakeable unto death.'[29] And the Augsburg merchant Georg Peyerle, describing the atrocities committed by Boris's troops in the Seversk district, commented that '[i]t was impossible not to be amazed by the joyful manner in which innocent people endured torment and torture for the sake of Dimitry, whom they had never seen, considering death itself a

---

[24] Golubtsov, ' "Izmena" smol'nyan', p. 232. Emphasis in the original.

[25] *Ibid.*, p. 246. On popular miracle cults in sixteenth-century Russia, see Bushkovitch, *Religion and Society*, chs. 4–5.

[26] Pirling, *Iz smutnogo vremeni*, p. 139; Pierling, *La Russie et le Saint-Siège*, vol. 3, p. 129. Pierling's source appears to be the unpublished diary of the Polish Jesuit Father Andrzej Lawicki, who accompanied the pretender on his march to Moscow.

[27] On the significance of the term 'sun of righteousness' (*pravednoe solntse*) see Uspenskii, 'Tsar' i samozvanets', p. 203. Cf. the Old Testament prophecy (Malachi, 4.2): 'But for you who fear my name the sun of righteousness shall rise with healing in its wings.'

[28] Yves-Marie Bercé has argued that although the image of the mythical 'returning king' in early modern Europe may be based on that of Christ, it involves no miraculous resurrection (*Le roi caché*, pp. 228–9), and in so far as popular hopes vested in these kings can be described as messianic, it is a messianism of a purely secular character (*ibid.*, p. 312). K. V. Chistov also makes a clear distinction between 'religious-messianic legends' about 'saviours' and 'legends of a socio-political character' about 'returning tsar(evich)-deliverers' (*Russkie narodnye*, p. 24, cf. pp. 224–5, 338–9). My argument here is that Dimitry was believed, at least by some, to have been miraculously resurrected from the dead, and to that extent his support had elements of religious messianism. For discussion of millenarianism and messianism see, for example, Cohn, *The Pursuit of the Millennium*; Worsley, *The Trumpet Shall Sound*.

[29] Massa, *A Short History*, p. 77.

blessing, if they perished for his sake!'[30] Massa too states that in the Seversk lands, as in the Komaritskaya district, the inhabitants 'repudiated the tsar of Moscow, and despite intensified tortures, they would maintain to their dying breath that Dmitry was their true sovereign. Even some who had not seen him affirmed that they knew him, and held to this despite the most terrible torments.'[31]

In spite of the improbabilities it contained, Vishnevetskii's report to King Sigismund had been an attempt to provide a 'scientific' explanation of Dimitry's reappearance, based on the sort of rational assumptions about evidence that were likely to be held by the pretender's potential patrons in the *Rzeczpospolita*. The 'witnesses' who had attested to Dimitry's royal identity also provided a scientific form of evidence. It is worthy of note that the physical characteristics by which the pretender was 'recognised' in Poland were ordinary identifying marks which he supposedly shared with Dimitry of Uglich: a wart on his cheek beside his nose, and one arm that was longer than another. These are very different from the mystical 'royal signs', such as crosses or stars on the body, which were exhibited by some later Russian pretenders as 'proof' of their identity.[32] One contemporary source, however, attributes such 'royal marks' to Dimitry. The Pole Martyn Stadnicki claims that when the pretender declared himself to Prince Adam Vishnevetskii, he 'proved' his identity by displaying not only a diamond cross which had been given to the tsarevich at his christening, but also a depiction of the Muscovite eagle on his arm. (Stadnicki adds, however, that the Russian government claimed that this mark was evidence of corporal punishment inflicted upon the impostor.)[33] Another foreign source affirms that Dimitry proved his identity to Jerzy Mniszech by showing him 'a certain mark that was branded with a red-hot iron on the shoulders of all those of the Muscovite blood royal'.[34]

In the historical song about the First False Dimitry, the pretender is described as having the mark of a cross on his chest – the sign of a true tsarevich – but he is said to have falsely acquired this sign by means of his magic powers. In one version of this song, Mariya Nagaya explains to the boyars, after the pretender's marriage to Marina Mniszech, that he is not her son. Tsarevich Dimitry, she says, is dead and buried,

> But this is Grisha-Rosstrizhka, the son of Otrep'ev,
> He sat in prison for a full thirty years,
> He grew a cross on his white breasts,

[30] Paerle, 'Zapiski', p. 167.
[31] Massa, *A Short History*, p. 81.
[32] Uspenskii, 'Tsar' i samozvanets', pp. 205–6.
[33] Stadnitskii, 'Dnevnik', p. 133.
[34] Bercé, *Le roi caché*, pp. 94, 385, citing G. Tomasi, *Delle guerre e rivolgimenti del regno di Ungheria*, Venice, 1621.

> So the dog called himself the rightful tsar,
> The rightful tsar, Tsar 'Mitry,
> Tsarevich 'Mitry of Moscow.[35]

A peasant who sang a variant of this song for the folklorist P. N. Rybnikov in the nineteenth century provided the following explanation of this passage: 'Grishka spent thirty years in prison and in that time he deliberately grew a cross on his white breasts, in order to resemble Tsarevich Dimitry. For the real tsarevich, when he was born, had a cross on his white breast.'[36] Thus even if Dimitry himself did not claim to have 'royal signs' on his body as a mark of his divine preordination as a true tsar, it seems that the popular consciousness attributed such signs to him. The belief in his 'royal marks' survived his discrediting as an impostor and sorcerer: but it was subsequently explained in the folklore that he had acquired the marks by magical means.

Vishnevetskii's report to King Sigismund, and the 'recognition' of the pretender by various witnesses who claimed to have known the young Tsarevich Dimitry of Uglich, had represented attempts to provide proof of the pretender's identity. However clumsy and fraudulent these efforts might appear to us, they were nevertheless based on rational assumptions about evidence, such as those that might be required in a contemporary European court of law:[37] the pretender was expected to provide a plausible explanation of his escape from death and of his subsequent fate prior to his arrival in Brahin; and to provide witnesses to testify that he bore some physical resemblance to Dimitry of Uglich. In Poland, Dimitry had attempted to supply his patrons with such proofs of his identity, tailored for an educated foreign audience. Addressing himself to the Russian population of the south-west frontier region, however, with its religious and magical mentality, he was content to appeal to the role of Divine Providence, implying a miraculous aspect to his reappearance which was not inconsistent with the idea of resurrection. The

---

[35] *Istoricheskie pesni XVII veka*, no. 8, p. 33; cf. no. 10, p. 35; no. 15, p. 39.
[36] *Ibid.*, p. 336.
[37] Compare Natalie Zemon Davis's account of the type of proof of identity required by sixteenth-century French courts such as that which tried the famous case of the false Martin Guerre (Davis, *The Return of Martin Guerre*, p. 63):

> But how, in a time without photographs, with few portraits, without tape recorders, without fingerprinting, without identity cards, without birth certificates, with parish records still irregular if kept at all – how did one establish a person's identity beyond doubt? You could test the man's memory, though there was always the possibility that he had been coached. You could ask witnesses to identify him, and hope that they were accurate and truthful. You could consider special marks on his face and body, but their significance could only be established by witnesses who recollected the earlier person. You could look to see whether he resembled other members of the family. You could check his handwriting, but only if he and the earlier person could both write and you had samples of the latter's work. The court of Rieux had to try to extract some kind of truth from such evidence ...

'sacralisation' of the monarchy in the sixteenth century facilitated popular acceptance of the idea of a martyred tsarevich who could imitate not merely Lazarus but even Christ by rising from the dead,[38] and the concept of the sacred character of the tsar's power also gave rise to a belief in 'royal signs' as proof of the divine election of the true tsar.[39] The pretender was able to capitalise on these notions, even if he did not actively promote them.

The rising in the capital

After his retreat to Putivl', Dimitry had had to take stock of his position.[40] In an attempt to gain new allies among the Tatars, he sent envoys to the Crimean khan and to Prince Ishterek of the Great Nogai Horde on the Volga. Ishterek recognised Dimitry, but no military assistance was forthcoming from either the Crimean or the Volga Tatars. The pretender also renewed his contacts with Poland, but the *Sejm* was opposed to breaking the treaty with Boris, and the pretender had to content himself with the recruitment of a few more mercenaries.

Two curious episodes at Putivl' enabled Dimitry to reinforce his claim to be the youngest son of Ivan the Terrible. Peyerle relates how three monks appeared in the town, sent from Moscow by Boris as secret envoys to denounce Dimitry to the people as an impostor. When they were exposed as spies, Dimitry summoned them to appear before him, but he asked one of his Polish courtiers to play the part of the tsarevich. The monks accused this supposed Dimitry of being an impostor, but when one of them was granted a private audience with the 'real' Dimitry, he immediately 'recognised' him as the true tsarevich, and disclosed that he and his companions were involved in a plot with two of Dimitry's boyars to poison him. The boyars confessed, and were condemned to death. Dimitry then graciously acceded to a request from the people of Putivl' that they should be allowed to execute the traitors. The townspeople seized the boyars, stripped them naked, tied them to a post in the public square and shot them to death with their bows and muskets. The monk who had revealed the plot was generously rewarded by Dimitry, but his two companions were thrown into prison.[41] As Pierling comments,[42]

---

[38] Sacralisation involved the drawing of an analogy between the tsar and God or Christ: Uspenskii, 'Tsar' i samozvanets', pp. 202–3; Zhivov and Uspenskii, 'Tsar' i bog'.

[39] Such notions were not unique to Russia – the Habsburg princes, for example, were popularly believed to be born with the mark of a gold cross on their backs – and they reflect, in the view of Yves-Marie Bercé, a popular concept of natural, divinely ordained royal legitimacy: *Le roi caché*, pp. 378–401.

[40] For a detailed account of the later stages of Dimitry's march on Moscow, see Skrynnikov, *Sotsial'no-politicheskaya bor'ba*, pp. 217ff.

[41] Paerle, 'Zapiski', pp. 167–9.

[42] Pierling, *Rome et Démétrius*, p. 59.

Peyerle's account has certain 'legendary' features, but it does correspond in its essentials with the contemporary account of Dimitry's two Jesuit companions, Lawicki and Czyrzowski, who reported in a letter of 7/17 March 1605 that three elderly monks had arrived in Putivl' in order to denounce Dimitry as an impostor, but had ended up acknowledging him as the true tsarevich.[43]

The most probable explanation of this episode is that the pretender himself had prearranged it in order to bolster his claim to be Tsarevich Dimitry. The incident of the 'false Grisha Otrep'ev' served a similar function. In a letter of 26 February/8 March 1605 the Jesuits reported that Grishka Otrep'ev, a well-known Russian magician and scoundrel (*celebris Magus et nequam per totam Moschoviam*), had arrived at Putivl'. Since Boris had declared that the pretender was Grisha Otrep'ev, the appearance of this man made it clear to the Russians that Dimitry and Otrep'ev were two different individuals, and therefore strengthened the case for Dimitry's authenticity.[44] Other sources too speak of Grisha and the pretender as separate people.[45] Jacques Margeret, who believed firmly that the pretender was Dimitry of Uglich, insisted that Otrep'ev was an older monk who accompanied the tsarevich on his flight to Poland, and then returned with him to Russia, where 'everyone who wanted to could see him'.[46] The alternative explanation, as Pierling has pointed out, is that the Grisha Otrep'ev who appeared at Putivl' was not the real Grisha (who in his turn was probably the pretender), but was rather a third party who was playing the part of Grisha, on Dimitry's prompting, in order to discredit Boris's assertions that the pretender was Otrep'ev.[47] Russian sources suggest that when Grisha declared himself to be Dimitry in Lithuania, he made one of his companions, the monk Leonid, 'call himself by his own name, Grishka Otrep'ev'.[48] The appearance in Dimitry's camp of a real or false Grisha was to create problems for Boris's propaganda effort against the pretender, which had based its entire case on his identification as Otrep'ev. It has also led a number of historians to conclude that the pretender was not Grishka Otrep'ev.[49]

At Putivl' Dimitry began to call himself 'tsar', rather than 'tsarevich' or 'grand prince'. He formed a boyar duma and court from captured nobles and

[43] *Ibid.*, pièces justificatives, no. 4, pp. 204–5; Pierling, *La Russie et le Saint-Siège*, vol. 3, pp. 156–7. See also Baretstsi, 'Povestvovanie', p. 11.

[44] Pierling, *Rome et Démétrius*, p. 59; pièces justificatives, no. 3, p. 204; Pierling, *La Russie et le Saint-Siège*, vol. 3, pp. 420–1; Frantsev, 'Istoricheskoe i pravdivoe povestvovanie', p. 17.

[45] *SIRIO*, vol. 137, p. 580; Baretstsi, 'Povestvovanie', p. 11; De-Tu, 'Skazaniya', p. 333.

[46] Margeret, *The Russian Empire*, pp. 81–2.

[47] Pierling, *La Russie et le Saint-Siège*, vol. 3, p. 421; Pirling, *Iz smutnogo vremeni*, pp. 229–33.

[48] *RIB*, vol. 13, cols. 155–6; cf. cols. 48, 797. On Leonid see also Golubtsov, ' "Izmena" smol'nyan', pp. 235–6.

[49] See, for example, Kostomarov, *Kto byl pervyi Lzhedimitrii?*, pp. 31–4; Kostomarov, *Smutnoe vremya*, p. 120; Ilovaiskii, *Smutnoe vremya*, pp. 329–31.

commanders whom he rewarded generously with titles and honours. In this way he hoped to persuade other members of the Russian ruling elite to transfer their allegiance to him. Members of the lower classes had been encouraged to acknowledge the pretender by their realisation that his identification of Boris as a traitor and usurper freed them from any obligation to render dues and taxes to Moscow. The petty nobles of the southern garrison towns expected to be rewarded for their switch of loyalty by additional grants of land and money. Dimitry appears to have made little use of terror against those who opposed him. Apart from the two boyars who were implicated by the monks in a plot against him, the sources refer only to his execution of a Russian who had written to Boris offering to capture the pretender alive and hand him over.[50]

On 13 April 1605 Boris Godunov died suddenly in Moscow. Godunov's death was to contribute more to the success of the pretender's cause than were any of Dimitry's own actions. The boyars in Moscow, the overwhelming majority of whom had remained loyal to Boris,[51] now had to decide whether their personal ambitions would be better served by recognition of Dimitry than by allegiance to Boris's young son. Immediately after Godunov's death, however, his courtiers were quick to recognise Fedor Borisovich and to organise the swearing of the oath of loyalty to the new tsar. The text of the oath referred to the rival candidate for the throne as 'the rogue who calls himself Prince Dimitry of Uglich'.[52] Unlike the earlier denunciations of the pretender that had been issued in Boris's lifetime, it did not name him as Grisha Otrep'ev. Presumably news of the appearance of a Grisha Otrep'ev at Putivl' had reached Moscow, and Fedor's advisors had decided that it was best not to mention his name. But their sin of omission made matters worse, and led to suspicions that the Moscow government no longer knew who the pretender was. And if he was not Grisha, might he not in fact be Dimitry of Uglich?[53] Rumours spread that Boris himself had been unsure of the pretender's identity, and had killed himself in fear of the return of Tsarevich Dimitry, thirsting for revenge.[54] In an attempt to quash such rumours, Prince Vasilii Shuiskii, who had headed the commission of enquiry into the events at Uglich in 1591, declared publicly that Tsarevich Dimitry was truly dead, and that he himself had placed him in his coffin with his own hands.[55]

The reign of Tsar Fedor Borisovich began inauspiciously. Doubts about the stability of his rule gave rise to allegations that he was planning to seek

[50] Baretstsi, 'Povestvovanie', p. 11.
[51] Pavlov, *Gosudarev dvor*, p. 78.
[52] *SGGiD*, vol. 2, no. 85, p. 192.
[53] Pierling, *La Russie et le Saint-Siège*, vol. 3, pp. 164–5.
[54] *RIB*, vol. 13, col. 39; Massa, *A Short History*, pp. 90–1, 93–4.
[55] Massa, *A Short History*, p. 97.

asylum in England. The report of Sir Thomas Smith's embassy relates that after Boris's death the English ambassador was anxious to leave Russia as soon as possible because of the spread of rumours which were 'so innumerable and uncertaine, as they were doubtfull and fearefull'. The elaborate provision which was made for the envoys' journey downriver from Vologda to Kholmogory, 'especially the large and well builded Boats', led to rumours that Fedor Godunov was planning to flee to England with them.[56]

These uncertainties and doubts contributed to the low morale of the government army besieging Kromy, where there was some reluctance on the part of the troops to take the oath to Fedor.[57] Peter Basmanov, the new commander appointed to lead Godunov's army, soon learned from his spies that 'there were more supporters of Dimitry among the soldiers than there were of the Muscovites'. According to Isaac Massa, it was this realisation that persuaded Basmanov himself to join the conspiracy at Kromy in favour of Dimitry.[58] The appointment behind his back of Prince A. A. Telyatevskii to a senior command position finally destroyed Basmanov's loyalty to the Godunovs. When the nobility of Ryazan', led by Prokopii Lyapunov, headed a mutiny in the camp on 7 May, Basmanov, together with the two Princes Golitsyn, openly went over to the pretender's side. It was only at this stage that the boyar elite divided and began to defect to Dimitry.[59]

After the success of the mutiny, its leaders sent Prince Ivan Golitsyn to Putivl', to report to Dimitry that the government's main army now acknowledged him as tsar. Golitsyn explained the defection of the army in terms of the suspicious wording of the oath of loyalty to Fedor Godunov. Because it did not mention Grisha Otrep'ev, the troops had concluded that Dimitry really was the son of Ivan the Terrible, and they had decided to swear allegiance to him instead.[60] Dimitry sent Prince B. M. Lykov to Kromy with a gracious proclamation thanking the soldiers for their expression of loyalty to him, and granting them leave to return to their homes.[61]

Dimitry himself left Putivl' on 16 May, and arrived at Kromy on 19 May to find the camp already virtually deserted. He continued his advance to Moscow via Orel and Tula. *En route* he was met by delegations from various towns, reporting their adherence to his cause. They brought with them their local commanders, most of whom swore allegiance to the 'true tsar'. Those who refused were imprisoned. The townspeople flocked to welcome him, greeting him as the true son of Tsar Ivan, 'the sun which had set, which they

---

[56] Smith, *Voiage*, ff12–12v.
[57] *RIB*, vol. 13, col. 40; *PSRL*, vol. 34, p. 206.
[58] Massa, *A Short History*, p. 98.
[59] Pavlov, *Gosudarev dvor*, pp. 78–9.
[60] *SGGiD*, vol. 2, no. 87, pp. 196–7.
[61] Massa, *A Short History*, p. 101.

desired to see rising, and which, when it shone out, would be seen by all'.[62]

From Krapivna, near Tula, Dimitry sent two envoys, Gavrila Pushkin and Naum Pleshcheev, to Moscow with a proclamation calling on the inhabitants of the capital to acknowledge him as their sovereign. On the morning of 1 June, Pushkin and Pleshcheev entered Moscow and read out Dimitry's proclamation to the people of the capital assembled on Red Square. This proclamation was much fuller than the pretender's earlier proclamation of November 1604 to the townspeople of the Seversk frontier.[63] It was addressed specifically to Prince F. I. Mstislavskii and the Princes V. I. and D. I. Shuiskii, as well as to the boyars in general and all the descending ranks of Muscovite society, down to the 'merchants and the best trading people, and the middle and all the common (*chernym*) people'.[64] Dimitry reminded his subjects that after the death of his father, Tsar Ivan, he had been exiled to Uglich by (unnamed) traitors who had then made various attempts to kill him. God, however, had saved him from their nefarious intents and had preserved him till adulthood. The traitors had told the Russian people that the tsarevich had died and been buried at Uglich. When his brother Tsar Fedor had died, the people, not realising that Dimitry was still alive, had sworn allegiance to 'our traitor Boris Godunov', who had already become the virtual ruler of Muscovite state during Fedor's reign, when 'he rewarded and executed whomever he pleased'.[65]

Dimitry then indicated that he was willing to pardon the Muscovites for fighting against him. He recognised that when he had appeared and had announced that he was willing to reclaim his kingdom without bloodshed, they had opposed him out of ignorance and out of fear of Boris.[66] The pretender then listed all his triumphs and successes. He had a large army, he said, of Russians and Lithuanians and Tatars. Many towns had sworn allegiance to him and promised to support him against the traitors. Most recently, he added, the Volga towns had acknowledged him and were sending their governors to his camp: even the *voevody* of distant Astrakhan' were on their way to Voronezh.[67] The Nogai horde under Ishterek had also offered to help him, but – the pretender assured his audience – as a Christian tsar he did not want to encourage Tatars to enter the heartland of Muscovy.[68]

---

[62] Aleksandrenko, comp., 'Materialy', pp. 398–9, 533 (a report by Lawicki, dated 21 September 1605, to the Jesuit General Claudio Aquaviva).

[63] *AAE*, vol. 2, no. 34, pp. 89–91; cf. no. 26, p. 76.

[64] *Ibid.*, no. 34, p. 89.

[65] *Ibid.*, pp. 89–90.

[66] *Ibid.*, p. 90.

[67] Skrynnikov points out that at the time this proclamation was written, Dimitry's cossacks were still besieging Astrakhan'. His second envoy to Moscow, Naum Pleshcheev, however, had been the *voevoda* of Tsaritsyn, which lent credence to the pretender's claims about his support in the Volga towns: Skrynnikov, *Sotsial'no-politicheskaya bor'ba*, p. 268.

[68] *AAE*, vol. 2, no. 34, p. 90.

Dimitry then began to catalogue the abuses which the country had suffered at the hands of the Godunovs. The dowager tsaritsa Mariya Grigor'evna and her son Fedor did not care for the country – which was not surprising, he added, since it did not belong to them. They had devastated the Seversk lands and laid waste many towns and districts. However, Dimitry did not hold the boyars and servicemen responsible for this, since they had acted out of ignorance and in fear of their lives. He addressed each social group, reminding them of the oppression to which Boris had subjected them. The boyars had suffered dishonour; the nobles and *deti boyarskie* had been ruined and exiled; the merchants and traders had their commercial freedom restricted and had heavy taxes imposed upon them. The persecution of innocent Orthodox Christians had been so great that even foreigners had pity on the Russians and, recognising Dimitry as the true tsar, had gladly served him and spilt their blood in his cause.[69]

In conclusion, Dimitry called on the Muscovites of all ranks to swear allegiance to him. He promised graciously to reward them for their loyalty. The boyars would be honoured and preferred; not only would they retain their existing estates, but they could also hope for additional lands. The nobles and officials would be favoured; the merchants and traders would benefit from tax reductions; and as for the ordinary people, 'all Orthodox Christians will live in peace and tranquillity and prosperity'. But if they did not recognise him as tsar and beg for his pardon, they would have to render their account to God on the Day of Judgement. They could not hide from God's righteous anger, nor from Dimitry's royal hand.[70]

As R. G. Skrynnikov has pointed out,[71] Dimitry's most fulsome promises at this final stage of his campaign for the throne were directed towards the upper classes, whose support was essential for his success. Many of the boyars were present on Red Square to hear his proclamation. The English author of the report of Sir Thomas Smith's embassy claims that their presence was enforced by the crowd: 'many came; the Commons being resolved, else to fetch them out'.[72] According to Conrad Bussow, the proclamation had an immediate effect on the ordinary people, who cried out, 'Please God that the true sun rise again over Russia. Until now we have been sitting in darkness, but now the true light has dawned.'[73] The solar imagery here, as before, echoes not only the 'good tsar' of folklore, but also Biblical imagery relating to Christ as Messiah.

---

[69] *Ibid.*
[70] *Ibid.*, pp. 90–1.
[71] Skrynnikov, *Sotsial'no-politicheskaya bor'ba*, p. 275.
[72] Smith, *Voiage*, fK3.
[73] Bussov, *Moskovskaya khronika*, p. 106.

The popular uprising in the capital against the Godunovs began with an attack on the city jails to release political detainees – Polish prisoners of war and previous envoys sent earlier by Dimitry to Moscow. Some foreign accounts state that Dimitry's envoys chided the Muscovites for their imprisonment and ill-treatment of previous messengers,[74] and this may have led to the release of these men. The English report describes how, before Pleshcheev had finished reading the proclamation, some of the crowd rushed into the Kremlin, where they met two of the newly released messengers. The graphic account which these men gave of their 'torturing, whipping and roasting' at the hands of the Godunovs' officials served to inflame the people further.[75] Some of the crowd attacked the royal palace, while others raided the Godunovs' mansions in the suburbs of the city. Subsequently the mob looted houses belonging to other members of the Godunov family, and to their kinsmen the Saburovs and Vel'yaminovs. The movement spread, turning into a more general attack by the lower orders on the property of the rich. There are no reports, however, of killings or lynchings: the only victims, according to some accounts, were looters who died of alcoholic poisoning after drinking too deeply of plundered wine and spirits.[76]

In the aftermath of the Moscow rising, Boris's body was disinterred from its ceremonial resting-place in the Archangel Cathedral in the Kremlin. Having been subjected to various forms of abuse and defilement, the corpse of the 'traitor and usurper' was reburied in the grounds of the modest Varsunof'ev Convent.[77] Various rumours were spread in Moscow about Boris after his disinterment. According to Isaac Massa: 'Suddenly, most of the people began to believe that Boris was not dead, even though they themselves had buried him twice. Some said that he had fled, and someone else had been put in the tomb in his place.'[78] Massa further relates that when the mobs ransacked Boris's palace some people claimed that they had seen the former tsar alive and well in the cellars. In the palace they discovered a wax figure of an angel, which was to have served as the model for a gold statue for a church. It was said that this figure had been found in Boris's coffin, and so constituted evidence that he was not dead.[79]

---

[74] *Ibid.*, p. 105; Smith, *Voiage*, fK3v.
[75] Smith, *Voiage*, fL.
[76] Skrynnikov, *Sotsial'no-politicheskaya bor'ba*, p. 282.
[77] *Ibid.*, p. 290.
[78] Massa, *A Short History*, p. 106.
[79] *Ibid.*, pp. 106–7. Other contemporary accounts also mention rumours about a statue found in Boris's palace. According to these sources, Godunov had allegedly booby-trapped his mansion by placing gunpowder in the cellars, with a fuse attached to a lamp in the hands of a statue. See Frantsev, 'Istoricheskoe i pravdivoe povestvovanie', pp. 31–2; *Moskovskaya tragediya*, p. 36.

According to Massa, the rumours that Godunov was still alive were so strong that messengers were sent out far and wide to look for him. Some people said that he had gone to Tatary, and cossacks ostensibly searching for the fugitive tsar ransacked villages on the Volga. Others claimed that he had left for Sweden, but most were convinced that the English merchants had taken him with rich treasures to their own country.[80] The foreign merchants, including Massa himself, who left Moscow at this time for the White Sea port of Archangel, were in constant fear of attack, since it was widely believed that they were smuggling Boris and his treasury out of Russia.[81] Massa describes the rumours about Boris as evidence of the 'most ridiculous blindness' on the part of the credulous Russians.[82] His own account, however, suggests that there was some method in the Russians' apparent madness, since the rumours clearly served as a pretext for looting and pillaging by those who claimed to be searching for Boris and his treasure.

K. V. Chistov, noting the similarity of these rumours to some of the motifs of the 'socio-utopian legends about returning tsar-deliverers', states that nevertheless no such legend was formed about Boris, since no-one wanted him to reappear. Unlike Tsarevich Dimitry, Boris was an all too familiar and discredited figure, with whom popular socio-utopian expectations could not be associated.[83] Subsequently, however, as we shall see below, the Poles were to find a use for the rumours about Boris, when they threatened Dimitry with the spectre of a false Boris.[84]

Foreign accounts based on reports by the Polish Jesuit Andrzej Lawicki suggest a possible alternative explanation of these rumours about Boris Godunov. Lawicki states that on his arrival in Moscow the pretender ordered Godunov's palace to be razed to its foundations, 'fearing spells and magic', since Boris in his desperation had resorted towards the end of his life to sorcery as a weapon against the pretender.[85] Certainly there is evidence that Boris had long been interested in magic: Horsey, who knew him before he became tsar, describes him as 'affected much to necromancy'.[86] But, as B. A. Uspenskii has noted, Dimitry and his supporters would in any case have regarded Boris as a sorcerer, in so far as they viewed him a false tsar –

[80] Massa, *A Short History*, p. 106.
[81] *Ibid.*, p. 107.
[82] *Ibid.*, p. 107.
[83] Chistov, *Russkie narodnye*, p. 47.
[84] For discussion of the rumours about Boris, see Perrie, ' "Popular Socio-Utopian Legends" ', pp. 23–6.
[85] Aleksandrenko, comp., 'Materialy', pp. 400, 535; Frantsev, 'Istoricheskoe i pravdivoe povestvovanie', p. 31; *Moskovskaya tragediya*, pp. 35–6.
[86] Berry and Crummey, eds., *Rude and Barbarous Kingdom*, p. 362.

a usurper or 'pretender on the throne'.[87] (This was of course the counterpart of Boris's own depiction of Grisha Otrep'ev as a black magician.) Rumours that Boris was not dead may have reflected the popular belief that the earth would not accept the body of a sorcerer. Similar rumours, as we shall see, were to surround the death and burial of the First False Dimitry himself in 1606.

After the Moscow rising, Bogdan Bel'skii took over the administration of the capital in Dimitry's name. Bel'skii, who had been in disgrace since the Tsarev-Borisov incident in 1600, had returned to Moscow only as a result of the political amnesty declared on Boris's death. According to the English report, it was Bel'skii who succeeded in persuading the boyars to acknowledge Dimitry as tsar:

The Nobles ioyning in one Counsell for the present ordering of these suddaine accidents, and for answere to the *P[rince] Dem[etrie] Euanich*, who suddenly was by generall consent concluded (by the perticular knowledege of *Bodan Belsekey* a great Counseller, that was privie to his departure, and some others) to be their right and lawfull Emperour.[88]

In reality, of course, the boyars recognised Dimitry not because they believed him to be the true tsarevich, but because acknowledgement of the pretender was the only way they could hope to survive the popular uprising and regain control of events.

On 5 June Dimitry learned of the rising in Moscow, and left Krapivna in order to begin his triumphal march on the capital. At Tula, where the new tsar was welcomed with great pomp, he received a delegation from Moscow. This was headed not by the chief boyars, but by second-rank figures. The pretender, clearly feeling slighted by this, snubbed the delegation by receiving envoys from the Don cossacks ahead of the Moscow notables. The boyars were mocked and derided by the cossacks, aided and abetted by Dimitry, who, in the words of the chronicler, 'chastised and cursed them like a real tsar's son'.[89] The lesson was not lost on the leaders of the boyar duma. When Dimitry reached Serpukhov he was met with great honour by Prince F. I.

---

[87] Uspenskii, 'Tsar' i samozvanets', pp. 216–17. For the same reasons, Vasilii Shuiskii believed that Dimitry's palace was bewitched. Isaac Massa (*A Short History*, p. 166) tells us that after he succeeded to the throne, Shuiskii had a new residence built, because: 'He had not wished to live in Dmitry's sumptuous palace for fear of a nocturnal visit from the Demon, for he still held Dmitry to have been a sorcerer, and all the places he inhabited were thought impure.'

[88] Smith, *Voiage*, fL2. Skrynnikov's account of Bel'skii's role appears to be based on a mistranslation in the Russian edition of this source: Skrynnikov, *Sotsial'no-politicheskaya bor'ba*, p. 285. Bel'skii was able to persuade the boyars to recognise Dimitry because he had been 'privy to his departure' from Uglich (see below, p. 80), not because he 'had heard of his departure from his camp' at Tula.

[89] *PSRL*, vol. 14, p. 65, para. 104.

Mstislavskii and Prince D. I. Shuiskii, and a lavish banquet was arranged to welcome him.

The pretender had obtained the support of the boyars, but he had not yet been recognised by the Holy Synod. In proclamations which he had sent to the provinces on dates when he was still at Tula, but which were written as if he was already established in Moscow, Dimitry had claimed that he had been acknowledged as tsar by Patriarch Iov and by the Synod,[90] but this was untrue. Iov had remained loyal to the Godunovs until the end, and had suffered for this in the course of the Moscow rising, when the mob had dragged him from the altar of the Uspenskii Cathedral in the Kremlin and subjected him to all kinds of abuse. While Dimitry was still outside the capital, his new lieutenant P. F. Basmanov stripped Iov of his robes of office. The pretender nominated as Iov's successor the Archbishop of Ryazan', Ignatii, who had been the first senior prelate to recognise him. A meeting of the Holy Synod after Dimitry entered the capital agreed to Iov's retirement on the grounds of ill-health, and elected Ignatii as the new Patriarch.

At Serpukhov, it seems, the boyars had agreed to Dimitry's demand that before he entered the city the previous occupant of the throne, and his mother, should be 'got out of the way'.[91] Soon after the boyars returned to Moscow, it was announced that Tsar Fedor and Tsaritsa Mariya had committed suicide. When their bodies were publicly displayed, eyewitnesses noticed rope-marks on their necks, indicating that they had been strangled.[92] According to the *New Chronicle*, they were murdered on the orders of Prince Vasilii Golitsyn. Fedor and his mother were buried alongside Boris in the Varsunof'ev monastery. Fedor's sister Kseniya survived as a prisoner;[93] subsequently she was allegedly raped by the pretender before being forced to take the veil.[94] Much later, in 1609, a rumour was reported from Poland that Tsar Fedor Borisovich was alive and living at the court of the Holy Roman Emperor,[95] but no false Fedor appeared in Russia during the Time of Troubles.

Moscow and coronation

Dimitry made his triumphal entry into Moscow on 20 June. The streets were thronged with his jubilant subjects. Some cried out, 'May He who preserved Thee in miraculous fashion preserve Thee further in all Thy endeavours!'

---

[90] Proclamation to Sol' Vychegodsk, dated 6 June 1605: *AAE*, vol. 2, no. 35, p. 92; proclamation to Pelym, dated 11 June: *SGGiD*, vol. 2, no. 89, p. 200.

[91] Bussov, *Moskovskaya khronika*, p. 107.

[92] Petrei, *Istoriya*, p. 205.

[93] *PSRL*, vol. 14, p. 66, para. 106.

[94] Massa, *A Short History*, p. 119.

[95] *AI*, vol. 2, no. 199, p. 231.

Others greeted him as 'the true sun shining upon Russia'.[96] Dimitry entered the Kremlin, and wept over the graves of his supposed father and brother, Tsars Ivan and Fedor, in the Archangel Cathedral. At the Cathedral of the Assumption, the archpriest Terentii greeted him with a flowery speech whose imagery, reflecting the Church's official view of the new tsar as a sacred figure, was not dissimilar from that of the voices in the crowd. Terentii rejoiced that God had blessed Dimitry in his mother's womb, preserved him with His invisible power from all his enemies, and set him on his royal throne. Describing the new tsar as the defender of the Orthodox faith, 'shining more brightly than the sun in the heavens', the archpriest called on him to imitate Christ in his mercy towards the people.[97]

Then Bogdan Bel'skii addressed the crowds on Red Square. Bel'skii claimed to be Dimitry's godfather, appointed as his guardian by Tsar Ivan. According to Conrad Bussow, Bel'skii ostentatiously swore on the cross before the citizens that their new tsar was indeed Dimitry Ivanovich, whom he himself had 'sheltered on his bosom' and was now restoring to them.[98] A Russian source also states that Bel'skii claimed to have preserved Dimitry, and to have suffered for this at Boris's hands.[99] What significance should we attach to Bel'skii's claim to have been Dimitry's saviour?

In his proclamations to the provinces issued after the Moscow rising, Dimitry had continued to use the same vague formulae about his escape from death as had been used in his earlier manifestos: Divine Providence had saved him from an evil death at the hands of the traitor Boris Godunov, and God had graciously preserved him in safety until he reached manhood, etc.[100] The version that Bogdan Bel'skii saved Dimitry from death is contained in the report of Sir Thomas Smith's embassy. The English party left for home from the White Sea at the beginning of August 1605,[101] so that this account must reflect rumours current in Moscow at the time of Dimitry's first entry into the capital. The author describes how on Tsar Ivan's death Boris had become regent for Tsar Fedor Ivanovich, and had exiled Dimitry to Uglich. Bogdan Bel'skii, Andrei Shchelkalov and Andrei Kleshnin were at first close associates of Boris, but Godunov, being jealous of their influence, sought to distance them from positions of power, 'by throwing discontents upon one of

[96] Bussov, *Moskovskaya khronika*, pp. 109, 235. Bussow even attempts to reproduce the Russian words in his German text: 'Thy brabda Solniska'. Zhivov and Uspenskii ('Tsar' i bog', p. 57) translate this as *solntse pravednoe*, i.e. 'sun of righteousness'.
[97] *AAE*, vol. 2, no. 224, pp. 383–5.
[98] Bussov, *Moskovskaya khronika*, p. 109.
[99] Belokurov, ed., *Razryadnye zapisi*, p. 5.
[100] *AAE*, vol. 2, no. 37, pp. 92–3; no. 38, p. 93; *SGGiD*, vol. 2, no. 90, p. 201.
[101] Smith, *Voiage*, fM.

them and a slightly-regarding of the other'.[102] Bogdan Bel'skii was forced to leave Moscow, but his two former colleagues kept him informed of happenings at court. Bogdan then

(knowing the ambitious thirst of *Borris* to extirpate the race of *Evan Vassiliwich* himselfe now but an *Usurper*) took deliberation with the old *Empresse* (mother to *Demetre*) for the preservation of the child. And seeing afarre off, arrowes aimed at his life, which could very hardly be kept off, it was devised to exchange *Demetre* for the child of a churchman (in yeares and proportion somewhat resembling him) whilst the other (by this meanes) might live safe, though obscure.

This counterfet Churchmans Sonne being then taken for the lawful *Prince*, was attended on and associated according to his State: with whome one day, another child, (that was appointed to bee his play fellow) disporting themselves, finding faulte that the collor which the supposed *Demetre* wore about his necke (as the fashion of the Countrey is) stood awry, preparing to mende it, with a sharpe knif (provided as seems of purpose) cut his throat.[103]

Boris had made a hypocritical show of grief, and had sent a commission of inquiry to investigate the circumstances of Dimitry's death. The tsarevich's guardians were imprisoned, and some of them were put to death.

But heaven protected the lawfull, to be an instrument for the *Usurpers* confusion. Obscurely livd this wronged *Prince*, the changing of him being made private to none but his owne mother (Sister as is said before to *Boris*) who is now living, and to *Bodan Belskey*: but upon what wheele his various fortunes have bin turned, (which of necessity must needs be strange) came not within the rech of our knowledge being there.[104]

As the historian Kostomarov pointed out last century, this version of Dimitry's escape from death, in which the substitution took place long before 15 May 1591, is much more convincing than the pretender's own account, given to Vishnevetskii in Poland, in which the tsarevich's tutor intervened with a replacement child on the day itself.[105] Jacques Margeret too stated that Dimitry's substitution took place before 1591, but he attributed the ruse to 'Dmitrii's mother and some of the high nobles who were left, like the Romanovs, the Nagois, and others'.[106] Foreign contemporaries, such as Margeret and the author of the English account, believed that the man who was crowned in Moscow in July 1605 really was Tsarevich Dimitry, saved by

---

[102] *Ibid.*, fM2. Andrei Kleshnin and Vasilii Shchelkalov (the brother of Andrei) were later named by the Second False Dimitry as allies of Bogdan Bel'skii in thwarting Boris's plans to murder him at Uglich: Buturlin, *Istoriya smutnogo vremeni*, vol. 2, prilozheniya no. 7, p. 49.

[103] Smith, *Voiage*, fM2.

[104] *Ibid.*, fM2v–[M3]. Dimitry's mother was not of course Boris's sister.

[105] Kostomarov, *Kto byl pervyi Lzhedimitrii?*, pp. 35–40.

[106] Margeret, *The Russian Empire*, p. 81.

the boyars from Boris's attempt to kill him.[107] Kostomarov, while rejecting the view that Dimitry had avoided death at Uglich, suggests that a group of boyars including Bel'skii was responsible for setting up the pretender.[108] Bearing in mind the discrepancy between the English account and the pretender's own story of his escape, however, it is more likely that his supporters in Moscow, such as Bogdan Bel'skii, tried to provide a more credible version of his biography, for the benefit of the citizens of the capital, than the vague talk of Divine Providence which was contained in Dimitry's own proclamations. Thus in addition to the 'religious-miraculous' version of the tsarevich's escape from death that circulated in the Seversk region, a new variant of the 'scientific-rational' explanation was produced for the more sophisticated inhabitants of Moscow.

The problem of persuading people of his identity as Dimitry Ivanovich was one which arose particularly acutely for the pretender on his first appearance in the capital. According to the *New Chronicle*, many Muscovites recognised him immediately as Grisha Otrep'ev and were bitterly disillusioned.[109] Some accounts state that Dimitry began secretly to dispose of anyone who doubted his royal birth. A wave of arrests, tortures, exiles and killings was instituted.[110] Two public executions took place: the nobleman Peter Turgenev and the townsman Fedor Kalachnik were beheaded on Red Square for refusing to accept the pretender as the son of Tsar Ivan. Kalachnik is said to have denounced Dimitry on the scaffold not only as 'the emissary of Satan' but also as 'the image of the Anti-Christ'[111] – the direct antithesis of his supporters' view of Dimitry as the Christ-like 'sun of righteousness'.

Soon after Dimitry entered Moscow, the Shuiskii brothers were arrested and brought to public trial, accused of plotting to kill the new tsar. All three were found guilty. Prince Vasilii Shuiskii was sentenced to death, but was reprieved at the last moment and sent into exile with his brothers. It was widely rumoured that his real offence was to have initiated a whispering campaign that Dimitry was an impostor. R. G. Skrynnikov makes the plausible suggestion that Dimitry's prompt removal of the Shuiskiis was not undertaken in response to any rash action on their part, but was rather a preemptive strike by the pretender against the heads of the princely clan with the most valid claim to the throne.[112]

---

[107] For the rather more sceptical view of a member of Sir Thomas Smith's party, see William Scott's report to Lord Salisbury: Aleksandrenko, comp., 'Materialy', pp. 246–7.

[108] Kostomarov, *Kto byl pervyi Lzhedimitrii?*, pp. 41–9.

[109] *PSRL*, vol. 14, p. 67, para. 107.

[110] Popov, *Izbornik*, p. 329; Massa, *A Short History*, p. 113.

[111] Palitsyn, *Skazanie*, p. 111; *PSRL*, vol. 14, p. 67, para. 111.

[112] Skrynnikov, *Sotsial'no-politicheskaya bor'ba*, pp. 308–9; Skrynnikov, *Rossiya v nachale XVII v.*, p. 238. Skrynnikov makes no attempt to reconcile Dimitry's persecution of the Shuiskiis with his theory that this clan had been responsible for setting up the 'pretender intrigue'.

If anyone doubted his identity, however, the pretender had a trump card to play. Tsaritsa Mariya Nagaya, the mother of Dimitry of Uglich, was still living as the nun Marfa in the remote northern convent to which she had been exiled after the death of her son. As we have noted, the captured nobleman Peter Khrushchov had told the pretender on the eve of his incursion into Russia in 1604 of rumours that Boris had summoned Mariya to Moscow to interrogate her, but there appears to have been no substance to these. In his proclamations of June 1605 to the Siberian towns of Sol' Vychegodsk and Pelym, Dimitry had called upon his loyal subjects to pray not only for himself but also for 'Our mother, the Great Sovereign Tsaritsa and Grand Princess the nun Marfa Fedorovna of All Russia'.[113] According to the text which was circulated at the same time, the oath of allegiance was to be taken to Marfa Fedorovna as well as to her son.[114] The practice of naming the dowager tsaritsa in the oath of allegiance had been introduced by Boris Godunov, who derived his claim to the throne from his sister Irina, the widow of Tsar Fedor Ivanovich. The precedent had been mechanically copied by Tsar Fedor Borisovich. For Dimitry, as for Boris, it served the additional purpose of stressing his link with the old dynasty.[115]

When he reached Moscow, Dimitry sent his trusted boyar Prince Vasilii Mosal'skii to escort Mariya to the capital. But he had prepared the ground in advance, having already despatched Semen Shapkin, a relative of the Nagois whom the pretender had appointed to the rank of chamberlain (postel'nichii), to persuade Mariya to acknowledge Dimitry as her son. According to one Russian source, the 'persuasion' was to take the form of a threat to kill her if she did not recognise him.[116] The New Chronicle, however, admits that no-one knows why Mariya acknowledged the pretender: from fear of her life, or of her own volition.[117] Not surprisingly, after the murder of the First False Dimitry Mariya herself claimed that she had acted under duress.[118]

In reality, the pretender hardly needed to resort to threats to induce Mariya to recognise him as her son. While he was still encamped at Tula, Dimitry had sent messengers to the obscure provincial towns where the surviving senior members of the Nagoi family were serving in the minor posts which Boris had allowed them to occupy after their years of imprisonment and exile. Dimitry generously rewarded his closest 'relatives'. Mariya Nagaya's brother Michael Fedorovich Nagoi was made a boyar and equerry to the tsar;

[113] AAE, vol. 2, no. 35, p. 92; SGGiD, vol. 2, no. 89, p. 200.
[114] AAE, vol. 2, no. 38, p. 94; SGGiD, vol. 2, no. 91, pp. 202–3.
[115] Skrynnikov, Sotsial'no-politicheskaya bor'ba, p. 289; Perrie, 'Female Rule', pp. 4–5.
[116] Belokurov, ed., Razryadnye zapisi, p. 6.
[117] PSRL, vol. 14, p. 67, para. 109.
[118] SGGiD, vol. 2, no. 146, p. 307; no. 147, p. 312; no. 149, p. 317; AAE, vol. 2, no. 48, p. 111.

her other brother, Grigorii, and her cousins Andrei, Afanasii and Michael Aleksandrovich Nagoi were also made boyars. They were all allocated estates and mansions which had been confiscated from the Godunovs.[119] This dramatic improvement in the fortunes of her kinsmen, as well as an understandable tendency to wishful thinking, must undoubtedly have influenced Mariya's attitude towards her supposed son.

In addition to the Nagois, Dimitry generously rewarded members of other boyar families who had been in exile and disgrace in Boris's reign. The brothers I. P. and V. P. Golovin were made *okol'nichie*, as was the *d'yak* V. Ya. Shchelkalov. Ivan Nikitich Romanov was made a boyar. His brother Fedor, whom Boris had obliged to become the monk Filaret, returned to Moscow from the Antoniev Siiskii monastery, and was appointed Metropolitan of Rostov. The agents who kept watch on Filaret had reported that in February 1605, when news of the pretender's successes first reached him, the reluctant elder had undergone a marked change in his behaviour. Filaret had begun laughing to himself, threatening his jailors, and reminiscing about his former life as a layman, with his hawks and his hunting dogs – a life to which he clearly hoped soon to return.[120] This evidence has served for some historians as confirmation of their hypothesis that these boyar families were responsible for setting up the pretender.[121] But it is just as reasonable to assume that Dimitry, in need of allies in the boyar duma, realised that men and women who had been exiled by Boris would not require too stringent proofs of his identity, and would be willing to 'recognise' and support him in return for their rehabilitation and reinstatement.

On 17 July the nun Marfa reached the village of Taininskoe, on the outskirts of Moscow. Dimitry went to meet her there, and a touching scene ensued in which mother and son were reunited after fourteen years. The next day Dimitry escorted the dowager tsaritsa into the capital, where they were greeted by cheering crowds on Red Square and attended a service of thanksgiving in the Kremlin. Three days later, on 21 July 1605, the pretender was crowned as tsar in the Uspenskii cathedral. According to the Pole Stanisław Niemojewski, when Dimitry was riding to his coronation, the people of Moscow hailed him as the 'true tsarevich and our legitimate sovereign, our true sun (*prawotne solnyszko nasze*)'.[122]

---

[119] Skrynnikov, *Sotsial'no-politicheskaya bor'ba*, p. 314.
[120] *AI*, vol. 2, no. 54, pp. 64–6.
[121] E.g. Kostomarov, *Kto byl pervyi Lzhedimitrii?*, pp. 48–9; Platonov, *Ocherki*, pp. 186–7.
[122] Nemoevskii, 'Zapiski', p. 114. Although the Russian re-translation is *istinnoe solnyshko nashe*, the original was probably *pravednoe solnyshko*, i.e. 'sun of righteousness'.

3   The pretender on the throne

True tsar; good tsar?

After his coronation, Dimitry disbanded his foreign mercenaries, whose behaviour in the capital had caused tensions with the Muscovites. He also dismissed most of his cossacks, whom the boyars had not forgiven for their insulting behaviour at Tula. The cossacks were generously rewarded, but this did not stop them grumbling about their treatment. Isaac Massa presciently commented that 'Each of these malcontents would have liked to have been tsar himself!'[1]

Meanwhile King Sigismund was anxious to put pressure on his protégé, the new tsar of Russia, to provide military assistance to the *Rzeczpospolita* against Charles IX of Sweden. In August 1605 Dimitry received the Polish ambassador, Alexander Gosiewski, in secret audience. Gosiewski repeated to Dimitry a tale which, he said, had been told him in Poland by a former official in Boris's administration. This story was as follows. When he had received news of the pretender's successful invasion of Russia, Boris Godunov had consulted his soothsayers. They had told Boris that as long as he remained in Moscow, the tsardom would be vulnerable to the pretender; but if Boris left Russia, and his son Fedor became tsar, Muscovy could resist Dimitry. Boris had acted on this advice. He had ordered his own death to be announced, poisoned another man who resembled him, and ordered him to be buried as if he were the tsar. Boris had then collected a mass of gold and other treasures, and fled to England in the guise of a merchant. Gosiewski added solicitously that Sigismund had ordered enquiries about this to be made in England, and the king had also told his commanders on the Ukrainian frontier to be ready to assist Dimitry in the case of any eventuality.[2] Dimitry replied that he had no reason to doubt that Boris Godunov was dead, but he thanked Sigismund for his kindness in informing him of the rumour, and for the orders he had given to his commanders.[3]

---

[1] Massa, *A Short History*, p. 112.

[2] *SGGiD*, vol. 2, no. 96, pp. 213–14.

[3] *Ibid.*, no. 97, p. 216.

Gosiewski's tale incorporated elements of the rumours about Boris that had been current in Moscow at the time of the uprising in favour of Dimitry. But Gosiewski was not of course simply repeating idle gossip when he reported this story to the new tsar. There was a thinly veiled threat in the ambassador's tale: he was warning Dimitry that it would be just as easy for the Poles to set up a false Boris to overthrow him, if necessary, as it had been for them to support a false Dimitry against Boris. After the pretender's death, the Poles did not forget this threat, and similar rumours about Boris were conveyed to Tsar Vasilii Shuiskii's envoys to Poland in 1606.[4]

After this preliminary skirmish, the ambassador proceeded to the true business of his embassy, the military alliance against Sweden. But here Dimitry was not willing or able to commit himself, complaining that Sigismund had not accorded him the title of 'tsar'.[5] Subsequently the question of titles became even more contentious, when Dimitry adopted the title of emperor (*tsesar'*) as well as tsar. For the moment, however, Dimitry could not afford to antagonise Sigismund too far. He was still anxious to marry Marina Mniszech, and a marriage ceremony was conducted in Craców in November 1605, with the Russian *d'yak* Afanasii Vlas'ev standing proxy for the tsar.

In domestic politics, as in his foreign relations, Dimitry's dubious legitimacy was his Achilles' heel. In March 1606 doubts arose even among Dimitry's own Russian bodyguard of musketeers (*strel'tsy*) as to whether he truly was the son of Ivan the Terrible. According to Massa, when these doubts were reported to Dimitry by Basmanov, the pretender assembled all the musketeers in the Kremlin, and challenged them to provide proof that he was an impostor. He charged them with ingratitude, telling them that he had risked his life to regain his throne, not from a desire for personal power, 'but through pity for you, to deliver you from the depths of misery and fearful slavery into which you were about to be plunged by [the Godunovs,] these traitors and oppressors of the land'.[6] Having roused the *strel'tsy* to a frenzy of loyalty by his oratory, Dimitry called on them to kill the seven alleged ringleaders of the whispering campaign against him. The men were then torn to pieces by their former comrades with their bare hands.[7]

In his speech to the *strel'tsy*, Dimitry's account of his escape from Uglich had been typically vague: 'God has delivered me from the mortal snares with which I was surrounded and singularly preserved me.' But he had assured them that his 'mother and all the lords here present' could vouch for him.[8]

---

[4] *SIRIO*, vol. 137, pp. 306, 307.
[5] *SGGiD*, vol. 2, no. 96, pp. 214–15; no. 97, p. 216.
[6] Massa, *A Short History*, p. 122. Cf. Koretskii, *Formirovanie krepostnogo prava*, p. 243.
[7] Massa, *A Short History*, pp. 122–3. See also Bussov, *Moskovskaya khronika*, pp. 112–13; Petrei, *Istoriya*, p. 212; *PSRL*, vol. 14, p. 68, para. 116; *AAE*, vol. 2, no. 48, pp. 108–9; *RIB*, vol. 13, pp. 78–9; Platonov, *Ocherki*, pp. 222–3.
[8] Massa, *A Short History*, p. 122.

There is some evidence, however, that Marfa Nagaya's willingness to testify to Dimitry's authenticity had already begun to weaken. Soon after he had come to the throne, apparently in an attempt to give credence to the story that a substitute child had been buried in the place of the young tsarevich, Dimitry had ordered the tomb at Uglich to be opened and the 'false' remains removed. But Marfa Nagaya, knowing that the body buried at Uglich was indeed that of her son, had objected strongly and had prevented the pretender from carrying out his plan. According to the Polish hetman Żółkiewski, Dimitry's tactless proposal antagonised Marfa so much that she sent a message to King Sigismund through the agency of a certain Swede, to warn the king that his protégé was an impostor.[9] R. G. Skrynnikov speculates that this Swede was Petrei (Peer Persson), who had an audience with King Sigismund in December 1605. Petrei tells a very similar story in his account of the Time of Troubles, adding that Marfa had acknowledged the pretender as her son only in order to gain recognition for herself and to obtain revenge against Boris Godunov.[10] According to Bussow, even Basmanov, the tsar's closest Russian confidant, privately conceded that Dimitry was an impostor.[11]

Historians have offered conflicting assessments of Dimitry's conduct as tsar. The problem of obtaining a balanced assessment is intensified by the lack of official sources for his reign, since these were largely destroyed after his overthrow. Dimitry's relationship with the boyars is particularly problematic. Godunov's boyars had been obliged to recognise the pretender in order to survive the Moscow rising; and the duma had subsequently been expanded by Dimitry's new appointees. But according to R. G. Skrynnikov, Dimitry soon became a virtual prisoner of his boyars. By the end of 1605 he had had to agree to the pardon of the Shuiskiis, whose lands and offices were also returned to them. From then onwards, boyar opposition meant that Dimitry was unable to implement any of his proposed innovations.[12] Skrynnikov's 'revisionist' account is not very convincing, however, and it does not adequately rebut the more traditional view that Dimitry was overthrown by the boyars because they resented the changes that he was introducing.[13]

It is clear that many of Dimitry's actions challenged the norms of the Muscovite court, with its elaborate rituals. He often insisted on going out and about unaccompanied by the boyars, sometimes on foot or on horseback, rather than in the conventional carriage used by previous tsars. He wore

---

[9] Zholkevskii, *Zapiski*, pp. 10–11.

[10] Petrei, *Istoriya*, pp. 243–4; Petrei, *Relyatsiya*, pp. 98–100; Skrynnikov, *Smuta v Rossii*, pp. 24–5.

[11] Bussow, *Moskovskaya khronika*, p. 132; cf. Petrei, *Istoriya*, p. 244.

[12] Skrynnikov, *Samozvantsy*, pp. 154–74; Skrynnikov, *Smuta v Rossii*, pp. 12–23.

[13] See, for example, the assessments by Solov'ev and Kostomarov. For criticism of Skrynnikov's interpretation of Dimitry's relationship with the boyars, see Dunning, 'R. G. Skrynnikov', p. 76.

Western dress, and built himself a new palace in the Kremlin, expensively furbished in the latest Polish taste. He expressed an interest in declaring religious tolerance, and planned to follow Boris's example in sending Russian youths to study abroad. Presiding over the boyar duma, he criticised his elderly counsellors for their ignorance, and suggested that foreign travel might broaden their minds. Certainly, Dimitry's 'heretical' behaviour as tsar is entirely consistent with the characterisation of Grisha Otrep'ev as a rebel against Orthodoxy that was provided by Boris Godunov's government before the pretender had crossed the Russian frontier. Tsar Dimitry's interest in Western innovations has led some historians to suggest that in many respects he foreshadowed Peter the Great.[14] Richard Hellie, describing him as 'one of the few really enlightened rulers Russia has ever had', notes that '[a]ll of his actions reflected the modernizing, rationalizing tendencies which led to his early murder'.[15]

R. G. Skrynnikov does not deny that Dimitry implemented a number of measures which were relatively enlightened by Muscovite standards. But in Skrynnikov's view these simply demonstrate that Dimitry was a skilful demagogue who was concerned to create an image of himself as a 'good' tsar. To this end, he issued pardons to the Godunovs and their kinsmen, and made an example of corrupt officials. He invited his provincial subjects to send him petitions about abuses by local governors, and promised to deal with any complaints. He exempted the inhabitants of Putivl' and its district from taxes for ten years, and promised the people of Tomsk that he would not levy taxes which were disproportionate to their ability to pay. Skrynnikov presents all of these policies as evidence of demagogic tendencies on the part of the pretender.[16] But we have no reason to doubt Dimitry's sincerity when he asserted his intention to rule with justice and mercy, and there is evidence that he was able to implement some positive measures of reform.

There has been considerable debate among Soviet historians about the nature of Dimitry's social legislation. This centres on two decrees relating to the position of slaves and peasants respectively. A law of 7 January 1606 forbade the joint assignment of a bondslave to more than one master, such as a father and son, and also freed anyone who had previously been enslaved in this way.[17] This decree has to be interpreted in relationship to the earlier decree of 1 February 1597 which had stated that slaves should be freed on their masters' deaths, and not transferred to their wives or children.[18] It seems

---

[14] Ikonnikov, 'Kto byl pervyi samozvanets?', p. 12; Barbour, *Dimitry*, p. 160.
[15] Hellie, *Enserfment and Military Change*, p. 49.
[16] Skrynnikov, *Samozvantsy*, pp. 157–60, 161–2, 168–9; Skrynnikov, *Smuta v Rossii*, pp. 14–15, 17–18, 22. Cf. Dunning, 'R. G. Skrynnikov', pp. 75–6.
[17] *Zakonodatel'nye akty*, no. 54, p. 73.
[18] *Ibid.*, no. 47, para. 5, p. 65.

that some nobles had attempted to circumvent this 1597 legislation by assigning their slaves to more than one master in a single document, in the expectation that a slave in joint bondage to a father and son, for example, would not be freed on the death of the older lord, but would remain in bondage to the son. The law of 7 January 1606 sought to close this loophole and to guarantee that slaves would be freed on their master's death.[19]

The law of 1 February 1606 on fugitive peasants was rather more complex. It ordered that peasants who had fled from their masters in the year preceding or in the years following the famine years should be returned to them. This in effect restated the provision in a decree of 24 November 1597 for the return of fugitive peasants within a five-year period of their departure. In addition, the law of 1606 stated that peasants who had fled during the famine years, but not out of dire necessity, were also to be returned to their former masters. Peasants who had absconded during the famine out of need, however, because their masters were unable to feed them, were not to be returned, but were to remain as slaves or serfs of their new masters.[20]

Soviet historians' discussion of the significance of these two pieces of legislation formed part of their broader debates about the nature of the movement in support of the first pretender and about the chronological parameters of the 'first peasant war'. In a popularising work on Russian history, written immediately after the revolution, M. N. Pokrovskii had presented the First False Dimitry as a cossack tsar who headed a popular rising against feudal oppression. Dimitry's decrees of 7 January and 1 February 1606, in Pokrovskii's not unreasonable assessment, made concessions to the bondslaves and peasants respectively.[21] From the mid-1930s, however, the official Soviet campaign against Pokrovskii, inspired by Stalin, criticised his depiction of the First False Dimitry as the leader of a peasant rising, and presented the pretender instead as the puppet of Polish interventionists. In an article published in 1938, I. I. Smirnov put forward the extraordinary argument that the decrees of the First False Dimitry reinforced restrictions on bondslaves and peasants, rather than relaxing them, as Pokrovskii had asserted. The law of 7 January 1606, as Smirnov speciously pointed out, did not prevent slaves from being assigned to more than one master in separate documents; and although peasants who had been forced to flee during the famine were not to be returned to their former masters, the law of 1 February did not free them but confirmed their enserfment to their new masters.[22]

---

[19] Hellie, *Slavery in Russia*, pp. 76–7.
[20] *Zakonodatel'nye akty*, no. 55, pp. 73–4; cf. no. 48, pp. 66–7.
[21] Pokrovskii, *Izbrannye proizvedeniya*, vol. 3, pp. 60–4; cf. vol. 1, pp. 356–63, where he put more emphasis on the effect of this legislation on various categories of landowners.
[22] Smirnov, 'K kharakteristike', pp. 186–207.

In the debate about the 'first peasant war' which he initiated after Stalin's death, A. A. Zimin, while agreeing with Smirnov that the general effect of Dimitry's legislation was to enforce serfdom, nevertheless argued that the decrees made some concessions to the peasants and bondslaves. These concessions endowed Dimitry with the aura of a 'good tsar' and contributed to the subsequent formation of his positive popular image.[23] The most recent contribution to this debate has come from R. G. Skrynnikov. Skrynnikov regards the decree of 7 January 1606 on bondslaves as a concession to the latter, at the expense of the interests of the feudal lords. The main beneficiaries of the law of 1 February 1606, however, in Skrynnikov's interpretation, were the landowners of the south, who were not required to return peasants who had fled to their estates during the famine years (the direction of peasant flight in the famine years had been predominantly southward). These decrees therefore benefited two social groups to whom Dimitry was particularly endebted for his success: the servicemen of the southern frontier, and the military bondslaves. Skrynnikov, like Smirnov, argued that the peasants did not gain from Dimitry's legislation, since those who had fled in the famine years remained enserfed to their new masters. Thus in relation to the peasants Dimitry was pursuing an 'even more conservative course' than Boris Godunov, who had partially restored their right of departure on St George's Day in 1601 and 1602.[24] It is however difficult to agree with Skrynnikov that Dimitry's legislation brought no gains to the peasants. Although those who had been forced to flee south during the famine were not to be freed, it seems reasonable to assume that they would have preferred to stay with the new masters who had taken them in and fed them, rather than be returned to the old ones who had turned them out in time of dearth.[25] And while Skrynnikov may be correct to note that Dimitry, unlike Boris, did nothing to restore the peasants' freedom to move on St George's Day, it could be maintained that the famine years had been exceptional, and that Dimitry was doing nothing more than restoring the *status quo ante*.

Dimitry planned to codify the laws of Russia, and on the basis of an analysis of the materials that the tsar's officials had collected for this purpose, V. I. Koretskii concluded that he intended to grant the peasants greater freedom than they had enjoyed at the time of Tsar Ivan's codification of 1550. According to Koretskii, Dimitry's legislation of February 1606 marked only the first stage of his policy towards the peasants. By the spring of 1606,

---

[23] Zimin, 'Nekotorye voprosy', pp. 99–100. Smirnov reasserted his previous views, but Zimin found some support for his interpretation in I. M. Sklyar's contribution to the debate: Smirnov, 'O nekotorykh voprosakh', pp. 117–20; Sklyar, 'O nachal'nom etape', pp. 100–1.

[24] Skrynnikov, *Smuta v Rossii*, pp. 15–18.

[25] In his authoritative study of enserfment, the American historian Richard Hellie interprets this provision as a concession to the peasantry: Hellie, *Enserfment and Military Change*, p. 107.

Koretskii contended, popular disillusionment with the pretender threatened to lead to a new outburst of Peasant War. This led Dimitry to reassess his social policies, and to consider far-reaching concessions to the peasantry. The pretender was overthrown, however, before he was able to restore the peasants' right of departure on St George's Day in the autumn of 1606.[26] R. G. Skrynnikov has dismissed Koretskii's claims about Dimitry's plans to free the peasants in his new Law Code, claiming that it is impossible to draw such a radical conclusion from an incomplete assemblage of materials.[27] But Skrynnikov agrees with Koretskii that by the spring of 1606 Dimitry was facing the prospect of discontent among the very social groups who had initially supported him. One symptom of this growing popular unrest, in the view of both historians, was the appearance on the Volga of a cossack army led by a new pretender, 'Tsarevich Peter'.[28]

Tsarevich Peter

According to Jacques Margeret, who was in Moscow at the time as captain of the tsar's palace guard:

At the end of April the Emperor Dmitrii received news that between Kazan and Astrakhan about four thousand Cossacks had assembled. . . . They were said to have with them a young prince named Tsar Petr who was the true son (as they had it bruited about) of the Emperor Fedor Ivanovich and of the sister of Boris Fedorovich, who reigned after the said Fedor.[29]

There was of course no historical Tsarevich Peter: Tsar Fedor had only a daughter, Tsarevna Feodosiya, who was born in 1592 and died two years later. The new pretender's supporters apparently alleged that Irina's real child had been a son, for whom the infant Feodosiya had been substituted. According to Margeret's account, Peter 'was supposedly born around the year 1588 and a girl was supposedly put in his place secretly, who died at the age of three'.[30] There is no evidence that such a rumour about Feodosiya – which Chistov characterised as 'yet another anti-Godunov legend'[31] – existed before 1606. We do know, however, that the dynastic problems created by Fedor's childlessness and Boris's presumed ambition to succeed his brother-in-law had given rise to a number of rumours of this kind. In 1588, for example,

---

[26] Koretskii, *Formirovanie krepostnogo prava*, pp. 243–9. Richard Hellie accepts Koretskii's arguments on this point: Hellie, *Enserfment and Military Change*, pp. 107–8.
[27] Skrynnikov, *Smuta v Rossii*, pp. 15–16.
[28] Koretskii, *Formirovanie krepostnogo prava*, p. 253; Skrynnikov, *Smuta v Rossii*, p. 28.
[29] Margeret, *The Russian Empire*, pp. 70–1.
[30] *Ibid.*, p. 71.
[31] Chistov, *Russkie narodnye*, p. 49.

it had been reported by Polish agents that Boris had tried to substitute a baby boy for a daughter supposedly born to Irina.[32] The appearance of the First False Dimitry in Russia would have revived gossip about the old dynasty; and Dimitry's own account of his escape from death at the hands of Boris's agents might have given currency to tales about substituted royal children. The story of an infant tsarevich replaced at birth by a baby girl was an ingenious variation on the False Dimitry's explanation of his escape from Uglich.

For a long time no-one in Moscow seemed to know who the false Peter was. Various rumours circulated about his identity. Niemojewski relates that soon after Vasilii Shuiskii came to the throne in May 1606 the new tsar's supporters claimed that 'Petrashka' was

the son of one of the boyars of the duma, Prince Vorotynskii, born out of wedlock to a disssolute woman from Pskov, whom he sent back to Pskov with the child when he subsequently married. The boy, when he grew up, went to join the Don cossacks, and remained constantly in their ranks, but now, in the present troubles, he has called himself the son of Grand Prince Fedor Ivanovich.[33]

In April 1607, however, Shuiskii's envoy to the Crimean khan was instructed to describe 'Tsarevich Peter' as Ileika, a Terek cossack, 'the slave of the *syn boyarskii* Grigorii Elagin, and his mother and his wife and sisters are from the black [i.e. tax-paying] ploughing folk and they are still living'.[34] Finally, after his surrender in October 1607 Tsarevich Peter himself provided Shuiskii with his detailed biography.

According to his own testimony, the pretender was a young man called Il'ya Korovin. He had been born in the town of Murom – hence his nickname, Il'ya of Murom (Ileika Muromets): by an ironical coincidence, the name of the most famous warrior hero of the Kievan cycle of *byliny* (epic songs). His mother, Ul'yanka, was the wife of a tradesman, Tikhon Yur'ev, but Il'ya was her illegitimate son by one Ivan Korovin. After Ivan's death Ul'yanka had entered a convent. When she too died, the orphan Ileika was taken to Nizhnii Novgorod, on the Volga, by a trader from that town named Taras Grozil'nikov. Il'ya lived with Taras in Nizhnii for three years, selling apples and pottery in his market-stall.[35] He then hired himself out as a ship's cook to a merchant called Koz'ma Ognev, and went with him down the Volga to Astrakhan', where he spent the winter, trading in leather and shoes in the Tatar

---

[32] Skrynnikov, *Rossiya nakanune*, p. 56.

[33] Nemoevskii, 'Zapiski', p. 120.

[34] Gnevushev, ed., 'Akty', no. 102, p. 244.

[35] *VIB*, p. 223. Some sources describe the pretender as a potter (*gonchar*), or attribute to him a surname or nickname associated with Russian words for potter (Goncharovskii, Gorchakov): Popov, ed., *Izbornik*, pp. 195, 196; *RIB*, vol. 13, p. 97.

bazaar. In the spring he took to the river once more, and voyaged upstream to Kazan' and to Vyatka, before returning to Astrakhan'. There he spent another winter, living with a *strelets* called Khariton, and again working in the bazaar. The following spring he made further trips upriver, first to Nizhnii Novgorod, then to Tsaritsyn.[36]

Subsequently there was a change in Il'ya's career. From being a 'cossack' in the sense of a peripatetic ship's hand and market-stall trader on the Volga and its tributaries, he became a military-service cossack.[37] He was recruited in Astrakhan' by the *voevoda* Stepan Kozmin to go to the River Terek, and subsequently went to Tarki in the North Caucasus on Tsar Boris's disastrous campaign in the summer of 1604. On his return from the campaign Il'ya spent the winter in the town of Terek, on the Caspian Sea, where, being presumably destitute, he sold himself into slavery to Grigorii Elagin.[38]

In the summer of 1605 Il'ya returned to Astrakhan', having joined up with some Don and Volga cossacks. His account of his subsequent activities is very laconic. He left his companions, he said, in order to spend four weeks in Astrakhan', then rejoined the cossacks and sailed upriver with them. At Ploskii island they met the newly appointed governor of Astrakhan', Prince Ivan Khvorostinin, and returned with him to Astrakhan'.[39] R. G. Skrynnikov suggests that Il'ya's account of his activities at this time is heavily self-censored.[40] Astrakhan' had been under siege by cossack forces supporting Dimitry since the winter, and surrendered only in May 1605. It is likely that Il'ya took part in the siege of Astrakhan', and entered the city after its capitulation.[41] Once Tsar Dimitry's new governor was installed in Astrakhan', Il'ya entered his service, and in the autumn of 1605 he was sent to the Terek in a party of cossacks.[42]

While wintering on the Terek, the cossacks began to discuss their plans for the spring. According to Il'ya's testimony, 'the cossacks as an entire band began to think about going to the River Kura, to the [Caspian] Sea, to raid the Turkish people on their ships; and if it turned out that there was no booty to be had there, they would go and serve the Persian Shah Abbas'.[43]

---

[36] *VIB*, pp. 223–4.

[37] As I. I. Smirnov notes, Il'ya's recruitment as a service cossack may have been facilitated by contacts made through his former landlord, the Astrakhan' *strelets* Khariton: Smirnov, *Vosstanie Bolotnikova*, p. 225.

[38] *VIB*, p. 224. According to Avraamii Palitsyn, Tsarevich Peter was 'the slave of Grigorii Elagin, a musketeer captain from Sviyazhsk': Palitsyn, *Skazanie*, p. 116. The *New Chronicle* describes him as Ilyushka, the slave of Vasilii Elagin: *PSRL*, vol. 14, p. 71, para. 128.

[39] *VIB*, pp. 224–5.

[40] Skrynnikov, *Rossiya v nachale XVII v.*, p. 221.

[41] For a detailed and well documented account of events in Astrakhan' in 1605, see Smirnov, *Vosstanie Bolotnikova*, pp. 217–22.

[42] *VIB*, p. 225.

[43] *Ibid.*, p. 225.

Some of the band, however, still had their sights set on Russia rather than on Turkey or Persia. They apparently felt aggrieved that they had not been adequately remunerated for their service to the new tsar: 'And these words were heard among the cossacks on the Terek: "His Majesty wanted to reward us, but the boyars are evil; the boyars have intercepted our reward and will not give us it."'[44] A group of about 300 cossacks, headed by the *ataman* Fedor Bodyrin, began to formulate their own plans separately from the rest of the band. They decided 'to go to the Volga, to raid the merchant ships'. And they also proposed to call one of their number the son of Tsar Fedor Ivanovich. The cossacks selected two youths as possible candidates for the role of Tsarevich Peter: Ileika and a cossack called Mitka, the son of a *strelets* from Astrakhan'.[45] Mitka disqualified himself by saying that he had never been to Moscow, whereas Il'ya had once spent some time in the capital.[46]

Once Bodyrin's cossacks had decided on their plan, they went down the River Terek to the Caspian Sea. The *voevoda* of Terek, Peter Golovin, heard of their escapade and sent the cossack chief Ivan Khomyak to persuade Il'ya to come into the fortress. The cossacks, however, realising that Golovin regarded the pretence as a 'great affair', i.e. a political crime against the state, refused to hand him over, and they set up their base on an island in the Caspian Sea near the mouth of the Terek. There they were joined by cossacks from all the settlements (*yurty*), and having gathered their forces in defiance of the *voevoda*, they set off for Astrakhan'. They were not allowed to enter the city 'for fear of looting', and continued up the Volga towards Moscow, 'to the court of Grishka Rostriga'. When they reached Samara, they were met by a messenger from 'the Rostriga', telling them to come to the capital with all haste. The cossacks, however, got no further than the Vyazovye heights, 10 versts north of Sviyazhsk, when they were met by a messenger from Moscow who told them that Grishka had been killed in Moscow 'by the entire community' (*mirom vsem*), and they retreated back down the Volga to the River Kamyshenka.[47]

---

[44] *Ibid.*, p. 225.

[45] The evidence which Il'ya's confession provides about his own humble background and that of Mitka, together with some information he supplies about his 'comrades' among the cossack participants in the pretence, led I. I. Smirnov to conclude that the 300 men who devised the pretence comprised the poorer cossacks, recruited primarily from bondslaves and the urban lower orders: Smirnov, *Vosstanie Bolotnikova*, pp. 366–7.

[46] There seems to be no grounds for Skrynnikov's assertion – apparently based on Il'ya's testimony that he had lived in Moscow 'from Christmas to St Peter's Day' – that he had spent the period 25 December 1604 to 29 June 1605 in the capital: Skrynnikov, *Rossiya v nachale XVII v.*, p. 222. Il'ya has already said that he spent the winter of 1604/5 in the town of Terek as a slave of Grigorii Elagin; here he says that he went to Moscow 'from Nizhnii', i.e. presumably when he had lived in Nizhnii Novgorod in his youth with the trader Taras Grozil'-nikov: *VIB*, pp. 223–5.

[47] *VIB*, p. 226.

Il'ya's testimony is of exceptional interest, but it poses major problems of interpretation. We must first of all enquire how trustworthy it is: it was after all a confession, obtained presumably under torture. There is of course no doubt that Il'ya did call himself 'Tsarevich Peter': we may question, however, how far this pretence was imposed upon him by his fellow cossacks, as he himself asserts. Il'ya presumably hoped that Shuiskii would regard it as less culpable of him to have been 'elected' tsarevich by his band of cossacks than to have proposed himself for the role. In the absence of evidence to the contrary, however, we must take the pretender's word for it. Indeed Margeret partly confirms Il'ya's account when he tells us that the cossacks 'had it bruited about' that Peter was with them.[48]

Thus there can be little doubt that Tsarevich Peter's immediate entourage, at least, knew perfectly well that he was an impostor. Il'ya's pretence may have been inspired by Boris Godunov's allegations that Tsarevich Dimitry was Grisha Otrep'ev.[49] Patriarch Iov's proclamation of January 1605 had described Grisha as a labourer (*stradnik*) and rogue (*vor*) as well as an unfrocked monk, and had alleged that he had gone marauding (*vorovati*) with the Zaporozhian cossacks before declaring himself to be Tsarevich Dimitry.[50] After Grisha's extraordinary success in coming to the throne, other cossack bands may well have wondered whether one of their number too might turn out to be a long-lost descendant of Ivan the Terrible. This does not necessarily mean that the Terek cossacks believed that Dimitry was an impostor. But it does indicate that the idea of falsely calling oneself a scion of the old dynasty had acquired broad currency. The cossacks, in particular, were able and willing to exploit the possibilities for mischief that it created. The fact that the act of setting up a false tsarevich was viewed as sacrilegious by the Orthodox Church was unlikely to trouble such men, whose banditry already placed them largely outside the bounds of conventional morality and religion.

Il'ya's confession made it clear that piracy on the Volga was a major aim of the cossacks' expedition, but he was understandably silent about the details of their activities. Margeret, however, noted that Tsarevich Peter's cossacks 'caused harm along the Volga',[51] and Isaac Massa asserted that they 'wrought

---

[48] Russian sources also suggest that Peter's pretence was a collective cossack action. The Russian envoys to Poland informed their hosts in December 1606 that the cossacks had elected a rogue from amongst themselves as Tsarevich Peter: *SIRIO*, vol. 137, p. 352. The *New Chronicler* says that the cossacks, inspired by the devil, called Ilyushka 'Tsarevich Peter': *PSRL*, vol. 14, p. 71, para. 128. The 'Karamzin Chronograph' states that the cossacks on the Terek called a cobbler's son the son of Tsar Fedor Ivanovich: Popov, ed., *Izbornik*, pp. 330, 331–2.

[49] On the imitative aspect of Ileika's pretence see Solov'ev, 'Zametki o samozvantsakh', p. 270; Kostomarov, *Smutnoe vremya*, p. 289; Ilovaiskii, *Smutnoe vremya*, p. 87; Platonov, *Ocherki*, p. 251.

[50] *AAE*, vol. 2, no. 28, pp. 78–9.

[51] Margeret, *The Russian Empire*, p. 71.

great depredations, plundering loaded boats which came from Astrakhan and causing millions in losses'.[52] In December 1606 the Russian envoys in Craców were to tell the Poles that during the reign of the First False Dimitry the Volga and Terek cossacks had committed major acts of piracy against merchant shipping on the Volga, taking goods worth hundreds of thousands of zlotys and roubles.[53] Thus at one level the pretence may be seen as a device to justify piracy: no doubt the merchants were attacked as 'traitors' and their property subjected to punitive confiscation when they refused to recognise Peter as a tsarevich. The legitimising function of pretence was well understood by contemporaries such as Margeret, who commented that, 'This Tsar Petr could have been aged from sixteen to seventeen years if their story had been true, but it was well known that this was only a pretext to pillage the land.'[54]

The cossacks' attitude towards Dimitry is difficult to establish. It seems probable that many of them had, like Ileika himself, fought for Dimitry in 1605, but had subsequently become disillusioned. Margeret stated that Peter's cossacks 'were discontented with Dmitrii, reckoning that they had not been recompensed by him as they had hoped to be';[55] but Il'ya himself, as we have seen, attributed to his comrades the view that the tsar had wanted to reward them, but the wicked boyars had appropriated their reward. This anti-boyar sentiment may have been genuine, but it also provided a convenient legitimation for the cossacks' defiance of Dimitry's *voevody* in Terek and Astrakhan'.

It appears from Il'ya's confession that the cossacks planned to go to Moscow to confront the tsar. Their precise aims, however, are unclear. Il'ya's testimony implies that they simply wanted to petition Dimitry about their 'reward'. But another source suggests that Tsarevich Peter aimed to replace Dimitry on the throne. A unique version of the *New Chronicle* states that Peter wrote to Dimitry, claiming that he was the true heir and threatening to overthrow him.[56] But most historians are sceptical about this piece of testimony. I. I. Smirnov suggested that it reflects a later gloss on the original text of the chronicle by an editor who knew that, according to the principle of primogeniture, Tsar Fedor's son would have had a stronger claim to the

---

[52] Massa, *A Short History*, p. 148.
[53] *SIRIO*, vol. 137, pp. 351–2. The envoys stated that it was only after Shuiskii came to the throne and took firm measures against the cossacks that they had decided to set up a pretender (p. 352) – disingenuously, they claimed not to have heard of Peter before their departure from Russia (p. 351).
[54] Margeret, *The Russian Empire*, p. 71. Since Feodosiya was born in 1592, any real Tsarevich Peter would have been only fourteen in 1606.
[55] *Ibid.*, p. 71.
[56] *Novyi letopisets . . . po spisku knyazya Obolenskogo*, p. 78.

throne than his younger half-brother.[57] But in the eyes of the cossacks themselves, it seems, the older principle of collateral succession held sway, and the uncle had seniority over the nephew. The balance of the evidence suggests that Peter regarded himself not as a rival to Dimitry, but rather as a supplicant towards him, and an advocate of the cossacks' cause. Thus Il'ya's adoption of the role of Tsarevich Peter may be viewed as a device to give status to the cossacks' demands. It is significant that when they learned of Dimitry's murder, the cossacks retreated back down the Volga, instead of proceeding towards Moscow. If their aim had really been to put Peter on the throne in Dimitry's place, they would surely have continued to head for the capital.

What was Dimitry's attitude towards the new pretender? Both Russian and foreign sources confirm Il'ya's assertion that Dimitry invited the cossacks to the capital. The *New Chronicle* states that after Peter had written to Dimitry, the latter 'ordered him to come to Moscow'.[58] Margeret tells us that when Dimitry heard about Peter, he wrote him a letter, 'by which he sent for him, saying that if he were the true son of his brother Fedor he would be welcome. All provisions . . . for his journey would be provided by the emperor. However, Dmitrii also wrote, if he were not the true son of Fedor, he should withdraw from the emperor's lands.'[59] Niemojewski states that Dimitry, having investigated the cossacks' claims, acknowledged Peter as his nephew, and invited him to come to Moscow, promising him an appanage principality (*państwo*, translated as *udel'noe knyazhestvo*). But the Pole adds that this may have been only a ruse to lure Peter to Moscow so that Dimitry could get his hands on him and prevent him from gaining support – including assistance from the Tatars – and causing him problems. Alternatively, Niemojewski adds, Dimitry may have intended to treat his supposed nephew well.[60]

V. I. Koretskii believed that Dimitry's main aim in inviting Peter to Moscow was to try to 'neutralise' his campaign. But Koretskii suggested that Dimitry may also have had an ulterior motive: to use Peter's cossacks against the boyars.[61] Isaac Massa states that after his death Dimitry was accused by the boyars of having 'provoked the appearance of an impostor who was to come and lend him assistance in case of danger'.[62] In his discussion of this evidence, Koretskii rejected any implication that Dimitry himself might have set up Peter's pretence, but he accepted the possibility that Dimitry invited Peter to Moscow so that the cossack pretender could render him aid.[63] By the spring of 1606, Koretskii argued, Dimitry found himself 'between the

---

[57] Smirnov, *Vosstanie Bolotnikova*, pp. 369–70.
[58] *PSRL*, vol. 14, p. 71, para. 128.
[59] Margeret, *The Russian Empire*, p. 71.
[60] Nemoevskii, 'Zapiski', pp. 119–20.
[61] Koretskii, *Formirovanie krepostnogo prava*, p. 256.
[62] Massa, *A Short History*, p. 148.
[63] Koretskii, *Formirovanie krepostnogo prava*, pp. 256–7.

hammer and the anvil': 'On the one hand, there was a growth of popular discontent, which for the time being was directed against the boyars, but which could at any moment break on his own head; on the other hand, the boyars were spinning the web of a new conspiracy.'[64] In this situation, Dimitry's invitation to Peter and his cossacks was a desperate attempt to save himself.[65] It seems unlikely, however, that Dimitry would have risked forming an alliance with such a blatant impostor as Tsarevich Peter. Peter's most likely fate, if he had come to Moscow, would have been that of the later cossack 'tsareviches' who were hanged by the Second False Dimitry.

Death and denunciation

Within a few months of his coronation, many of the boyars had become disillusioned with their new tsar. His planned wedding to Marina Mniszech, it seems, was a particular sticking point, since it infringed the Russian tradition of royal marriage alliances with leading boyar families. After the return of the Shuiskiis to Moscow at the end of 1605, secret plots against Dimitry gathered strength. Some Russian boyars who opposed the pretender established contacts with the Polish king. Hoping to gain Sigismund's benevolent neutrality, if not his active support for their conspiracy, they offered the Russian throne to his son Władysław.[66] Foreign observers report various attempts to assassinate Dimitry at the beginning of 1606, for which they blame Prince Vasilii Shuiskii.[67] After the executions of the *strel'tsy* in March 1606, opposition to the new tsar appeared to have been suppressed. The pretender's opponents, however, were merely biding their time.

On 2 May 1606 Marina Mniszech arrived in Moscow and made a grand entry into the capital. The bridal party numbered 2,000 people, and Marina's attendants included Polish cavalrymen and haiduks.[68] This open display of military strength alarmed the Russians, who enquired of foreign residents whether it was normal practice abroad for wedding guests to carry weapons and wear armour.[69] The insolent behaviour of Mniszech's men antagonised the Muscovites and played into the hands of Dimitry's enemies.

Dimitry's marriage to Marina was celebrated on 8 May. The wedding was preceded by Marina's coronation, an unprecedented ceremony in Russia for a queen-consort. Pierling suggests that this innovation was introduced in an

---

[64] *Ibid.*, p. 257.
[65] *Ibid.*, p. 257. For a similar interpretation, see Skrynnikov, *Smuta v Rossii*, pp. 30, 153; for an expression of scepticism, see Dunning's editorial note to Margeret, *The Russian Empire*, n. 259, pp. 168–9.
[66] Zholkevskii, *Zapiski*, pp. 9–10.
[67] Massa, *A Short History*, p. 121; Margeret, *The Russian Empire*, p. 70.
[68] Massa, *A Short History*, pp. 127–8; Margeret, *The Russian Empire*, p. 72.
[69] Bussov, *Moskovskaya khronika*, p. 115.

attempt to circumvent the problem of Marina's Catholicism. Marina had refused to convert to Orthodoxy, and the Pope was unwilling to grant her a dispensation to perform Orthodox rituals. The more extreme Russian churchmen insisted on a second baptism as a token of her renunciation of Catholicism. A compromise proposal, however, which was accepted by Patriarch Ignatii, required Marina only to undergo anointing with holy oil as a sign of her acceptance of Orthodoxy. Anointing, of course, was also part of the coronation service, and Pierling suggests that its great advantage was that 'the same ceremony could serve in the eyes of some as a royal consecration, and in the eyes of others as a renunciation of Catholicism'. The implementation of this 'Machiavellian plan' did not however save Dimitry from the charge of apostasy, after his overthrow, on the grounds that he had married an unbaptised Catholic and allowed her to be crowned.[70] To make matters worse, the marriage ceremony took place, contrary to Orthodox custom, on a Thursday, the eve of a fast-day which was also the feast of St Nicholas. The wedding celebrations spilled over to the Friday, scandalising the pious Russians. Folksongs about Grisha Otrep'ev, transcribed more than two centuries later, recalled that he chose a heretical Lithuanian as his wife and married her on St Nicholas' Day.[71]

The festivities in the capital involved much public drunkenness and led to street fights between Russians and Poles. In the week following the tsar's marriage, the situation became increasingly tense. The boyar conspirators decided to take advantage of the heightened anti-Polish feeling in Moscow in order to rid themselves of Dimitry. In the early morning of Saturday 17 May they raised the cry that the Poles were attacking the tsar. The Muscovites who rushed to the Kremlin to protect Dimitry fell upon the foreign mercenaries in whom the pretender had placed his hopes of safety. Meanwhile, the boyars themselves sought to assassinate the tsar in his inner apartments. Dimitry managed to escape the first attempt to kill him, but he was eventually surrounded by the conspirators and their agents.

At this stage the accusation was made that the tsar was an impostor and heretic. Dimitry was then subjected to ribald abuse before the *coup de grâce* was administered. According to Bussow, the Russians mocked the pretender as the Jews had mocked Christ (i.e. they treated him as a false Messiah). They stripped him of his royal attire and dressed him in the grubby tunic of a pie-seller. One shouted ironically, 'Behold the tsar of all the Russias!', while another exclaimed, 'I've got a tsar like that in my stable at home!' Others abused him as a 'Polish buffoon (*skomorokh*)'. A merchant fired at

---

[70] Pierling, *La Russie et le Saint-Siège*, vol. 3, p. 301; *SGGiD*, vol. 2, no. 146, pp. 306–7; no. 147, p. 309; *AAE*, vol. 2, no. 48, p. 107. See also Perrie, 'Female Rule', pp. 5–6.
[71] *Istoricheskie pesni XVII veka*, nos. 4–10, pp. 27–35.

Dimitry and wounded him, whereupon the rest set up a cry of 'Crucify him!' and the princes and boyars slashed and stabbed him to death.[72]

Even in death, indignities continued to be heaped upon Dimitry. His naked body, and that of Basmanov, who had been killed trying to protect his master, were dragged out of the Kremlin and publicly displayed in the market-place. During the looting of the tsar's apartments the mob had found some theatrical masks which Dimitry had been preparing for a masquerade which was to form part of the entertainments for the wedding celebrations.[73] A Polish source states that the conspirators told the crowd that they had found one of these masks hanging over Dimitry's bed, where the icons should have been; and that they had found the icons under the bed.[74] According to Massa, the Russians were naive enough to believe that the masks were the pretender's gods.[75] This is confirmed by Peyerle, who relates that a mask was laid on Dimitry's belly, whereupon the Muscovites shouted, 'Behold thy God!'[76] In Bussow's account, a boyar placed the mask over the pretender's genitals and stuck the chanter of a bagpipe in his mouth. 'You've made us whistle for you for long enough', he said, '. . . now you can whistle for us for a bit.'[77] Prince Ivan Golitsyn obtained the boyars' permission to bury his kinsman Basmanov the next day, but Dimitry's body lay in the square for three days and nights, and was subjected to terrible abuse by the Russians.[78]

B. A. Uspenskii has provided an illuminating interpretation of the symbolism of this vilification of Dimitry's body. By adorning the corpse with a mask and bagpipe – the accoutrements of a minstrel (*skomorokh*) – his murderers were depicting Dimitry as a sorcerer, for minstrelsy and sorcery were closely identified with one another in old Russian culture.[79] The accusation that the tsar kept the icons under his bed was particularly indicative of sorcery, since icons and crosses were laid on the ground or trampled underfoot during acts of black magic.[80] The placing of the mask on Dimitry's groin, rather than on his face, was an 'exchange between top and bottom', a kind of inversion typical of the blasphemous anti-behaviour of mummers who depicted unclean spirits at Yuletide and other festivals.[81]

---

[72] Bussov, *Moskovskaya khronika*, p. 121. See also Massa, *A Short History*, pp. 137–8.
[73] Massa, *A Short History*, p. 138.
[74] 'Dnevnik Mariny Mnishek', p. 238. For the motif of icons under the pretender's bed, see also *Istoricheskie pesni XVII veka*, no. 4, pp. 27–9.
[75] Massa, *A Short History*, p. 138.
[76] Paerle, 'Zapiski', p. 196. See also Nemoevskii, 'Zapiski', pp. 80, 98.
[77] Bussov, *Moskovskaya khronika*, p. 128. Cf. also Howe, ed., *The False Dmitri*, p. 47.
[78] Bussov, *Moskovskaya khronika*, p. 128.
[79] Uspenskii, 'Tsar' i samozvanets', pp. 214–15, 216.
[80] *Ibid.*, pp. 214–15.
[81] *Ibid.*, p. 216.

Further evidence that Dimitry was regarded as a sorcerer is provided by descriptions of the disposal of his body.[82] The fullest account is supplied by Bussow, who relates how on the third night after Dimitry's murder the watchmen on the market square brought strange reports to the boyars, of flames leaping from the ground on either side of the table on which the pretender's corpse was displayed. The watchmen were particularly terrified to observe that the flames disappeared when they approached the body, but reappeared as soon as they moved further away. The boyars came to see for themselves. The same eerie phenomenon occurred, and they hastily ordered the body to be taken to the poor-house next day and discarded. Early in the morning the corpse was removed, but it was accompanied on its journey through the city by a terrible whirlwind which left a path of destruction in its wake. At the poor-house Dimitry's body was flung into an open pit where the bodies of paupers and suicides lay; but the next morning it was found lying outside the locked gates of the building. Two doves were perched on Dimitry's corpse. Whenever anyone approached the body, they flew away; but they returned as soon as it was left alone. Then the boyars ordered that the body be thrown again into the pit, and this time covered with earth. A few days later, however, on 27 May, the pretender's remains were found in another cemetery, some distance from the poor-house.[83] Uspenskii notes that it was widely believed in this period that the earth would not accept the body of a sorcerer,[84] and this is confirmed by Bussow's account of the comments made by contemporary Muscovites. Some said that Dimitry could not have been an ordinary mortal, if his body would not stay in the earth. Others whispered that he must have been the devil, who was directing his machinations against mankind. And yet others said that he was a black magician who had learned his arts from the Laplanders, who were well known for being able to raise themselves from the dead.[85]

Peyerle describes rumours that not only flames but also 'cheerful music' emanated from Dimitry's grave.[86] Russian sources enable us to appreciate the significance of this, as they describe 'devils playing like *skomorokhi* over the False Dimitry's body',[87] with dancing and music of drums and pipes, as Satan rejoiced at his coming.[88] Isaac Massa describes rather different prodigies: on

---

[82] *Ibid.*

[83] Bussov, *Moskovskaya khronika*, pp. 128–9.

[84] Uspenskii, 'Tsar' i samozvanets', p. 216.

[85] Bussov, *Moskovskaya khronika*, p. 129. Isaac Massa states that Russians considered Dimitry to be 'Satan himself', or 'a sorcerer in communication with the Devil' (Massa, *A Short History*, pp. 144, 147).

[86] Paerle, 'Zapiski', p. 197. See also Nemoevskii, 'Zapiski', pp. 103–4.

[87] Uspenskii, 'Tsar' i samozvanets', p. 216.

[88] *RIB*, vol. 13, cols. 59, 831. See also 'Latukhinskaya Stepennaya Kniga', cited by Karamzin, *Istoriya*, vol. 3, primechaniya k XI tomu, col. 82, no. 574.

the day on which Dimitry's body was buried, all plants and trees within a 20 mile radius of Moscow were scorched as if by fire; and on the day Shuiskii was elected tsar, an unseasonal frost destroyed all the crops.[89] Again, the Russian sources help us to understand this in the context of ideas about the earth's refusal to accept the body of a sorcerer:[90]

the earth disdained to carry upon it the accursed and vile corpse, and the air was poisoned and would not send rain from the heavens; where the accursed corpse lay, the earth brought forth no fruit and the sun would not shine because of the foul stench, and the stench covered all the fruits and they dried up; and the Lord took away from the earth both wheat and grapes until the corpse had disappeared.[91]

Eventually it was decided to burn Dimitry's body and scatter his ashes to the wind, and this was duly done in the village of Kotly on the outskirts of the capital.[92] Niemojewski relates that the wooden gates of the city, through which Dimitry's remains were taken to be burned, collapsed a few hours afterwards, and that this was regarded by many as a portent (*prodigium*).[93] Captain Gilbert, a Scottish member of Dimitry's bodyguard, reports that, 'Demetrius his body was plucked out of the graue and burnt, the ashes throwne into the aire, the seeds, as the sequele seemed to shew, of many Demetris after.'[94] According to Peyerle, Dimitry's ashes were loaded into an enormous cannon and fired out of the gate through which he had entered Moscow, 'so that not even his dust remained'.[95]

Immediately after their coup against Dimitry, the boyars met to decide on the succession. Two days later it was announced that Prince Vasilii Ivanovich Shuiskii had been elected tsar. Shuiskii lost no time in sending out proclamations to all the provinces, denouncing Dimitry as a pretender, justifying his death, and informing his subjects of his own accession to the throne. Dimitry was depicted in the most lurid colours. The late tsar was identified as the unfrocked monk (*rostriga*) Grishka Otrep'ev, and he was also described as a scoundrel (*vor*), an apostate, a heretic, a black magician and an agent of Satan. Shuiskii and the boyars made more specific charges against the pretender, however, and they were able to back them up with evidence. They had found papers in his apartments relating to his dealings with the Poles

[89] Massa, *A Short History*, pp. 144–6. Margeret also refers to a severe frost: *The Russian Empire*, p. 73.
[90] Uspenskii, 'Tsar' i samozvanets', p. 216.
[91] *RIB*, vol. 13, col. 831; cited in David Budgen's translation in Uspenskij, 'Tsar and Pretender', p. 276. See also *RIB*, vol. 13, col. 59.
[92] *PSRL*, vol. 14, p. 69, para. 118; Massa, *A Short History*, p. 145; Bussov, *Moskovskaya khronika*, p. 129.
[93] Nemoevskii, 'Zapiski', p. 104.
[94] Howe, ed., *The False Dmitri*, p. 63.
[95] Paerle, 'Zapiski', p. 197.

and with the Vatican, which bore witness to Dimitry's promises of territorial concessions and religious tolerance. The boyars had interrogated Jerzy Mniszech, who had confirmed the authenticity of the marriage contract that he and the pretender had signed. Within a fortnight, translations had been made of these incriminating documents, which were circulated to the provinces.[96]

Shuiskii also accused Dimitry of plotting to massacre the boyars. Dimitry's Polish secretaries, Stanisław and Jan Buczynski, had testified that the pretender planned to invite all the Russian nobility to accompany him outside the city on 18 May for military exercises. His Polish and Lithuanian mercenaries would then have fallen upon them and killed them all. Their lands and property were to have been distributed among the Poles, as a preliminary to the introduction of Roman Catholicism into Russia.[97] These allegations appear to have been totally spurious, devised solely in order to justify Dimitry's murder by presenting it as a pre-emptive strike by the boyars, an act of self-defence. But the accusations might well have gained some credibility with the Muscovites, who had been struck by the pretender's passion for military exercises involving artillery bombardments.[98] In winter he had devised a war-game in which he and his foreign mercenaries defended a fortress made of snow that had to be stormed by the Russian commanders, both sides being armed only with snowballs.[99] The Russians were particularly intrigued by a kind of siege-engine which Dimitry had set up on the ice of the Moscow River. The machine was painted all over with flames, and the gun-embrasures took the form of demons' heads, so that the Russians called it 'the monster from hell'. This contraption seemed to the more superstitious Muscovites to confirm the allegations that Dimitry was in league with the devil, and according to Isaac Massa it was burned at Kotly along with the pretender's body.[100] In later Russian literary accounts the military purpose of the engine is completely ignored, and it is depicted solely as a model of hell which the pretender had had made as a reminder of his 'eternal dwelling-place with his father the Devil and Satan', and into which he threw Orthodox Christians who denounced him as a heretic.[101] Boris Uspenskii comments that the description of the object in these tales 'corresponds fairly closely to

---

[96] *AAE*, vol. 2, no. 44, pp. 100–1; no. 48, pp. 106–15; *SGGiD*, vol. 2, no. 144, pp. 302–4; no. 147, pp. 308–125. Massa states that these and other accusations were read aloud to the Muscovites on Red Square on 30 May: Massa, *A Short History*, pp. 146–9.

[97] *AAE*, vol. 2, no. 44, p. 100; no. 48, pp. 108–10; *SGGiD*, vol. 2, no. 140, pp. 296–8. The accusations are repeated by Massa, who appears to believe them: Massa, *A Short History*, pp. 142–3.

[98] Massa, *A Short History*, p. 117.

[99] Bussov, *Moskovskaya khronika*, p. 113.

[100] Massa, *A Short History*, pp. 117–18, 145, 147.

[101] *RIB*, vol. 13, cols. 55–6, 818–20.

the depiction of hell in the form of a fire-breathing dragon (for example, ...
in Russian icons of the Last Judgement)'.[102]

Cynical foreign contemporaries regarded the Russians' elaborate attempts
to discredit Dimitry as a heretic and magician as evidence of their grossly
superstitious outlook.[103] But it must be borne in mind that in killing the pretender the Russians were not simply ridding themselves of a clever confi-
dence-trickster. Less than a year earlier, Dimitry had been euphorically welcomed to Moscow as a Christ-like saviour, the last true scion of the old
dynasty miraculously protected by divine providence from his enemies; and
he had been properly crowned and anointed as tsar. In order to legitimise
his murder, his opponents needed to depict him in the worst possible light,
as the very antithesis of what he had previously appeared to be. Hence the
rituals embodying the belief that they were ridding themselves of an agent
of the devil.[104]

There was of course a real basis for the allegations that Dimitry was a
'heretic'. The pretender had secretly converted to Catholicism in Poland; his
marriage to Marina Mniszech and his general disregard for Orthodox traditions strengthened suspicions that he planned to introduce the Roman faith
into Russia. The American scholar Daniel Rowland has noted that Dimitry
was depicted in seventeenth-century Russian literary sources as the Anti-
Christ and instrument of Satan not only because he was an impostor, but
also because he favoured Catholicism and Catholics. His critics drew on
Byzantine images of rulers, such as Julian the Apostate, who were seen as
destroyers of Orthodox Christianity. Dimitry, like Julian, was portrayed as
an 'anti-tsar' – a 'tormentor' (*muchitel'*) who had to be overthrown rather
than obeyed.[105]

Like the allegation of Dimitry's heresy, the accusation that he was a sorcerer reflected the fact that he was regarded as an impostor. Pretence was
perceived as a form of 'anti-behaviour', and as such was associated with
black magic.[106] But there may have been real grounds for this accusation too.
As we have seen, Boris Godunov had alleged that Grisha Otrep'ev dabbled
in magic while he was a still a monk in Moscow, and some sources suggest
that the pretender practised necromancy after he came to the throne. Isaac
Massa tells us that after Dimitry's death the boyars accused him

---

[102] Uspenskii, 'Tsar' i samozvanets', p. 216.
[103] Massa, *A Short History*, p. 147.
[104] The French historian Yves-Marie Bercé uses the term 'desacralisation' (*désacration*) to refer
to this process, and notes that similar rituals of humiliation to those directed against Dimitry
were used against the Pseudo-Baldwin of Flanders, the False Edward VI of 1555, and the
Venetian Don Sebastian: Bercé, *Le roi caché*, pp. 366–7.
[105] Rowland, 'Did Muscovite Literary Ideology Place Limits', pp. 136–9.
[106] Uspenskii, 'Tsar' i samozvanets', pp. 213–17.

of having been a sorcerer in communication with the Devil. His tutor, a Pole, came
to affirm that he was devoted to magic and other occult sciences, and the Muscovites
supported this opinion with various conjectures, such as the 'Monster of Hell' he had
built, and other fables of the same sort.[107]

Later, Shuiskii's envoys to Poland were to report that Dimitry's favourite
Michael Molchanov had practised magic with the tsar in the royal apartments.[108] The image of the pretender as a sorcerer proved to be an enduring
one. In Russian folklore Grisha Otrep'ev is depicted with a book of magic
spells; he abuses holy icons and crosses, and visits the bath-house to fornicate
with Marina instead of attending the Easter mass at church.[109]

In the folksong about Grisha Otrep'ev, before murdering Dimitry the
boyars appeal to Marfa Nagaya to tell them whether the tsar is really her
son. This reflects historical fact, since the dowager tsaritsa was indeed
recruited into Shuiskii's campaign of denunciation of Dimitry. There is conflicting evidence, however, as to when exactly Marfa publicly renounced her
supposed son as an impostor. According to the *New Chronicle*, during the
riot of 17 May the *strel'tsy* had insisted that Marfa be questioned about Dimitry, and they allowed him to be killed only after she had repudiated him.[110]
Peyerle states that Dimitry himself had demanded that Marfa Nagaya be
found and asked to vouch for him, but Prince Golitsyn had informed the
crowd that Marfa had long since renounced her 'son'.[111] According to other
accounts, Marfa was questioned only after the pretender's death. A Polish
source relates that when Dimitry's body was taken from the Kremlin, the
mob halted outside the convent where the tsaritsa was living. When they
summoned her to appear before them and tell them whether the dead man
was her son, Marfa had replied, somewhat cryptically: 'You should have
asked me that while he was still alive; but now that he is dead, he is not
mine.'[112]

It may well be true that Marfa hesitated before denying that Dimitry was
her son. Shuiskii's first proclamations on his accession, dated 19–20 May,
do not cite her testimony in support of his accusation that the late tsar was
a pretender.[113] On 21 May, however, Marfa herself issued a statement
denouncing Dimitry as the impostor Grishka Otrep'ev. Her son had been
killed at Uglich on the orders of Boris Godunov, she said, in her presence

[107] Massa, *A Short History*, p. 147.
[108] *SIRIO*, vol. 137, p. 344.
[109] Uspenskii, 'Tsar' i samozvanets', pp. 213–17; *Istoricheskie pesni XVII veka*, nos. 4–23,
pp. 27–44.
[110] *PSRL*, vol. 14, p. 69, para. 118.
[111] Paerle, 'Zapiski', p. 191; also 'Dnevnik Mariny Mnishek', p. 238.
[112] 'Dnevnik Mariny Mnishek', p. 238. See also Kostomarov, *Smutnoe vremya*, p. 223.
[113] *SGGiD*, vol. 2, no. 141, pp. 299–300; *AAE*, vol. 2, no. 44, pp. 100–1.

and that of her brothers. She had acknowledged Grishka as Dimitry only under duress, when the pretender had threatened to kill her and all her clan if she did not recognise him. She had however secretly informed the boyars that he was not her son; and now she and her brothers had publicly stated that Grishka was a scoundrel who had falsely called himself Tsarevich Dimitry.[114]

Shuiskii's master-stroke, however, in his campaign to discredit the dead tsar, was his decision to send a commission to Uglich to bring the remains of Tsarevich Dimitry to Moscow. It is not clear exactly when this delegation was despatched to Uglich, but it must have been within a few days of Shuiskii's election, since the commission was already reporting on its findings on 28 May. The decision appears to have been taken partly to counter the rumours of Dimitry's second escape from death that had begun to spread in Moscow (see below, pp. 109–15). The pretender in his time, it will be recalled, had thought of opening the tomb at Uglich, which he claimed to contain only the bones of the child who had been substituted for the real tsarevich; but Tsaritsa Marfa had objected. Now Shuiskii's aim was to demonstrate that the grave contained the real Dimitry Ivanovich, and thereby to prove conclusively that the tsar who had been killed on 17 May was an impostor. Marfa Nagaya had stated in her proclamation of 21 May that her son had been killed on Boris's orders. This allegation of course was consistent with the accusations which the Nagois had made against Godunov in 1591 itself. Although the Nagois' allegations had been rejected then by the official commission of inquiry – headed by none other than Prince Vasilii Shuiskii – in favour of a verdict of accidental death, it was very convenient for Shuiskii in May 1606 to accept that Dimitry had been murdered by Boris. The 'innocent lamb' could now be depicted as a saintly martyr; and, Tsar Vasilii claimed, many miracles had been reported at his tomb at Uglich.[115]

The commission which Shuiskii despatched to Uglich to bring the miracle-working relics of the tsarevich to Moscow was headed by Metropolitan Filaret of Rostov (the former Fedor Nikitich Romanov). It included Archbishop Feodosii of Astrakhan' and the boyars Prince I. M. Vorotynskii, P. N. Sheremetev, and two of the Nagois: Grigorii Fedorovich and Andrei Aleksandrovich. On 28 May they wrote to Shuiskii to report their wondrous discovery: when the coffin was opened, the entire cathedral was filled with an exquisite fragrance, and the body of the tsarevich was found to be perfectly preserved – an irrefutable sign of sainthood. His regal clothing too remained intact: his shoes were entire, although the soles of his socks had come off. They had even found a handful of fresh nuts in the coffin; the tsarevich had been eating these at the time of his death, and they had been buried with him because

---

[114] *SGGiD*, vol. 2, no. 146, pp. 306–7. See also no. 142, p. 300.
[115] *AAE*, vol. 2, no. 48, p. 110.

they had been splashed with his blood. The members of the commission added that they had collected written testimony from people who had been cured of various illnesses over the years by Dimitry's relics, and they would bring this evidence of his miracle-working with them when they brought the body to Moscow.[116] These affidavits were undoubtedly forged: there is no evidence that miracles had been reported in Uglich before May 1606. Sceptical foreign observers claimed that the unputrefied corpse was also a fabrication, Shuiskii having ordered the nine-year-old son of a priest to be killed, and his body substituted for the decomposed remains of Dimitry of Uglich.[117]

On 3 June the corpse was brought to Moscow. Tsaritsa Marfa accompanied Shuiskii to meet the solemn procession on the outskirts of the city, and publicly pronounced that this was indeed the body of her son, intact and uncorrupted. They escorted the relics to the Kremlin, where they were reburied in the church of the Archangel Michael. During the ceremony Marfa begged forgiveness for all the harm she had caused by her failure to denounce the pretender, and Shuiskii magnanimously forgave her, on his own behalf and that of the late Tsar Ivan and Tsarevich Dimitry.[118]

In his proclamation of 6 June, Shuiskii reported that Dimitry's remains had continued to work miracles even as they were being carried into Moscow: along the route they cured people of various illnesses. The miracles continued when the tsarevich was reinterred in the Archangel cathedral: thirteen people were healed on the first day after his reburial, and twelve on the second day.[119] The foreign sceptics claimed that these 'miracles' were all fakes, and that various 'worthless people' from outside Moscow had been bribed by the authorities to pretend to have been cured of their feigned blindness or paralysis. Unfortunately for Shuiskii, one of these fraudulent invalids died in the church, and soon afterwards the public were kept away from the tomb of the new saintly martyr.[120]

---

[116] *Ibid.*, pp. 110–11.
[117] Bussov, *Moskovskaya khronika*, pp. 134–5; Massa, *A Short History*, p. 159.
[118] *AAE*, vol. 2, no. 48, pp. 111–12.
[119] *Ibid.*, p. 111.
[120] Massa, *A Short History*, pp. 160–1; Bussov, *Moskovskaya khronika*, p. 135.

Part 2

Rebels in the name of Tsar Dimitry

4   Tsar Dimitry lives!

Rumours in Moscow

Stories of Dimitry's escape from death arose within days or even hours of his murder. Bussow says that the rumours circulated on the very day of the riot.[1] The Dutchman Herckman reports that when Dimitry's body was publicly displayed in the marketplace a nobleman (*syn boyarskii*) rode up, inspected the body, and cried out, 'The man you have killed is not the true Dimitry – he has escaped!' The horseman then galloped off, and no-one could discover where he had gone.[2]

There are various versions of the rumours about Dimitry's escape from death. According to Margeret:

Some days after Dmitrii's murder, there began to circulate a rumor that the emperor had not been killed, but rather it was one who resembled him, whom Dmitrii had put in his place. This was done after Dmitrii had been informed some hours in advance of what was about to happen and had left Moscow to see just what would occur.[3]

Other sources provide variants to some of the details in Margeret's account. For example, the man who was substituted for Dimitry is variously described as a Lithuanian, a German, or 'one of Dimitry's German bodyguards, a native of Prague, very similar to him in appearance'.[4] Isaac Massa reports a version in which the victim was a damask weaver whom Marina Mniszech had

---

[1] Bussov, *Moskovskaya khronika*, p. 129.

[2] Gerkman, 'Istoricheskoe povestvovanie', p. 294. Margeret, however, states that the rumours began a few days after the riot (Margeret, *The Russian Empire*, p. 75); and Niemojewski dates their appearance to several days after Dimitry's body was burned: Nemoevskii, 'Zapiski', p. 119.

[3] Margeret, *The Russian Empire*, p. 75. Massa states that it was rumoured that Dimitry had taken flight 'two or three days before the revolt': Massa, *A Short History*, p. 156.

[4] The victim was described as a Lithuanian in the account of Prince Katyrev-Rostovskii (*RIB*, vol. 13, cols. 584, 661); as a German by Bussow and the *New Chronicler* (Bussov, *Moskovskaya khronika*, p. 129; *PSRL*, vol. 14, p. 70, para. 124); as a 'native of Prague' by Peyerle (Paerle, 'Zapiski', p. 213). In 1608 the Second False Dimitry was to claim that 'a German named Artsykalus' had been killed in his stead (Buturlin, *Istoriya smutnogo vremeni*, vol. 2, prilozheniya, no. 7, p. 51.).

brought with her from Sandomierz in Poland. This man closely resembled Dimitry, and on the morning of the murder he was acting the part of the tsar in the royal apartments, Dimitry having already taken flight. When the assassins burst in, the weaver, who thought he was playing Dimitry's role for 'a diversion, a wager or masquerade', cried out 'I am not Dimitry!' But the conspirators, thinking that he was the tsar admitting to be an impostor, 'began striking the harder'.[5]

An even more fantastic account was reported in Poland by two former soldiers in Dimitry's army. They told Father Bartch, King Sigismund's confessor, that Dimitry had had two doubles, who resembled him in every way except for the prominent wart beside his nose. Whenever Dimitry had wanted to be free of court ritual, he made one of his doubles apply a false wart to his face, and dress in the royal robes. On 17 May a certain Borkowski was acting as the tsar's substitute, and it was he who was killed by the conspirators, after Dimitry himself had fled from Moscow.[6]

Soon these rumours were followed by the appearance in Moscow of letters in Dimitry's name, stating that he was alive and would soon return to avenge himself on those who had attempted to kill him.[7] The Pole Chwalibog reports that proclamations of this kind were found nailed to the gates of the boyars' mansions within a few days of Dimitry's death. These proclamations were attributed to Patriarch Ignatii, as a result of which he was deposed and replaced by Germogen, the Metropolitan of Kazan'.[8] Such letters continued to appear over the next few weeks. Polish sources relate that on 22 July/1 August there was a riot in the capital because of letters distributed in Dimitry's name. The authorities made all the *d'yaki* assemble, in order to compare their handwriting with that of the subversive documents, but they were unable to identify the culprit.[9] Margeret says that letters appeared in August, stating that Dimitry would return on the first day of the new year (1 September 1606).[10]

Bussow claims that the rumours of Dimitry's escape were devised by the Poles,[11] but other evidence contradicts this. Many Poles did not believe the rumours;[12] and some, 'fearing another revolution', even defended Shuiskii against hostile Muscovites who were evidently inflamed by the rumours of

---

[5] Massa, *A Short History*, p. 157.
[6] Pierling, *La Russie et le Saint-Siège*, vol. 3, pp. 345–6.
[7] Margeret, *The Russian Empire*, p. 76. Peyerle reports that those who said Dimitry was still alive produced 'written proofs' (Paerle, 'Zapiski', p. 213).
[8] Khvalibog, 'Donesenie', pp. 3–4.
[9] See 'Dnevnik Mariny Mnishek', p. 177; Dyamentowski, 'Dyariusz', p. 76 (*VIB*, p. 166); Stadnitskii, 'Dnevnik', p. 172.
[10] Margeret, *The Russian Empire*, p. 76.
[11] Bussov, *Moskovskaya khronika*, p. 129.
[12] 'Dnevnik Mariny Mnishek', p. 177; Dyamentowski, 'Dyariusz', p. 75 (*VIB*, p. 166); Stadnitskii, 'Dnevnik', p. 171.

Dimitry's escape.[13] In the riot that had followed the tsar's murder on 17 May many Poles had been killed, and their property looted. Marina and her father were placed under house arrest, as were the Polish envoys to Russia. It seems unlikely that in such circumstances they would have been able to influence popular opinion in Moscow. It is more probable that the rumours about Dimitry's escape from death were invented by Russian opponents of Vasilii Shuiskii, as Margeret asserts.[14] The Poles naturally welcomed the rumours: when Mniszech heard from Russians about Dimitry's escape, he reportedly 'was glad of it';[15] and Marina's French cook told Margeret that when his mistress heard that Dimitry was alive, 'she appeared much more cheerful than before'.[16] The Mniszechs subsequently became active disseminators of the rumours about Dimitry.[17]

In the view of certain Soviet scholars, the circulation of these rumours reflected the formation of a new version of the 'popular socio-utopian legend' about Dimitry. K. V. Chistov argues that after the death of the First False Dimitry, 'the legend acquired new features and turned into an anti-boyar legend about Tsar Dimitry as a "deliverer" '. While recognising that the evidence concerning Dimitry's policy towards the peasantry is contradictory, Chistov asserts that his reign was so short that the masses retained their illusions about him, and 'his overthrow was interpreted as a boyar conspiracy against a tsar who supposedly wanted to liberate the people from feudal obligations'.[18] And although R. G. Skrynnikov regards Dimitry's peasant policy as a feudal one, he argues that 'the brief reign of the False Dimitry not only failed to destroy faith in the "good tsar" but facilitated an even wider dissemination of utopian views and hopes amongst the *narod*'.[19] The rumours that Dimitry was still alive were assiduously disseminated by the Mniszechs and other Poles but, in Skrynnikov's view, 'the basis for the myth was the popular mood, and faith in the "good tsar" '.[20]

There is no evidence, however, that the rumours about Dimitry that circulated in the summer of 1606 had any 'socio-utopian' content: contemporaries did not seem to believe that the boyars had overthrown the tsar because he wanted to restore peasant freedom. But it is not impossible that the idea of Dimitry's second escape from death might have arisen spontaneously. As we have seen, the culture of the age allowed for both miraculous and magical

---

[13] Khvalibog, 'Donesenie', p. 4.
[14] Margeret, *The Russian Empire*, p. 76. For a review of the evidence, see Dolinin, 'K izucheniyu', p. 476.
[15] *SIRIO*, vol. 137, p. 373.
[16] Margeret, *The Russian Empire*, p. 77.
[17] Skrynnikov, *Smuta v Rossii*, pp. 60–1.
[18] Chistov, *Russkie narodnye*, p. 52.
[19] Skrynnikov, *Smuta v Rossii*, p. 39.
[20] *Ibid.*, p. 60.

resurrections. In 1604–5 support had been mobilised for the pretender by the image of Tsarevich Dimitry as a Christ-like figure risen from the dead. And we have also noted that there was a popular Russian belief that a sorcerer could raise himself from the grave. Thus those who considered that Dimitry was the true tsar might have expected him to escape death again by a second miracle, while those who regarded him as an impostor could anticipate that he might survive because of his magical powers. There is evidence that both of these notions were current in the capital in May 1606. When Shuiskii's envoys to Poland attempted to refute the rumours that Dimitry was still alive, they were told that the Poles who had been in Moscow reported two alternative versions of how Dimitry might have escaped: 'either God concealed him manifestly, or he himself substituted someone in his place by his devilish thoughts and necromancy'.[21]

But although some may have believed that Dimitry had escaped death through the intervention of supernatural agencies, malignant or benign, other contemporaries were led by more rational and scientific considerations to question whether he had indeed died. Genuine doubts were expressed as to whether the corpse which lay in the market-place really was that of the tsar. Isaac Massa recounts that some Russians had assured him that the body was so muddy and mutilated that it was completely unrecognisable. Others who had examined the body swore that it could not be Dimitry's, because the hair was too long; the famous wart was not visible; or the toenails were uncut.[22] Jacques Margeret cites similar testimony: he was informed that the dead man had longer hair than the tsar; and he had signs of a beard, whereas Dimitry had been clean-shaven. Margeret adds that he was told by Stanisław Buczynski, one of the tsar's Polish secretaries, 'that there was a young Russian noble, much loved and favoured by Dmitrii, who strongly resembled the emperor, except that he had a little beard. According to what Russians say, no trace of this young noble was ever found, and no-one knew what had become of him'.[23] Massa confirms that the Buczynskis played a part in spreading doubts about the identity of the body: one of the brothers, having been in the habit of frequenting the bath-house with the tsar, claimed to know that Dimitry had a birthmark on his left breast. No such birthmark, however, was evident on the naked body displayed in the market-place. Massa, however, questioned whether this birthmark had ever existed, since 'The secretary could very well have said it in his own interest rather than in the interest of truth.'[24]

[21] *SIRIO*, vol. 137, p. 306.
[22] Massa, *A Short History*, pp. 156–8.
[23] Margeret, *The Russian Empire*, pp. 76–7.
[24] Massa, *A Short History*, pp. 156, 157–8. The Buczynskis continued to spread rumours about Dimitry. On 5 January 1607 Jan Buczynski arrived in Lwów from Yaroslavl', where the Poles had been interned by Shuiskii, and assured the Jesuit Andrzej Lawicki that Dimitry had escaped death: Pierling, *La Russie et le Saint-Siège*, vol. 3, p. 347.

Many of the superstitious beliefs which surrounded the disposal of Dimitry's body helped to feed the rumours that the corpse in the market-place was not that of the tsar. Herckman states that it was because of popular doubts about the identity of the body that the boyars had decided to bury it. Then, as the rumours about Dimitry's escape continued, the magnates feared that attempts might be made to dig up the corpse and examine it, in order to establish the dead man's identity. Thereupon the monks of the Androniev monastery, where the body had been buried, invented rumours about strange happenings which occurred at the grave, claiming that fires and devils had been seen there. The monks had said that they were so afraid of these evil spirits that they did not dare to go to the chapel in the mornings for matins. Since it was intolerable that divine service should be disrupted in this way, the body was then ordered to be burned.[25] Thus Herckman provides a 'rational' explanation for the strange rumours that surrounded the disposal of the corpse. Massa too states that some of Dimitry's supporters claimed that the body was burned to prevent it from being identified; but Massa himself prefers to explain it in terms of the Russians' magical beliefs: 'If they burned him, it was in accordance with the wishes of the people who cried that they wanted to see him reduced to ashes because his spirit was still casting spells, as witnessed by the drying up of the crops around Moscow, a scourge of which they accused him as the cause.'[26]

The rumours about Dimitry's escape from death were amplified by tales of mysterious horsemen who had left the capital on the night before the murder. Margeret relates that the Russians who believed in the tsar's survival claimed that three Turkish horses had disappeared from the palace stables on the eve of the rising, and that Dimitry had been recognised by the owner of the house in which he first sought shelter after his escape from the capital.[27] The most likely basis for these rumours was the flight from Moscow soon after Dimitry's murder of the pretender's close confidant Michael Molchanov. Chwałibog relates that on the day of Dimitry's death twenty-five horses had disappeared from the royal stables, and at the same time 'the eminent boyar Mikhailo Molchanov' had vanished. This gave rise to the rumour that Dimitry had secretly left the capital with Molchanov and some others. The missing animals included Dimitry's favourite Turkish horse, which later reappeared in Poland.[28] Isaac Massa relates that:

[25] Gerkman, 'Istoricheskoe povestvovanie', pp. 295–6.
[26] Massa, *A Short History*, pp. 157, 158. On the burning of the body to prevent identification, see also the letter of Father Bosgraven to Possevino, 12 August 1606, cited by Pierling, *La Russie et le Saint-Siège*, vol. 3, p. 344.
[27] Margeret, *The Russian Empire*, p. 76. On missing horses, see also *Moskovskaya tragediya*, p. 71; Stadnitskii, 'Dnevnik', p. 180.
[28] Khvalibog, 'Donesenie', pp. 3, 4. For other references to Molchanov's flight from Moscow at this time, see *SIRIO*, vol. 137, p. 302; Nemoevskii, 'Zapiski', p. 119.

After the tsar's assassination, when the tidings of it spread, Mikhail Molchanov, one of his secret counsellors in both his acts of tyranny and his debauches, took flight and went to Poland. After his departure the disappearance of a sceptre and a crown was noticed, and there was no doubt that he had taken these objects with him.[29]

Conrad Bussow tells a similar story, although in his account the fugitive is named as Prince Grigorii Shakhovskoi, and the item of regalia which he allegedly took with him is the royal seal.[30] During the riot of 17 May, Bussow relates, Prince Shakhovskoi stole the golden seal of state and fled from Moscow in the direction of Putivl' with two Poles in Russian dress. Below Serpukhov he crossed the River Oka and gave the ferryman six Polish guilders as a tip. He then asked the ferryman if he knew who his passengers were; and on receiving a negative reply, he told him that he had just carried Tsar Dimitry across the river. Pointing to one of the Poles, Shakhovskoi avowed that this man was Dimitry, who had escaped an attempt on his life and was going to Poland to obtain troops. When he returned, the tsar would generously reward the ferryman for assisting his escape. Shakhovskoi had told a similar story to the German widow who cooked them a meal at Serpukhov, and repeated the device at every inn and post-house on the road to Putivl'. The news spread rapidly, until 'the whole country from Moscow to the Polish border believed that Tsar Dimitry had indeed escaped and was still alive'. When the rumours reached Moscow, they caused 'wild and absurd thoughts' to arise among the common people.[31]

Margeret too relates that stories of Dimitry's escape from death were spread by the three horsemen who fled from the Kremlin on the night before the murder; and he links these with the appearance of Dimitry's letters in the capital:

they allege that the master of the first lodging where Dmitrii would have eaten after his departure from Moscow attested to speaking to Dmitrii. This man even brought a letter written by Dmitrii (so he said) in which the emperor complained about the Russians, reproaching them for their ingratitude and disregard for his kindness and clemency, and assuring them that he would soon revenge himself on the guilty. Moreover there were found several notes and letters scattered on the roads saying the same thing. Dmitrii was even recognised at most of the places where he had taken posthorses.[32]

Herckman notes that news of Dimitry's flight to Poland via Putivl' was brought to Moscow by a series of messengers from the Seversk lands.[33] And

---

[29] Massa, *A Short History*, p. 144.
[30] On Bussow's confusion of Shakhovskoi with Molchanov, see Smirnov, *Vosstanie Bolotnikova*, pp. 100–4. Stadnicki too identifies the new false Dimitry as Shakhovskoi: Stadnitskii, 'Dnevnik', p. 180. See also pp. 117–18 below.
[31] Bussov, *Moskovskaya khronika*, pp. 135–6.
[32] Margeret, *The Russian Empire*, p. 76.
[33] Gerkman, 'Istoricheskoe povestvovanie', p. 295.

Peyerle, who was under house arrest in Moscow with the Polish envoys, and obtained most of his news from the Russian *strel'tsy* guarding them, reports rumours in July that Dimitry was in the Seversk district, where the inhabitants had recognised him as tsar and were resorting to arms to restore him to his throne.[34]

In Moscow, as elsewhere, rumours about Dimitry's second escape from death served as a unifying and legitimising slogan for opposition to the new tsar Vasilii Shuiskii, the validity of whose election had been questioned from the outset.[35] Margeret describes protests before and after Shuiskii's coronation (which took place on 1 June) and on 3 June, the day when the remains of Dimitry of Uglich were brought to Moscow for reburial. On one occasion Shuiskii was obliged to resort to the device of offering to abdicate, in order to calm the crowds.[36] Sporadic unrest continued in July and August. These incidents in the capital appear to have been triggered by the distribution of proclamations in Dimitry's name, and by rumours that he had been recognised by the population of the border towns, and was preparing to march on Moscow in order to regain his throne.[37]

Shakhovskoi and Molchanov

One of Shuiskii's first actions on his accession had been to send new governors to provincial towns. Prince Grigorii Shakhovskoi was assigned to Putivl' to replace Dimitry's appointee, Prince Bakhteyarov-Rostovskii. According to an English account, after the new governor was sent to Putivl', Shuiskii 'despatched a Gentleman presently after him to sweare the people of that place to his Alleageance'.[38] This envoy was probably Gavrilo Shipov, who was sent to Putivl' by Shuiskii in May 1606.[39] In Putivl' Shipov encountered Molchanov, whom the English author describes as 'a speciall favorite of the slayne Emperour called Mutcham (whoe escapeinge thether had drawne many Gentlemen and Soldiers of those partes from acknowledginge the present Emperour)'.[40] Molchanov then 'seduced' Shipov to join the rebellion against Shuiskii.[41]

The English account states that the new governor opposed the rebellion, and was killed.[42] Russian sources, however, demonstrate that it was the old

[34] Paerle, 'Zapiski', pp. 214–15.
[35] On the circumstances of Shuiskii's election, see Skrynnikov, *Smuta v Rossii*, pp. 40–8.
[36] Margeret, *The Russian Empire*, pp. 77–9.
[37] Dyamentowski, 'Dyariusz', pp. 75–8; 'Dnevnik Mariny Mnishek', pp. 177–8; for a review of the sources, see Smirnov, *Vosstanie Bolotnikova*, pp. 279–81.
[38] Smirnov, *Vosstanie Bolotnikova*, p. 553.
[39] Gnevushev, ed., 'Akty', no. 1, pp. 1–3.
[40] Smirnov, *Vosstanie Bolotnikova*, p. 553.
[41] *Ibid.*
[42] *Ibid.*

governor, Bakhteyarov-Rostovskii, who was killed, and Shakhovskoi who headed the revolt.[43] We can only speculate about the reasons for Shakhovskoi's defection from Shuiskii.[44] Prince Grigorii, together with his father Prince P. M. Shakhovskoi, had been enthusiastic supporters of the pretender, and it may be that his appointment as governor of Putivl' was intended by Shuiskii as a form of exile from the capital for a potential political opponent. In the context of the growth of rumours about Dimitry's escape from death, this proved to be a costly error of judgement by the new tsar.[45]

Prince Shakhovskoi told all the inhabitants of Putivl' that Dimitry had escaped and had gone to Poland to gather a new army. He said that Dimitry had asked him to persuade the people of Putivl' to support their true tsar and recruit troops to help him to regain his throne.[46] According to the English account, the leaders of the revolt in Putivl' argued, in order to obtain support, that the Muscovites had had no right to depose the tsar and elect a new one without consulting the provinces. This arbitrary act was a 'greate disparagement to the Borderers and remote partes of Russia'.[47] For that reason, 'they tooke occasion to refuse the oath of Alleageance, and resolved to call them of the Mosco to an Accompte of their former proceedings'. In the view of the English author, the rumour that Dimitry was still alive was disseminated by the anti-Shuiskii faction in Putivl' primarily as a device to give legitimacy to their rebellion: 'And the better to countenance their proceedinges they gave out that Demetrie was yett liveinge and had solicited them to reestablishe him in the Kingdome.'[48]

Putivl', of course, had been Dimitry's 'capital' at a key stage in his campaign for the throne in 1605, and it is not surprising that the town and its surrounding district should have manifested a particular loyalty to 'Tsar Dimitry'. Massa states that Shuiskii's accession was greeted with joy, except in the towns through which Dimitry had passed on his route to Moscow.[49] Peyerle claims that Dimitry's supporters spread the rumour in the Seversk lands that Shuiskii planned to punish the inhabitants of that region for having been the first to recognise the pretender,[50] so that fear of reprisals by the new

---

[43] *Ibid.*, pp. 97–9.
[44] R. G. Skrynnikov suggests that it was Molchanov who incited Shakhovskoi to defect. Skrynnikov speculates that Molchanov, disguised as a Pole, may have travelled to Putivl' in the company of Shakhovskoi. Thus Skrynnikov ingeniously reconciles Bussow's evidence about Shakhovskoi's journey to Putivl' with that of other sources concerning Molchanov's flight: Skrynnikov, *Smuta v Rossii*, pp. 65–7.
[45] Solov'ev, *Istoriya Rossii*, vol. 4, p. 468; Skrynnikov, *Smuta v Rossii*, pp. 78–9.
[46] Bussow, *Moskovskaya khronika*, p. 136; *PSRL*, vol. 14, p. 70, para. 124.
[47] Smirnov, *Vosstanie Bolotnikova*, p. 553. See also Paerle, 'Zapiski', p. 215; Massa, *A Short History*, p. 151.
[48] Smirnov, *Vosstanie Bolotnikova*, p. 553.
[49] Massa, *A Short History*, p. 149.
[50] Paerle, 'Zapiski', p. 215.

tsar served as an incentive for their revolt. According to the English report, the people of Putivl′ were inclined to reject Shuiskii, 'for as much as Demetrius had for speciall service freed that Province of all Taxes and impositions for 10 yeares wch by his death was absolutely lost'.[51]

The defection of Putivl′ was followed by that of other towns in the Seversk region. The English report states that the rumour that Dimitry was alive enjoyed such success among the 'discontented and factious' inhabitants 'that most [of] the Townes in those partes revoulted from their Alleageance to the present Emperour, and took a newe oathe to the supposed liveinge Demetrie'.[52] Bussow relates that the Putivlans sent to the 'wild field' and soon assembled several thousand cossacks from the steppe, in addition to 'all the princes and boyars living in the Putivl′ district' (the local service nobility) – a further several thousand men. This army, headed by the *syn boyarskii* Istoma Pashkov, was intended to recapture the fortresses and towns which had renounced Dimitry after Shuiskii's accession. But in fact, as soon as the inhabitants of these towns heard that Dimitry was still alive, they surrendered voluntarily and swore allegiance to him.[53] By the summer of 1606, the towns of Chernigov, Ryl′sk, Starodub, Kromy, Kursk and Elets had rejected Shuiskii as tsar.[54] In August, Pashkov's army headed for Moscow.[55]

Soon rumours began to spread in Poland that Dimitry was residing in Sambor with his mother-in-law, Jerzy Mniszech's wife. At the beginning of September (NS) 1606, the papal nuncio Rangoni reported to Cardinal Borghese in Rome a piece of news which was being disseminated in Poland by an Italian merchant, Francesco Talamio, who had recently returned to Galicia from the fair at Yaroslavl′. According to Talamio, Dimitry was alive and well and hiding in a Bernardine convent at Sambor, well guarded from prying eyes. He had arrived in Sambor in a closed carriage, accompanied by two horsemen who had travelled with him from Moscow. After they reached Sambor, the travellers were not seen again, but a wonderful transformation took place in Lady Mniszech. Previously grief-stricken at the fate which had befallen her husband and daughter in Moscow, she now dried her tears and began to smile. One of her maids, gossipping at the local market, revealed the secret of her mistress's joy: Tsar Dimitry was at Sambor.[56]

It seems most likely that the part of Dimitry was played at Sambor by Molchanov, who had gone there from Putivl′. According to Bussow, the two Poles who had accompanied Shakhovskoi from Moscow to Putivl′ continued

[51] Smirnov, *Vosstanie Bolotnikova*, p. 553.
[52] *Ibid.*
[53] Bussov, *Moskovskaya khronika*, p. 136.
[54] Skrynnikov, *Smuta v Rossii*, p. 79.
[55] Bussov, *Moskovskaya khronika*, p. 140.
[56] Pierling, *La Russie et le Saint-Siège*, vol. 3, pp. 344–5.

their journey to Poland, to report the recent events in Moscow to Lady Mniszech. They told her that Shakhovskoi had a plan to avenge Dimitry's death. He proposed to write to them in Poland as if Dimitry were there with them, and they in their turn were to reply in Dimitry's name.[57] I. I. Smirnov plausibly concludes that one of these 'Poles' was in fact Molchanov, who continued to play the part of Dimitry at Sambor.[58] It seems likely, as R. G. Skrynnikov suggests, that Lady Mniszech received Molchanov at the request of her husband and daughter: although under house arrest in Yaroslavl', they managed to maintain contacts both with Moscow and with Sambor.[59]

Molchanov appears to have begun to issue proclamations in Dimitry's name from Sambor. Having stolen the seal of state, he was able to give his letters an appearance of authenticity. A letter from an insurgent leader on the Volga in November 1606 refers to a proclamation from Tsar Dimitry 'with a red seal'.[60] It seems, however, that it was not widely known in Russia where 'Dimitry' was to be found: Father Bartch reported to Rangoni in August 1606 that a delegation from the Seversk lands had arrived in Kiev in the hope of finding the former tsar in some Polish castle.[61] R. G. Skrynnikov suggests that Lady Mniszech may have been afraid that an open claim that Dimitry was at Sambor would bring Russian reprisals against Marina and Jerzy Mniszech, who were still held as hostages in Yaroslavl'.[62] The Russian and Polish authorities, however, soon learned of the new intrigue.

In the late summer of 1606 the Russian envoys Prince G. K. Volkonskii and the *d'yak* Andrei Ivanov, who were detained at Grodno, were told by their Lithuanian hosts that they had definite evidence that Dimitry was at Sambor. The tsar had made his escape from Moscow disguised as a monk, and Lady Mniszech had supplied him with new clothing and a retinue of servants. He had been recognised as Tsar Dimitry by many people who had known him in Russia, and Russians, Poles and Lithuanians were flocking to his banner.[63] Prince Volkonskii replied that the so-called Dimitry was probably Michael Molchanov, who had fled from Moscow at the time of the pretender's death. Further enquiries about the supposed Dimitry convinced the Russians that he was indeed Molchanov. Tsar Dimitry had been pale, with reddish hair, whereas the Poles described the man who had sought refuge at Sambor as having a swarthy complexion, dark hair, a small moustache and

---

[57] Bussov, *Moskovskaya khronika*, p. 136.
[58] Smirnov, *Vosstanie Bolotnikova*, p. 105. Skrynnikov, as we have already noted, believes that Molchanov travelled all the way from Moscow to Putivl' in the guise of one of Shakhovskoi's Polish companions: *Smuta v Rossii*, pp. 66–7.
[59] Skrynnikov, *Smuta v Rossii*, pp. 60–1.
[60] *VIB*, p. 208.
[61] Pierling, *La Russie et le Saint-Siège*, vol. 3, p. 345.
[62] Skrynnikov, *Smuta v Rossii*, pp. 68–9.
[63] *SIRIO*, vol. 137, pp. 301, 306.

a clipped, greying beard. Both men had facial warts: but where Dimitry's wart had been on the side of his nose, Molchanov's was on his cheek.[64] Molchanov, Volkonskii added, had lived in the pretender's apartments and had practised black magic with him. He had once been flogged for villainy (*vorovstvo*) and necromancy, and could be recognised by the marks of the knout on his back.[65]

It is not clear whether the allegations of sorcery which the Russian envoys made against Molchanov had any real basis, or whether they were simply a standard form of denigration of a pretender (similar allegations, we may recall, were made about Grisha Otrep'ev after his flight to Poland). But what little we know about Molchanov's biography is not inconsistent with his having an interest in the black arts. He was well educated – the envoys told the Poles that he could speak and write Polish, and knew Latin[66] – but was of dubious moral character. I. I. Smirnov cites documents from Boris's reign, which suggest that Molchanov had a reputation for dishonesty and was regarded as politically suspect.[67] The *New Chronicle* names him as one of the murderers of young Fedor Godunov.[68] Isaac Massa describes him as 'a rogue and a flatterer, one who feared neither God nor man'. Massa states that Molchanov had first joined the supporters of the First False Dimitry in Poland; in Moscow he served as the tsar's procurer, bringing girls to the bath-house, and often enjoying their favours himself after his master had finished with them.[69]

The supposed Dimitry was so well concealed at Sambor that no-one was able to see him. In October 1606 the Jesuit Father Andrzej Lawicki, who had accompanied the pretender to Moscow, went to Sambor to try to discover for himself whether it was true that the tsar had escaped, but he was not allowed to inspect him.[70] Then the Bernardine monks in Craców sent a member of their order on an official mission to enquire whether the rumours about Dimitry were true, but he returned with an affidavit signed by the monks of Sambor, to the effect that they had seen nothing of Dimitry since his departure in 1604.[71] When Leo Sapieha, the Lithuanian chancellor, dispatched one of his servants to Sambor to investigate the identity of the sup-

---

[64] *Ibid.*, pp. 301, 306, 313, 361, 368.
[65] *Ibid.*, p. 302. R. G. Skrynnikov assumes that Molchanov's flogging took place after the coup of 17 May 1606 (Skrynnikov, *Smuta v Rossii*, pp. 63, 64), but the sources make it clear that it occurred earlier than this (*SIRIO*, vol. 137, p. 368). Karamzin is probably right to assert that Molchanov's flogging for necromancy was administered 'in Boris's time' (Karamzin, *Istoriya*, vol. 3, t. 12, col. 18).
[66] *SIRIO*, vol. 137, pp. 306, 313.
[67] Smirnov, *Vosstanie Bolotnikova*, pp. 102–3.
[68] *PSRL*, vol. 14, p. 66, para. 106.
[69] Massa, *A Short History*, p. 119.
[70] Pierling, *La Russie et le Saint-Siège*, vol. 3, p. 346.
[71] *Ibid.*, pp. 346–7.

posed tsar, even he was not allowed to see Dimitry. Sapieha's agent was told that the pretender was living incommunicado in the local monastery, attired as a monk, and doing penance for his sins.[72]

The new pretender at Sambor therefore appeared to be strangely reluctant to assume the role of Tsar Dimitry in public, and to head the revolt against Shuiskii that was gathering momentum in Russia. This may be explained partly in terms of Molchanov's personal cowardice or caution, and partly in terms of the political situation in Poland, where the *rokosz*, a rebellion against King Sigismund led by Nicholas Zebrzydowski, provided the main preoccupation for the nobility of the *Rzeczpospolita*. Many of the Polish backers of the First False Dimitry had participated in the *rokosz*, and there is some evidence that they were eager to support the new pretender too.[73] But the Russian envoys to Poland were informed by one of their guards that the fugitive at Sambor was reluctant to approach the *rokoszanie*, fearing that they would hold him responsible for the massacre of their fellow-countrymen in Moscow.[74] Whatever his reasons, Molchanov remained in hiding at Sambor while the rebellion in the name of Tsar Dimitry spread rapidly in Russia.

Ivan Bolotnikov

At some time in the summer of 1606 there arrived in Putivl′ a certain Ivan Isaevich Bolotnikov, who was subsequently to be hailed in Soviet historiography as the leader of the 'first peasant war' in Russia. Little is known about Bolotnikov's biography. Russian sources describe him as the slave of Prince Andrei Telyatevskii.[75] A short chronicle characterises him as a *sluga*, that is, military bondsman of Telyatevskii, and V. I. Koretskii has suggested that he may have belonged to an impoverished family of petty military servitors who were forced to sell themselves into slavery in the second half of the sixteenth century.[76] Isaac Massa states that Bolotnikov fled from Prince Telyatevskii and took refuge with the cossacks on the steppe,[77] and the English report depicts him as a former Volga cossack ('an olde Robber or Borderer of the Volga').[78]

The fullest account of Bolotnikov's adventures before his arrival in Putivl′ is provided by Conrad Bussow. According to Bussow, Bolotnikov was a Russian who had in his youth been captured on the steppe by the Tatars and

[72] *SIRIO*, vol. 137, pp. 307, 312.
[73] Pierling, *La Russie et le Saint-Siège*, vol. 3, pp. 273–5, 345.
[74] *SIRIO*, vol. 137, p. 312.
[75] 'Prince A. A. Telyatevskii's man': *PSRL*, vol. 14, p. 71, para. 129; '*kholop* of Prince Andrei Telyatevskii': *VIB*, p. 111 ('Iz "Karamzinskogo khronografa" '); Palitsyn, *Skazanie*, p. 116.
[76] Koretskii, 'O formirovanii', pp. 122–4.
[77] Massa, *A Short History*, p. 155.
[78] Smirnov, *Vosstanie Bolotnikova*, p. 555.

sold as a slave to the Turks. He spent several years as a galley-slave before he was rescued by German vessels which defeated the Turks in a naval battle. He disembarked at Venice, and returned to Russia through Germany and Poland, where he hoped to learn about 'the amazing changes which had taken place in his native land in his absence'.[79] In Poland, Bussow tells us, Bolotnikov heard that Tsar Dimitry had escaped from his enemies in Moscow and was in Sambor with Lady Mniszech. Bolotnikov immediately went to Sambor, where 'the man who claimed to be Dimitry' interrogated him. Realising that Bolotnikov was 'an experienced warrior', the 'tsar' asked him whether he was willing to serve him against the traitors in Russia. Bolotnikov exclaimed that he was willing to lay down his life for his true sovereign, whereupon the presumed Dimitry gave him 30 ducats, a sword and a cloak, and despatched him to Putivl' with a letter for Prince Shakhovskoi. 'Dimitry' assured Bolotnikov that on receipt of the letter Shakhovskoi would give him 'sufficient' money from his treasury, and would make him the chief commander of his army of several thousand soldiers. Bolotnikov was to lead this army against the traitors in Dimitry's stead. The 'tsar' added that Bolotnikov was to be sure to tell the Putivlans that he had seen Dimitry and spoken to him, and that he had received his letter of appointment from the tsar's own hands.[80] When Bolotnikov arrived at Putivl', Bussow continues, he was received 'joyfully and kindly'. His arrival, and his news, convinced the Putivlans of the truth of Prince Shakhovskoi's assurances that Dimitry was alive. Having been appointed commander-in-chief, Bolotnikov was sent with 12,000 soldiers through the Komaritskaya district to join Istoma Pashkov at Moscow.[81]

This is of course an extremely improbable story, as V. I. Koretskii has pointed out:[82] it indicates that Bolotnikov's only recent military experience had been that of a galley-slave, and it is unlikely that a solitary ex-captive would have been appointed as head of Dimitry's army. Koretskii finds Isaac Massa's account of Bolotnikov's appointment more convincing than Bussow's. Massa makes no mention of Bolotnikov's visit to Sambor, but states that Bolotnikov, while serving as a cossack, had gone

on campaign in Hungary and Turkey, and, finally, joined the rebels with a party of ten thousand Cossacks. He was a big, strong and very courageous man, who distinguished himself in the wars of the Cossacks by his bravery and boldness. Although he was a Muscovite by birth, they appointed him hetman, or chief general, of their army.[83]

[79] Bussov, *Moskovskaya khronika*, p. 138.
[80] *Ibid.*
[81] *Ibid.* pp. 138–9.
[82] Koretskii, 'O formirovanii', p. 128.
[83] Massa, *A Short History*, p. 155.

In Koretskii's opinion, Bolotnikov's command of 10,000 cossacks provides a much more likely explanation for his appointment as general of the insurgent army than the meeting with Dimitry in Sambor to which Bussow attributes it.[84] R. G. Skrynnikov, however, prefers Bussow's account, pointing out that Bussow, who served Bolotnikov at Kaluga in 1606–7, is likely to have been better informed about his biography than Massa.[85] But although Bussow may have known Bolotnikov better, this may simply mean that he reproduces Bolotnikov's own justification of his right to command 'Tsar Dimitry's' army. Bussow himself later describes two occasions on which Bolotnikov publicly referred to his meeting with Dimitry. The first was on his arrival in the rebel camp outside Moscow, when he claimed seniority of command over Istoma Pashkov on the grounds that he, unlike Pashkov, had been personally appointed supreme commander by Tsar Dimitry. The second occasion occurred during the siege of Moscow. When a deputation of sceptical inhabitants of the capital demanded proof that the former tsar was still alive, Bolotnikov assured them that he had personally seen Dimitry in Poland.[86] One cannot help suspecting that Bolotnikov might have invented his meeting with the tsar, in the interests of his own greater credibility as a general.

On the other hand, Bussow's story of Bolotnikov's meeting with Dimitry in Poland is not altogether impossible. There is evidence that Molchanov had previously attempted to send an emissary to Russia, an émigré Russian named Zabolotskii.[87] And although 'Tsar Dimitry' had been inaccessible to other visitors to Sambor, Skrynnikov points out that since Bolotnikov had come from the west, and had never seen the First False Dimitry, 'it was not difficult to deceive him'.[88] Molchanov had to take his visitor's military experience on trust; but, as his subsequent career was to demonstrate, Bolotnikov did possess some qualities of leadership, and Molchanov may genuinely have been impressed by his personality. Or he may simply have been desperate to respond to the growing demands from his associates in Russia for the appearance of the 'true tsar'. Molchanov dared not show his own face in Putivl', where the inhabitants knew the First False Dimitry well by sight; but he could try to reinforce their faith in Dimitry's escape by sending them a 'witness' of his presence at Sambor. As for Bolotnikov himself, we can only speculate as to whether he was a witting or an unwitting dupe of Molchanov and Lady Mniszech.

[84] Koretskii, 'O formirovanii', p. 129.
[85] Skrynnikov, Smuta v Rossii, p. 75. Koretskii had attempted to reconcile Bussow's evidence with Massa's, but Skrynnikov finds the two sources completely incompatible.
[86] Bussov, Moskovskaya khronika, p. 139. See also pp. 126, 129 below.
[87] Skrynnikov, Smuta v Rossii, pp. 63, 70–1, 74, 76.
[88] Ibid., p. 76.

While Shakhovskoi and Bolotnikov were spreading propaganda in the Seversk region about Dimitry's escape from death, Shuiskii attempted to respond in kind. The ex-tsaritsa Marfa Nagaya was persuaded to follow up her proclamation of 21 May with a further denunciation of the First False Dimitry as a pretender. In August 1606 Marfa sent her brother Grigorii Nagoi to Elets with an icon of the newly canonised tsarevich Dimitry and a letter to the inhabitants of the town, in which she refuted the claims of the 'Lithuanians' that the former tsar was still alive. Tsar Dimitry, Marfa asserted, had really been killed in Moscow; and, in any case, he was not her son, who had died at Uglich, and whose miracle-working remains were now providing proof of this.[89] But Marfa's exhortations failed to dislodge Elets from its allegiance to Dimitry.

There has been much dispute among Soviet historians about the timing and military course of the insurgents' campaign against Moscow, and many of the details are still unclear.[90] It seems certain, however, that the rebels marched against the capital from Putivl' in two separate armies. The first, headed by Istoma Pashkov, went first to Elets and then followed a circuitous route which encompassed the lands to the south-east of Moscow, where they were joined by the servicemen of Ryazan' under Prokopii Lyapunov. The second army, commanded by Bolotnikov, followed a more direct and northerly path, via Kromy, Orel and Kaluga. The two armies joined forces at Kolomenskoe, on the outskirts of Moscow, at the beginning of November, and laid siege to the capital.

Following a line of interpretation first drawn by the pre-revolutionary scholar S. F. Platonov, Soviet historians argued that the armies led by Bolotnikov and Pashkov were of different social composition, and that this influenced their behaviour both *en route* to Moscow and during the siege of the capital.[91] According to V. I. Koretskii, Bolotnikov's army comprised primarily cossacks, peasants and bondslaves; and although it also included many nobles and *deti boyarskie*, these 'occupied a subordinate position'.[92] Conversely, Pashkov's forces included cossacks, peasants, bondsmen and townsmen, but they were subordinated to the noble commanders such as Pashkov and Lyapunov.[93] *En route* to Moscow, according to Koretskii, Bolotnikov encouraged

[89] *SGGiD*, vol. 2, no. 149, pp. 316–18.
[90] Smirnov, *Vosstanie Bolotnikova*, pp. 136–200; Ovchinnikov, 'O nachal'nom periode', pp. 116–20; Zimin, 'Nekotorye voprosy', pp. 109–13; Ovchinnikov, 'Nekotorye voprosy', pp. 69–81; Koretskii, *Formirovanie krepostnogo prava*, pp. 258–94; Skrynnikov, *Smuta v Rossii*, pp. 74–116; Skrynnikov, 'Spornye problemy'; Nazarov, 'K nachal'noi istorii'.
[91] Platonov, *Ocherki*, pp. 241–57; Smirnov, *Vosstanie Bolotnikova*, pp. 136–200, 255–324; Ovchinnikov, 'Nekotorye voprosy', pp. 69–81.
[92] Koretskii, *Formirovanie krepostnogo prava*, pp. 280–2.
[93] *Ibid.*, p. 282.

class reprisals by peasants and slaves against their masters.[94] In the territory occupied by Pashkov and Lyapunov, by contrast, although the townsmen and peasants killed some landowners and officials who remained loyal to Shuiskii, the leaders themselves, influenced by feelings of class solidarity with fellow nobles, remained 'within a framework of "legality" ' and sent captured *voevody* as prisoners to Putivl'.[95]

According to R. G. Skrynnikov, however, there is no evidence that the treatment of landowners and other nobles who remained loyal to Shuiskii was significantly different in the areas occupied by the two armies.[96] In Kolomna, for example, which was occupied by Istoma Pashkov, the *dvoryane* and *deti boyarskie* and leading townspeople had been the victims of attacks by the insurgents.[97] Nor were there significant differences in the composition of the two armies. Both were socially heterogeneous, and in the towns on both routes many of the local *dvoryane* and *deti boyarskie* went over to 'Tsar Dimitry' along with the townsmen and the peasants of the surrounding district.[98] In Skrynnikov's view, the presence of so many nobles in his army 'undermines the hypothesis that Bolotnikov fought under the slogan of the physical elimination of the feudal lords and the confiscation of their property, thereby advocating a programme of opposition to enserfment'.[99]

Skrynnikov is undoubtedly correct to state that Dimitry's supporters included representatives of all social groups. But the privileged classes were disproportionately represented on Shuiskii's side, and the evidence suggests that the victims of the executions and tortures ordered by the insurgents on both Pashkov's and Bolotnikov's routes were drawn primarily, if not exclusively, from the upper classes. The 'Karamzin Chronograph' describes how in the south-western towns the inhabitants put the boyars, *voevody* and others to death by various means, throwing some from the tops of towers, hanging others by their legs and nailing them to the town walls. The rich were robbed, 'and those who were killed and looted were called traitors, for they [the insurgents] supposedly stood for Tsar Dimitry'.[100] Sources relating to the fate of various individual noblemen confirm this general account. In the reign of Tsar Michael Romanov, the Mtsensk landowners D. D. and S. D. Sukhotin described how their father had been killed by being thrown from a tower, and all their property had been looted. Another landowner from Mtsensk, S. Ragozin, was also thrown from the tower, but survived and was put in prison. In Odoev, the landowner Nikita Kolupaev was thrown to his death

---

[94] *Ibid.*, pp. 267–80.
[95] *Ibid*, pp. 267–8
[96] Skrynnikov, *Smuta v Rossii*, pp. 130–1.
[97] Morozov, 'Vazhnyi dokument'; Skrynnikov, *Smuta v Rossii*, p. 131.
[98] Skrynnikov, *Smuta v Rossii*, pp. 131–4.
[99] *Ibid.*, pp. 133–4.
[100] Popov, ed., *Izbornik*, p. 331 (*VIB*, p. 110).

from a tower, 'because he did not kiss the cross to the scoundrels and traitors from the *ukraina*', and his house and property were plundered.[101] In Bolkhov the nobleman Afanasii Pal'chikov, an opponent of the First False Dimitry and critic of Bolotnikov, was nailed to the town walls, left there all day until evening, and then killed by being thrown from a tower. As V. I. Koretskii suggests, the cruel, prolonged and public form of execution to which Pal'chikov was subjected was no doubt designed to have a deterrent effect on others who might doubt whether Tsar Dimitry really was alive.[102] In general, the insurgents' tortures and executions of 'traitors' assumed the form of ritualistic punishments, involving the symbolic 'casting down' of the victims from towers, and their public humiliation before the crowd.

Thus although the rebels may not have called for the mass extermination of property owners, but only for the punishment of 'traitors' to Tsar Dimitry, many members of the nobility suffered cruel deaths at the hands of the insurgents. This suggests that in the course of the uprising the resentments of the 'have-nots' in Russian society were able to find an outlet in attacks on the rich and powerful, legitimised as reprisals directed against opponents of the true tsar, Dimitry. These social antagonisms, already evident in the risings in the towns of the south-west, became even more noticeable during the siege of Moscow.

The siege of Moscow

There has been much debate amongst historians about the rebels' aims and about their intentions towards the inhabitants of Moscow. An early seventeenth-century literary source, the 'Continuation of the History of Kazan'', suggests that the insurgents had a radical social programme. It states that Bolotnikov's men, *en route* to Moscow, had said to one another, 'Let us all go and take Moscow and destroy those living in it, and possess it, and share out the houses of the magnates and the strong, and take their noble wives and daughters as wives for ourselves.'[103] V. I. Koretskii argues that this source describes the aim of the rising as 'the seizure of power in the capital and the implementation of a political and social revolution: the destruction of the lords and the confiscation and division of their property'.[104] R. G. Skrynnikov, however, speculates that the author of the 'History' was simply reproducing Shuiskii's propaganda. Tsar Vasilii, Skrynnikov believes, tried to rally support for himself in the capital by claiming that the rebels planned

---

[101] Koretskii, *Formirovanie krepostnogo prava*, pp. 268–9.
[102] *Ibid.*, pp. 270–1; Koretskii, ed., 'Novoe', pp. 100–3.
[103] *VIB*, p. 105.
[104] Koretskii, *Formirovanie krepostnogo prava*, p. 259.

to exterminate the entire population of Moscow.[105] In reality, however, their aims were much more limited.[106]

There is certainly some evidence that the insurgents initially tried to persuade the Muscovites to surrender peacefully, and to acknowledge 'Tsar Dimitry'. Only the Shuiskiis were to be held responsible for the events of 17 May. Bussow states that when Istoma Pashkov arrived at Kotly, on the outskirts of Moscow, 'In the name of his sovereign Dimitry he demanded the surrender of the city and also the handover of the three brothers Shuiskii, as traitors to the tsar and instigators of the present rising and the terrible bloodshed.'[107] But the absence of Tsar Dimitry in the besiegers' camp made the inhabitants of the capital sceptical about the claims that he was still alive. Bussow describes how the citizens of Moscow sent a delegation to Bolotnikov with an ultimatum. If the former Tsar Dimitry was present in his camp or in some other place, they said, Bolotnikov was to produce him or send for him, so that they could see him with their own eyes. If he did so, they would submit to Dimitry, humbly beg his pardon and surrender to him. Bolotnikov replied that he had himself seen the tsar in Poland and that he was shortly expected to come to Moscow. But the Muscovites assured Bolotnikov that Dimitry had indeed been killed on 17 May, and invited him to surrender to Shuiskii. Bolotnikov defiantly replied that he would remain loyal to Dimitry, and would see them all hanged. At this point the negotiations were broken off, and Bolotnikov wrote urgently to Prince Shakhovskoi, telling him to bring Dimitry to Moscow as soon as possible, since his appearance in the besiegers' camp would lead to the immediate surrender of the capital. Dimitry need delay no longer, for the prospect of a peaceful transfer of power meant that there was no necessity for him to recruit more troops.[108] Prince Shakhovskoi in his turn, on receiving Bolotnikov's letter, sent an urgent message to Poland,

but he who by agreement with him had promised to give himself out to be Dimitry and pretend to be him, could not steel himself for such a subtle ploy. He did not want to become Dimitry, and he remained in Poland as a fine gentleman and left whomever wanted to do so to fight for the Muscovite tsardom.[109]

Bolotnikov's inability to produce Tsar Dimitry in person, Bussow concludes, raised morale among the defenders of the capital.[110]

[105]   Skrynnikov, *Smuta v Rossii*, p. 120.
[106]   *Ibid.*, pp. 134–5.
[107]   Bussov, *Moskovskaya khronika*, p. 138.
[108]   *Ibid.*, pp. 139–40.
[109]   *Ibid.*, p. 140.
[110]   *Ibid.*

It is not unreasonable to assume that the failure of Tsar Dimitry to appear in the rebel camp also weakened the morale of the besiegers. Nevertheless, many members of Bolotnikov's army remained fanatical believers in Dimitry, asserting him to be alive even when they were under torture and threat of death. The English report describes a rebel prisoner who 'was sett uppon a Stake and at his death did constantly affirm that the late Emperour Demetrie did live and was at Poteemoe [Putivl']'.[111] Isaac Massa states that prisoners who were executed by drowning 'held to their last breath that Dimitry was not dead'; others insisted under torture 'that they have seen him with the same sceptre and crown as he had worn in Moscow'.[112] Massa also relates that even two defectors to Shuiskii 'swore that Dimitry was still alive, and that they had seen him'.[113] Some of these accounts were very specific. In November 1606, for example, it was reported on the Volga that Dimitry was at Kolomna.[114] And in March 1607 the Polish exiles in Rostov met a Don cossack who said he had been imprisoned for bearing one of Dimitry's proclamations to Moscow. He insisted that Dimitry was alive, and swore on oath that he himself had seen him.[115] This evidence suggests that in the case of some of Dimitry's supporters, at least, their belief that the 'true tsar' had again escaped death was held with a quasi-religious fervour.

V. I. Koretskii speculates that while Bolotnikov – according to Bussow, at least – asserted that Dimitry was still in Poland, Istoma Pashkov may have been responsible for spreading false information that the tsar had already returned to Russia, thereby undermining Bolotnikov's position in his negotiations with the delegation of Muscovites.[116] In practice, however, it seems likely that rumours that Dimitry was somewhere in Russia, or even present in the rebel camp, arose spontaneously, possibly on the basis of the proclamations in his name which were widely disseminated by the insurgents. But it is certainly true that Bolotnikov's inability to produce Dimitry in person weakened the credibility of the insurgent leaders.

After their failure to persuade the Muscovites to surrender, the rebels attempted to foment an uprising in the capital. Patriarch Germogen's *gramota* of 29 November 1606 to Metropolitan Filaret of Rostov states that

these villains are encamped outside Moscow at Kolomenskoe, and they are writing their accursed leaflets to Moscow and telling the boyars' bondslaves to kill their masters, and they promise them their wives, and hereditary and service lands; and they are telling the clowns and obscure rogues to kill the merchants and all the traders

[111] Smirnov, *Vosstanie Bolotnikova*, p. 555.
[112] Massa, *A Short History*, pp. 156, 157.
[113] *Ibid.*, p. 163.
[114] *VIB*, p. 208.
[115] Dyamentowski, 'Dyariusz', p. 94; *VIB*, p. 169.
[116] Koretskii, *Formirovanie krepostnogo prava*, pp. 296–302.

and to take their property; and they are calling on these villains to join them and they are offering to give them the ranks of boyar and *voevoda* and *okol'nichii* and *d'yak*.[117]

The English report provides similar evidence, asserting that the rebel army 'continued the Seige and Writt ltres to the Slaves wth in the Towne, to take Armes against their Masters and to possesse themselves of their Goodes and substance'.[118] The older generation of Soviet historians, following Platonov,[119] argued that these sources show that Bolotnikov's aim was a fundamental social revolution with an anti-feudal content.[120] R. G. Skrynnikov, however, is much more sceptical about this, observing that, while the sources are too tendentious to provide an accurate picture of the rebels' 'programme', there is no evidence that they planned to abolish serfdom, and therefore no reason to describe the revolt as a 'peasant war'.[121] The sources do however suggest that Bolotnikov sought to take advantage of social antagonisms between the rich and poor elements in the capital. His proclamations, it seems, identified the chief traitors to Tsar Dimitry as nobles, and he incited their slaves to attack them, by promising to reward them with shares of their masters' property. But this was hardly a programme for social revolution: indeed, it was little more than an extension of the actions of Ivan the Terrible and Boris Godunov, who had encouraged slaves to denounce their masters as traitors, and rewarded them with landed estates and noble rank. Far from abolishing 'feudalism', Bolotnikov's victory might have seen some former slaves and serfs become noble proprietors of landed estates, but the institutions of slavery and serfdom would have remained, along with the hierarchical Muscovite system of ranks.

Bolotnikov's appeals struck terror into the hearts of the Muscovite elites: according to the author of the English report, the 'Nobles and better sorte of Cittizens' of the capital were very fearful of the possibility of a revolt by 'the Comon sorte of people whoe lately infected wth robbinge and spoyleinge of the Poales were very unconstent and readie to Mutine uppon every reporte, as hopeinge to share wth Rebells in the spoyle of the Cittie'.[122] The anxiety of the upper classes was further intensified when 'In the ende the Rebells writte letres into the Towne requireinge by name divers Noble men and some principall Cittizens to be delivered unto them as cheefe Actors in murtheringe

---

[117] *AAE*, vol. 2, no. 57, p. 129. Cf. also no. 58, p. 132.

[118] Smirnov, *Vosstanie Bolotnikova*, pp. 553–5.

[119] Platonov, *Ocherki*, pp. 252–7. The Marxist historian M. N. Pokrovskii, however, in a work written before the Revolution, had rejected Platonov's view that the aim of the Bolotnikov rising was 'not only a political but also a social revolution': Pokrovskii, *Izbrannye proizvedeniya*, vol. 1, pp. 371–2.

[120] Smirnov, *Vosstanie Bolotnikova*, p. 283; Koretskii, *Formirovanie krepostnogo prava*, pp. 306–11.

[121] Skrynnikov, *Smuta v Rossii*, p. 135; Skrynnikov, 'Spornye problemy', pp. 105–6, 108.

[122] Smirnov, *Vosstanie Bolotnikova*, p. 555.

the late Emperour'.[123] No popular uprising, however, was to materialise in Moscow. Tsar Vasilii apparently succeeded in persuading the inhabitants that the rebels posed a threat to them all, and not just to the propertied classes. Isaac Massa, who was in the capital during the siege, states that the citizens took a new oath of loyalty to Shuiskii, 'swearing to defend him and fight for him as they would for themselves, their wives and their children. They were well aware that the rebels had resolved not to spare a living soul in Moscow, intent on holding them all responsible for Dmitry's death.'[124]

Divisions within the insurgents' camp led to the defection of both Lyapunov and Pashkov. Lyapunov and the servicemen of Ryazan' went over to Shuiskii on 16 November. Fighting occurred on 26 November, but the decisive battle took place on 2 December, when Tsar Vasilii's troops made a sortie from Moscow to attack the cossack camp at Zabor'e. In the course of the fighting, Pashkov and 500 of his men defected to Shuiskii, and the remainder of the cossacks soon surrendered.[125]

Personal rivalry had existed between Bolotnikov and Pashkov since the beginning of the siege. According to Conrad Bussow, when Bolotnikov arrived at Moscow with his army he had demanded that Pashkov cede to him the better position and the supreme command. Bolotnikov claimed seniority to Pashkov, on the grounds that the latter had been appointed *voevoda* only by Prince Shakhovskoi, whereas he, Bolotnikov, had received his letters of appointment from Tsar Dimitry himself. Pashkov yielded with a very bad grace, and in order to gain his revenge on Bolotnikov he entered into secret negotiations with Shuiskii. Having received generous payments of gold and silver from Tsar Vasilii, Pashkov revealed that no-one at Putivl' had seen Dimitry, and that they still knew no more about him than Shakhovskoi had told them at the very outset, namely that he was alive and in Poland. Noting that Bolotnikov claimed to have met Dimitry in Poland and to have been appointed by the tsar as senior commander in his place, Pashkov hinted that this supposed Dimitry might have been a new pretender: 'He could not tell whether it was true that Dimitry had escaped to Poland and had himself sent this Bolotnikov, having appointed him in his stead, or whether the Poles and Shakhovskoi had fostered a new Dimitry, but, as he had said, so far

---

[123] *Ibid.* V. I. Koretskii argues that the demand that the Muscovites hand over several nobles and merchants reflects Bolotnikov's political programme, which was more radical than that of Pashkov, who had requested the surrender only of the Shuiskiis (Koretskii, *Formirovanie krepostnogo prava*, pp. 290, 304–6). R. G. Skrynnikov, however, argues that the expansion of the list of traitors was undertaken with the agreement of all the leaders of the rebellion after the failure of negotiations with the townspeople had demonstrated that 'all the boyars and the "best people" supported the traitor Shuiskiis' (Skrynnikov, *Smuta v Rossii*, p. 134).

[124] Massa, *A Short History*, p. 155.

[125] Skrynnikov, *Smuta v Rossii*, pp. 140–5.

no-one had seen Dimitry in Muscovy.'[126] According to the English report, Pashkov told Shuiskii that 'the Rumor of Demetrius liveinge was but a forged conceipte'.[127]

Bussow explains Pashkov's desertion from the insurgent camp in terms of his personal rivalry with Bolotnikov, but Soviet historians have placed greater emphasis on the alleged social differences between the two leaders' armies. The radicalism of Bolotnikov's anti-feudal programme, they argue, alienated the noble servicemen, and led to the defection first of Lyapunov and then of Pashkov to Shuiskii's side.[128] Even R. G. Skrynnikov believes that social tensions contributed to the nobles' abandonment of the rebel camp. Bolotnikov's appeal to the lower classes in Moscow, Skrynnikov suggests, alarmed the noblemen in the besieging army, and drove them into Shuiskii's arms.[129] We can of course only speculate about the noble defectors' motives, which were undoubtedly complex, but it is not impossible that social as well as personal conflicts played their part.

Some contemporaries suggested that Pashkov's defection to Shuiskii during the fighting on 2 December was the major reason for the rebels' failure to take the capital,[130] but I. I. Smirnov observed that in reality the outcome of the siege was determined by 'other, more profound factors',[131] of which their unwarranted faith in 'Tsar Dimitry' was one of the most important.[132] Certainly Bolotnikov's inability to prove to the Muscovites that Dimitry was alive played into the hands of Shuiskii's propagandists. After the battle, Bolotnikov retreated from his camp at Kolomenskoe to Kaluga, with his forces more or less intact.

---

[126] Bussov, *Moskovskaya khronika*, p. 139.
[127] Smirnov, *Vosstanie Bolotnikova*, p. 555.
[128] *Ibid.*, pp. 282–4, 293–8; Koretskii, *Formirovanie krepostnogo prava*, pp. 289–92, 307–8.
[129] Skrynnikov, *Smuta v Rossii*, p. 137.
[130] Massa, *A Short History*, p. 163; Smirnov, *Vosstanie Bolotnikova*, p. 555; Paerle, 'Zapiski', p. 217.
[131] Smirnov, *Vosstanie Bolotnikova*, p. 313.
[132] *Ibid.*, pp. 509–11.

5   The uprising continues

The Astrakhan' tsareviches

From the summer of 1606 there developed on the Volga a rebellion in favour of Tsar Dimitry which was largely independent of the revolt in the Seversk lands. The first major Volga city to reject Shuiskii was Astrakhan', the great commercial port at the mouth of the river, on the Caspian Sea.[1] Immediately after the overthrow of the First False Dimitry, Astrakhan' had sworn loyalty to Shuiskii. The citizens' acceptance of the new tsar, however, was half-hearted from the outset, and within a few days an incident occurred which led to their rejection of Vasilii. On 17 June 1606, soon after Shuiskii's official proclamation announcing his accession had been received in Astrakhan', the mounted *strelets* Vas'ka Eremeev arrived from Kazan' with a document in Dimitry's name. Although this was dated earlier than Shuiskii's proclamation, the people of Astrakhan' chose to take it as evidence that Dimitry was still alive, and used it as a pretext for renouncing their allegiance to Shuiskii. An uprising took place, in which the *d'yak* Afanasii Karpov and the nobleman Tret'yak Kashkarov were killed for their continued support of Shuiskii. Many other people were put to death by means of the *raskat* – that is, they were hurled from the top of a high watchtower in the Astrakhan' kremlin.[2] The city governor, Prince I. D. Khvorostinin, transferred his loyalty to Dimitry.

Shortly before his overthrow, the First False Dimitry had sent F. I. Sheremetev to replace Prince Khvorostinin as governor of Astrakhan'. Sheremetev, who was accompanied by a substantial contingent of troops to reinforce or replace the city garrison, was still *en route* for Astrakhan' when Dimitry was killed. Shuiskii confirmed his appointment, but before Sheremetev could reach his destination, the uprising against Shuiskii occurred. The people of Astrakhan' refused to let Sheremetev enter the city, and he was obliged to establish a camp on the island of Balchik, a few miles upstream. The men

---

[1] The fullest and most authoritative account of events in Astrakhan' after the death of the First False Dimitry is provided by Smirnov, *Vosstanie Bolotnikova*, pp. 222ff.

[2] *PSRL*, vol. 14, p. 72, para. 131; Smirnov, *Vosstanie Bolotnikova*, pp. 250–2.

of Astrakhan', together with cossacks from the Terek, Volga, Don and Yaik, twice attacked Sheremetev's camp at Balchik at the beginning of September 1606.[3] Prince Khvorostinin himself appears to have played an active role in the Astrakhan' rising, and he remained governor of the city after the revolt.

Important evidence about events on the Volga in 1606–7 is provided by the reports of a party of Spanish and Italian monks who were travelling down the river to Persia. These Carmelite missionaries had left Moscow on 12/22 March 1606 with documents from the First False Dimitry guaranteeing them safe passage. They were accompanied by Zenil Kambey (Zain-ul-'Abidin Baig), a Persian envoy to the Holy Roman Emperor who was returning home through Russia from Prague.[4] The party had reached Kazan' when news arrived of Dimitry's death and Shuiskii's accession. The governor of Kazan' swore allegiance to Shuiskii, and imprisoned the Carmelites until he received orders from Moscow concerning them. On 10/20 July Shuiskii's reply was brought by two ambassadors whom the new tsar was sending to Persia. Vasilii was willing to allow the Carmelites to continue to Persia in the company of his own envoys, and at the expense of the Russian government.[5]

The missionaries left Kazan' on 14/24 July and on 10/20 August they reached Tsaritsyn.[6] There they learned of the major rising against Shuiskii that had broken out downstream. This revolt on the lower Volga was led by three new pretenders. Not only was the story of Dimitry's supposed escape from death spreading far and wide, the Carmelites discovered, but 'an intriguer, who claimed to be the brother of this prince [Dimitry] was making skilful use of the general rumour, and had succeeded in raising Astrakhan' and the surrounding area against Shuiskii'. This pretender had had little difficulty in obtaining support from the Don cossacks, whose zeal for Dimitry's cause was intensified by the presence in their midst of

two nephews of Dimitry, sons of Fedor, who had entrusted themselves to their loyalty and had been living amongst them since the period of Boris's usurpation. Under the leadership of the elder of these two brothers an army of cossacks, reinforced by the adhesion of a large number of Muscovites, was marching on Moscow with the aim of restoring Dimitry's rights.[7]

---

[3] *VIB*, p. 236.

[4] On the background to the Carmelite mission, see Pierling, *La Russie et le Saint-Siège*, vol. 3, pp. 237–9; Pirling, *Iz smutnogo vremeni*, pp. 54–66; *A Chronicle of the Carmelites*, vol. 1, pp. 104–11. The fullest account of their voyage down the Volga is provided in Berthold-Ignace, *Histoire*, pp. 135–203; see also Pirling, *Iz smutnogo vremeni*, pp. 64–6; Florencio, *A Persia*, pp. 67–86; *A Chronicle of the Carmelites*, vol. 1, pp. 111–12. Only Pirling and the *Chronicle* have been used by Soviet historians.

[5] Berthold-Ignace, *Histoire*, pp. 135–46.

[6] *Ibid.*, pp. 147, 150.

[7] *Ibid.*, pp. 151–2.

The Carmelites do not name the Astrakhan' pretender who claimed to be Dimitry's brother, but it is clear from their subsequent account of his activities that he was 'Tsarevich Ivan Augustus', who claimed to be the son of Tsar Ivan the Terrible. Russian sources do not refer to this pretender until the following year, when he sailed up the Volga towards Moscow (see pp. 147–8 below), but it is evident from the Carmelites' information that he played a part in the Astrakhan' rising virtually from the outset, and had the backing of the neighbouring cossacks. It seems likely that his pretence was modelled on that of Tsarevich Peter, whose campaign in the spring of 1606 had been supported by the Terek, Don and Volga cossacks.

Little is known about the background of Tsarevich Ivan Augustus. In a paragraph entitled 'The rogues (*vory*) of Astrakhan', who called themselves tsareviches', the *New Chronicle* includes 'Augustus, the son of Tsar Ivan' in its list of three pretenders who appeared in Astrakhan' while the Second False Dimitry was encamped at Tushino (i.e. in 1608–9) – the other two being Osinovik, the son of Tsarevich Ivan Ivanovich, and Laver (Lavrentii), the son of Tsar Fedor Ivanovich. The chronicler comments indignantly that a boyar's man (a bondslave) and a ploughing peasant had dared to call themselves tsareviches at this time, but does not specify which of the Astrakhan' pretenders these were.[8] I. I. Smirnov sees the chronicle's information about the lower-class origins of the Astrakhan' tsareviches as evidence of the social character of the rising in the city: such pretenders, he argues, could have been acknowledged as 'tsareviches' only by members of their own social milieu. Smirnov adds that by declaring a bondsman and a peasant to be tsareviches, the oppressed masses were demonstrating their concept of a 'good tsar' as one recruited from their own ranks.[9] R. G. Skrynnikov speculates that Ivan Augustus was a fugitive bondsman, put up by the Volga cossacks;[10] but we cannot be certain that he was of slave or peasant origin. One of the most intriguing features of the Astrakhan' tsarevich is his choice of name. Augustus (Avgust) was not a common Russian name. It echoes the sobriquet of King Sigismund II Augustus of Poland, Ivan the Terrible's opponent in the early years of the Livonian War; and it also recalls Ivan's own attempt, as part of his justification for adopting the title of tsar (Caesar, emperor), to claim descent from the Roman Emperor Augustus Caesar. These resonances, if conscious, suggest a higher level of education and culture on the part of the pretender or his advisers than is consistent with the hypotheses of Soviet historians about their lower-class background.

We do not know how, if at all, Ivan Augustus justified his claim to be the son of Tsar Ivan. According to a proclamation of the Second False Dimitry,

[8] *PSRL*, vol. 14, p. 89, para. 195.
[9] Smirnov, *Vosstanie Bolotnikova*, p. 254.
[10] Skrynnikov, *Smuta v Rossii*, p. 222.

dated 24 April 1608, Tsarevich Ivan Augustus called himself the son of Tsar Ivan Vasil'evich by his fourth wife Anna Koltovskaya – a claim which the pretender derided, reminding the Russians that Tsar Ivan had been married to Koltovskaya for only seventeen weeks.[11] (Since Koltovskaya had been sent to a convent after her shortlived marriage to the tsar, however, it is not altogether impossible that she could have borne Ivan a son.) According to R. G. Skrynnikov, the pretender's knowledge about Koltovskaya suggests that he had been to Moscow and learned something about the life of the royal court.[12] Koltovskaya's wedding to Ivan had taken place in 1572, so any son of the marriage would have been aged about 33 in 1606. Like Tsarevich Peter, he would have had a stronger claim to the throne (by the principle of linear succession) than Tsarevich Dimitry of Uglich, but what little evidence we have of the activity of Ivan Augustus suggests that – again like Peter – he was willing to act in a subordinate role to 'Dimitry'.

It is more difficult to identify the 'two nephews of Dimitry, sons of Fedor' who, according to the Carmelites' information, were active among the Don cossacks in 1606. The elder of these, who was supposedly leading an army against Moscow, was probably Tsarevich Peter. The identity of the younger is more problematic. The Second False Dimitry, in his proclamation of 24 April 1608, named no less than eight pretenders – in addition to Tsarevich Peter – who had appeared in the cossack settlements on the steppe (*pol'skie yurty*), all claiming to be sons of Tsar Fedor Ivanovich,[13] but it is not clear when these pretenders first manifested themselves. One of them, Tsarevich Fedor Fedorovich, came to the Second False Dimitry's camp at Bryansk in the autumn of 1607, accompanied by a band of Don cossacks, and it may be that he was the second 'son of Fedor' that the Carmelites heard about on the Volga in the summer of 1606.[14]

Tsarevich Peter at Putivl'

Tsarevich Peter had heard at Sviyazhsk of the death of the First False Dimitry, and had then retreated down the Volga with his cossacks. According to several sources, they looted as they went. The *New Chronicle* states that the cossacks plundered many towns on the Volga, and that at Tsaritsyn they killed the Russian envoy to Persia, Prince Ivan Petrovich Romodanovskii, and the *voevoda* Fedor Akinfov (Akinfeev), before going to the Don and

---

[11] Buturlin, *Istoriya smutnogo vremeni*, vol. 2, prilozheniya, no. 7, p. 56 (*VIB*, pp. 229–30). The Second False Dimitry also names a second Astrakhan' tsarevich, Lavrentii. See below, ch. 6, p. 176.

[12] Skrynnikov, *Smuta v Rossii*, p. 222.

[13] Buturlin, *Istoriya smutnogo vremeni*, vol. 2, prilozheniya, no. 7, pp. 56–7 (*VIB*, p. 230).

[14] *PSRL*, vol. 14, p. 77, para. 153. See also below, ch. 6, pp. 174–5.

wintering there.[15] The 'Karamzin Chronograph' says that they committed acts of piracy on the Volga and then turned west before reaching Tsaritsyn and went along the River Kamyshenka to Voronezh.[16] According to Margeret,

before my departure from Russia, these Cossacks sacked three castles situated along the Volga, captured some small cannon and other munitions of war, and separated. Most of them went into the plains of Tartary. The others withdrew to a castle which is halfway between Kazan and Astrakhan, hoping to rob the merchants taking goods to Astrakhan or at least to force them to come to terms. But while I was at Archangel I received news that all was calm along the Volga and that the cossacks had all left.[17]

Il'ya's own testimony, not surprisingly, does not mention his piratical activity. He states that when the cossacks, on their retreat down the Volga, reached the Kamyshenka, they crossed overland to the River Ilovlya, a tributary of the Don. They then rowed down the Don to Monastyrskoe, and from there went up the Donets. After they had ascended the Donets 100 versts, they were met by one Goryaino, a messenger from Putivl'. He handed them a letter from Prince Grigorii Shakhovskoi, requesting them to come in haste, since Tsar Dimitry was alive and was heading for Putivl' from Lithuania with many men. As a result of this invitation the cossacks crossed from the Donets to Tsarev-Gorod (Tsarev-Borisov) and from there they went to Putivl'.[18]

It is not entirely clear from these sources why Peter should have decided to leave the Volga in the summer of 1606. One factor may have been the troops which Shuiskii sent against the Volga pirates as soon as he came to power. The Russian envoys to Poland claimed in December 1606 that the Volga and Terek cossacks had fled from the Volga when Tsar Vasilii sent troops after them.[19] Another consideration for Peter and his cossacks may have been the presence of rival 'tsareviches' further downstream, at Astrakhan'.

Nor is it clear why Prince Shakhovskoi should have invited Peter to Putivl'. As we have noted, the absence of 'Tsar Dimitry' in Russia was an increasing embarrassment to the rebel movement by the autumn of 1606, and Shakhovskoi may have felt that any pretender, even a cossack tsarevich, was better than none. According to Bussow, Prince Shakhovskoi intended Peter to be

---

[15] *Ibid.*, p. 71, para. 128. In fact, both Romodanovskii and Akinfov were killed on the orders of Tsarevich Ivan Augustus (see pp. 145, 147 below).

[16] *VIB*, p. 110.

[17] Margeret, *The Russian Empire*, p. 71. R. G. Skrynnikov wrongly attributes the capture of the fortresses and cannon to the period of Peter's upriver journey: *Smuta v Rossii*, p. 29.

[18] *VIB*, p. 226.

[19] The envoys stated that it was only after their departure from the Volga that the cossacks set up a pretender in order to sow dissension between Poland and Russia and to save themselves from death: *SIRIO*, vol. 137, p. 352.

only a temporary replacement for Dimitry: he was to help the deposed tsar to regain his patrimony until Dimitry arrived from Poland with fresh troops, for which service his 'uncle' would reward him with 'the best principality'. Bussow adds that Shakhovskoi hoped that if no-one came from Poland to play the part of Dimitry, Tsarevich Peter would be accepted by the Russians as their tsar, 'in so far as he was the true son of Fedor Ivanovich and therefore the rightful heir to the state'. In the meantime, however, everything had still to be done in Dimitry's name.[20] Peter, according to his own testimony, accepted the invitation to Putivl' in the expectation that Tsar Dimitry himself would soon appear there. This would seem to suggest that his aim, as on his journey up the Volga towards Moscow in 1606, was still to try to forge some kind of alliance with Dimitry, rather than to oppose or to supplant him.

Peter and his cossacks arrived in Putivl' around November 1606,[21] having occupied Tsarev-Borisov on their route from the Donets. There they had executed the *voevody* Mikhail Bogdanovich Saburov and Prince Yurii Priimkov Rostovskii,[22] and threatened to kill an elderly monk (*starets*) called Iov, who tried to persuade people to oppose the pretender.[23] In Putivl', too, Peter launched a reign of terror. Many captured noblemen who had refused to recognise 'Tsar Dimitry' during the insurgents' march on Moscow had been sent to Putivl', where Prince Shakhovskoi held them in prison until Dimitry should arrive and pass judgement on them. Peter, however, evidently felt able to order the executions of these prisoners, in lieu of Dimitry. The Russian chronicles provide long lists of Peter's eminent victims, and describe the cruel deaths to which he subjected them.[24] According to the *New Chronicle*, some were thrown from a tower, some were dropped from a bridge into the moat, some were hung upside down, and others were spreadeagled with their arms and legs nailed to a wall and shot at with guns.[25] Other sources refer to deaths by disjointing, dismemberment, scalding and impaling.[26] The *Piskarev Chronicle* suggests that the cruellest tortures were reserved for those who denounced Peter as an impostor.[27] Not even the clergy were exempt. Abbot Dionisii of the Molchinskii monastery condemned Peter as a pretender, for which he was thrown from the top of a tower.[28] According to the author of the *Kazanskoe skazanie*, public executions of this type took place at the

[20] Bussov, *Moskovskaya khronika*, p. 141.
[21] Smirnov, *Vosstanie Bolotnikova*, p. 372; Nazarov and Florya, 'Krest'yanskoe vosstanie', p. 339.
[22] *PSRL*, vol. 14, p. 74, para. 141.
[23] Novombergskii, ed., *Slovo i delo gosudarevy*, vol. 1, pp. 12–13.
[24] *PSRL*, vol. 14, p. 74, para. 141; *PSRL*, vol. 34, p. 211 (*VIB*, p. 131).
[25] *PSRL*, vol. 14, p. 74, para. 141.
[26] *VIB*, pp. 104, 132, 243.
[27] *PSRL*, vol. 34, p. 214 (*VIB*, p. 132).
[28] Koretskii, 'Aktovye i letopisnye materialy', pp. 57–8.

rate of seventy per day. The property of the victims was confiscated, and their wives and daughters were raped.[29] The *New Chronicle* adds that Peter personally 'took to himself for shame to his bed' the daughter of Prince Andrei Bakhteyarov-Rostovskii, the former governor of Putivl'.[30]

The forms assumed by Tsarevich Peter's terror, like that of Bolotnikov *en route* to Moscow, were savage in their cruelty. R. G. Skrynnikov has noted that the horrific deaths that Peter imposed on his victims resembled the types of executions of 'traitor-boyars' that Ivan the Terrible had implemented in the period of the *oprichnina*.[31] In 1570, for example, the state treasurer Nikita Funikov had been boiled alive, and the *d'yak* Ivan Viskovatyi was hacked to pieces by the *oprichniki*. Skrynnikov does not draw any conclusions from these similarities, but it could be argued that the rebels' perception of Dimitry was similar to the folk image of Ivan Groznyi: a just but terrible tsar whose terror was directed exclusively against traitors.[32] Like Bolotnikov, Peter did not exterminate nobles indiscriminately (he even had his own 'loyal' boyars, such as Prince Shakhovskoi). But the execution of traitors to 'Tsar Dimitry' may have served as an outlet for the cossacks' traditional hatred for nobles and officials.

More broadly, the forms assumed by these executions owed much to the popular culture of the age, which was fascinated by grotesque punishments. In Western Europe, medieval mystery plays depicted with relish the dismemberment of bodies in hell, and their roasting, burning and mutilation.[33] In Russia, the torments of hell were depicted in icons and frescoes of the Last Judgement, and were graphically described in unofficial Apocryphal writings, which influenced popular oral culture. The Russian scholars Panchenko and Uspenskii have argued that Tsar Ivan regarded himself as God's representative on earth, whose duty was to administer punishment to sinners on the model of divine retribution in hell. Accordingly, all the most grotesque forms of *Groznyi*'s terror – including the baiting of victims with dogs and bears, and their boiling alive – had their analogies in the descriptions of hell in the Apocrypha.[34] In his famous book on Rabelais and the popular culture of his age, Mikhail Bakhtin noted that Ivan the Terrible's *oprichnina* was influenced by popular forms of mockery and derision,[35] and S. K. Rosovetskii has detected echoes of medieval comic culture and of semi-pagan customs not only in Ivan's terror but also in the forms of executions carried out in the

---

[29] *VIB*, p. 104.
[30] *PSRL*, vol. 14, p. 74, para. 141.
[31] Skrynnikov, *Smuta v Rossii*, p. 158.
[32] Perrie, *The Image of Ivan the Terrible*, pp. 60–5.
[33] Bakhtin, *Rabelais*, p. 347.
[34] Panchenko and Uspenskii, 'Ivan Groznyi i Petr Velikii', pp. 66–78.
[35] Bakhtin, *Rabelais*, pp. 270–1: see also Likhachev, Panchenko and Ponyrko, *Smekh v drevnei Rusi*, pp. 48–9.

course of popular uprisings in seventeenth-century Russia.[36] Like those of
Ivan Groznyi, the tortures and executions conducted by Bolotnikov and Tsarevich Peter in the name of Tsar Dimitry involved ritualistic humiliation of
the victims. The casting down of nobles from the tops of towers, or from
city walls and bridges, clearly involved their symbolic debasement, while the
hanging of their bodies upside down echoed carnivalesque overturning and
reversal.

The throwing of victims from towers (*raskat*) may have involved an
element of audience participation. According to R. G. Skrynnikov, such punishments asssumed the form of 'popular reprisals', in which the crowd
assembled at the foot of the tower was allowed to decide whether or not
each victim was to be hurled to the ground.[37] An account of executions of
this kind in Astrakhan', probably written later in the seventeenth century,
describes how the crowd were invited to decide the fate of each prisoner.[38]
Such punishments were subsequently recalled with mixed feelings. In 1623,
when Vasilii Ivanov, a priest in the town of Kashira, advocated a more democratic form of administration, involving consultation of the community (*mir*),
his enemies claimed that the priest's concept of justice derived from the
period of Tsarevich Peter's rule, and that he 'wanted to kill nobles and *deti
boyarskie* and throw them from towers'.[39]

It is not clear how relations developed at Putivl' between Tsarevich Peter
and Prince Shakhovskoi and the other magnates. Skrynnikov describes Peter's arrival as constituting a kind of coup by the cossacks within the rebel
camp.[40] The numerous executions which followed Peter's arrival at Putivl'
suggest that they were a result of the cossacks' influence. On the other hand,
Skrynnikov argues, by assuming the role of *de facto* regent for the absent
Dimitry, Peter was obliged to accept the advice of a 'boyar duma' comprising
Prince Shakhovskoi, Prince Telyatevskii, the Princes Mosal'skii and other
prominent noblemen who were present at Putivl'. Peter also – unlike Bolotnikov, in Skrynnikov's assessment – began to allocate landed estates to his
supporters.[41] But Skrynnikov provides no evidence that the titled nobles who
formed Peter's 'suite' at Putivl' were in any meaningful sense a 'boyar
duma'; and Peter at least nominally acted in Tsar Dimitry's name.

Shakhovskoi took advantage of Peter's arrival at Putivl' in order to renew
his attempts to gain support from Poland. On 26 December the Poles told
Shuiskii's envoys in Craców that Peter was sending ambassadors to the king.

---

[36] Rosovetskii, 'Ustnaya proza', pp. 90–2.
[37] Skrynnikov, *Smuta v Rossii*, pp. 220–1.
[38] Smirnov, *Vosstanie Bolotnikova*, pp. 251–2. Such executions are also described by eyewit-
    nesses of Razin's capture of Astrakhan' in 1670 (see Plate 2).
[39] Stanislavskii, ed., 'Novye dokumenty', nos. 8–11, pp. 80–1.
[40] Skrynnikov, *Smuta v Rossii*, pp. 153–4.
[41] *Ibid.*, pp. 156–7, cf. Koretskii, *Formirovanie krepostnogo prava*, pp. 268–75.

Plate 2 The *raskat*: victims are thrown from the top of a tower in the Astrakhan′ kremlin. Detail from a contemporary engraving of the capture of Astrakhan′ by Sten′ka Razin in 1670

Janusz Ostrozhskii had received a letter from Putivl′ to say that Peter's envoys were on their way to Kiev.[42] The Russian envoys declared that Peter must be an impostor, and demanded that the Poles should not offer him any assistance. The Poles, however, saw the new pretender as a useful bargaining

[42] *SIRIO*, vol. 137, pp. 330, 346, cf. p. 352.

counter in their negotiations for the release of the Mniszechs and other Poles still held in Russia. They hinted that they might be less inclined to support 'Dmitryashka and Petrushka' if the hostages were freed.[43]

It was probably after his arrival in Putivl' that Peter's new advisors found it expedient to provide their protégé with a convincing 'biography'. As we have already noted, when Peter first appeared on the Volga in the spring of 1606, he claimed simply to be the son of Tsar Fedor. Jacques Margeret, who left Russia in September 1606, tells us that Peter said he had been secretly replaced by the baby girl who became Tsarevna Feodosiya.[44] In Margeret's account, it is not clear who substituted Feodosiya for Peter, or when, or why. In December 1606 the Russian envoys to Poland were told by their hosts that 'this Peter says that when he was born, he was replaced by a daughter on Boris Godunov's orders, so that he should not have the kingdom'.[45] At the next audience, one of the envoys, Prince Grigorii Volkonskii, recalled that his own sisters had been in attendance on the tsaritsa at the time of Feodosiya's birth, and he claimed that if any substitution had taken place, he would have known about it.[46] The Russian envoys poured scorn on the idea that it would have been possible for a child to have been secretly substituted in the Russian royal household.[47]

Various other versions of Peter's biography appear to have gained currency at this time. According to Niemojewski, Peter was the son of Tsar Fedor, and Boris Godunov had wanted to kill him, just as he had killed Dimitry,

but the mother of this Petrashka noticed this and spread the rumour that he had died, and in his place they buried some little girl who had died; Petrashka himself was given to a certain simple woman to bring up, and then, when he was older, the boy joined the Don cossacks and remained amongst them in concealment until the present time.[48]

Kostomarov cites a more detailed version of Peter's story, in which the new-born tsarevich was substituted at birth by his mother, Irina, to protect him from Boris. This account, which Kostomarov found in a manuscript in the Krasiński library in Warsaw, bears certain similarities to those versions of the biography of the First False Dimitry in which his mother saved the tsarevich by substituting another boy:

The wife of Tsar Fedor Ivanovich feared her brother Boris, who already aimed at the throne. The time came for her to give birth. She gave birth to a son. But to prevent

[43] Ibid., pp. 345–6.
[44] Margeret, The Russian Empire, p. 71.
[45] SIRIO, vol. 137, p. 345. This information appeared to have reached the Poles from Janusz Ostrozhskii, the son of the governor of Kiev: pp. 346, 352.
[46] Ibid., p. 351.
[47] Ibid., pp. 345, 351.
[48] Nemoevskii, 'Zapiski', p. 119.

Boris from harming the infant she substituted for him a girl, said that she had given birth to a daughter, and gave her son to Andrei Shchelkalov to bring up, and entrusted him to the guardianship of Prince Mstislavskii. The tsarevich lived for eighteen months with the wife of Shchelkalov, who brought him up as her own son, then he was given to Fedor (or Grigorii) Vasil'evich Godunov, who also knew the secret; he lived with him for two years, then handed him over to a monastery, not far from Vladimir on the River Klyaz'ma, and the abbot there taught the child to read and write. When he had learned to read and write, the abbot wrote to ... Vasil'evich Godunov, thinking that the boy was his son, but he was no longer alive, and his relatives said: 'our nephew (i.e. kinsman) did not have a son; we don't know where this boy has come from'. And they turned to Boris, who wrote to the abbot, asking him to send the boy to him. And they took the boy to Boris. But the tsarevich guessed that something bad was threatening him, and he escaped *en route,* fled to Prince Baryatinskii and took refuge with him, and later ran off to join the Don cossacks, where he declared himself.[49]

Kostomarov does not tell us anything about the provenance or date of his source, but he suggests that this story was devised and spread by Prince Shakhovskoi after the latter had adopted Peter as a figurehead for his rebellion.[50]

There is another, less well known version of Peter's history in a Belorussian manuscript which was discovered by the historian Bodyanskii in the Poznań public library and published by him in 1846.[51] This is dated January 1607 and is in the form of a report of the interrogation of 'the Muscovite, Peter-the-Bear' (Niedźwiadko, Medved'ko), who had appeared in Orsha, claiming to be the son of Tsar Fedor. This man said that when he was born his mother Irina, fearing her brother Boris, had hidden the baby boy and told Boris that she had given birth to a monster, half bear and half human.[52] Irina gave the boy Peter to a peasant woman, a widow called Hannah, who lived in the village of Protoshino, 30 versts from Moscow, and who told her neighbours that he was an orphan who had been found by the wayside. The boy lived with Hannah until he reached the age of reason, and Irina then told Boris that she had given birth to a daughter.[53] When Fedor died – the tale continues – Boris succeeded to the throne, and put Irina into a convent. Later Boris learned from his wise women that Tsarevich Dimitry, whom he thought he had killed, was alive. When rumours started to spread in Moscow that

---

[49] Kostomarov, *Smutnoe vremya,* pp. 291–2.

[50] *Ibid.,* p. 291.

[51] Bodyanskii, 'O poiskakh moikh', pp. 3–6.

[52] There is clear folklore influence on this part of the story. The hero of some Russian folk-tales, Ivashko or Ivanko Medvedko (Ivan-the-Bear), is half-bear, half-human, having been born to a human mother, with a bear for a father. For two tales with this motif, see Afanas'ev, *Narodnye russkie skazki,* vol. 1, pp. 303–7, 338–40. The Russian for bear is *medved'*; *niedźwiadek* is the Polish for bear-cub.

[53] Bodyanskii, 'O poiskakh moikh', pp. 3–4. This last point makes little sense, as Medved'ko has earlier said that Irina told Boris that she had given birth to a monster.

Tsarevich Dimitry was in the Crimea, Boris went to his sister and asked her whether she knew anything about the truth of these rumours. Irina replied that it was true that Dimitry was alive, but she did not know where he was. Boris was angry, and struck his sister so hard that she died instantly.[54]

Later Peter was adopted by a *strelets* called Fedor from Astrakhan', who had come to Moscow on the tsar's orders, and he went with him to Astrakhan' in the hope of finding out about his uncle Tsarevich Dimitry. He lived with this *strelets* in Astrakhan' for two years before Godunov's death, without revealing his identity to anyone. But when Dimitry came to the throne after Godunov's death, Peter decided to go to him in Moscow. He asked a merchant from Astrakhan', Koshel, to take him to Moscow in his ship. When Koshel expressed some reluctance to do so, Peter explained that he was the son of Tsar Fedor, and Koshel then agreed to give him a passage. They reached Moscow, however, on the day after Dimitry's murder. Because of the upheaval in the capital, Koshel returned straightaway to Astrakhan', but Peter stayed in Moscow with a butcher called Ivan on Pokrovskaya street. When Shuiskii became tsar, rumours spread in Moscow that Tsarevich Dimitry was alive and living in Lithuania, and that a German had been killed in his place. Peter then decided to go and find Dimitry. He travelled to Smolensk in the company of some merchants, and stayed there with a merchant called Bogdan Kushner, who traded across the Lithuanian frontier. Peter went with Bogdan's goods to the village of Vasil'evich, near the border, and there met a Lithuanian, Stepan Logun, from the village of Romanovo. He told Logun that he wanted to go to Lithuania to meet his uncle, Tsar Dimitry Ivanovich, and Logun took him over the border at night to Romanovo.[55]

There is much that is puzzling about this report, and historians have interpreted it in different ways. Bodyanskii himself argued that this Medved'ko could not have been Peter-Ileika.[56] S. F. Platonov regarded 'Niedźwiadko, who was sometimes confused with Ileika', as one of the petty cossack pretenders who were denounced by the Second False Dimitry in 1608.[57] The Polish historian Hirschberg, however, did identify Peter-Ileika with Medved'ko, and was able to add some information about his presence in Orsha, taken, apparently, from unpublished Polish sources. Hirschberg states that while Tsarevich Peter was at Putivl', his supporters tried to spread rumours in Poland about him. To this end he was brought to Orsha at the end of December 1606 by two Polish soldiers, Pan Zenovich and Pan Senkevich,

---

[54] *Ibid.*, p. 4. Peter Khrushchov had told a similar story about Irina to the First False Dimitry in September 1604: *SGGiD*, vol. 2, p. 178. See above, ch. 2, p. 61.

[55] Bodyanskii, 'O poiskakh moikh', pp. 4–6.

[56] *Ibid.*, pp. 42–4. Bodyanskii's own theory is that Peter-the-Bear subsequently became the Second False Dimitry: *ibid.*, pp. 44–5. See below, ch. 6, p. 164.

[57] Platonov, *Ocherki*, p. 453, n. 105 to pp. 250–2.

who claimed to have accidentally met him in the village of Romanovo when they were travelling to Orsha from Mogilev. They had taken him to Andrzej Sapieha, the governor of Orsha, to whom he had told his story. Sapieha had made a transcript of his account and sent it to King Sigismund. He had intended to send Peter himself to the royal court, but the soldiers managed to disappear from Orsha together with the 'tsarevich'.[58]

R. G. Skrynnikov also identifies Peter-Ileika with Peter-the-Bear. Skrynnikov asserts that the biographical information which Peter provided in Belorussia in January 1607 corresponds in its essential points with Ileika Korovin's testimony to Shuiskii in October 1607,[59] but this is very doubtful. Peter-Ileika, like Peter-the-Bear, had lived for a time in Astrakhan′ with a *strelets*; and when Dimitry came to the throne, both Peter-the-Bear and Peter-Ileika sailed up the Volga to meet him: but the similarity in their stories ends there. It seems inherently improbable that Peter-Ileika, who, as we have seen, was in the process of establishing formal diplomatic relations with King Sigismund in December 1606, should have taken the risk of leaving Putivl′ to go to Orsha in person. Medved′ko may have been an agent of Peter-Ileika who was simply 'testing the ground' in Orsha with regard to Polish support for the latter. The very crudeness of his story, however, suggests that he was a separate and independent pretender, possibly a cossack from the Volga who knew about Peter-Ileika's pretence, but did not know that the latter had turned up in Putivl′ in the autumn of 1606. Later Polish sources confuse Peter-Ileika with Peter-Medved′ko,[60] but this is not surprising, since news about both pretenders must have reached Cracow at about the same time in the winter of 1606–7.

From his headquarters at Putivl′, Peter began in the winter of 1606/7 to extend his authority to other parts of the Seversk lands. On 31 December the Poles told the Russian envoys in Cracow that the governor of Mstislavl′ in Belorussia had written to inform them that 'Peter, who calls himself the son of Grand Duke Fedor, is acquiring the Muscovite state for Dimitry, who is said to be dead, but is alive; and this Peter has beleaguered the Seversk land as far as the forest of Bryansk, and has captured some towns.'[61] In

---

[58] Girshberg, *Marina Mnishek*, pp. 49–50. See also Nazarov and Florya, who accept Hirschberg's identification of Peter-Medved′ko with Peter-Ileika, and assert that the probable aim of his visit to Belorussia was to attempt to gain military support from Polish nobles: 'Krest′-yanskoe vosstanie', p. 339.

[59] Skrynnikov, *Smuta v Rossii*, p. 162, n. 23a.

[60] For example, a draft speech of Leo Sapieha to the *Sejm* in 1611 refers to Bolotnikov's companion at Tula as 'Peter the Bear-Cub' (Piotr Niedźwiadek, Petr Medvezhenok): Lyubavskii, 'Litovskii Kantsler', pp. 9, 10. The 'History of the False Dimitry' describes Petr Fedorovich, Bolotnikov's ally at Putivl′, as Nedvyadko: *RIB*, vol. 1, col. 122. The Belorussian *Barkulabovo Chronicle* refers to a pretender called Nedvedok who appeared in Russia in 1607: *PSRL*, vol. 32, p. 192 (Mal′tsev, 'Barkulabovskaya letopis′', p. 318).

[61] *SIRIO*, vol. 137, pp. 356–7.

January 1607 a substantial force of Zaporozhian cossacks arrived at Putivl',
and in February Peter moved his troops from Putivl' to Tula, in order to
offer support to Bolotnikov, who was besieged by Shuiskii's forces in nearby
Kaluga. An attempt by the cossacks to lift the siege of Kaluga led to their
defeat by Shuiskii's troops at the battle of the River Vyrka, and they retreated
to Tula. It was not until another two months had passed that the insurgents
at Tula again attempted to relieve Kaluga. This time they enjoyed greater
military success, at the battle of Pchel'na on 3 May 1607. Bolotnikov was
able to break out of Kaluga and rout the remains of the besieging army,
before withdrawing the main body of his troops to Tula. Shuiskii regrouped
his forces in Moscow, and set out again against the rebels at the end of May.
Peter sent forces commanded by Bolotnikov and Prince Andrei Telyatevskii
to meet them. Tsar Dimitry's men were defeated on the River Vosma, near
Kashira, and again on the River Voron'ya, outside Tula. They retreated to
Tula and prepared to withstand a siege by Shuiskii's forces. On 30 June Tsar
Vasilii and his main army arrived outside the walls of the fortress, and the
siege began.[62]

The lower Volga: Tsaritsyn and Astrakhan'

We left the Carmelite missionaries at Tsaritsyn, on the lower Volga, where
they had arrived in August 1606 in the company of the two Russian envoys
whom Vasilii Shuiskii was sending to Persia. Because of the uprising in
Astrakhan', it was dangerous to continue their voyage downriver. The
ambassadors decided to spend the winter in Tsaritsyn, and insisted that the
Carmelites and the Persian envoy, Zenil Kambey, do likewise.[63] In the winter
of 1606/7 various tensions arose in Tsaritsyn between pro- and anti-Shuiskii
factions.[64] The town governor, F. P. Akinfov, was loyal to Tsar Vasilii, but
many of the inhabitants were on Dimitry's side.[65] Divisions emerged between
the two Russian ambassadors. The senior envoy, Prince I. P. Romodanovskii,
was a staunch partisan of Shuiskii, while the sympathies of the other were
for Dimitry.[66]

---

[62] Skrynnikov, *Smuta v Rossii*, pp. 163–72, 211–17.
[63] Berthold-Ignace, *Histoire*, pp. 153–6; Florencio, *A Persia*, pp. 75–6.
[64] For discussion of events in Tsaritsyn at this time, see Smirnov, *Vosstanie Bolotnikova*,
pp. 245–50.
[65] Berthold-Ignace, *Histoire*, p. 153. For the name of the governor of Tsaritsyn, see Smirnov,
Vosstanie Bolotnikova, p. 247.
[66] Berthold-Ignace, *Histoire*, pp. 160–1. Prince I. P. Romodanovskii had originally been
appointed as ambassador to Persia by the First False Dimitry, but was confirmed in his post
by Shuiskii: Pirling, *Iz smutnogo vremeni*, p. 65, cf. *PSRL*, vol. 14, p. 71, para. 128. I have
not been able to identify the second envoy.

Rumours that Dimitry was still alive continued to circulate, and seemed to acquire substance: it was even said that the deposed tsar was marching on Moscow at the head of a mighty army to reclaim his throne.[67] On Whit Monday (3 June N.S.) three messengers from Astrakhan' arrived at Tsaritsyn and confirmed these rumours, not only in words, but also by producing a letter ostensibly written in Dimitry's own hand, calling on all his subjects to retain the loyalty they had sworn towards him as their legitimate sovereign. Their arrival served as a spark to ignite the discontent with Shuiskii's representatives which had long been evident in the town. Governor Akinfov, together with Ambassador Romodanovskii, barely succeeded in suppressing the first manifestations of unrest. Two days later, a new and better organised uprising took place. In the middle of the night, roused by the sound of trumpets, the people of Tsaritsyn rushed to the main square, where they assembled in bands. At daybreak they mounted an assault on the fortress and on the ambassadors' residence and the houses of those nobles who supported Shuiskii. They imprisoned Akinfov, Romodanovskii and others. The second ambassador was made governor, and the insurgents swore loyalty to Dimitry. The deposed governor was bound and sent to Astrakhan' with an armed escort, whose commander was instructed to inform Tsarevich Ivan Augustus of all that had happened, and to request him to send immediate troop reinforcements to Tsaritsyn. On his arrival at Astrakhan', Akinfov was tried, sentenced to death and executed.[68] Russian sources confirm the Carmelites' account of the fate of the governor of Tsaritsyn. In a petition addressed to Tsar Michael Romanov in April 1618, Fedor Akinfov's son Ivan described how 'when a rogue on the lower Volga called himself Tsarevich Ivan Augustus, then, sire, the people of Tsaritsyn, the *strel'tsy* and cossacks, bound my father and sent him to the rogue at Astrakhan', and the rogue executed my father'.[69]

Soon after the rising in Tsaritsyn, a judge arrived in the town, who had been sent from Astrakhan' by Tsarevich Ivan Augustus to try the prisoners. He put some to death and condemned others to flogging. Ambassador Romodanovskii was amongst those who were merely flogged: the tsarevich himself wanted to preside over his trial in Astrakhan'. The judge assured the people of Tsaritsyn that 400 soldiers were on their way to reinforce them, and returned to Astrakhan'. The Carmelite fathers entrusted him with a letter to

[67] Berthold-Ignace, *Histoire*, p. 182.
[68] *Ibid.*, pp. 182–6.
[69] Stanislavskii, ed., 'Novye dokumenty', pp. 75–6, 79–80. See also the petition of Ivan Akinfov and his brother Arkhip, dated 9 March 1627, requesting Tsar Michael's permission to rebury their father: *VIB*, pp. 318–19. See also Smirnov, *Vosstanie Bolotnikova*, pp. 247–9, 250; Skrynnikov, *Smuta v Rossii*, pp. 222–3.

Ivan Augustus, asking him to grant them permission to come to Astrakhan', and thence to continue their journey to Persia.[70]

Two days after the judge left for Astrakhan', a detachment of twenty-five soldiers arrived at Tsaritsyn, an advance party from an army of 7,000 men that Shuiskii was sending against Astrakhan'. They did not know that Tsaritsyn had defected to Dimitry, and entered the town quite unsuspecting. They were seized and put in irons, and their leaders were thrown from the top of a tower. The next day, another band of twenty-five men encountered the same fate. On the evening of the following day the entire army arrived at Tsaritsyn. They were taken by surprise by the townspeople, who were reinforced by the 400 soldiers who had been sent from Astrakhan', and by a band of cossacks. Shuiskii's troops were forced to retreat to the opposite bank of the Volga. The next day the defenders of Tsaritsyn launched an attack on the government army but, having lost the advantage of surprise and being heavily outnumbered, they had to withdraw to the town. Their opponents, however, misled by a prisoner into believing that an army of 10,000 soldiers was daily expected from Astrakhan', failed to follow up their victory. Shuiskii's troops saw a detachment of cavalry heading towards them and, apparently assuming that this was the vanguard of the army from Astrakhan', they re-embarked and retreated upriver, abandoning their arms and provisions in the course of their hasty flight.[71] (The government troops may have come from Saratov, as there is evidence that Sheremetev had requested assistance from the Saratov *voevody* Z. I. Saburov and V. V. Anichkov.)[72] The troop of cavalrymen whose approach had put Shuiskii's army to flight turned out to comprise a mere 200 men and, according to the Carmelites, they were escorting an envoy whom Dimitry was sending to his brother in Astrakhan' to inform him of his military successes. (This may be a reference to the lifting of the siege of Kaluga.) The news of Dimitry's victory, coming so soon after their own rout of Shuiskii's army, led to great rejoicing in Tsaritsyn.[73]

Soon afterwards letters were received from Ivan Augustus, granting permission for the missionaries to continue their voyage, and instructing the authorities in Tsaritsyn to send them immediately to Astrakhan'. The Persian envoy Zenil Kambey was to accompany them, as was the imprisoned Russian ambassador, Prince Romodanovskii. Since Sheremetev's besieging army was still encamped some distance upstream from Astrakhan', the pretender sent a detachment of 2,000 cossacks to protect the travellers.[74]

---

[70] Berthold-Ignace, *Histoire*, pp. 186–7.
[71] *Ibid.*, pp. 187–90.
[72] Gnevushev, ed., 'Akty', p. 174.
[73] Berthold-Ignace, *Histoire*, pp. 190–3.
[74] *Ibid.*, p. 193.

The Carmelites left Tsaritsyn on 24 July.[75] On the ninth day of their voyage, when they were still two days' journey from Astrakhan', the flotilla encountered Ivan Augustus, who was sailing upstream from Astrakhan' with 7,000 men to join Dimitry. The tsarevich was accompanied by Father Francisco da Costa, a Portuguese monk who was returning to Rome from Persia;[76] and by two Persian ambassadors, one of whom was assigned to Pope Paul V, and the other to the King of Poland. Ivan Augustus ordered his fleet to halt, and set up camp on the bank of the Volga in order to receive Zenil Kambey and the Carmelite fathers. They spent two days together, and the pretender acted very graciously towards the missionaries.[77]

During this halt, however, the captive Russian ambassador was murdered by the pretender's troops, in spite of the tsarevich's own expression of his willingness to pardon him as a result of the missionaries' intercession on his behalf. Ivan Augustus was however apparently unable to control his own followers: 'the ferocious soldiers whom he commanded, carried away by their fury against all supporters of the usurper, threw themselves on the ambassador and massacred him without pity. It was almost a revolt. It subsided of its own accord as a result of the shedding of the hated blood, and Dimitry's brother found it prudent to acquiesce.'[78]

Very little of the detailed information in the Carmelite reports of these events can be confirmed or refuted by Russian sources. As we have already noted, the *New Chronicle* states that Prince Romodanovskii was killed at Tsaritsyn along with the governor, Fedor Akinfov, but it attributes their deaths to the action of Tsarevich Peter's cossacks as they retreated down the Volga.[79] The fact of Tsarevich Ivan Augustus' voyage up the Volga is confirmed by the 'Karamzin Chronograph', which states that in the year 7116 [1607/8] 'rogues' from Astrakhan' came to Saratov with 'Tsarevich Ivan Ivanovich, the son of Tsar Ivan Vasil'evich'. They laid siege to Saratov, but were repulsed by the garrison, commanded by Z. I. Saburov and V. V. Anichkov, and retreated to Astrakhan', where the boyar F. I. Sheremetev was encamped on the island of Balchik.[80] As Russian historians have pointed out, the chronograph entry should probably be dated 7115 [1606/7], since Sheremetev left Balchik in October 1607.[81] I. I. Smirnov concludes that the evidence of the Carmelites confirms that the siege of Saratov by Ivan

---

[75] *Ibid.*
[76] *Ibid.*, p. 194; for further details on da Costa, see *A Chronicle of the Carmelites*, vol. 1, pp. 80–93.
[77] Berthold-Ignace, *Histoire*, pp. 194–5.
[78] *Ibid.*, p. 195.
[79] *PSRL*, vol. 14, p. 71, para. 128.
[80] Popov, ed., *Izbornik*, p. 339 (*VIB*, p. 119).
[81] Smirnov, *Vosstanie Bolotnikova*, pp. 244–5; *VIB*, n. 110, pp. 361–2.

Augustus took place in the summer of 1607.[82] On the basis of the Carmelites' assertion that Ivan Augustus was going up the Volga to join Dimitry, both I. I. Smirnov and R. G. Skrynnikov infer that he was planning to come to the assistance of Bolotnikov, who was then besieged at Tula.[83] It is possible that Ivan Augustus' journey upriver was undertaken in response to the messenger from 'Dimitry' who, according to the Carmelites, had passed through Tsaritsyn *en route* to Astrakhan'.

After their encounter with Tsarevich Ivan Augustus, the missionaries continued on their way on 25 July/4 August.[84] The pretender had reinforced the Carmelites' escort with a further 1,000 cossacks of his own, to defend them against possible attack by Sheremetev's army, which lay between them and Astrakhan'. Their flotilla was indeed ambushed, but after a fierce fight they succeeded in putting the government troops to flight.[85] The dating of this battle in the materials of the Carmelite mission appears to correspond to an episode described in the petition to Tsar Vasilii of Prokofii Vrazskii, an interpreter from Astrakhan', dated 1 March 1608. Vrazskii states that on 30 July 1607 Sheremetev had sent troops against 'the traitors from Astrakhan' and the rebel (*vorovskie*) cossacks from Tsaritsyn' who had gone past his camp.[86]

On 28 July/7 August 1607 the missionaries finally reached Astrakhan'. They were warmly welcomed by the governor, Prince Khvorostinin, whom they described as 'one of the foremost dukes or satraps of Russia'. The next day, at a public audience, he asked them whether they had with them any letters from Dimitry. When they gave a negative reply, he said regretfully that he could not permit them to travel further without permission from Dimitry's brother. In vain did the Carmelites refer to their meeting with Tsarevich Ivan Augustus, his favourable dealings with them, and his verbal assurances. The governor was adamant: they would have to remain at Astrakhan' until he had written to the tsarevich and received his reply. The pretender's permission was soon received, and the Carmelites finally left Astrakhan' for Persia at the end of August.[87]

I. I. Smirnov, who used the Carmelites' reports only in the very brief versions provided by Pierling and the author of the English 'Chronicle', notes that they provide valuable information about the relationship between the governor of Astrakhan', Prince Khvorostinin, and the pretender Ivan

[82] Smirnov, *Vosstanie Bolotnikova*, pp. 246–7.
[83] *Ibid.*, p. 247; Skrynnikov, *Smuta v Rossii*, p. 223.
[84] Florencio, *A Persia*, p. 79.
[85] Berthold-Ignace, *Histoire*, pp. 195–8; Florencio, *A Persia*, pp. 79–80.
[86] Gnevushev, ed., 'Akty', no. 96, p. 204 (*VIB*, pp. 237–8). For information about Vrazskii, see Smirnov, *Vosstanie Bolotnikova*, pp. 234–6.
[87] Berthold-Ignace, *Histoire*, pp. 198–202; Florencio, *A Persia*, pp. 80–4; *A Chronicle of the Carmelites*, vol. 1, p. 112.

Augustus. The fact that Khvorostinin would not allow the missionaries to continue on their way until he had obtained the tsarevich's agreement suggests that he 'regarded himself as a person subordinate to the "tsarevich" Ivan Augustus', and that his relationship with the pretender was similar to that which developed at Putivl' between Prince Shakhovskoi and Tsarevich Peter.[88] The fuller accounts of the Carmelites' journey contained in the French and Spanish histories of their mission enable us to confirm and amplify Smirnov's view that the insurgents in Astrakhan' had established their own organs of power, including a system of justice with trials, judges and a range of sentences for their political opponents.[89] It is clear from the Carmelites' reports that the writ of Tsarevich Ivan Augustus extended up the Volga at least as far as Tsaritsyn, to which he sent his 'judge' to try the 'traitors' to Tsar Dimitry.

The siege of Tula

At Tula, the forces of Bolotnikov were united for the first time with those of Tsarevich Peter. R. G. Skrynnikov suggests that this meant a demotion for Bolotnikov. Prince Andrei Telyatevskii, Bolotnikov's former master, had become Peter's chief general, and in the hierarchical structure of Peter's court Bolotnikov could not lay claim to membership of the 'boyar duma', although he still enjoyed great authority among the insurgents.[90] A contemporary Polish report claimed that many people in the Seversk lands wanted Peter to be their tsar, but it also noted that he was universally regarded as an impostor.[91]

The cossacks remained a major force in the insurgent camp at Tula, just as they had been at Putivl', and executions of 'traitors' to Tsar Dimitry continued to take place in the besieged fortress.[92] After the battle of Pchel'na the prisoners were taken to Tula, where, according to one Russian source, Peter ordered them to be executed at the rate of ten a day or more, having some thrown alive to wild animals for them to eat.[93] Other sources enable us to establish that these animals were bears. The petition which Ishei Barashev, a Tatar *murza* (nobleman) in Russian service, submitted to Shuiskii on 13 October 1607, states that when he was a prisoner at Tula he was subjected to all kinds of tortures: not only was he flogged with the knout, taken to the

---

[88] Smirnov, *Vosstanie Bolotnikova*, p. 253; for a similar assessment, see Skrynnikov, *Smuta v Rossii*, p. 222.

[89] Smirnov, *Vosstanie Bolotnikova*, pp. 250–3.

[90] Skrynnikov, *Smuta v Rossii*, pp. 157, 211–12, 219.

[91] Nazarov and Florya, 'Krest'yanskoe vosstanie', pp. 347–8.

[92] Skrynnikov, *Smuta v Rossii*, pp. 220–1.

[93] *VIB*, p. 106 ('Iz "Kazanskogo skazaniya" ').

top of a tower, and put into prison, but he was also mauled by a bear.[94] In a petition of October 1633 the *syn boyarskii* Bogdan Koshkin claimed that while imprisoned by Tsarevich Peter at Tula he had been 'tortured by various tortures' and set upon by bears.[95] R. G. Skrynnikov recalls that torture by bears was also enjoyed by Ivan Groznyi, who had used them to kill monks suspected of treason, in scenes that resembled the Ancient Roman arenas.[96] Even more obviously than the other methods of torture and execution in which Peter imitated his presumed grandfather, this baiting with bears derived from the carnivalesque popular culture associated with the *skomorokhi*.[97]

The fullest narrative account of the siege of Tula is provided by Conrad Bussow, whose son was in the beleaguered fortress. Bussow describes the dreadful situation in which the defenders of the town found themselves by the autumn of 1607. Shuiskii had built a dam on the River Upa downstream from Tula, which caused the town to flood. All communications were completely cut off, so that the inhabitants suffered terrible hunger and hardship. The citizens were reduced to eating cats and dogs, carrion from the streets, and the hides of horses, cows and oxen. Prices of rye and salt rocketed, and many people died of starvation and associated illnesses.[98]

Tsar Dimitry still failed to put in an appearance. According to Bussow, Bolotnikov continued to write and send messengers to Poland requesting aid, but there was no response. This caused growing disenchantment in the besieged fortress. Bussow relates that, 'The cossacks and all the inhabitants of Tula were very embittered against Bolotnikov and Shakhovskoi and they wanted to seize them and send them to the enemy, Shuiskii, for having invented such a fairytale and assuring them that Dimitry was still alive.'[99] Even Bolotnikov himself, apparently, was by now beginning to have doubts about the existence of Dimitry in Poland. According to Bussow, he repeated to his followers the tale of how he had met a young man in Poland who claimed to be Dimitry, and how he had sworn a solemn oath to serve him loyally. Bolotnikov then admitted the weakness of his testimony: 'Whether he was the true Dimitry or not, I cannot tell, for I never saw him on the throne in Moscow. According to descriptions of the man who occupied the throne, he looked exactly like him.'[100] Then the besieged Tulans turned on Prince Shakhovskoi, and threw him into prison, saying that they would not release him until Dimitry arrived to rescue them. If Dimitry did not appear,

[94] *VIB*, p. 227.
[95] Koretskii, Solov'eva and Stanislavskii, eds., 'Dokumenty', pp. 38–9.
[96] Skrynnikov, *Smuta v Rossii*, p. 221; Berry and Crummey, eds., *Rude and Barbarous Kingdom*, pp. 283–4.
[97] Belkin, *Russkie skomorokhi*, pp. 147–8; Zguta, *Russian Minstrels*, pp. 111–12.
[98] Bussov, *Moskovskaya khronika*, p. 143.
[99] *Ibid.*, pp. 143–4.
[100] *Ibid.*, p. 144.

they would hand Shakhovskoi over to Shuiskii as the main instigator of the civil war and of all the bloodshed it had caused, since it was he who had insisted that Dimitry had escaped from Moscow on 17 May 1606.[101]

Eventually, according to Bussow, Tsarevich Peter and Bolotnikov opened negotiations with Shuiskii. They offered to surrender the fortress immediately if he agreed to spare their lives; if not, they would hold out to the bitter end. Shuiskii consented to their terms, and on 'the day of Simon Judas' Tula surrendered to Tsar Vasilii.[102] Bussow attributes to Bolotnikov a typically flowery gesture and speech. Prostrating himself before Shuiskii in his tent, Bolotnikov put his sword to his neck, and said:

I have been true to the oath which I swore in Poland to the man who called himself Dimitry. Whether he was Dimitry or not, I cannot tell, for I had never seen him before. I served him on trust, but he has deserted me, and now I am here in your power and at your command. If you want to kill me, here is my own sword ready for the deed; if, on the other hand, you are willing to pardon me on my oath and promise, then I shall serve you faithfully, just as I have served him by whom I have been deserted.[103]

Shuiskii again agreed to spare Bolotnikov's life, but did not keep his promise, as both Bolotnikov and Tsarevich Peter were subsequently put to death.[104]

Bussow's account of the surrender of Tula has generally been regarded by historians as reliable, when due allowance is made for some artistic licence on the author's part.[105] A. A. Zimin, however, prefers the evidence of Russian sources, such as the Karamzin Chronograph, which state that the Tulans themselves entered into negotiations with Shuiskii, offering to hand over Bolotnikov and Tsarevich Peter if the rest of the defenders were spared. Zimin speculates that these 'capitulators' in Tula were headed by Prince Telyatevskii and Prince Shakhovskoi, whom he regards as typical 'noble fellow-travellers' in the 'peasant war'. Bolotnikov himself, in Zimin's somewhat tendentious view, remained until his death 'an uncompromising fighter against the serf-owner government of Vasilii Shuiskii'.[106] I. I. Smirnov and R. G. Skrynnikov see some degree of truth in both the Russian and the foreign

---

[101] *Ibid.*
[102] *Ibid.*, p. 146. The 'day of Simon Judas' was 18/28 October. This date for the fall of Tula is also found in some Russian sources, but most historians prefer to accept the date of 10 October (O.S.) which is found in contemporary official documents: Smirnov, *Vosstanie Bolotnikova*, pp. 467–8.
[103] Bussov, *Moskovskaya khronika*, p. 146.
[104] *Ibid.*, p. 147.
[105] For reviews of the sources and historiography relating to the fall of Tula, see Smirnov, *Vosstanie Bolotnikova*, pp. 469–92; Zimin, 'I. I. Bolotnikov', pp. 52–64; Skrynnikov, *Smuta v Rossii*, pp. 234–41.
[106] Zimin, 'I. I. Bolotnikov', pp. 63–4.

sources. Skrynnikov argues that Shuiskii negotiated simultaneously both with Bolotnikov and with some of the inhabitants of Tula. However in the event the Tulans let Shuiskii's troops into the city and handed their leaders over to Tsar Vasilii.[107]

Shuiskii did not execute Bolotnikov and Peter immediately after the surrender of Tula, and this was seen by I. I. Smirnov as evidence that Tsar Vasilii had promised clemency to the leaders of the rising.[108] Tsarevich Peter was interrogated straight away, and his confession of his pretence, made 'before the sovereign's boyars and before all the land', was circulated to the provinces in November and December 1607.[109] Peter was executed in Moscow at the end of January 1608, after spending several weeks in prison.[110] Predictably, rumours soon spread that he had escaped death. In April 1609 a Russian agent reported from Lithuania that 'the Petrushka who was besieged at Tula, and who you said had been executed, – that Petrushka, they say, is now alive and in Lithuania, but in what town, he does not know; but they say he really is Tsar Fedor's son; and a peasant was hanged in his stead'.[111] Nothing more, however, appears to have been heard of this rumoured Tsarevich Peter.

Bolotnikov was exiled at the end of February 1608. The Pole Dyamentowski, who was living in Yaroslavl', noted in his diary on 10 March (N.S.) that Bolotnikov was brought through the town on his way to Kargopol'. The local nobles were surprised to see him unchained, and enquired of his escort why he enjoyed such freedom. Bolotnikov, overhearing them, retorted, 'I'll soon put you in chains and sew you into bearskins.'[112] This threat echoes another form of punishment associated with Ivan the Terrible. According to the Pskov chronicler, in 1575 Tsar Ivan had had the disgraced Archbishop Leonid of Novgorod sewn into a bearskin and had set dogs on him.[113] This torture – a variant of the sport of baiting bears with dogs[114] – evidently made a strong impression on the Russian popular imagination. In some texts of the folksong about Ivan and his son, the tsar threatens to sew the boyar Nikita Romanovich into a bearskin and feed him to the dogs.[115] In a treason case of 1626 Tsar Michael was criticised by a prison guard for his weakness in failing to prevent his mother's interference in his marriage plans. Michael had been reluctant

---

[107] Smirnov, *Vosstanie Bolotnikova*, pp. 469–92; Skrynnikov, *Smuta v Rossii*, pp. 234–9.

[108] Smirnov, *Vosstanie Bolotnikova*, p. 491.

[109] *AAE*, vol. 2, no. 81, pp. 173–6 (*VIB*, pp. 222–6); Smirnov, 'Kogda byl kaznen Ileika Muromets?', pp. 111–15.

[110] *VIB*, p. 182. For a review and discussion of the sources relating to Peter's execution, see Smirnov, 'Kogda byl kaznen Ileika Muromets?'

[111] *AI*, vol. 2, no. 199, p. 231.

[112] Dyamentowski, 'Dyariusz', p. 128 (*VIB*, pp. 174–5).

[113] *PL*, vol. 2, p. 262.

[114] See Belkin, *Russkie skomorokhi*, p. 147.

[115] *Istoricheskie pesni XIII–XVI vekov*, nos. 218, 219, pp. 351–7.

to treat his mother harshly, unlike 'former sovereigns' who had sewn such troublemakers into bearskins and baited them with dogs.[116] Bolotnikov's words to his tormentors therefore not only demonstrate his defiance, but also indicate that his notions of an appropriate fate for 'traitor-boyars' may have been derived – like those of Tsarevich Peter – from folk traditions about the rough justice dispensed by Ivan the Terrible.

According to Bussow, Bolotnikov was imprisoned for a time at Kargopol', before being blinded and drowned.[117] R. G. Skrynnikov suggests that Shuiskii's decision to kill Tsarevich Peter and Bolotnikov was taken in response to the threat of a new campaign against Moscow by the Second False Dimitry at the beginning of 1608.[118] Prince Shakhovskoi, however, did not share the fate of Bolotnikov and Peter. Bussow relates indignantly that when Shuiskii entered Tula, Shakhovskoi was released with all the other prisoners in the town jail. Prince Grigorii told the tsar that the insurgents had imprisoned him because they had learned that he planned to transfer his allegiance to Shuiskii. Tsar Vasilii believed him, and let him go free, but Shakhovskoi subsequently switched his loyalty to the Second False Dimitry.[119] Shuiskii's proclamations on the fall of Tula, however, describe Shakhovskoi as surrendering along with the other leaders of the rising,[120] and the *New Chronicle* states that he was sent 'to Kamenoe'.[121] Shakhovskoi's exile was shortlived: Bussow is correct when he says that Prince Grigorii subsequently joined the supporters of the Second False Dimitry. The fate of Prince Telyatevskii is unclear. Bussow states that he defected to Shuiskii at the battle on the River Vosma before the siege of Tula began,[122] but other sources state that he was present during the siege and surrendered with the other leaders.[123]

---

[116] Novombergskii, ed., *Slovo i delo gosudarevy*, vol. 1, no. 30, p. 40.

[117] Bussov, *Moskovskaya khronika*, p. 147; cf. *VIB*, p. 118 ('Iz "Karamzinskogo khronografa" ').

[118] Skrynnikov, *Smuta v Rossii*, pp. 240–1. I. I. Smirnov, by contrast, links the timing of first the despatch to the provinces of Peter's confession, and then his subsequent execution, to the appearance of 'Tsarevich' Fedor Fedorovich at the Second False Dimitry's camp at Bryansk in November 1607, and Dimitry's execution of the rival pretender: Smirnov, 'Kogda byl kaznen Ileika Muromets?', pp. 115–19. On Fedor Fedorovich, see below, ch. 6, pp. 174–5.

[119] Bussov, *Moskovskaya khronika*, p. 147.

[120] *SGGiD*, vol. 2, no. 154, p. 325; *AAE*, vol. 2, no. 81, p. 173 (*VIB*, pp. 221, 222).

[121] *PSRL*, vol. 14, p. 77, para. 150. The editors of the *New Chronicle* index this as Kamennoe gorodishche in Putivl' uezd.

[122] Bussov, *Moskovskaya khronika*, p. 143.

[123] See Solov'ev, *Istoriya Rossii*, vol. 4, pp. 480, 703–4; Skrynnikov, *Smuta v Rossii*, pp. 213–14, 237–8.

Part 3

The final stages of the Troubles

6   The Second False Dimitry: from Starodub to Tushino

Tsar Dimitry at Starodub

The Second False Dimitry appeared in Russia well before the fall of Tula. The pretender revealed himself in the town of Starodub, in the Seversk district, in June 1607.[1]

There has been much debate about the identity of the Second False Dimitry.[2] Shuiskii's government was unable to discover who he was, and referred to him simply as a *vor* (scoundrel, rogue).[3] Years later, the *New Chronicle* reported that no-one knew who the 'scoundrel' was, nor where he came from; it was known only that he did not belong to the nobility ('he was not of service origin'), and it was surmised that he was the son of a priest or a church sexton, because of his familiarity with clerical matters.[4] The view that he was a priest's son was quite widespread among contemporaries: Avraamii Palitsyn calls him 'the priest's son Matyushka Verevkin from the Seversk towns',[5] and one of the pretender's commanders, captured by Shuiskii's men in December 1608, stated under torture that the *soi-disant* tsar was Mit'ka, a priest's son from a church on the Arbat in Moscow.[6] The pretender's clerical connections are also stressed in a chronicle from Novgorod, which names him as Ivashko, and states that he had been a church sexton in Lithuania, and had taught children their letters.[7] Others however did believe him to belong to the petty nobility. The *Piskarev Chronicle* says that he was a *syn boyarskii* called Verevkin from the Seversk region,[8] and the Pole Marchocki

---

[1] For the date of Dimitry's appearance in Starodub, see *RIB*, vol. 1, col. 123; Platonov *Ocherki*, p. 268; Skrynnikov, *Smuta v Rossii*, p. 197.

[2] For the fullest review of the sources, see Ilovaiskii, *Smutnoe vremya*, pp. 289–92.

[3] E.g. *AAE*, vol. 2, no. 90, pp. 183–4; no. 93, pp. 188–90.

[4] *PSRL*, vol. 14, p. 89, para. 195.

[5] Palitsyn, *Skazanie*, p. 116.

[6] *AAE*, vol. 2, no. 94, p. 192; Gnevushev, ed., 'Akty', no. 25, p. 29.

[7] *Novgorodskie letopisi*, pp. 473–4. Other more detailed sources also affirm that the pretender had been a schoolteacher: see below, p. 161.

[8] *PSRL*, vol. 34, p. 212. The surname Verevkin derives from a certain Gavrila Verevkin, whom the *New Chronicle* describes as being a leading supporter of the pretender in Starodub: *PSRL*, vol. 14, p. 76, para. 149; Skrynnikov, *Smuta v Rossii*, p. 199.

describes him as a *syn boyarskii* from Starodub.[9] The most fanciful explanation of his origin was the view, reported in Tot'ma in 1608, that he was
the son of Prince Andrei Kurbskii, the opponent of Ivan the Terrible who
had fled to Lithuania in 1563.[10] Most contemporaries, however, depicted him
as a man of lower-class origins: the Swedes described him as a labourer
(*stratnik, Stratenick, stratenik*), a drummer and former servant of Grishka
Otrep'ev;[11] and a French agent portrayed him as 'a simple soldier, the son
of a blacksmith or coachman'.[12] One Russian source states that he was a
cossack whom Tsarevich Peter and Prince Shakhovskoi secretly dispatched
from Tula to Starodub under cover of darkness during the siege, in the company of the Princes Zasekin.[13] There is general agreement that the Second
False Dimitry was a much coarser and cruder character than his predecessor.
The Pole Maskiewicz describes him as an 'uncouth peasant, foul-mouthed
in his conversation and with vile. habits'.[14]

A number of sources state that Dimitry was of Jewish origin.[15] Metropolitan Isidor of Novgorod described the pretender as 'the Jew (*zhidovin*) Bogdashko' in July 1612,[16] and in November 1613 Tsar Michael's envoys to
Denmark characterised him as 'a Jew by birth' (*rodom zhidovin*).[17] The fact
that Dimitry is said to have been of Jewish origin in official documents of
Michael Romanov's government serves for R. G. Skrynnikov as proof of its
verisimilitude, since Michael's father, Filaret, had been very close to the
Second False Dimitry at Tushino. Skrynnikov also claims that a seventeenth-
century Polish engraving of the pretender depicts him as having Semitic features (see Plate 3).[18]

The Poles alleged that after the pretender's flight from Tushino at the end
of 1609 a Talmud was found among his papers.[19] Similar rumours were
spread after his death at Kaluga in December 1610. Stadnicki states that, 'It
is most probable that this murdered fraudster was a Jew by origin, since
amongst his things in a box they found a Hebrew Talmud, and a number of

[9] Marchocki, *Historya*, p. 6.
[10] *AAE*, vol. 2, no. 91, p. 186.
[11] *Ibid.*, no. 108, p. 210; Forsten, 'Politika Shvetsii', pp. 339–40.
[12] Zholkevskii, *Zapiski*, prilozheniya, no. 21, col. 54.
[13] *VIB*, pp. 108–9.
[14] Maskevich, 'Dnevnik', p. 29; see also *RIB*, vol. 1, col. 514.
[15] See, for example, Widekind, *Historia*, p. 212; Zholkevskii, *Zapiski*, prilozheniya, no. 44, col. 192.
[16] *AAE*, vol. 2, no. 210, p. 357.
[17] *RIB*, vol. 16, no. 99, col. 435; no. 100, col. 467. Cf. *AAE*, vol. 3, no. 29, p. 67. See also Karamzin, *Istoriya*, vol. 3, primechaniya k XII tomu, col. 33, no. 138; Ilovaiskii, *Smutnoe vremya*, p. 290.
[18] Skrynnikov, *Smuta v Rossii*, pp. 201–2. The engraving is reproduced in his 'V to smutnoe vremya . . .', p. 46. There is no evidence that it was taken from life.
[19] *RIB*, vol. 1, p. 527.

Plate 3 The Second False Dimitry. A seventeenth-century Polish engraving

other Hebrew letters and papers written in Hebrew.'[20] It is of course possible that the allegations about Dimitry's Jewishness were untrue, and were made with the sole aim of discrediting him. Russian Orthodoxy regarded Judaism as apostasy, and in the late fifteenth century a 'Judaising' heresy was identified and suppressed in Novgorod and Moscow. There is evidence of hostility to Jews who had come to Russia from the *Rzeczpospolita* with the First False Dimitry. As early as January 1605 Patriarch Iov had accused that pretender

---

[20] Stadnitskii, 'Dnevnik', p. 204. Cf. Karamzin, *Istoriya*, vol. 3, primechaniya k XII tomu, col. 33, no. 138.

of planning to replace Russia's Orthodox churches with 'Latin and Lutheran and Jewish temples (*kostely*)'.[21] And the confirmatory charter (*utverzhdennaya gramota*) of May 1613 on Michael Romanov's election to the throne condemned Grisha Otrep'ev for bringing 'heretics' to Moscow: not only Catholics and Protestants of various types, but also 'deicidal Jews'.[22] Russian literary publicists subsequently criticised the First False Dimitry for having imported Jews as well as Poles and Lithuanians into Muscovy.[23] A Jewish danger was also perceived to have been present in the later stages of the Time of Troubles. In 1611 the author of the patriotic 'New Tale of the Glorious Russian Tsardom' listed 'the kinsmen of Judas, the betrayer of Christ' among the enemies threatening Russia.[24]

In Russian Orthodox culture the suggestion that the Second False Dimitry was a Jew was at least as damaging as the allegations of heresy and necromancy that were made against the First False Dimitry. An interest in Judaism could be seen as a form of that 'anti-behaviour' which was *a priori* attributed to pretenders in Old Russian culture. But whereas the charges of heresy and sorcery were made against the First False Dimitry in his lifetime, the second Dimitry appears to have been accused of Judaism only after his death. The danger of Jewish infiltration was only a minor hazard in the Time of Troubles, compared to that of Catholic domination,[25] and it seems improbable that the allegation of Dimitry's Jewishness should have been invented by the clergy solely in order to discredit him posthumously. Since it does not seem, therefore, that the rumours about his Judaism formed part of an official propaganda campaign against the Second False Dimitry in his lifetime, they may actually have had some factual basis: he may indeed have been a baptised Jew whose conversion to Christianity was only skin-deep. As in the case of the First False Dimitry, an alienation from Orthodoxy may have facilitated the pretender's willingness to play the part of a false tsar.

Some sources describing the origins of the Second False Dimitry are more detailed than the rumours we have previously reviewed, and may therefore be based on more reliable information. In April 1609 a Russian agent informed Michael Shein, the governor of Smolensk, that he had been told in Velizh, in Belorussia, that the pretender was called Bogdashko (a diminutive form of Bogdan). At the time of the murder of the First False Dimitry this Bogdashko had come from Belaya to Velizh, where he claimed that he was the late tsar's personal secretary. He remained in Velizh for six weeks before

---

[21] *AAE*, vol. 2, no. 28, p. 79.

[22] 'Utverzhdennaya gramota', p. 31.

[23] *RIB*, vol. 13, cols. 166, 820, 824–5, 827, 829, 830; Palitsyn, *Skazanie*, pp. 112, 263.

[24] *PLDR*, pp. 36/7.

[25] John Klier undoubtedly exaggerates when he states that alongside fear of Catholicism, Muscovites during the Time of Troubles 'showed equal concern with Judaism': Klier, *Russia Gathers her Jews*, p. 27.

departing for Vitebsk in the company of a Lithuanian, 'and from Vitebsk he went to Poland, and from Poland he declared himself in the scoundrel's name'.[26]

The Polish Jesuit Wielewicki concurs with some of these details. He states that the pretender was a baptised Jew called Bogdanka who had served the First False Dimitry as a clerk, composing letters for him in Russian.[27] After Dimitry's death this man had fled to Lithuania, where he wandered for a few months before turning up in Mogilev. Here an archpriest befriended him. He employed him as a teacher in the Russian school attached to his church, and allowed him to lodge in his house. Bogdanka, however, abused the archpriest's hospitality by having an affair with his wife, whereupon the archpriest beat him and threw him out. After this escapade, Bogdanka decided to return to Russia and assume the role of Tsar Dimitry.[28]

Other sources also state that the pretender was employed as a teacher in a church school, but unlike Wielewicki they do not describe him as a former servant of the First False Dimitry. The Belorussian author of the *Barkulabovo Chronicle* asserts that 'Dimitry Nagoi' first worked as a schoolteacher for a priest in the town of Shklov, then moved to Mogilev, where he taught village children in the school run by the priest Fedor Sasinovich Nikol'skii, and also worked as an odd-job man for the curate Tereshko of the church of St Nicholas. The teacher was poor and badly dressed, wearing an old coat and a sheepskin hat even in summer. 'When they began to recognise that Dimitry Nagoi' as Tsar Dimitry, he fled from Mogilev to the town of Propoisk.[29] Conrad Bussow also describes the pretender as a former schoolteacher and priest's servant from Belorussia.[30] His name was Ivan, and at the time he undertook his pretence he was employed by a Belorussian priest in Shklov. Ivan was a Russian by birth, who had lived in Belorussia for many years and could speak, read and write perfectly in both Russian and Polish.[31]

According to Wielewicki, the idea of passing himself off as Tsar Dimitry, his former master, came to Bogdanka spontaneously after he had been thrown out of the archpriest's house in Mogilev:

Not daring to show his face any longer in Lithuania, Bogdanka decided to return to Russia. He was a cunning and inventive fellow; he knew many of Dimitry's secrets;

---

[26] *AI*, vol. 2, no. 199, p. 231.

[27] Zholkevskii, *Zapiski*, prilozheniya, no. 44, col. 192. Wielewicki's diary is based on the notes of the Jesuit Sawicki who accompanied the First False Dimitry to Russia. See Ilovaiskii, *Smutnoe vremya*, p. 291; Pirling, *Iz smutnogo vremeni*, pp. 255–8.

[28] Zholkevskii, *Zapiski*, prilozheniya, no. 44, col. 192.

[29] *PSRL*, vol. 32, p. 192. On the likely authorship of this chronicle, see *ibid.*, pp. 9–12; Mal'tsev, ed., 'Barkulabovskaya letopis'', pp. 291–5.

[30] Bussow, *Moskovskaya khronika*, p. 175.

[31] *Ibid.*, p. 144. This evidence about the pretender's employment as a teacher in a church school is of course consistent with the assertion of the *New Chronicler* about his clerical knowledge.

he could see that the news of his supposed escape was spreading, and that the Seversk land was in turmoil; therefore he decided to make use of all these circumstances, and to give himself out to be Dimitry.[32]

The *Barkulabovo Chronicle* also implies that the pretender acted independently. Bussow, however, states that the schoolteacher was persuaded to assume the role of Dimitry by friends of the Mniszechs, in response to the desperate pleas of Bolotnikov and Prince Shakhovskoi that someone should be found to act as the tsar. These agents taught him everything he needed to know, and sent him to Russia with Pan Miechowicki.[33] Maskiewicz identifies Miechowicki as a former intimate of the First False Dimitry who knew all his secrets, and describes him as the mentor of the new pretender.[34] But in Maskiewicz's account Miechowicki acted on his own initiative, rather than as an agent of the Mniszechs at Sambor. In 1607 Miechowicki found 'a Muscovite similar in build to the late [tsar], decided to elevate him, and began to announce to the people that Dimitry had escaped from the murderous hands of the Muscovites by the same means as he had escaped in childhood from Godunov'.[35]

A number of sources state that after leaving Mogilev the pretender was imprisoned in a Lithuanian frontier fortress. According to Wielewicki's Diary, Bogdanka was arrested as a spy and incarcerated first in Velizh and then in 'another fortress close to Russia', but no charge of treason could be proved against him, and he was soon released.[36] Marchocki states that the pretender was imprisoned for a week in Propoisk as a Russian spy.[37] The Belorussian chronicler also says that he was imprisoned in Propoisk; then a local official (*vryadnik*), Pan Ragoza, from nearby Chechersk, released him and, with the knowledge of his superior, Pan Zenovich, the governor (*starosta*) of Chechersk, escorted him to Popova Gora, on the Russian side of the frontier.[38]

Historians have long disagreed on the question of how far the Second False Dimitry was a puppet created by the Poles. Many pre-revolutionary scholars, basing themselves on the evidence of Bussow and Maskiewicz about Miechowicki's role, viewed the pretender as a Polish creation from the outset.[39]

---

[32] Zholkevskii, *Zapiski*, prilozheniya, no. 44, col. 192.

[33] Bussov, *Moskovskaya khronika*, p. 144.

[34] Maskevich, 'Dnevnik', pp. 21, 29.

[35] *Ibid.*, p. 29. For details of Miechowicki's biography, see Soloviev, *History of Russia*, vol. 15, n. 72, pp. 305–6.

[36] Zholkevskii, *Zapiski*, prilozheniya, no. 44, cols. 192–3.

[37] Marchocki, *Historya*, p. 6.

[38] PSRL, vol. 32, p. 192. Marchocki names one of Dimitry's companions in Starodub as Pan Rogozinski, the burgrave of Propoisk: Marchocki, *Historya*, p. 6.

[39] E.g. [Shcherbatov], *Kratkaya povest'*, pp. 85–6; Karamzin, *Istoriya*, vol. 3, t. XII, cols. 35–6; Klyuchevskii, *Sochineniya*, vol. 3, p. 40.

Ilovaiskii went further than most, seeing in the appearance of the Second False Dimitry the result of a conspiracy on the part of the same Polish–Lithuanian families who, he believed, were responsible for setting up the first pretender – the Mniszechs, Sapiehas and Vishnevetskiis – together with the Różyńskis.[40] Other pre-revolutionary scholars, while acknowledging that Dimitry obtained Polish military support very soon after he was recognised as tsar in Starodub, were more non-committal about the Poles' complicity in his first appearance.[41] Most Soviet historians have seen the second Dimitry, albeit in somewhat general terms, as a Polish creation.[42]

R. G. Skrynnikov, however, argues that the Mniszechs at Sambor had nothing whatever to do with the appearance of the new pretender. The initiative for the new 'pretender intrigue' came not from the Polish nobility, in Skrynnikov's view, but from the Russian insurgents, and especially from Tsarevich Peter. Peter had come to Orsha in December 1606, and had conducted negotiations with Andrzej Sapieha. Having received no encouragement for his hopes of obtaining military support from the king, Peter had returned to Putivl'. But when he was in Belorussia he had persuaded Polish veterans of the First False Dimitry's campaign to find a new pretender to assume the role of Dimitry. And they had succeeded in doing so. Skrynnikov draws attention to a 'slight, but very significant coincidence': ' "Tsarevich Peter" was accompanied on his travels in Belorussia by the *szlachcice* [Polish noblemen] Pan Zenovich and Pan Senkevich. A short time passed, and the aforementioned Pan Zenovich escorted to the Russian frontier that "Tsar Dimitry" whom "Peter" had sought so assiduously in Belorussia.'[43] As he so often does, however, Skrynnikov here draws inferences that go beyond the evidence. In the first place, it is not at all clear that the 'soldier' Zenovich who escorted Tsarevich Peter to Orsha at the end of 1606 was the governor of Chechersk who authorised the deportation of the Second False Dimitry to Russia in May 1607.[44] And in the second place, and more significantly, it is highly improbable, as we have already noted (pp. 141–3 above), that the Tsarevich Peter (Medved'ko or 'Peter-the-Bear') who turned up in Orsha in

---

[40] Ilovaiskii, *Smutnoe vremya*, pp. 91, 291–2. Prince Roman Różyński was one of the Second False Dimitry's generals at Tushino.

[41] Solov'ev, *Istoriya Rossii*, vol. 4, pp. 477–8; Kostomarov, *Smutnoe vremya*, pp. 299–301; Platonov, *Ocherki*, pp. 267–9.

[42] Smirnov, *Vosstanie Bolotnikova*, p. 458; Shepelev, *Osvoboditel'naya i klassovaya bor'ba*, pp. 40–2; Zimin, 'Nekotorye voprosy', pp. 101–2; Makovskii, *Pervaya krest'yanskaya voina*, pp. 401–4.

[43] Skrynnikov, *Smuta v Rossii*, p. 193.

[44] The source for the role of 'two Polish soldiers' (*pana soldata*), Zenovich and Senkevich, as companions of 'Tsarevich Peter' in Orsha at the end of December 1606 is Girshberg, *Marina Mnishek*, p. 49 (see above, ch. 5, pp. 142–3). The Barkulabovo chronicler states that 'Dimitry Nagoi' was escorted from Propoisk to the Russian frontier by Pan Ragoza, 'with the knowledge of his gracious lord Zenovich, the *starosta* of Chechersk': *PSRL*, vol. 32, p. 192.

December 1606 was Peter-Ileika, who had arrived in Putivl' in November 1606. And if 'Peter-the-Bear' is not Peter-Ileika, then Skrynnikov's theory about the complicity of the Russian insurgents at Putivl' in setting up the new 'pretender intrigue' has no validity.

There may well, however, have been a connection between Peter-the-Bear and the Second False Dimitry. Many years ago the historian Bodyanskii suggested that Medved'ko himself subsequently assumed the identity of the tsar. Might not Medved'ko, Bodyanskii asked, having fruitlessly wandered the length and breadth of Russia in the role of Tsarevich Peter, have decided to exchange it for the more promising role of Dimitry? Medved'ko (whom Bodyanskii does not identify with Peter-Ileika) had vanished from the scene in January 1607; less than six months later, the Second False Dimitry had appeared in Belorussia.[45] Bodyanskii's hypothesis, while not entirely implausible, is even more fanciful than Skrynnikov's. The most that we can safely conclude from the evidence is that the appearance of Tsar Dimitry in Belorussia rather than at Sambor may not have been unconnected with the arrival of Medved'ko in Orsha in the winter of 1606/7.

R. G. Skrynnikov speculates that Zenovich, Miechowicki and others started to prepare the new 'pretender intrigue' at the beginning of 1607, soon after the appearance of 'Tsarevich Peter' in Orsha.[46] On the basis of a chance encounter, they chose as Tsar Dimitry a poor schoolteacher in Mogilev who had been dismissed from his post for 'immoral behaviour'. Selectively combining pieces of evidence from various sources, Skrynnikov constructs the following imaginative narrative:

The vagrant found himself on the street without a crust of bread. At that moment he was spotted by some veterans of the First False Dimitry's Moscow campaign. One of them, Pan Miechowicki, drew attention to the fact that the ragamuffin was 'similar in build to the late tsar'. Obsequiousness and cowardice conflicted in the teacher's soul. In spite of his destitution, he did not immediately succumb to the blandishments of Miechowicki and his friends. The fate of Otrep'ev frightened him.[47]

The reluctant pretender fled to Propoisk, where he was thrown into prison:

His flight from Mogilev to Propoisk did not save him. Miechowicki had influential confederates and accomplices in the persons of the local officials from Propoisk and Chechersk, Pan Zenovich and Pan Ragoza. Thanks to this he was able to blackmail the imprisoned vagrant. The teacher was faced with a choice: either to rot alive in jail (he could also have been hanged as a Russian spy); or to agree to be a tsar. In the end, he chose the crown.[48]

---

[45] Bodyanskii, 'O poiskakh moikh', pp. 44–5.
[46] Skrynnikov, *Smuta v Rossii*, p. 197.
[47] *Ibid.*, p. 194.
[48] *Ibid.*, pp. 194–5.

Thus according to Skrynnikov the new pretender was the unwitting victim of a group of Polish–Belorussian nobles who press-ganged him into service as the tsar, and then sent him across the Russian frontier with only a handful of companions, and no armed escort. This is rather an unconvincing scenario, however. Skrynnikov presents the pretender as a weak and cowardly figure who was simply the puppet of his Polish manipulators. But it seems much more reasonable to assume that the pretender either initiated the intrigue himself, or was a willing participant in it. Skrynnikov ignores the many sources that suggest that the second Dimitry had served the previous pretender, and that he himself decided to assume the role of the Russian tsar. And if the new Dimitry were such a reluctant pretender, why did his Polish masters leave him virtually unattended on the border? Skrynnikov can only suggest that according to the Poles' agreement with their Russian collaborators, their role was to be limited to finding a pretender and taking him to the frontier: the rest was to be up to the Russians.[49]

The sources offer a range of versions of where and how the pretender first revealed himself in Russia as Dimitry. The *Barkulabovo Chronicle* depicts 'Dimitry Nagoi' as still acting alone, and describes his ecstatic reception in the town of Popova Gora. The Russians recognised him as 'the true and undoubted tsar of the east, the sun of righteousness', because of his 'royal marks' (*znaki tsarskie*) and the proclamations which he distributed.[50] The townspeople rejoiced and dressed him in rich attire, and he was soon joined by 700 cavalrymen. Then he went to Starodub, where more recruits began to rally to his banner.[51]

Other sources, however, agree that the pretender first declared himself in Starodub. According to Wielewicki, when the teacher Bogdanka was released from prison, two agents of the Belorussian authorities were designated to follow him to the border and keep an eye on him. Bogdanka, however, managed to persuade one of them that he was Dimitry. 'In confirmation of the veracity of his words, he produced some proofs, I do not know exactly what', and these served to convince his 'credulous companion'. The two men then went to Starodub, where at first they did not openly reveal Bogdanka's royal identity, but confided it secretly to various individuals. Rumours about Dimitry's re-appearance soon spread throughout the Seversk lands, and the people began to take up arms in his cause. He was accepted by some because he bore a certain resemblance to the first Dimitry, and because, having been his secretary, he knew a number of his secrets. Others realised that he was an

---

[49] *Ibid.*, pp. 195–6.
[50] *PSRL*, vol. 32, p. 192. B. A. Uspenskii cites this as probably the first case of the application of the term *pravednoe solntse* to a tsar ('Tsar' i samozvanets', p. 203) although, as we have seen, the term was also applied to the First False Dimitry.
[51] *PSRL*, vol. 32, p. 192.

impostor, but saw him as a suitable leader for an uprising against Shuiskii, and therefore supported him.[52]

Other sources attribute a greater role to Dimitry's companion. According to the *New Chronicle*, when the pretender arrived in Starodub he called himself Andrei Andreevich Nagoi, and he was accompanied by a man who claimed to be Aleshka (Aleksei) Rukin, a chancellery official (*pod'yachii*) from Moscow, although the chronicler notes that some people regarded this man as Nagoi's servant. Nagoi and Rukin told the people of Starodub that they had been sent by Tsar Dimitry, who was alive and in hiding nearby, to assess the attitudes of the townspeople towards him. When the Starodubtsy expressed their enthusiasm for Dimitry, Rukin revealed that his companion Andrei Nagoi was Tsar Dimitry. The townspeople were sceptical, and put Rukin to the torture, but when he continued to insist that Nagoi was Dimitry, they believed him and rang the bells for joy.[53] Another variant of the story is provided by the Pole Jozef Budzilo. According to Budzilo, four weeks after Andrei Andreevich Nagoi arrived in Starodub a Muscovite named Andrei Voevodskii-Rukin appeared in Chernigov and declared that Dimitry was alive. The people of Chernigov sent a delegation to Starodub, where Rukin was eventually prevailed upon to identify Nagoi as the tsar. Nagoi admitted that he was Dimitry, saying that he had 'in miraculous fashion escaped the death prepared for him by Shuiskii'.[54]

Conrad Bussow's account of Dimitry's appearance at Starodub is similar to that of the *New Chronicle*. According to Bussow, when Dimitry arrived in Starodub he was accompanied by two men, Grigorii Kashnets and a clerk (*pisets*) called Aleksei.[55] The pretender told the people of Starodub that he was 'the tsar's kinsman Nagoi', and that Tsar Dimitry himself was nearby with Pan Miechowicki and many thousand cavalrymen. When Dimitry and Miechowicki failed to appear, the people of Starodub flogged Aleksei, who admitted under torture that his companion Nagoi was in fact the tsar, who was concealing his true identity as a test of their loyalty and affection towards him. Thereupon the 'poor, pathetic, ignorant people' of Starodub immediately accepted 'Nagoi' as the true tsar Dimitry.[56] On that very same day, Miechow-

[52] Zholkevskii, *Zapiski*, prilozheniya, no. 44, cols. 193–4.
[53] *PSRL*, vol. 14, p. 76, para. 149.
[54] *RIB*, vol. 1, cols. 123–4.
[55] Bussov, *Moskovskaya khronika*, p. 144. According to Marchocki, he was accompanied by Hrycko (Grigorii), a tradesman from Propoisk, and by a certain Rogozinski, the burgrave of Propoisk: Marchocki, *Historya*, p. 6.
[56] Bussov, *Moskovskaya khronika*, pp. 144–5. In addition to Bussow and the *New Chronicle*, both Budzilo and Marchocki state that the pretender's accomplices revealed his 'true' identity in response to the use or threat of torture: *RIB*, vol. 1, col. 124; Marchocki, *Historya*, p. 7.

icki arrived in Starodub with some Polish cavalrymen.[57] Miechowicki's well-timed appearance at Starodub suggests that Polish military backing for the pretender was more important than R. G. Skrynnikov acknowledges, and that the entire scenario of Dimitry's 'recognition' in Russia was carefully pre-planned by his backers from the *Rzeczpospolita*.

The nineteenth-century historian N. M. Kostomarov took contemporary accounts of events at Starodub at face value, and presented the Second False Dimitry as an accidental pretender who acquired his royal name in a genuine case of mistaken identity. Kostomarov suggests that the poor school-teacher adopted the name of Dimitry's uncle, the Russian boyar Nagoi, in order to get himself released from prison at Propoisk. On returning to Russia he was naturally asked about his 'nephew', and he helped to spread the rumours that Tsar Dimitry was alive. When tortured in Starodub to make him reveal further details of the former tsar, his companion Rukin pointed to Nagoi, and the latter had little option but to accept this role.[58] Most historians, however, have concluded that the pretender's revelation of his identity at Starodub was carefully planned in advance, and that his companions were accomplices in the deception.[59] By first assuming the surname Nagoi, the pretender was bound to elicit questions about 'Tsar Dimitry'; the role of his associate, who confirmed under torture that Andrei Nagoi was in fact the rightful tsar of Russia, was a useful device to give the pretence greater credibility.[60]

According to Bussow, the pretender was also 'recognised' in Starodub by Ivan Martynovich Zarutskii, a cossack leader who had been dispatched by Bolotnikov from Tula to find Tsar Dimitry at Sambor and discover his intentions. Zarutskii, however, 'went as far as Starodub, did not dare to venture further, remained there and did not bring back any answer'.[61] When Zarutskii learned that Dimitry was in Starodub, he at once went to see him, to hand over the letters with which Bolotnikov had entrusted him. Zarutskii immedi-

---

[57] Bussov, *Moskovskaya khronika*, pp. 144–5. For Miechowicki's arrival in Starodub, with 5,000 Poles, on the day of Dimitry's revelation of his 'true' identity, see Buturlin, *Istoriya smutnogo vremeni*, vol. 2, p. 90.

[58] Kostomarov, *Smutnoe vremya*, pp. 299–300.

[59] E.g. Karamzin, *Istoriya*, vol. 3, t. XII, cols. 36–7; Ilovaiskii, *Smutnoe vremya*, pp. 92–3; Skrynnikov, *Smuta v Rossii*, p. 200.

[60] According to Marchocki, the pretender called himself the son of Andrei Nagoi in prison in Propoisk: Marchocki, *Historya*, p. 6. The pretender himself, in a proclamation of April 1608, confirmed that he had at first called himself Andrei Nagoi at Starodub, 'not wanting to reveal himself for fear of the traitors Vasilii Shuiskii and his henchmen': Buturlin, *Istoriya smutnogo vremeni*, vol. 2, prilozheniya, no. 7, p. 53.

[61] Bussov, *Moskovskaya khronika*, p. 144. Zarutskii was a Pole from Tarnopol who had been captured in childhood by the Tatars; he later escaped and joined the Don cossacks, and adhered with them to the forces of the First False Dimitry: Zholkevskii, *Zapiski*, p. 116.

ately realised that this Dimitry was not the tsar who had reigned in Moscow, but he nevertheless 'recognised' him, thereby convincing the Starodubtsy even more firmly that he was indeed the tsar. Bussow presents Zarutskii's arrival in Starodub, and his recognition of the new pretender as Tsar Dimitry, as a mere coincidence.[62] R. G. Skrynnikov, however, sees Zarutskii's presence in Starodub as evidence of the collusion of Bolotnikov and Tsarevich Peter with the pretender's Polish backers,[63] and it is not impossible that the Russian insurgents may have sought to make contact with the new Dimitry at this stage.

Certainly Zarutskii was willing to collaborate with the new Tsar Dimitry from the very outset, in a ploy that was evidently devised to test the credibility of his pretence. Bussow describes how on the day of his revelation as Tsar Dimitry the pretender instructed Zarutskii to go with him to the open ground beyond the town gates, where they would stage a jousting match. Zarutskii pretended to strike Dimitry a heavy blow with his lance; the tsar fell to the ground as if severely wounded, and Zarutskii fled from the scene. Then the people of Starodub indignantly declared Zarutskii to be a traitor, seized him, beat him up, and brought him to Dimitry, for the tsar to decide his fate.

When Dimitry saw how many people had attacked Zarutskii, he laughed and said, 'Thank you, good Christians. Now I am convinced for a second time that you are devoted to me. Thank God, nothing is the matter with me, I simply wanted to test you and therefore put Zarutskii up to this ploy'. They were amazed at his cunning, and laughed. And Zarutskii had to put up with this crude joke.[64]

The rallying of support

According to the author of the *Barkulabovo Chronicle*, as soon as the pretender had crossed the Russian border and been recognised as tsar in Popova Gora, he sent proclamations to all the frontier fortresses in Belorussia, calling on troops to join him.[65] From Starodub he wrote to the Lithuanian nobles, telling them that he had had to hide for a while in the *Rzeczpospolita* in order to escape from the traitor Vasilii Shuiskii, but now he had been able to return to Russia. He promised to reward them generously for their military support, offering to pay two or three times what they would have received in their own country.[66] Maskiewicz states that Miechowicki distributed proc-

[62] Bussov, *Moskovskaya khronika*, p. 145.
[63] Skrynnikov, *Smuta v Rossii*, pp. 197–8, 200–1.
[64] Bussov, *Moskovskaya khronika*, pp. 145–6.
[65] *PSRL*, vol. 32, p. 192.
[66] Girshberg, *Marina Mnishek*, pp. 53–4.

lamations in the tsar's name to whomever he chose, promising 70 zlotys to a hussar and 50 to a cossack.[67]

Dimitry also attempted to attract support from within Russia itself. According to Marchocki, even before he declared himself publicly the pretender sent a Russian (*Moskwicin*) called Alexander to the Seversk fortresses, including Putivl', to announce that Tsar Dimitry was at Starodub.[68] After he had been recognised in Starodub, he sent agents to all the major towns of the Seversk region with proclamations announcing that he had returned to Russia.[69] None of the pretender's early proclamations has survived, but in April 1608, in an appeal for support from the people of Smolensk, he rehearsed his biography since the attempt on his life at Uglich by Boris Godunov. He reminded them how God had punished Boris for his treason against the true heir to the throne, and implied that a similar fate lay in store for Vasilii Shuiskii, the architect of the second unsuccessful attempt to kill him. Dimitry was no more specific in describing his most recent escape from death than he (and the First False Dimitry) had been in explaining Tsarevich Dimitry's escape from Uglich. He had been warned of Shuiskii's evil intentions, he said, and God had preserved him with His divine providence. A German called Artsykalus had been killed in his place, while the tsar had gone to Lithuania for safety. (In case anyone believed that the tsar who had supposedly been killed on 17 May was Grisha Otrep'ev, as Shuiskii had claimed, the pretender assured his audience that everyone knew that Grisha Otrep'ev was a completely different individual.) After finding refuge in Lithuania, Dimitry continued, he had returned to Russia, to Starodub, where he had at first called himself Andrei Nagoi. But then his loyal subjects from many towns had recognised him as Tsar Dimitry, thereby earning his gratitude and generous rewards, which would be extended to all those who swore allegiance to him.[70]

Although the towns of the Seversk lands recognised the pretender as Tsar Dimitry and swore allegiance to him, there were few Russian servicemen left in the region to provide him with an effective army of an adequate size to raise the siege of Tula.[71] He therefore had to rely heavily on his ability to recruit mercenary troops from Poland–Lithuania. At first his appeals attracted

---

[67] Maskevich, 'Dnevnik', pp. 29–30. For examples of proclamations written in the names of Tsar Dimitry and Tsarevich Peter, and sent to Mstislavl' in Belorussia by Prince D. V. Mosal'skii, the *voevoda* of Roslavl', in June 1607, see *AI*, vol. 2, no. 75, pp. 100–1; Pyasetskii, *Materialy*, p. 19. See also Nazarov and Florya, 'Krest'yanskoe vosstanie', pp. 327–8, 339–40, 342–3, 349. R. G. Skrynnikov appears to believe that these proclamations were issued on behalf of the Second False Dimitry (Skrynnikov, *Smuta v Rossii*, pp. 206–7), while Nazarov and Florya ('Krest'yanskoe vosstanie', p. 349, n. 97) associate them with Bolotnikov.

[68] Marchocki, *Historya*, pp. 6–7.

[69] *PSRL*, vol. 14, p. 76, para. 149.

[70] Buturlin, *Istoriya smutnogo vremeni*, vol. 2, prilozheniya, no. 7, pp. 46–55.

[71] Skrynnikov, *Smuta v Rossii*, pp. 203–6.

recruits only from poor and destitute soldiers of fortune,[72] but after the defeat of the *rokosz* rebellion against King Sigismund in July 1607, the Polish nobility too began to flock to his banner. On 10/20 September 1607 Dimitry felt himself sufficiently strong to leave Starodub and begin his march on Tula to relieve Bolotnikov and Tsarevich Peter.[73]

Ahead of his army, the pretender sent a *syn boyarskii* from Starodub to Shuiskii's camp at Tula, with letters to Tsar Vasilii, demanding that he hand over the realm to its rightful sovereign. The envoy denounced Shuiskii as a usurper, and was burned at the stake. 'And he died, still uttering these same words', the chronicler commented, 'for the devil had so embittered his accursed soul, that he died for such a scoundrel.'[74] The Spanish missionary Nicolao de Mello claimed that Dimitry sent an envoy to Shuiskii with a letter in which the pretender offered to pardon him if he surrendered, and that this letter was delivered to Tsar Vasilii in his camp at Tula on 24 September/4 October.[75]

The pretender's advance towards Tula began well. A series of towns on his route northwards welcomed him with scenes of joy reminiscent of those which had greeted the First False Dimitry in 1605. On 8 October his troops relieved Kozel'sk, which was besieged by Shuiskii's troops, and Dimitry entered the town in triumph on the 11th. But news of the surrender of Tula on 10 October had a devastating effect on the pretender's army, and he retreated to Karachev. Many of his Polish mercenaries deserted him, as did a detachment of Zaporozhian cossacks who had joined his army only a couple of weeks earlier. The pretender himself was so demoralised that he twice attempted to flee. In November and December 1607 his army besieged the town of Bryansk, but had to retreat without capturing it. Dimitry spent the winter encamped near Orel, where he replenished his provisions and recruited reinforcements, in readiness for a new campaign in the spring of 1608.[76]

Many of the recruits to Dimitry's banner in the winter of 1607–8 were Poles. Jozef Budzilo had joined him at Starodub in August 1607; at the end of October, after his retreat from Karachev, the pretender met Samuel Tysz-kiewicz and Pan Walawski who were marching to join him. Prince Adam Vishnevetskii, the patron of the First False Dimitry, arrived at about the same time, and Alexander Lisowski in November. In March 1608 Prince Roman Różyński appeared in the pretender's camp at Orel with a large detachment

---

[72] *PSRL*, vol. 32, p. 192.
[73] *RIB*, vol. 1, col. 125.
[74] *PSRL*, vol. 14, p. 76, para. 149.
[75] Dyamentowski, 'Dyariusz', pp. 115–16; *VIB*, p. 173.
[76] *RIB*, vol. 1, pp. 125–30; Shepelev, *Osvoboditel'naya i klassovaya bor'ba*, pp. 46–56; Skrynnikov, *Smuta v Rossii*, pp. 228–30, 239–40.

of cavalry, and ousted Miechowicki as the commander-in-chief of his army.[77]

Large numbers of Russians too were rallying to Tsar Dimitry. After the fall of Tula, many former adherents of Bolotnikov and Tsarevich Peter joined the new pretender's army.[78] When Dimitry began his march on Moscow in the spring of 1608, supporters flocked to join him. According to Bussow, when the pretender advanced from Orel to Bolkhov, in April 1608, many Russians concluded

that since so many thousands of Poles had come to him he must be the true Tsar Dimitry. Therefore he was joined by many princes, boyars and Germans [i.e. by Russian servicemen and foreign mercenaries (M.P.)], to whom he immediately gave lands and peasants, more than they had previously had. This was why they remained permanently in his camp, although they could see perfectly well that he was not the first Dimitry, but someone else.[79]

But Dimitry did not gain support solely from Russian nobles; he also made a bid for the allegiance of the bondslaves. Bussow's account continues:

Dimitry had it announced everywhere where there were estates of the princes and boyars who had gone over to Shuiskii, that their slaves (*Knechte*) should come to him, swear allegiance, and receive from him the estates of their masters, and if their masters' daughters remained there, the slaves should take them as their wives, and serve him. Thus many poor slaves became nobles, wealthy and powerful to boot, while their masters had to go hungry in Moscow.[80]

This evidence of Bussow's has caused considerable interest among historians, especially when it is considered in conjunction with the following passage from the eighteenth-century historian Tatishchev:

Encamped at Orel, [Dimitry] sent out proclamations to all the towns, with great promises of favours, including for the peasants and *kholopy* the former freedom which Tsar Boris had taken from them (Petreus, p. 404), and thereby, it seems, he attracted all the simple people to him. And thus in all the towns the number of cossacks from the *kholopy* and peasants multiplied, and in every town they elected their *atamans*.[81]

[77] There is conflicting evidence about the dates at which the various Polish commanders joined the pretender's camp, and the number of troops which they brought with them. For a useful review of the sources and literature, see editors' notes 104 and 106, in Bussov, *Moskovskaya khronika*, pp. 367–8.

[78] *PSRL*, vol. 34, p. 247; Koretskii, *Formirovanie krepostnogo prava*, p. 344.

[79] Bussov, *Moskovskaya khronika*, p. 149.

[80] *Ibid.*, pp. 149, 281.

[81] Tatishchev, *Istoriya Rossiiskaya*, vol. 6, p. 320.

Although Tatishchev provides a reference only to Petreus (Petrei), whose account is similar to that of Bussow,[82] V. I. Koretskii suggested that he may also have used another source which has not survived, possibly the 'History' by the monk Iosif on which Tatishchev had based his previous discussion of the process of enserfment.[83] It may be, however, that Tatishchev's reference to the freeing of both peasants and *kholopy* by the Second False Dimitry is simply his own gloss on the statements of Bussow and Petrei about the pretender's rewarding of the *Knechte* of nobles who remained loyal to the 'traitor' Shuiskii. Tatishchev, however, implies a far-reaching abolition of serfdom, whilst the evidence of Bussow and Petrei indicates a more limited policy, involving the redistribution of the lands and property only of those nobles who were traitors to Tsar Dimitry. Certainly Bussow, who describes the pretender's allocation of both landed estates and peasants to his supporters, hardly presents Dimitry as promoting an 'anti-feudal' programme.

Surviving documents appear to confirm Bussow's version of Dimitry's social policy, rather than Tatishchev's. The pretender allocated estates and peasants to his supporters among the service nobility;[84] and he also gave lands confiscated from 'traitors' – Shuiskii's adherents – to their own or neighbouring peasants.[85] However, there appears to be no archival evidence of the blanket abolition of serfdom which Tatishchev implies: as Koretskii observes, the granting of estates to peasants and slaves would have led not to the abolition of serfdom, but to the 'feudal regeneration' of these former bondsmen, i.e. the conversion of individual peasants or slaves into landowners themselves.[86] Nevertheless, in allocating the lands of Shuiskii's adherents to their peasants and slaves, Koretskii argues, 'the pretender was in effect sanctioning the situation which had been created in the southern countryside as a result of a successful anti-feudal uprising'.[87]

There is certainly evidence of widespread attacks by bondsmen on noble landowners in this period. A literary source of the early seventeenth century describes how, during the siege of Bryansk by Dimitry's army at the end of 1607, about 1,000 nobles from that region had fled to Moscow, because their slaves and servants had attacked and beaten them and had taken their wives

---

[82] Cf. Petrei, *Istoriya*, p. 263. It is not clear whether Bussow based his account on that of Petrei, or *vice versa*.

[83] Koretskii, *Formirovanie krepostnogo prava*, pp. 344–6.

[84] For examples of these practices, see Bussov, *Moskovskaya khronika*, p. 368, n. 107.

[85] Examples of the latter practice were discovered by V. I. Koretskii: Koretskii, *Formirovanie krepostnogo prava*, pp. 348–50. Previous Soviet historians, familiar only with evidence of the pretender's 'feudal' allocation of populated estates, had interpreted Bussow's statement about the allocation of estates to bondslaves as evidence of 'social demagogy' on the pretender's part – that is, as empty promises made in the hope of attracting support from the 'masses'.

[86] *Ibid.*, pp. 347–51.

[87] *Ibid.*, p. 351.

and daughters 'as wives for themselves'.[88] This is partly confirmed by an appeal by Tsar Vasilii to the inhabitants of Perm', dated 7 September 1608, requesting funds to help him compensate nobles and servicemen (*dvoryane* and *deti boyarskie*) who had fled to Moscow in the past year from their estates in the *ukrainnye* and Seversk regions, which had been ruined 'by the traitors and scoundrels'.[89]

The sources do not permit us to judge whether these attacks by slaves on their masters were indiscriminate, or whether they were directed only against those who supported Shuiskii and hence could be viewed as 'traitors' to Tsar Dimitry. If they were undertaken in response to Dimitry's proclamations, it seems more likely that the latter was the case. Bondsmen who denounced their masters as traitors could appropriate a share of their property as a reward for their service to the true tsar. The social programme of the Second False Dimitry at this stage of his campaign appears to have had much in common with that of Bolotnikov, who had called on slaves to take the property and wives of their masters who were traitors to Tsar Dimitry. And as we noted in relation to Bolotnikov, this practice was not new: both Ivan the Terrible and Boris Godunov had allocated estates to bondsmen who denounced their lords for treason.   R. G. Skrynnikov has plausibly suggested that the Second False Dimitry's proclamations were addressed primarily to military bondsmen (*boevye kholopy*), who would have received land in return for military service to the 'tsar'.[90] Skrynnikov implies that there was nothing 'anti-feudal' in this practice; but he concedes that by offering the slaves not only their masters' lands, but also their daughters, the pretender was pursuing an 'anti-noble' policy.[91]

It seems, however, that by the spring of 1608 Dimitry was endeavouring to tone down the socially divisive aspects of his appeal, at least when he was bidding for support from 'respectable' townspeople. In his proclamation to Smolensk of 24 April 1608, Dimitry not only denounced the myriad cossack 'tsareviches' who had appeared on the Volga and on the steppe, and promised that he would deal harshly with them (see pp. 175–6 below); but he also dissociated himself from Tsarevich Peter. The aim of Dimitry's initial campaign, in the early autumn of 1607, had been to come to the assistance of Bolotnikov and Peter at Tula. But now the pretender realised that his potential supporters in Smolensk might be deterred by recollections of the reign of terror which Peter had introduced at Putivl' and Tula ('in other towns

---

[88] *VIB*, pp. 106–7.
[89] *AAE*, vol. 2, no. 87, p. 179.
[90] Skrynnikov, *Smuta v Rossii*, pp. 205–6. Skrynnikov relates this policy to the pretender's recruitment campaign at Starodub, in the summer of 1607, whereas Bussow dates it to his Bolkhov campaign in the spring of 1608.
[91] *Ibid.*, p. 206.

he subjected many of our loyal and innocent subjects to various torments'). He assured the people of Smolensk that he 'regretted and grieved at such a great sin, that so much innocent Christian blood was spilled'. And he promised them that they need not fear 'violence and killing and looting' from his Lithuanian soldiers and cossacks.[92]

At the end of April 1608 Dimitry marched from Orel towards Bolkhov, where Tsar Vasilii's army, commanded by his brother Prince Dimitry Shuiskii, was stationed. Dimitry's general Różyński inflicted a defeat on Shuiskii's army and occupied Bolkhov, before advancing on the capital via Kozel'sk, Kaluga, Borisov and Mozhaisk. The pretender's troops set up camp in the village of Tushino, near Moscow. On 25 June they defeated Shuiskii again at Khodynka, but were unable to follow up their victory by taking the capital.[93] The ensuing military stalemate was to last for over a year, and Tushino remained the headquarters of the Second False Dimitry until the end of 1609.

The cossack tsareviches

In the months following the surrender of Tula, there was a great proliferation of pretenders in Russia. The first new tsarevich appeared in the autumn of 1607, when the Second False Dimitry was besieging Bryansk. He called himself Tsarevich Fedor Fedorovich, the son of Tsar Fedor Ivanovich, and hence the 'nephew' of Tsar Dimitry and the brother of Tsarevich Peter. The fullest information which we have about this pretender is provided by a letter dated 20/30 November 1607, sent by the Pole Stanislav Kurovskii from Dimitry's camp at Bryansk to a certain Pan Rakovskii. According to Kurovskii, Fedor Fedorovich had recently joined their army with 3,000 Don cossacks. 'He himself and his warriors are subordinate to our tsar [Dimitry], and he serves him like any junior servitor (*syn boyarskii*), but stands high in the tsar's esteem.'[94] Dimitry's good relations with his supposed nephew did not last long, however. The *New Chronicle* tells us that, 'At Bryansk, the scoundrel who called himself Tsarevich Dimitry put to death that scoundrel Fedka whom the cossacks had brought from the Don.'[95] We know nothing more about this 'Tsarevich Fedor Fedorovich', but he may have been the younger of the two unnamed 'nephews of Dimitry, and sons of Fedor' about whom the Carmelite missionaries had learned at Tsaritsyn in August 1606, and who, according to their information, had been living among the Don cossacks since

---

[92] Buturlin, *Istoriya smutnogo vremeni*, vol. 2, prilozheniya, no. 7, pp. 57–8 (*VIB*, p. 231).
[93] Shepelev, *Osvoboditel'naya i klassovaya bor'ba*, pp. 60–88; Skrynnikov, *The Time of Troubles*, pp. 64–5.
[94] Girshberg, *Marina Mnishek*, pp. 55–6; see also Smirnov, 'Kogda byl kaznen Ileika Muromets?', p. 115.
[95] *PSRL*, vol. 14, p. 77, para. 153.

Boris's usurpation of the throne. (The elder of these two brothers, who was reported to be marching on Moscow with a cossack army, was most probably Tsarevich Peter-Ileika.)[96]

According to I. I. Smirnov, the evidence of the *New Chronicle* about the execution of Tsarevich Fedor demonstrates that Dimitry's 'esteem' for his nephew was purely superficial and ephemeral, and served to mask his real hostility towards another pretender who was potentially a rival claimant to the throne. Dimitry could not attack Fedka immediately, however, since the 3,000 Don cossacks were a valuable reinforcement for his army at the beginning of the siege of Bryansk. But as more and more Polish noblemen arrived to strengthen his forces, Dimitry became less dependent on Fedor's cossacks, and was able to dispense with him.[97] This view is shared by V. I. Koretskii, who presents Dimitry's treatment of Tsarevich Fedor as an example of the pretender's 'vacillation' in response to competing pressures within his camp from the former supporters of Bolotnikov on the one hand, and the Poles on the other. At first, when he needed cossack support, Dimitry treated Fedor with respect, but later, when significant Polish forces had joined him, he 'dropped his mask and executed his supposed "nephew" '.[98] It seems likely, in fact, that Dimitry executed Fedor not so much because he regarded him as a rival, but rather because he feared that an alliance with the cossack tsarevich would discredit his own campaign in the eyes of the Muscovite elites to whom he was now looking for support.

Apparently undeterred by the fate of Tsarevich Fedor, further pretenders had appeared by the spring of 1608. In his proclamation to Smolensk of 24 April 1608, 'Tsar' Dimitry reported that 'a great heresy' had manifested itself in his realm: many people, inspired by the wiles of the Devil, were calling themselves 'Muscovite tsareviches, true royal seed'. (Dimitry's characterisation of the claims of these new pretenders as 'heresy' appears to have been modelled on the denunciations of the First False Dimitry by Boris Godunov and Vasilii Shuiskii.) He reminded his subjects that he himself, the son of Ivan IV by Mariya Nagaya, was the only surviving member of the old dynasty. Tsar Ivan had had three sons by his first wife Anastasiya Romanova: but of these, Dimitry had died in infancy; Ivan had died without issue; and Fedor had had only a daughter, Feodosiya, who had died at the age of two. But now, he complained, many 'tsareviches' were appearing in Astrakhan' and in the cossack settlements on the steppe (*pol'skie yurty*).[99]

---

[96] Berthold-Ignace, *Histoire*, pp. 151–2. See above, ch. 5, pp. 132, 134.
[97] Smirnov, 'Kogda byl kaznen Ileika Muromets?', pp. 116–17.
[98] Koretskii, *Formirovanie krepostnogo prava*, p. 344.
[99] Buturlin, *Istoriya smutnogo vremeni*, vol. 2, prilozheniya, no. 7, pp. 55–6. Part of this document is reprinted in *VIB*, pp. 229–31.

Dimitry named the Astrakhan' tsareviches as Ivan Augustus, the son of Tsar Ivan by Anna Koltovskaya (see p. 134 above); and Lavrentii, the son of Tsarevich Ivan Ivanovich by Elena Sheremeteva. Their claims were absurd, he asserted, since everyone knew that the marriages of which they professed to be the offspring had been childless.[100] Tsarevich Peter, Dimitry continued, had come from the steppe; and now many more pretenders had appeared there, all claiming to be the sons of Tsar Fedor, and hence Dimitry's nephews: Tsareviches Fedor, Klementii, Savelii, Semion, Vasilii, Eroshka, Gavrilka and Martinka (see Figure 4).[101]

Dimitry rejected the claims of these pretenders to be sons of Tsar Fedor Ivanovich, reminding the people of Smolensk that Tsar Fedor's only child had been Tsarevna Feodosiya. The only living descendant of Tsar Ivan, he asserted brazenly, was himself, 'your merciful and righteous and generous and true tsar and grand prince Dimitry Ivanovich of all the Russias'.[102] There were apparently limits to Tsar Dimitry's mercy and generosity, however. He went on to inform the people of Smolensk that he had sent messengers to the Lower Volga towns and to the steppe settlements to search for 'those scoundrels who call themselves tsareviches'. When they were found, they were to be beaten with the knout and thrown into prison to await Dimitry's further instructions. When he ascended the throne of his ancestors in Moscow, he continued, he would deal with these impostors; and he would also fulsomely reward those who supported him and served him.[103]

Other sources confirm the names of some of these tsareviches. As we have already noted, the *New Chronicle* lists three Astrakhan' tsareviches: Avgust (Augustus), the son of Tsar Ivan; Osinovik, the son of Tsarevich Ivan Ivanovich; and Laver (Lavrentii), whom the chronicler describes as the son of Tsar Fedor.[104] A proclamation from Prince Dimitry Pozharskii of 7 April 1612 names the false tsars who had appeared at the time of the Second False Dimitry as 'Petrushka, and Avgust, and Lavrushka and Fedka, and many others'.[105] A literary work, the 'Lament for the captivity and complete destruction of the Muscovite State', lists Peter; Ivan, nicknamed Avgust; Lavrentii; and Gurii. (Although this passage is based on Pozharskii's proclamation, the name 'Gurii' is found only in the 'Lament' and works based on it.)[106] The names of Tsareviches Klementii, Savelii, Semion, Vasilii, Eroshka, Gavrilka and Martinka appear uniquely in the Second False Dimitry's procla-

---

[100] Buturlin, *Istoriya smutnogo vremeni*, vol. 2, prilozheniya, no. 7, p. 56.
[101] *Ibid.*, pp. 56–7.
[102] *Ibid.*, p. 57.
[103] *Ibid.*
[104] *PSRL*, vol. 14, p. 89, para. 195.
[105] *AAE*, vol. 2, no. 203, p. 344.
[106] *RIB*, vol. 13, p. 228 (*PLDR*, pp. 138–9, and note on p. 566); Tikhomirov, ed., 'Novyi istochnik', p. 127.

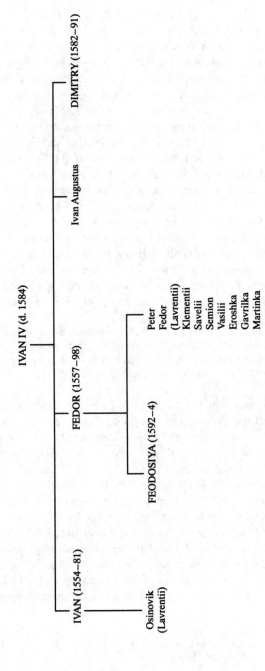

Figure 4 Real and false descendants of Ivan the Terrible.
Notes 1. The names of real descendants of Ivan IV are printed in capitals, false ones in lower case.
2. Lavrentii (Laver) is said in one source to have been the son of Tsarevich Ivan; in another, the son of Tsar Fedor.

IVAN IV (d. 1584)

IVAN (1554–81)

FEDOR (1557–98)

Ivan Augustus

DIMITRY (1582–91)

Osinovik (Lavrentii)

FEODOSIYA (1592–4)

Peter
Fedor
(Lavrentii)
Klementii
Savelii
Semion
Vasilii
Eroshka
Gavrilka
Martinka

mation of 24 April 1608. R. G. Skrynnikov states that the use of diminutive names such as Eroshka and Gavrilka shows that 'the cossack leaders operating in the south did not conceal their origins as slaves and peasants'.[107] It seems more likely, however, that these forms of their names were used not by the cossack pretenders themselves, but by the Second False Dimitry, with a pejorative intent. It is even possible that these names may have been intended as the Russian equivalent of 'Tom, Dick and Harry'.

Some Soviet scholars have suggested that the proliferation of petty cossack pretenders in 1607–8 was a symptom of the decline and fragmentation of the opposition to Shuiskii following the defeat of the Bolotnikov rising. According to D.P. Makovskii, after the fall of Tula the revolt became localised, and these pretenders were 'a peculiar kind of banner' for the various 'uncoordinated theatres of the peasant war'.[108] K. V. Chistov too associated the appearance of the numerous petty pretenders of 1607–8 with the defeat of Bolotnikov and disillusionment with the prospect of Tsar Dimitry's return to Russia.[109] These tsareviches, all claiming to be descendants of Ivan the Terrible, gained support mainly from the cossacks and urban soldiery, for whom their appearance served as an 'ideological and legal sanction for the individual outbreaks of a movement that was going into decline':

The appearance of several peripheral 'tsareviches' indicates the decline of the movement: the legends about the 'deliverers' had lost their highly important unifying and integrating function; and various groups were putting forward 'their own' tsareviches in accordance with their own narrow and localised interests.[110]

These explanations – which reflect the official Soviet view that the Bolotnikov revolt marked the culmination of the class struggle in the early seventeenth century – are not very satisfactory, however. In the first place, the appearance of at least some of the cossack tsareviches preceded or accompanied the outbreak of the Bolotnikov revolt. Tsarevich Peter-Ileika declared himself before the death of the First False Dimitry; we know from the Carmelite sources that two other pretenders – probably Ivan Augustus and Fedor Fedorovich – were active on the Volga by the summer of 1606; and Peter-the-Bear arrived in Orsha in the winter of 1606/7. All of these pretenders acted in the name of Tsar Dimitry, even after the events of May 1606. It is perhaps more appropriate to see the new wave of pretenders in 1607–8 as a symptom of the revival of the opposition to Shuiskii after the failure of Bolotnikov's revolt, a revival inspired by the appearance of the

---

[107] Skrynnikov, *Smuta v Rossii*, p. 204.
[108] Makovskii, *Pervaya krest'yanskaya voina*, p. 408.
[109] Chistov, *Russkie narodnye*, pp. 60–1.
[110] *Ibid.*, p. 64.

Second False Dimitry. Just as the First False Dimitry had served as a magnet for Tsarevich Peter in 1606, so did the Second False Dimitry attract a host of cossack tsareviches in 1607–8, all apparently hoping for 'rewards' from their royal relative. Although the Second Dimitry regarded these pretenders as an embarrassment, they themselves apparently acted towards him as junior kinsmen and supplicants, rather than as rivals.

These petty pretenders appeared almost exclusively amongst the cossacks, whose attitude towards the central power of the Russian state, embodied in the person of the tsar, had always been ambivalent. On the one hand, the cossacks sought autonomy, under their own elected leaders; on the other hand, they sought generous rewards from the Russian tsar for any services they might render him, and they remained dependent on the Muscovite frontier towns for many staples of their existence, from guns and ammunition to salt and cloth. Their ideal leader, in many ways, was their 'own' tsarevich, a cossack like themselves who was at the same time a member of the legitimate Muscovite dynasty, and could intercede with the tsar on their behalf. It seems likely that, following the example of 'Tsarevich Peter', the cossack pretenders justified piratical activity by their supporters as the punishment and expropriation of traitors, and hoped to be rewarded by 'Tsar Dimitry' with new rights and privileges.

They were to be disappointed, however. The new pretender understood that if he were to have any realistic chance of gaining the throne, he needed support from nobles who were likely to be alienated by his swarms of cossack 'relatives'. It is surely not coincidental that the Second False Dimitry condemned the cossack tsareviches in the same proclamation in which he dissociated himself from the bloody actions of Tsarevich Peter. Instead of expressing his gratitude to the cossacks for protecting his young kinsmen, 'Tsar Dimitry' denounced their 'tsareviches' as impostors and called for them to be handed over to him.

We do not know what happened to the pretenders from the steppes, but the Second False Dimitry was eventually able to rid himself of the Astrakhan' tsareviches. The *New Chronicle* tells us that the cossacks brought Ivan Augustus and Lavrentii to him at Tushino, having previously hanged the third pretender, Osinovik, on the Volga. Dimitry rewarded the cossacks, and had Augustus and Lavrentii hanged at Tushino, 'on the Moscow road'.[111] The date of this event is not clear. The positioning of the entry in the chronicle suggests 1609, and this is the year to which it is allocated by nineteenth-century historians such as Karamzin and Kostomarov.[112] I. I. Smirnov, however, has suggested that it took place in the summer of 1608, soon after

[111] *PSRL*, vol. 14, p. 89, para. 195.
[112] Karamzin, *Istoriya*, vol. 3, t. XII col. 99; Kostomarov, *Smutnoe vremya*, p. 373.

Dimitry's arrival at Tushino, and this dating has been followed by other Soviet historians.[113] R. G. Skrynnikov sees the execution of the Astrakhan' tsareviches as evidence that by the time of his arrival at Tushino Dimitry had conclusively broken with the types of cossack insurgent who had earlier supported Bolotnikov.[114]

It is not clear what led the Volga cossacks to hand Ivan Augustus and Lavrentii over to the Second False Dimitry. As we have already noted, Ivan Augustus and his cossacks had sailed up the Volga in the summer of 1607. After their meeting with the Carmelites they made an attempt to take Saratov, but this was unsuccessful, and they retreated to Astrakhan' (see pp. 147–8 above). In October 1607 Shuiskii's commander F. I. Sheremetev left his camp at Balchik, near Astrakhan', and withdrew his troops to Tsaritsyn.[115] Sheremetev's report to Moscow provides some relevant information about the situation on the lower Volga in the winter of 1607–8. On 11 November 1607 the news of the fall of Tula reached Tsaritsyn. Along with a proclamation about the surrender of the insurgents, Shuiskii sent Sheremetev a group of eight men who had come over to his side: *strel'tsy* from Astrakhan' and Terek cossacks who had followed Tsarevich Peter to Tula. Sheremetev decided to use these men for propaganda purposes. He sent them downstream with proclamations calling on the citizens of Astrakhan' and the Terek cossacks to denounce 'the scoundrels who had by their villainy incited them, and were still now inciting them' – presumably a reference to the 'tsareviches'. The envoys were to promise pardon and rewards to those who surrendered to Tsar Vasilii.[116]

On 12 January 1608 the envoys returned to Sheremetev at Tsaritsyn and reported on the outcome of their mission. At first they had enjoyed some success: they had been met by a detachment of cossacks who escorted them into Astrakhan', where many of the inhabitants, having listened to the proclamation, had expressed their willingness to surrender to Shuiskii. However, at that crucial moment a rival delegation of cossacks had arrived. The newcomers confirmed that Bolotnikov and Tsarevich Peter had surrendered to Shuiskii, but they added that Tsar Dimitry was alive and encamped at Orel. The people of Astrakhan' were greatly excited by this news, and immediately resolved to send a deputation of 150 *strel'tsy* and steppe Tatars to the *ukraina* to check out the information about Tsar Dimitry.[117]

---

[113] Smirnov, *Vosstanie Bolotnikova*, p. 253; cf. Shepelev, *Osvoboditel'naya i klassovaya bor'ba*, p. 242.
[114] Skrynnikov, *The Time of Troubles*, pp. 69–70.
[115] Gnevushev, ed., 'Akty', no. 93, p. 171.
[116] *Ibid.*, p. 180.
[117] *Ibid.*, pp. 180–1.

We may speculate that this delegation from Astrakhan' established contact with the Second False Dimitry in his camp at Orel at the beginning of 1608: this would explain why his proclamation to Smolensk of April 1608 contains much more detailed information about the Astrakhan' tsareviches Ivan Augustus and Lavrentii than it does about the other cossack pretenders from the steppe settlements. Dimitry, as we have seen, denounced all of these tsareviches as impostors, and called on his loyal subjects on the Volga to beat and imprison them. It seems likely that it was in response to this appeal, and in the hope of gaining a reward for their loyalty, that the cossacks brought the tsareviches to Dimitry's camp at Tushino, probably in the summer of 1608.

7   The Second False Dimitry: Tushino and Kaluga

The Tushino court

The advance of Dimitry's army from Bolkhov towards Moscow in the early summer of 1608 had created alarm and consternation in the capital. According to Bussow, the news that a number of noblemen had defected from Shuiskii's army convinced many Muscovites that the pretender really was Tsar Dimitry, and they feared that he would wreak a terrible vengeance on the city for the events of May 1606. Some ordinary citizens hoped to put all the blame on the boyars, but others feared that Dimitry's extraordinary powers would enable him to discover the true identity of those who had overthrown him:

> Someone said, 'I have heard that he is so clever that he can tell from looking at you whether you're guilty or not'. A certain butcher was very alarmed at this, and said, 'So much the worse for me. I daren't appear in his sight, for I killed five of his Poles with this very knife'.[1]

Shuiskii was able to use these fears to his advantage. Massa states that, as Dimitry's army approached Moscow,

> The tsar contrived to steady the people by his many exhortations, for he swore to them that the enemy would kill all the inhabitants, including women and children, if they surrendered. Since they had all been to some degree accomplices in Dmitry's murder, they once more resolved to stand firm.[2]

Thus although Bolotnikov's failure to take Moscow in the autumn of 1606 may partly be explained in terms of the absence of 'Tsar Dimitry' in the besieging army, the arrival before the capital of an apparently credible pretender in the summer of 1608 did not lead to a popular rising in his favour. Fear of reprisals united the Muscovites against Dimitry.

---

[1] Bussov, *Moskovskaya khronika*, p. 151.
[2] Massa, *A Short History*, p. 174.

When Dimitry's besieging army set up camp at Tushino, Shuiskii sought to break the military stalemate by diplomatic manoeuvres. King Sigismund's envoys had been in Moscow since the autumn of 1607, but their efforts to improve relations had foundered on Tsar Vasilii's refusal to release the Poles who had been imprisoned after the events of May 1606. Now Shuiskii was willing to make concessions, in the hope of eliminating Polish support for the pretender. The previous Polish envoys were released, and the Mniszechs were allowed to return to Moscow from their exile in Yaroslavl'. A delegation of Różyński's Poles from Tushino was even invited to take part in the negotiations.[3] A peace treaty was agreed on 25 July. The Polish hostages were to be released and granted a safe conduct to the Polish border. In return, Sigismund agreed not to assist Tsar Vasilii's enemies; the Poles at Tushino were to abandon Dimitry, and promise not to support any further pretenders; Jerzy Mniszech was not to refer to Dimitry as his son-in-law, nor to allow Marina to consort with him; and Marina was not to call herself Tsaritsa of Russia.[4] It soon became apparent that Shuiskii had been far too trusting towards the Poles. Taking advantage of his invitation to Moscow to participate in the negotiations, Różyński conducted a reconnaissance of Shuiskii's military dispositions, and launched a surprise attack on the Russians which they repulsed with some difficulty.[5] And after the hostages were freed, not only did the Poles fail to leave Tushino, but other Poles soon joined them. The most notable of the new arrivals was Jan-Piotr Sapieha, a nephew of the Lithuanian chancellor Leo Sapieha.

Having released the Mniszechs and the Polish envoys, Shuiskii dispatched them to the border with a military escort. They travelled by a circuitous route, designed to prevent them from falling into the hands of the pretender's troops. But a detachment of Dimitry's supporters, led by Prince Vasilii Mosal'skii, intercepted them in the Belaya district, near Smolensk, and took Marina and her father prisoner.[6] At Tsarevo-Zaimishche Mosal'skii joined forces with Jan-Piotr Sapieha, who was *en route* to Tushino, and Sapieha escorted Marina to the outskirts of Moscow. Finally, on 10/20 September 1608, Dimitry received Marina joyfully in Tushino, and Marina played the part of a loving wife reunited with a husband whom she had believed to be dead.[7]

It seems highly likely that the 'reunion' of Dimitry and Marina was the culmination of a lengthy period of collusion and negotiation between the pretender and Jerzy Mniszech. As early as January 1608 Dimitry had written to Mniszech, while the latter was still a prisoner at Yaroslavl', to inform him

[3] *PSRL*, vol. 14, p. 80, para. 161.
[4] Karamzin, *Istoriya*, vol. 3, t. XII, col. 51.
[5] *PSRL*, vol. 14, p. 80, para. 161.
[6] *Ibid.*, p. 81, paras. 165–6; Zholkevskii, *Zapiski*, prilozheniya, cols. 201–5.
[7] Hirschberg, ed., *Polska a Moskwa*, pp. 181–7; Bussov, *Moskovskaya khronika*, p. 153.

of his presence at Orel.[8] Karamzin plausibly speculated that secret contacts took place between the Mniszechs and Dimitry while the peace negotiations were being conducted in Moscow in July.[9] Żółkiewski reports that Mniszech deliberately delayed on his way to the frontier, so that Dimitry's forces could stage a pre-arranged 'rescue'.[10] Mniszech himself undoubtedly knew from the outset that this new pretender was not his son-in-law; and on his arrival at Tushino he drove a hard bargain with Dimitry, who had to promise him the Seversk lands and 300,000 roubles in order to gain his recognition.[11] Marina's position is rather more uncertain. Żółkiewski insists that she was even more anxious than her father to be 'rescued' by Dimitry's envoys. Although she had been reliably informed that the pretender was not her husband, she 'very much wanted to be tsaritsa'.[12]

Conrad Bussow, however, takes a more charitable view of the Mniszechs. They were delighted to be rescued by the Tushinites, he says, because they genuinely believed that Dimitry was Marina's husband; and the soldiers who were sent to intercept them were under strict orders not to reveal the truth. As the party approached Tushino, however, a young Polish nobleman, seeing that Marina was singing happily in her carriage in anticipation of her reunion with Dimitry, felt honour bound to dispel her illusions, and told her that the man she was about to meet was not her husband. Marina promptly burst into tears, and the Polish commander of the detachment, noticing her sudden change of mood, demanded to know the reason. Under his questioning, Marina eventually revealed the name of the man who had undeceived her. When confronted with Marina's testimony, the young Pole stated in his own defence that everyone at Tushino knew that the pretender was not who he claimed to be. This frankness did not help his case. He was bound hand and foot and sent to Dimitry, who had him impaled alive.[13]

Bussow's story appears somewhat fanciful, but there were clearly real problems involved in obtaining Marina's recognition of Dimitry. According to the laconic entries in Sapieha's diary, when the Poles approached Tushino on 1/11 September they were met by Różyński, who explained that Dimitry could not welcome them in person because of illness. 'The tsaritsa did not

---

[8] *SGGiD*, vol. 2, no. 156, pp. 326–7.

[9] Karamzin, *Istoriya*, vol. 3, t. XII, col. 53.

[10] Zholkevskii, *Zapiski*, pp. 14–15. The account of the Jesuit Wielewicki, however, insists that the Mniszechs were captured against their will: *ibid.*, prilozheniya, no. 44, col. 205.

[11] Buturlin, *Istoriya smutnogo vremeni*, vol. 2, prilozheniya nos. 9 and 10, pp. 71–3; *SGGiD*, vol. 2, no. 164, p. 340.

[12] Zholkevskii, *Zapiski*, p. 14. See also Stadnitskii ('Dnevnik', pp. 180–2), who suggests that Marina was motivated by a thirst for revenge against Shuiskii.

[13] Bussov, *Moskovskaya khronika*, pp. 152–3. According to Marchocki, however (*Historya*, p. 39) it was Mosal'skii who undeceived Marina, before defecting to Shuiskii.

want to go to the tsar's camp'; but her father went to see Dimitry. On 5/15 September Mniszech visited Dimitry at Tushino again, 'to ascertain whether or not he was the true tsar'. Apparently Mniszech was satisfied – with the terms offered, if not with the identity of the pretender – and on the next day Dimitry himself came to Sapieha's camp to meet Marina. 'There the tsaritsa greeted the tsar somewhat unwillingly and was ungrateful for his arrival.'[14]

Marina's evident reluctance to recognise Dimitry as her husband may have been the result of her genuine ignorance, until the last moment, that he was an impostor; of her unwillingness to go through with a charade to which she had thoughtlessly agreed at an earlier stage; or of a calculated desire to obtain the best possible recompense for her role in the deception. According to Bussow, before Marina would consent to stage a touching public reunion with her 'husband' at Tushino Dimitry had to agree to refrain from conjugal relations until he occupied the throne in Moscow.[15] Maskiewicz states that Marina and Dimitry were secretly married at Tushino, with the agreement of the Jesuits, and lived together as man and wife.[16] Another Pole, however, explicitly states that they were not married.[17] After a few months Jerzy Mniszech left Tushino to return to Poland, and his relations with his daughter were strained.[18] R. G. Skrynnikov speculates, somewhat pruriently, that Mniszech's estrangement from Marina may have been caused by her defiance of the prohibition of sexual intercourse with Dimitry before his restoration to the throne.[19]

Bussow asserts that Marina's recognition of Dimitry as her husband had a significant effect on the pretender's credibility, and attracted a multitude of 'princes and boyars' into his camp.[20] But Marina's initial reluctance to accept the new pretender was well known at Tushino, so that news of their reunion was more likely to have had a positive effect on public opinion outside Moscow, rather than in the capital.[21] It is improbable that anyone who had seen the First False Dimitry – and there must have been many such in the Tushino camp – could have believed that the second pretender was the same person. Nevertheless, Dimitry himself and his advisers evidently believed that there were sufficient gains to be made from Marina's recog-

---

[14] Hirschberg, ed., *Polska a Moskwa*, pp. 184–5.
[15] Bussov, *Moskovskaya khronika*, p. 153. This condition is also referred to in the report of the French agent of April 1610: Zholkevskii, *Zapiski*, prilozheniya, no. 21, cols. 47–56.
[16] Maskevich, 'Dnevnik', pp. 21, 31–2, 297.
[17] Stadnitskii, 'Dnevnik', p. 182.
[18] See her letters to her father of 26 January and 23 March 1609: *SGGiD*, vol. 2, nos. 173 and 178, pp. 353, 359.
[19] Skrynnikov, *The Time of Troubles*, p. 67.
[20] Bussov, *Moskovskaya khronika*, p. 153.
[21] Solov'ev, *Istoriya Rossii*, vol. 4, pp. 494–5; Kostomarov, *Smutnoe vremya*, pp. 322–3.

nition of him, in terms of the establishment of the pretender's credibility, for them to be willing to take the risks involved in bringing the ex-tsaritsa to Tushino.

Defections from Shuiskii to Dimitry had begun even before the pretender set up his headquarters at Tushino. After the fall of Bolkhov, while Tsar Vasilii was regrouping his forces for the defence of Moscow, a group of suspected traitors was arrested in the army. The noble ringleaders were exiled and imprisoned, while other less eminent conspirators were executed in Moscow.[22] In an attempt to rally support, Shuiskii addressed his troops and offered them the alternative of either renewing their oath of loyalty to him and withdrawing to Moscow to withstand the siege; or of quitting his camp without penalty. All chose to swear allegiance; but in the next few days, the chronicler tells us, many nonetheless defected to Tushino.[23] Some of these may have genuinely expected to find their former tsar at Tushino; on discovering the truth, they soon returned to Moscow and denounced Dimitry as an impostor.[24] But others simply sought their maximum advantage with either of the rival tsars; the 'Tushino period' became synonymous in Russian history with cynical switching of allegiance from one camp to another. Bussow names an Austrian mercenary, Johann Heinrich Carles, who transferred his loyalty no less than thrice,[25] while his Russian contemporary Avraamii Palitsyn alleges that some changed sides as many as ten times.[26] Palitsyn calls such people 'migratory birds' (perelety), and describes how after dining together in Moscow one group of friends would return to Shuiskii's palace in the Kremlin, while the others would go to Dimitry's encampment at Tushino. Some Russian families, according to Palitsyn, deliberately kept members in both camps, as a kind of insurance policy.[27] Such behaviour is consistent with the pious Russians' supposed reverence for the sacred figure of the tsar only if we assume that neither Dimitry nor Shuiskii enjoyed any legitimacy. Certainly the former was widely regarded as an impostor, and the latter was increasingly seen as a usurper whose continued rule served as a barrier to the restoration of social and political stability. But the boyars' behaviour is also consistent with the view that their belief in the tsar's sacred status was an elaborate fiction that cloaked the political reality of oligarchy.[28] Faced with rival tsars with competing claims to legitimacy, the boyars pursued their own interests rather than divinely ordained truth. 'They played with the tsar

[22] *PSRL*, vol. 14, pp. 79–80, para. 159.
[23] *Ibid.*, p. 82, para. 169.
[24] Prince Vasilii Mosal'skii was among the first to revert to Shuiskii: Bussov, *Moskovskaya khronika*, p. 153; Hirschberg, ed., *Polska a Moskwa*, p. 184.
[25] Bussov, *Moskovskaya khronika*, pp. 153–4.
[26] Palitsyn, *Skazanie*, p. 119.
[27] *Ibid.*, p. 117.
[28] Keenan, 'Muscovite Political Folkways', p. 142.

as with a child', Avraamii Palitsyn lamented.[29] But even the 'migratory birds', it seems, needed to be able to justify and legitimise their switch of support to the pretender; and Dimitry responded to this need by making his imposture appear as credible as possible.

By the autumn of 1608, Dimitry had acquired a court and a boyar duma consisting of a number of Muscovite nobles and aristocrats who were for various reasons discontented with Shuiskii.[30] A further boost was provided for his credibility when in October 1608 Metropolitan Filaret of Rostov (the former Fedor Nikitich Romanov) was brought to Tushino as a prisoner and appointed Patriarch. In contrast to the Mniszechs, Filaret was, at least initially, an unwilling prisoner. The Metropolitan had led the resistance to Dimitry's troops in Rostov.[31] Filaret refused to flee; he barricaded himself into the church with his supporters, and surrendered only when the enemy threatened to break down the doors.[32] He was stripped of his robes, mocked and humiliated, and taken to Tushino as a prisoner, dressed in 'pagan vestments', with a Tatar hat on his head, and wearing only sandals on his feet.[33] In spite of this treatment, however, Filaret agreed to accept the title of Patriarch from Dimitry.

Filaret's position at Tushino was highly ambivalent. His Moscow counterpart, Patriarch Germogen, was subsequently willing to concede that his rival was not a traitor, having been taken prisoner and obliged to recognise Dimitry under duress rather than of his free will.[34] But Filaret, whose candidacy for the Patriarchate had been rejected by Shuiskii in 1606, played the part with apparent relish. There was no love lost between the Romanovs and the Shuiskiis, and a number of Filaret's kinsmen transferred their allegiance to the Tushino camp.[35] Because of the Romanovs' connection by marriage with the old dynasty, the presence of Filaret at Tushino gave Dimitry's pretence a further element of credibility.

The struggle for the towns

At the end of September 1608 Sapieha and his men left Tushino to lay siege to the great Monastery of the Trinity and St Sergius, situated a few miles to

---

[29] Palitsyn, *Skazanie*, p. 119.

[30] On the character and composition of Dimitry's court, see Platonov, *Ocherki*, pp. 317–21.

[31] Bussov, *Moskovskaya khronika*, pp. 154–5.

[32] *PSRL*, vol. 14, pp. 82–3, para. 171.

[33] Palitsyn, *Skazanie*, p. 123. According to another source he was taken to Tushino on a cart with a whore (*s zhenkoyu*): *AAE*, vol. 2, no. 88, p. 180. These forms of ritual humiliation resemble the methods used by Ivan the Terrible's *oprichniki* against his clerical opponents Metropolitan Filip Kolychev of Moscow and Archbishop Pimen of Novgorod.

[34] *AAE*, vol. 2, no. 169, p. 288.

[35] On Filaret's role at Tushino, see Platonov, *Ocherki*, pp. 316–18.

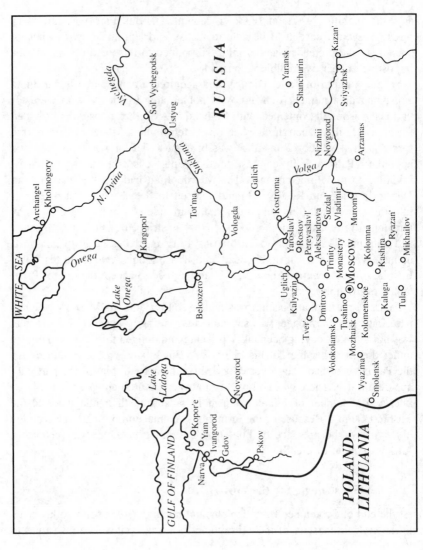

Map 4 Northern Russia. This map shows towns affected by fighting in 1608–12

the north-east of the capital. The siege was to last until January 1610, and the heroic resistance of the defenders constituted one of the most celebrated episodes of the Time of Troubles.[36] The rest of Dimitry's army remained at Tushino. The blockade of Moscow was not complete, since Ryazan', to the south-east, remained loyal to Shuiskii, and supplies were able to enter the capital by the Ryazan' road, which led through Kolomna.

When Shuiskii realised that his peace treaty with Poland was not going to lead to the withdrawal of the intervention forces, he turned for military assistance to Sweden. In August 1608 Tsar Vasilii sent his nephew, Prince Michael Skopin-Shuiskii, to Novgorod to negotiate with Charles IX.[37] Novgorod in the far north, together with Smolensk in the far west, were the only major cities to remain loyal to Shuiskii in the winter of 1608–9. On the Volga, Nizhnii Novgorod and Kazan' continued to be held by Tsar Vasilii's commanders.[38] They held out in the hope of reinforcement by the boyar Fedor Sheremetev who, having withdrawn from his camp outside Astrakhan' in the autumn of 1607, had established his headquarters at Tsaritsyn.[39]

In the autumn of 1608 Dimitry's commanders concentrated on securing the allegiance of those towns which lay to the north and east of Moscow. The first to surrender was Suzdal',[40] followed by Pereyaslavl'-Zalesskii. The citizens of Pereyaslavl' not only capitulated without a fight, but also sent troops to help take Rostov. Metropolitan Filaret of Rostov, as we have seen, made a stand against the Tushinites, who wreaked their vengeance by burning and looting the town.[41] Nearby Yaroslavl', hoping to avoid the fate of Rostov, negotiated terms for its peaceful surrender which were subsequently disregarded by the Poles.[42] Vologda, the other great trading centre of the north, agreed to surrender 'on pain of being razed to its foundations and seeing its inhabitants, men, women, and children, put to the sword if it refused'.[43]

Most of these towns acknowledged Dimitry as a result of the use or threat of force by raiding parties sent out from Tushino or from Sapieha's camp outside the Trinity monastery. But in some cases there appears to have been sympathy for Dimitry's cause on the part of the poorer townspeople. In Yaroslavl', the 'best people' fled, while the ordinary citizens (*chern'*), with the governor Prince Fedor Baryatinskii, offered to surrender the town and

---

[36] The fullest account of the siege of the Trinity monastery is that provided by its cellarer, Avraamii Palitsyn: *Skazanie*, pp. 126–97.

[37] *PSRL*, vol. 14, p. 84, para. 177.

[38] *Ibid.*, para. 174.

[39] See above, ch. 6, p. 180. On Sheremetev's advance up the Volga, see *PSRL*, vol. 14, p. 86, para. 182; p. 88, para. 190.

[40] *AI*, vol. 2, nos. 99–100, pp. 131–3.

[41] *PSRL*, vol. 14, pp. 82–3, paras. 171–2; Bussov, *Moskovskaya khronika*, pp. 154–5.

[42] Bussov, *Moskovskaya khronika*, p. 155; Massa, *A Short History*, pp. 175–6.

[43] Massa, *A Short History*, p. 176.

'kiss the cross' to Tsar Dimitry.[44] In Vologda, according to Isaac Massa, who was in the city at the time, the governor N. M. Pushkin and his *d'yak* R. M. Voronov were 'dismissed from their posts, shamefully treated, and although they were completely innocent, even thrown in jail by the city's inhabitants, who are cruel, stupid, blown with every wind, mindless of their past, present, and future oaths, and live like wild beasts'.[45]

The sources do not provide us with sufficient information to draw any firm conclusions about the nature of these conflicts within Yaroslavl' and Vologda. According to A. A. Zimin, the social struggle of the urban masses against the nobility and merchant elite in the autumn of 1608 represented an anti-feudal movement that signified the continuation of a peasant war, characterised by 'social demagogy' on Dimitry's part.[46] It does not seem, however, that the pretender's own proclamations of this period made any attempt to appeal particularly to the poorer citizens. Dimitry's proclamation to Suzdal' of 23 October made promises to all social groups indiscriminately: if they assisted him to regain his throne, he would reward the nobles with landed estates, the servicemen with money and cloth, and the rest of the population with tax concessions.[47] The pretender appealed for support on the basis of his legitimate claim to the throne; and the towns which swore allegiance to him claimed that they had been deceived by Shuiskii into believing Dimitry to be dead. When Yaroslavl' surrendered, its inhabitants begged Dimitry's pardon for having opposed him: the 'traitors' had told them that he had been killed in Moscow, 'and we thy slaves are guilty before thee our Sovereign, that we believed these traitors to thee our Sovereign'.[48]

In the case of Pskov, the detailed local chronicles demonstrate that the 'big people' supported Shuiskii, while the 'little people' sympathised with Dimitry.[49] Social conflict in Pskov dated back to 1606, when a dispute had arisen between the rich and poor over the distribution of a new tax imposed by Shuiskii. Some of the artisans had complained that they were being allocated an unfair share of the burden, and the rich merchants, supported by the governor, Peter Sheremetev, had accused them of treason. As a result of this episode, in the words of the chronicler, 'there was great depravity in

[44] *AAE*, vol. 2, no. 88, p. 180.
[45] Massa, *A Short History*, pp. 176–7.
[46] Zimin, 'Nekotorye voprosy', p. 101.
[47] *AI*, vol. 2, no. 10, pp. 132–3.
[48] *Ibid.*, p. 133.
[49] The events of the Time of Troubles in Pskov are described in two local chronicles, one of which was published in *PSRL*, vol. 4, pp. 322–30 and in *PL*, vol. 2, pp. 267–77; the other was published in *PSRL*, vol. 5, pp. 66–72 and in *PL*, vol. 1, pp. 134–40. This second account has also been published with a modern translation in *PLDR*, pp. 146–61.

Pskov, the great against the small, the small against the great, and thus it went on to the ruin of all'.[50]

In the spring of 1607 many *strel'tsy* and other servicemen from Pskov and its districts returned home from military service, and persuaded the inhabitants of the surrounding villages to swear allegiance to 'Tsar Dimitry'. Shortly after this there arrived in the Pskov region a certain Fedor Pleshcheev, an ardent supporter of the Second False Dimitry, who provided military reinforcement and leadership for Shuiskii's opponents in the area. For the time being the governor was able to keep the town itself loyal to Tsar Vasilii; but his task was not made easier when a delegation from Novgorod arrived in Pskov, to report that the Swedes would soon be coming to their assistance. 'Because of the Germans [Swedes]', however, the patriotic people of Pskov refused to ally with Novgorod. At this stage the pre-existing social tensions within Pskov expressed themselves in political divisions. The 'little people' suspected Sheremetev of planning to surrender the town to the Swedes; and they also accused him of wanting to arrest and execute many of the artisans and *strel'tsy* as traitors to Shuiskii. The 'big people' supported Sheremetev: and the two groups remained bitterly divided.[51]

In the early summer of 1608 news reached Pskov of the Second False Dimitry's defeat of Shuiskii's troops at Bolkhov. After his victory Dimitry sent envoys to various towns calling on them to swear allegiance to him; the delegation which he sent to Pskov brought with them a proclamation from Dimitry, which, according to the chronicler, created a highly favourable impression in the town. The envoys, however, were thrown into prison.[52] On St Simeon's Day (1 September) 1608, an uprising in Pskov led to the overthrow of Sheremetev and the merchant oligarchy, and the triumph of the 'little people' who sympathised with Dimitry. The rising began with the spread of false rumours that the Swedes were approaching, to lift the virtual siege of the town by Pleshcheev. The inhabitants of Pskov were divided in their reaction to this news. Most of the clergy and the 'big and middle people' still wanted to resist Pleshcheev, but during the ensuing unrest in the town the gates were opened by 'some crazy people, without the agreement or knowledge' of the townspeople. Pleshcheev's troops entered the town, and the next day the citizens of Pskov 'kissed the cross to Tsarevich Dimitry of Moscow'.[53]

During the uprising on 1 September, the 'best people' and the merchants had been thrown into prison by the insurgent townsfolk; and when Pleshcheev

[50] *PL*, vol. 2, p. 268.
[51] *Ibid.*, pp. 269–70.
[52] *Ibid.*, pp. 268–9.
[53] *Ibid.*, pp. 270–1.

entered Pskov, Sheremetev and his aides were also imprisoned. The property of the rich merchants was looted: in the words of the hostile chronicler, the townspeople 'began to live according to their own will ... and they went crazy through living according to their will, and in their avarice they became inflamed with passion for the wealth of others'.[54] Pleshcheev became governor of Pskov in Sheremetev's place, but in the autumn of 1608 new officials were sent to the town from Tushino. These men, according to the chronicler, were fanatical supporters of Dimitry, and they initiated a campaign of terror against the imprisoned supporters of Shuiskii: 'some were impaled, others beheaded, and the rest were tormented with various tortures, and their wealth was confiscated'.[55] This chronicler asserts that Sheremetev was strangled in prison; another source states that he was impaled.[56]

Pskov remained loyal to the Second False Dimitry, in spite of various attempts by Shuiskii's sympathisers to regain control. On 18 May 1609, Swedish and Russian troops from Novgorod tried to capture Pskov, taking advantage of a fire which had broken out in the town. They were repulsed, however, and a new wave of terror broke out, with the little people accusing the big people of starting the fire and of inviting the troops from Novgorod.[57] The leader of the 'little people' at this time was 'a simple peasant', Timofei Trepets, nicknamed Kuvekusha (or Kudekusha).[58] In August 1609, however, there was a counter-revolt against Dimitry's lower-class adherents. Trepets and his henchmen were killed by the clergy and the merchants, and the strel'tsy were driven out of town. But there was still sufficient support for Tsar Dimitry among the ordinary townspeople to prevent the oligarchs from surrendering Pskov to Shuiskii.[59]

In the towns of the north-east, by contrast, support for Dimitry proved to be short-lived. In Vologda, when a new governor and d'yak were sent from Tushino to replace N. M. Pushkin and R. M. Voronov respectively, the townspeople were immediately antagonised by the harsh actions of Dimitry's appointees. The new governor abused and threatened his predecessor, and made crude threats against the rich merchants. 'That same night', Isaac Massa continues, in his eye-witness account,

---

[54] *PL*, vol. 1, p. 134.
[55] *Ibid.*, pp. 134–5.
[56] Popov, ed., *Izbornik*, p. 354.
[57] *PL*, vol. 1, pp. 135–6; vol. 2, pp. 271–2. On the fire, see Lyubomirov, ed., 'Novye materialy', pp. 103–5.
[58] I. I. Smirnov, noting that the chronicler elsewhere refers to Timofei as a musketeer (*Timokha strelets*), suggests that Trepets is a corrupt form of '*strelets*': Smirnov, *Vosstanie Bolotnikova*, p. 207. D. P. Makovskii, however, more plausibly derives the name from *trepat'*, to scutch, and depicts Timokha as a scutcher, a hired worker in the flax or hemp-processing trade: Makovskii, *Pervaya krest'yanskaya voina*, p. 418.
[59] *PL*, vol. 1, p. 136; vol. 2, pp. 272–3.

some Poles who had been prisoners in the town of Vologda for a long time and had now regained their freedom attacked the peasants of the surrounding countryside, subjecting them to the cruellest of insults and despoiling them of everything, even their clothes. They came back into the city after this expedition with their sleds heaped with booty, intending to rejoin the army the next day. That same night, the peasants came to Vologda to lodge their complaints about these acts of brutality. The community, seeing the truth of their account, bitterly regretted rallying to Dmitry and swearing him allegiance.[60]

The townspeople released and reinstated Pushkin and Voronov, seized the new officials and the Poles,

and cut off their heads with axes. Then they rolled the heads and the bodies to the foot of the hill, into the stream called the Zolotitsa, where these human remains were frightful food for dogs and pigs. Having thus rallied openly to the Muscovite party, they swore to be forever faithful to the tsar and spill the last drop of their blood for him.[61]

Vologda reverted to Shuiskii in December 1608; Galich and Kostroma also rebelled against Dimitry at about the same time. According to Bussow, a major role in the defection of these towns was played by a Dutch salt entrepreneur from Yaroslavl', Daniel Eyleff, who wrote to tell them that they need not remain loyal to their oath. They had sworn allegiance to Dimitry Ivanovich, but he had incontrovertible proof that the 'tsar' at Tushino was neither the son of Ivan nor the man who had reigned in Moscow in 1605–6, but a new impostor. An uprising which Eyleff organised in Yaroslavl' was suppressed; and from Yaroslavl' Polish troops commanded by Lisowski quelled the revolts against Dimitry in Galich and Kostroma.[62] In the spring of 1609, however, when the Polish troops were withdrawn, these three towns again rebelled.[63]

These risings against the Tushinites were fuelled by the townspeople's resentment of the rapacity of the Poles and the cossacks. The Russian chronicler attributes a major part in the protests against Dimitry to the 'common people' (chernye lyudi).[64] And Conrad Bussow observes that the main role in the revolts against the depredations of the Poles was played by the peasants and the poor.[65] In other words, the ordinary people, who had often been the first to recognise the Second False Dimitry, were also amongst the first to

[60] Massa, A Short History, p. 177.
[61] Ibid., p. 178. On the events in Vologda, see also AAE, vol. 2, no. 88, pp. 179–81; no. 91, pp. 185–6; no. 94, pp. 191–2; no. 119, pp. 223–4; no. 126, pp. 233–4.
[62] Bussov, Moskovskaya khronika, p. 155.
[63] Massa, A Short History, p. 179; Kostomarov, Smutnoe vremya, pp. 362–9.
[64] PSRL, vol. 14, pp. 86–7, paras. 183–4.
[65] Bussov, Moskovskaya khronika, pp. 157–8.

reject him when he failed to live up to their expectations. A major part in the organisation of opposition to Dimitry fell to those northern towns, such as Novgorod and Ustyug, which remained free from the occupying forces. After its liberation, Vologda too played an important role.[66]

In their bids to rally support for Shuiskii, his adherents placed much emphasis on the heavy taxes and exactions which the Tushinites imposed on the towns which they controlled.[67] Shuiskii's propaganda stressed the threat to Orthodoxy which was presented by the invading Poles, who were allegedly despoiling churches and defiling icons and holy relics. Tsar Vasilii also attacked Dimitry as an impostor: both Dimitry of Uglich and 'the scoundrelly unfrocked monk Grishka Otrep'ev, who called himself by the name of Tsarevich Dimitry' were dead, so that those who kissed the cross to Dimitry did not know to whom they were swearing allegiance.[68] The correspondence among the northern towns also stressed Dimitry's imposture. The townspeople circulated copies of the interrogations of captured Tushinites which contained information that discredited Dimitry: 'this Tsarevich Dimitry is a scoundrel (vor) from Starodub, and the Lithuanians brought him'; 'Dimitry is a scoundrel and not a true tsarevich, but I don't know where he comes from'; 'in the scoundrel's regiments they call a scoundrel Dimitry, and Dimitry is not in the regiments, and the man they call Dimitry is not the scoundrel who was Grishka Otrep'ev in Moscow, but another scoundrel'.[69]

In February 1609 the Swedish commander Jacob Pontus De La Gardie arrived in Novgorod and concluded an agreement with Michael Skopin-Shuiskii. At the beginning of May a combined Russian and Swedish army defeated troops that had been sent from Tushino against Novgorod. On 10 May Skopin-Shuiskii left Novgorod to march on Moscow and lift the siege of the capital. News of his advance encouraged those northern towns which still recognised Dimitry to transfer their allegiance to Shuiskii; but Pskov, as we have seen, still held out, in spite of an attempt by Skopin's forces to capture the city on 18 May. In July 1609 Skopin occupied Tver', whence he moved east to link up with the levies from the north-eastern towns at the Kalyazin monastery. At Aleksandrova Sloboda, north-east of Tushino, they awaited the arrival of the boyar Fedor Sheremetev, who had been liberating the Volga towns to the south-east.[70]

On leaving Tsaritsyn in the spring of 1608, Fedor Sheremetev had secured Saratov and Kazan' for Shuiskii on his journey upriver. Nizhnii Novgorod, under its governor A. S. Alyab'ev, remained loyal to Shuiskii throughout.

---

[66] Platonov, Ocherki, pp. 291–2, 297–306.
[67] See, for example, AAE, vol. 2, no. 88, pp. 179–81.
[68] Ibid., no. 90, p. 183.
[69] Ibid., no. 91, pp. 186–7; no. 94, p. 191.
[70] Kostomarov, Smutnoe vremya, pp. 380–97.

Although the fortified towns on the Volga adhered to Tsar Vasilii, the surrounding countryside supported Dimitry. The indigenous Volga peoples –
the Mordvinians, the Cheremis and others – rose up against the Russian col-
onists in the name of Tsar Dimitry. In December 1608 they laid siege to
Nizhnii, where they were joined by the Tushino commander Prince Semen
Vyazemskii. The besiegers were however defeated by Alyab'ev in January
1609, and Vyazemskii was hanged.[71]

After their defeat at Nizhnii Novgorod, some bands of the Volga peoples
moved north-eastwards towards the lands of Vyatka and Perm'. Two Tatar
nobles (*murzy*) from Arzamas led their men from Koz'modem'yansk, on the
Volga, to capture the towns of Shanchurin and Yaransk.[72] In a petition to
Tsar Vasilii, the sexton of the cathedral in Yaransk, Pavlik Mokeev, described
how the town was obliged to swear allegiance to Dimitry. On 5 January 1609
the *murzy* arrived at Yaransk

with many villainous persons (*vorovskimi lyudmi*) – musketeers and cossacks and
Mordvinians and Chuvash and Cheremis – and they made the people of Yaransk kiss
the cross to the scoundrel who calls himself Prince Dimitry; and, Sire, they brought
the people of Yaransk to the oath to the scoundrel against their will, by the sword.

The arrival of the insurgents provoked an uprising in the town. All the 'best
people' were robbed, and some were cut to pieces. The official Peter Glukhov
was arrested and taken to the rebels' camp, whereupon the *syn boyarskii*
Osanchuk Gorikhvostov was elected by the community to run the town.
Pavlik Mokeev, according to his petition, had hidden in his house during the
uprising; but he was taken from the church by force and made to serve as
clerk (*pod'yachii*) to Gorikhvostov.[73] Thus the small towns in the districts
between the Rivers Volga and Vyatka were still being won over to Dimitry's
cause at a time when much of the rest of Russia had been reconquered for
Shuiskii. Although troops were sent from Vyatka against Yaransk and Shanchurin in April 1609,[74] bands of Cheremis were still active in the area in the
summer of 1610, when the authorities in Perm' and Vyatka corresponded
about the need to raise troops against the insurgents.[75]

In the course of 1609, the towns surrounding Moscow were recaptured for
Shuiskii. After freeing Nizhnii from its besiegers the city governor, Alyab'ev,

---

[71] *PSRL*, vol. 14, p. 86, para. 182; Platonov, *Ocherki*, pp. 282, 307–8.
[72] *AAE*, vol. 2, no. 100, p. 197.
[73] *Ibid.*, no. 116, pp. 220–1.
[74] *Ibid.*, no. 114, p. 216.
[75] *Ibid.*, no. 163, pp. 278–9. On events in the mid-Volga and Vyatka regions in 1608–10, see
Platonov, *Ocherki*, pp. 286–8; Shepelev, *Osvoboditel'naya i klassovaya bor'ba*, pp. 250–72;
Makovskii, *Pervaya krest'yanskaya voina*, pp. 428–30.

went on to the offensive and took Murom and Vladimir in March 1609.[76] When the governor of Vladimir refused to abandon his allegiance to Dimitry, the citizens arrested him, took him to the cathedral to receive the sacraments, and then stoned him to death as an 'enemy of the Muscovite state'. Then the townspeople attacked and routed the 'scoundrels', and took the oath to Tsar Vasilii.[77] Fedor Sheremetev arrived in Nizhnii in the spring of 1609. After an unsuccessful attempt to take Suzdal', he withdrew to Vladimir, whence he joined forces with Skopin-Shuiskii at Aleksandrova Sloboda towards the end of the year.[78]

The military successes of his commanders strengthened Shuiskii's position in Moscow in the second half of 1609. At the beginning of that year the Polish general Młocki had besieged Kolomna, impeding the supply of grain to the capital from the Ryazan' region. As food prices rose, so did discontent with Tsar Vasilii. In February 1609 an attempt to overthrow Shuiskii was made by some of his noble courtiers. The plot was thwarted mainly by Patriarch Germogen's stout defence of the tsar, and the ringleaders, including Prince Roman Gagarin, fled to Tushino. The boyar I. F. Kryuk-Kolychev organised another conspiracy on Palm Sunday, but this was discovered and Kryuk-Kolychev was executed. Soon after this, on 28 May, Prince Roman Gagarin returned to Moscow from Tushino and publicly denounced Dimitry as an impostor and tool of the Polish king. He also reported that the Swedes had arrived in Novgorod and had driven the Poles away. As a result of Gagarin's words, the chronicler tells us, the vacillations of the Muscovites ceased, and thereafter no-one transferred their allegiance to Tushino.[79]

Kaluga

The arrival of Sheremetev at Aleksandrova Sloboda, and the formation there of a united army in support of Shuiskii, caused panic at Tushino. The crisis was intensified with the arrival of envoys sent by King Sigismund to negotiate with Różyński and the other Polish leaders in Dimitry's camp. In the summer of 1609, angered by Swedish support for Shuiskii, Sigismund had decided to intervene directly in the Russian civil war, in order to obtain the Muscovite throne either for himself or for his son Władysław. In September he laid siege to the fortress of Smolensk, which was defended for Shuiskii by its governor M. B. Shein. News of Sigismund's action was not welcomed by the Poles at Tushino, who sent envoys to Smolensk to try to dissuade the king from his undertaking. But Sigismund in his turn made a bid for the

---

[76] Platonov, *Ocherki*, pp. 309–10.
[77] *PSRL*, vol. 14, p. 88, para. 191.
[78] Platonov, *Ocherki*, pp. 310–12.
[79] *PSRL*, vol. 14, p. 87, paras. 185–8; Platonov, *Ocherki*, pp. 330–2.

support of the Tushinites. A delegation from Smolensk arrived at Tushino in December 1609 to conduct negotiations with Różyński from which the pretender was excluded. Fearing treachery, Dimitry decided to flee. On 29 December he escaped from the camp on a manure cart, disguised as a peasant and accompanied only by his jester, Peter Koshelev.[80]

The town in which Dimitry sought refuge after his flight from Tushino was Kaluga, which lies to the south-west of the capital, near the confluence of the rivers Oka and Ugra. Kaluga had been Bolotnikov's headquarters after his retreat from Moscow in December 1606; and it had lain on Dimitry's route to Tushino in the early summer of 1608. Kaluga had a strong citadel, and had direct links with the Seversk towns, which comprised the main base of support for both the First and Second False Dimitrys. During the Tushino period, the pretender's supporters had sent their wives and children to Kaluga for safety, and he hoped that he could count on the loyalty of the townspeople.[81]

Instead of entering Kaluga immediately, however, Dimitry halted at a monastery on the outskirts, and sent some of the monks into the town with an appeal for support. These envoys told the citizens that Dimitry was seeking refuge from Różyński and his perfidious Poles at Tushino, who had been persuaded by King Sigismund to capture him and take him as a prisoner to Smolensk. Sigismund had demanded that Dimitry surrender the Seversk towns to Poland, but he had refused, 'so that the pagan faith should not take root in these lands'. If the Kalugans remained loyal to him, he would lead them against both Shuiskii and the Poles: 'He was ready to die alongside the people for the Muscovite Christian faith, and he would eradicate all other pagan faiths, and would not yield a single village or hamlet to the Polish king, let alone a town or principality.'[82] These patriotic and Orthodox appeals produced the desired effect on the Kalugans, who came to the monastery to welcome him with bread and salt – the symbols of hospitality – and accompanied him to the town governor's palace, where 'they gave him clothing and horses and sleds, and supplied him with food and drink'.[83]

By breaking with his Polish supporters and denouncing them as heretics and traitors, Dimitry was able to harness to his own cause the anti-Polish and anti-Catholic sentiments which had been aroused by the activities of the Tushinites. According to Bussow, Dimitry called on his Russian subjects to seize all the Poles they could find and to kill them, confiscate their property

---

[80] Bussov, *Moskovskaya khronika*, pp. 161–2; *PSRL*, vol. 14, p. 94, para. 219; Karamzin, *Istoriya*, vol. 3, t. XII, cols. 78–82, 104–12; Solov'ev, *Istoriya Rossii*, vol. 4, pp. 544–54; Kostomarov, *Smutnoe vremya*, pp. 400–15.

[81] Platonov, *Ocherki*, p. 315.

[82] Bussov, *Moskovskaya khronika*, p. 162.

[83] *Ibid.*

and send it to him at Kaluga. The ensuing bloodbath extended to Germans, Swedes and other foreigners who were suspected of having dealings with the Poles.[84] In Kaluga itself, the Polish governor Skotnicki was killed on Dimitry's orders on the basis of a false denunciation for treason.[85] Some sources suggest that social conflicts, as well as national and religious hatred, played their part at Kaluga. Avraamii Palitsyn tells us that Dimitry 'was welcomed in Kaluga by the boyars' slaves, and they served him as their tsar. And then Christian blood began to flow freely.'[86] Certainly, Poles and foreigners were not the only victims. The *okol'nichii* I. I. Godunov was thrown from a tower, then drowned in the River Oka[87] – the customary form of execution for a 'traitor-boyar' in the pretenders' camps.

Dimitry's flight from Tushino had been so precipitate that no-one there knew what had happened to him, and it was widely believed that he had been killed by the Poles.[88] This suspicion led to conflict between the Russians and the Poles at Tushino, and many Russians left the encampment. Some defected to Shuiskii in Moscow, and some returned to their homes, while others followed the pretender to Kaluga.[89] Marina found herself in a difficult position. Deserted by her husband, she at first tried to persuade the cossacks to remain loyal to Dimitry,[90] but meeting with no success, she resolved to make her own escape. On 12 January 1610, under pressure from Skopin's advancing troops, Jan-Piotr Sapieha abandoned the siege of the Trinity monastery and withdrew to Dmitrov.[91] Here Marina joined him on 16 February.[92] But as Skopin's forces were following in hot pursuit of Sapieha, Marina decided to seek refuge with her husband. Dressed in the red velvet coat of a Polish nobleman, and armed with a sword and a gun, she rode to Kaluga with an escort of cossacks and mercenaries provided by Sapieha, and was enthusiastically welcomed by Dimitry.[93]

After Marina's defection, Tushino was riven even further with divisions. At the end of January a group of Russian boyars at Tushino had sent a delegation to Smolensk, headed by M. G. Saltykov, who agreed terms with King Sigismund on 4 February for the offer of the Russian throne to Sigismund's son Władysław. At the same time, the Poles at Tushino also sent

[84] *Ibid.*, pp. 162–3.
[85] Bussov, *Moskovskaya khronika*, p. 164.
[86] Palitsyn, *Skazanie*, p. 205.
[87] Karamzin, *Istoriya*, vol. 3, primechaniya k XII tomu, cols. 113–14, no. 475; Bussov, *Moskovskaya khronika*, p. 367, n. 105.
[88] Bussov, *Moskovskaya khronika*, p. 162. This piece of disinformation was assiduously disseminated by Shuiskii's supporters: see *AAE*, vol. 2, no. 155, pp. 267–8.
[89] *PSRL*, vol. 14, p. 94, para. 219.
[90] Stadnitskii, 'Dnevnik', pp. 188–91.
[91] Palitsyn, *Skazanie*, p. 193.
[92] Hirschberg, ed., *Polska a Moskwa*, p. 250.
[93] Bussov, *Moskovskaya khronika*, pp. 164–5.

envoys to the king, demanding that he pay them the money which Dimitry owed them. Sigismund refused to agree to this, whereupon many of the Tushino Poles transferred their allegiance to the pretender at Kaluga.[94]

On 26 February, the day after Marina's departure from Dmitrov, the town was captured by Skopin's forces, and Sapieha was obliged to retreat further westward and set up a new camp on the banks of the River Ugra.[95] The reverses suffered by Sapieha depressed morale at Tushino still further. The Tushinites decided to withdraw *en masse* to Volokolamsk, after which each would be free to go his own way.[96] On 6 March the notorious encampment was burned by its remaining occupants.

Soon after the abandonment of Tushino, Skopin-Shuiskii entered Moscow in triumph, having liberated Russia almost single-handed. Tsar Vasilii, however, was rumoured to be jealous of his nephew's success and popularity. The tsar's brother, Prince Dimitry Shuiskii, had even more reason to be envious, since Skopin-Shuiskii was now widely regarded as the heir to the throne – a role which Prince Dimitry himself had previously hoped to fulfil, Tsar Vasilii having no sons. Thus when Prince Michael died suddenly on 23 April, after dining with Dimitry Shuiskii, it was widely believed that the latter had had him poisoned.[97]

Although the eastern part of Russia had been cleared of the Tushinites, threats still remained to Shuiskii's power: King Sigismund was encamped at Smolensk; and Dimitry was gaining adherents at Kaluga. Tsar Vasilii appointed his brother Dimitry as commander-in-chief in place of Michael Skopin-Shuiskii, and despatched him towards Smolensk with the Swedish general De La Gardie. Sigismund sent his most talented commander, the Hetman Stanisław Żółkiewski, to meet the advancing Russians. On 24 June 1610 Żółkiewski defeated the Russians at Klushino, and occupied Mozhaisk.

Simultaneously with Żółkiewski's advance into the heartland of Russia, the pretender left Kaluga and began to march on Moscow. Dimitry's army had been growing steadily. By the spring of 1610 he had attracted the support of Prince Grigorii Shakhovskoi and several thousand cossacks who had been encamped at Tsarevo-Zaimishche, near Vyaz'ma.[98] Some of Ivan Zarutskii's Don cossacks made their way from Tushino to Kaluga,[99] as did many Poles.[100] At the end of March Różyński died at Volokolamsk, and thereafter many of his troops and Sapieha's joined forces with Dimitry.[101] The adhesion of these

[94] Karamzin, *Istoriya*, vol. 3, t. XII, cols. 115–19; Zholkevskii, *Zapiski*, p. 37.
[95] Hirschberg, ed., *Polska a Moskwa*, pp. 255–6.
[96] *RIB*, vol. 1, col. 184.
[97] *PSRL*, vol. 14, pp. 96–7, paras. 226–7.
[98] Bussov, *Moskovskaya khronika*, p. 162.
[99] *Ibid.*, p. 163; Stadnitskii, 'Dnevnik', p. 191.
[100] *RIB*, vol. 1, col. 186.
[101] Bussov, *Moskovskaya khronika*, pp. 165–6.

Polish troops brought the pretender's army to a strength of about 10,000 men at the time of his second march on Moscow.[102] Shuiskii had called on the Crimean Tatars for military assistance against Dimitry, but the pretender defeated them at Borovsk, and they fled to the steppe.[103] The towns of Kolomna and Kashira went over to Dimitry and on 16 July, having captured the Pafnut'ev monastery and killed many of its defenders, he set up camp at Kolomenskoe, on the outskirts of Moscow.

Vasilii Shuiskii now found himself in an even more desperate situation than he had faced during the Tushino period. The main threat came not so much from the armies encamped at Kolomenskoe and Mozhaisk, as from his opponents within Moscow. Largely as a result of the rumours concerning the death of Skopin-Shuiskii, Tsar Vasilii's own position was much weaker than it had been in 1609, when he had had little difficulty in suppressing the conspiracies against him. The tsar's most bitter enemy was Prokopii Lyapunov, the erstwhile ally of Bolotnikov. Lyapunov, who had been appointed governor of Ryazan' by Shuiskii, raised the region against the tsar, accusing him of the murder of Prince Michael Skopin-Shuiskii.[104] After Żółkiewski's defeat of Dimitry Shuiskii at Klushino, Lyapunov established links with Prince Vasilii Golitsyn in Moscow, to plan the overthrow of Tsar Vasilii.[105] They made contact with Dimitry's supporters and arranged a meeting with them at the Danilov monastery. The Muscovites proposed that they would depose Tsar Vasilii, while at the same time the pretender's supporters would overthrow Dimitry, and then both sides would combine to elect a new tsar acceptable to both sides. On 17 July Prokopii Lyapunov's brother, Zakhar, raised a crowd on Red Square against Shuiskii, and this put pressure on the boyars to force the tsar's abdication. Only Patriarch Germogen opposed the action.[106] Dimitry's supporters, however, double-crossed the Muscovites, and refused to topple the pretender. 'You may have betrayed your oath of allegiance by dethroning your tsar,' they said mockingly, according to the *New Chronicle*, 'but we shall die for ours.'[107] According to Avraamii Palitsyn, the pretender's adherents said, 'You have done right in overthrowing your false tsar; now serve our true tsar as your rightful sovereign.'[108] Patriarch Germogen suggested that Tsar Vasilii be restored to power, but it was too late, and the conspirators had Shuiskii forcibly tonsured.[109]

---

[102] *RIB*, vol. 1, col. 198.
[103] *PSRL*, vol. 14, p. 98, para. 232.
[104] *Ibid.*, p. 97, para. 229.
[105] *Ibid.*, p. 98, para. 231.
[106] *Ibid.*, pp. 99–100, para. 235.
[107] *Ibid.*, p. 100, para. 236.
[108] Palitsyn, *Skazanie*, p. 207.
[109] *Ibid.*, p. 207.

The aim of the plotters in Moscow had clearly been to pre-empt Żółkiewski by uniting the pretender's supporters with Shuiskii's under the banner of a new, elected tsar. Although this plan had been aborted by the deceitfulness of Dimitry's adherents, the boyars at first held to their idea of electing a new tsar who would lead them against both Żółkiewski's Poles and Dimitry's 'scoundrels'. In proclamations to the provinces, the boyars announced the formation of a provisional government headed by Prince F. I. Mstislavskii, which would hold power until an election could be held by 'all the land'.[110] The oath of loyalty to the boyar government specifically called on the people to reject Dimitry's claim to the throne.[111]

This position, however, proved not to be a viable one, in view of the immediate threats posed by the pretender and Żółkiewski. The only real choice facing the Muscovites was to decide whether Dimitry or Władysław was the lesser evil. Opinions in part divided along class lines: Maskiewicz asserts that 'the common people wanted to put [the pretender] on the throne, but the boyars wanted the king's son [Władysław]'.[112] Bussow recounts that a number of boyars and cossacks fled to Dimitry's camp to tell him that the 'little people' in the capital were on his side and would rise up against the 'big people' on his behalf.[113] According to Avraamii Palitsyn, the defectors were motivated by their own fear of a popular uprising in Moscow: 'And these people said, "It is better to serve the tsarlet (*gosudarich*) than to be beaten by our slaves and to suffer eternal torment working for them."'[114] Patriarch Germogen suggested the names of possible Russian candidates for the throne: Prince Vasilii Golitsyn, the aspirant favoured by the clergy; or Michael Romanov, the young son of Filaret, whose claim was based on his kinship with Tsar Fedor's mother, Anastasiya.[115] But Mstislavskii and the boyars preferred the Polish prince, as a less divisive contender.

On 24 July Żółkiewski arrived outside Moscow and set up camp at Nekhoroshevo. His negotiations with the boyars led to an agreement on 17 August, in which Władysław was offered the Russian throne. The terms included an undertaking by Żółkiewski to assist the boyars to capture or kill the pretender, after which the Poles would withdraw to Mozhaisk. If Dimitry attempted to attack Moscow, Żółkiewski would oppose him, and would endeavour to detach Sapieha and his troops from the pretender's camp. The Hetman also promised not to refer to Marina as the tsaritsa of Russia, and agreed to take her back to Poland.[116] In the absence of instructions from Sigismund,

---

[110] *AAE*, vol. 2, no. 162, pp. 277–8; *SGGiD*, vol. 2, no 197, pp. 388–9.
[111] *SGGiD*, vol. 2, no. 198, p. 390.
[112] Maskevich, 'Dnevnik', p. 43.
[113] Bussov, *Moskovskaya khronika*, p. 176.
[114] Palitsyn, *Skazanie*, p. 208.
[115] Zholkevskii, *Zapiski*, pp. 74–5.
[116] *SGGiD*, vol. 2, no. 199, pp. 396–7.

Żółkiewski had negotiated these terms very much on his own initiative, basing himself on the agreement which the Tushino boyars had reached with the king at Smolensk in February 1610. Two days after the Muscovites had taken the oath of allegiance to Władysław, however, a messenger arrived from Sigismund, instructing the Hetman to agree terms with the boyars for an offer of the throne not to Władysław, but to Sigismund himself. Żółkiewski, realising that the king's candidature would be totally unacceptable to the Russians, thought it prudent to keep these instructions secret.[117]

Dimitry too had tried to do a deal with the Poles. On 24 July, as Żółkiewski approached the outskirts of Moscow, he was met by a delegation from the pretender's army, headed by the Pole Janikowski. They were on their way to Sigismund's camp at Smolensk, with an offer from Dimitry to cede the Seversk lands to the king, and to pay him vast sums of money, in return for Sigismund's support for his claim to the throne. Janikowski sought to gain Żółkiewski's backing, but the Hetman refused to commit himself.[118] After the conclusion of his agreement with the Moscow boyars, however, Żółkiewski established contact with Sapieha, calling on him to persuade Dimitry to submit to the king. If he did so, the Hetman asserted, he was willing to ask Sigismund to reward the pretender with the town of Grodno or Sambor. But if Dimitry were unwilling to surrender voluntarily, Sapieha was to hand him over or drive him out of his camp.[119]

Sapieha himself was prepared to accommodate Żółkiewski, but his men refused to betray Dimitry. The Hetman then resorted to a show of force. He agreed with the boyars that they would send troops from Moscow to stand alongside his own army – instructing them to garrison the capital securely behind them, since he knew 'that many people there were well-disposed to the impostor'. But Żółkiewski was reluctant to shed the blood of fellow Poles; and Sapieha accepted his offer of negotiations. Sapieha agreed that the terms which the Hetman had proposed to Dimitry were reasonable, and expressed his willingness to hand the pretender over if he himself refused to accept them. Dimitry and Marina were holding court at the nearby monastery of St Nicholas on the River Ugresha, and when they were offered the choice of Grodno or Sambor in exchange for renouncing their claim to the Russian tsardom, they understandably declined.[120]

On receiving the news of Dimitry's refusal to surrender voluntarily, Żółkiewski combined with the Russian troops to surround the monastery. Fore-

---

[117] Zholkevskii, *Zapiski*, pp. 78–9.

[118] *Ibid.*, pp. 72–3, and prilozheniya, no. 33, cols. 99–102.

[119] *Ibid.*, pp. 79–80. Sigismund had earlier promised the envoys of the Tushino Poles at Smolensk that he would make provision for Dimitry and Marina, if they surrendered to him: Karamzin, *Istoriya*, vol. 3, t. XII, cols. 118–19.

[120] Zholkevskii, *Zapiski*, pp. 80–3.

warned by one of his supporters in Moscow, however, the pretender was able to make his escape at night, with Marina and her ladies, escorted only by Zarutskii and a few hundred Don cossacks. They headed for Kaluga, and had such a good start that Żółkiewski was obliged to abandon his plans to pursue them. The next day, the Russians who remained in Dimitry's camp at Kolomenskoe took the oath of loyalty to Prince Władysław. In spite of Żółkiewski's insistence that the pretender's boyars should retain the rank which Dimitry had conferred on them, the Moscow boyars refused to recognise them as their equals, whereupon several of them 'again escaped to the impostor'.[121]

The flight of the pretender from his camp outside Moscow removed the only serious rival to Władysław's candidature for the Russian throne, and Żółkiewski was quick to consolidate his position. He ensured that the Russian delegation which was sent to Smolensk to offer the throne to Władysław included both Prince Vasilii Golitsyn, the Russian candidate favoured by the Orthodox Church, and Filaret, the father of the other main contender, Michael Romanov.[122] In practice, these Russian envoys became hostages in the hands of the king. Then, on the pretext that the people of Moscow might revolt in favour of the pretender, Żółkiewski moved his army into the capital, in direct contravention of the terms of his agreement of 17 August with the Moscow boyars.[123] Finally, having made all the arrangements that he could to secure his control over Russia, and leaving Alexander Gosiewski in command of Moscow, Żółkiewski departed for Smolensk. He took with him into captivity the deposed tsar, Vasilii Shuiskii, and his brothers Dimitry and Ivan.[124] Żółkiewski aimed to confront the king personally about his desire to acquire the Muscovite throne for himself rather than for his son.[125] Sigismund, however, remained adamant in his desire to be tsar. In his negotiations with the Russian envoys he insisted that he could not send his son to Moscow until he had brought about the surrender of Smolensk, whose inhabitants he suspected of sympathising with the pretender, and until he had captured Dimitry at Kaluga. It soon became clear to the Russians that in swearing allegiance to Władysław, and allowing Żółkiewski to occupy the capital, they had in effect delivered the country over to King Sigismund. Growing opposition to the Polish occupation began to play into the hands of the pretender.

After the boyars' agreement with Żółkiewski on 17 August, most of the towns which had previously recognised Shuiskii swore allegiance to Prince

---

[121] *Ibid.*, pp. 83–5.
[122] *Ibid.*, pp. 86–9.
[123] PSRL, vol. 14, p. 102, para. 242; Zholkevskii, *Zapiski*, pp. 89–90.
[124] PSRL, vol. 14, p. 103, para. 247.
[125] Zholkevskii, *Zapiski*, pp. 90–9.

Władysław.[126] Many of the Seversk towns still remained loyal to Dimitry, in spite of attempts by King Sigismund's forces to capture them. Astrakhan' too adhered to the pretender, as did Pskov and some other northern towns. The situation in the north-west of Russia at this time was very complex. The towns were being harassed by the Swedes, who were bitterly opposed to the Polish bid for the Russian throne. The boyar Ivan Saltykov was sent from Moscow to Novgorod to clear the region of the Swedes, but Saltykov soon discovered that the inhabitants of the city had reservations about taking the oath of allegiance to Władysław. They allowed him to enter Novgorod only after he had promised not to bring any Polish troops into the city with him. Saltykov reported to King Sigismund that the depredations of the Poles were deterring many towns from acknowledging Władysław.[127]

Pskov remained loyal to Dimitry. In the spring of 1610 Shuiskii had sent envoys to the town to report the fall of Tushino. This led to rejoicing among the 'big people', but the little people, fearing a coup by the oligarchs, invited the *strel'tsy* back into the town to protect them. Many of the 'best people' fled to Novgorod and Pechory, leaving Dimitry's supporters more securely entrenched in Pskov than before.[128] When after Shuiskii's overthrow messengers arrived in Pskov from Moscow and from Novgorod, calling on the town to swear allegiance to Władysław, the clergy and the 'big people' wanted to unite with the Novgoroders, but they did not dare to act, 'fearing the *strel'tsy* and the little people and the cossacks'.[129] But as the Swedes continued to harass the north, the people of Pskov invited the Polish commander Alexander Lisowski to enter the town to protect them. The behaviour of Lisowski's troops soon led the Pskovans to regret their invitation, and they managed to persuade him to go to defend nearby Ivangorod against the Swedes. Subsequently they refused to let Lisowski and his Poles back into Pskov, but he remained in the neighbourhood, harassing the town and its surrounding district.[130]

By the end of the year it had become clear in the provinces that the Poles had in fact taken control of the capital, and that the new tsar was not the potential convert to Orthodoxy, Prince Władysław, but the ardent Catholic King Sigismund. In January 1611 the inhabitants of Kazan' wrote to the Vyatkans to report that they had sworn allegiance to Dimitry, because they had heard that the boyars in Moscow wanted to take the oath of loyalty to King Sigismund. Dimitry was seen in Kazan' as a defender of Orthodoxy

---

[126] *Ibid.*, pp. 85–6. For the wording of the oath, see *AAE*, vol. 2, no. 164, p. 280.
[127] *SGGiD*, vol. 2, nos. 209–10, pp. 452–63.
[128] *PL*, vol. 1, pp. 136–7; vol. 2, pp. 274–5.
[129] *PL*, vol. 2, pp. 273–4.
[130] *PL*, vol. 1, p. 138; vol. 2, p. 275. On Lisowski, see also *PSRL*, vol. 14, p. 102, para. 243; Bussov, *Moskovskaya khronika*, p. 160.

against the dangers of 'the evil and accursed Catholic faith'; and the oath called on his faithful subjects to reject the claims of the king and the prince to the Russian throne, and to oppose the Poles by all possible means.[131] It did however recognise that Dimitry's supporters included undesirable elements, against whom they needed to take precautions:

As for the cossacks from the Volga, the Don, the Terek and the Yaik, and the *strel'tsy* from Astrakhan', we shall not let them into the town in large numbers, and we shall not obey their orders; but we shall let the cossacks into the town for trade in smaller numbers, ten, or twenty, or thirty at a time, but we shall not let them stay in the town for long.[132]

The Vyatkans, on receiving this news from Kazan', also took the oath to Dimitry, and wrote to nearby Perm' to persuade its inhabitants to do likewise. The people of Perm', however, were more circumspect, and while promising in their reply to unite with the Vyatkans to defend the Orthodox faith against its destroyers, they did not commit themselves to swearing allegiance to the pretender.[133]

The situation in Kazan' itself appears to have been more complex than its inhabitants had admitted to the Vyatkans. The town governor was the veteran intriguer Bogdan Bel'skii. Bel'skii had been named as one of the authors of the letter to Vyatka, but he subsequently turned against Dimitry. According to the *New Chronicle*, Bel'skii tried to persuade the citizens of Kazan' 'not to kiss the cross to the Rogue, but to kiss the cross to whoever would be [elected] sovereign of the Muscovite state'. The *d'yak* Nikinor Shulgin, on behalf of the pretender's supporters, ordered Bel'skii's execution, and the governor suffered the classic fate of a 'traitor-boyar' when he was thrown from the top of a tower. Three days later, a messenger arrived in Kazan' from Kaluga with the news of Dimitry's death.[134]

After his second flight from the outskirts of Moscow to Kaluga, the pretender had been understandably discouraged. According to Bussow, he was so disillusioned by the treachery of the Russians and the Poles that he proposed to recruit Tatars and Turks to assist him to regain his throne. At Kaluga his closest and most trusted adherents were cossacks and Tatars. In an attempt to revenge himself on the Poles, he sent the Tatars out in raiding parties to seize any Polish nobles and merchants they could find and confiscate their property. The Poles were brought as prisoners to Kaluga, where they were tortured to death or drowned in the River Oka. The pretender also made plans

[131] *AAE*, vol. 2, no. 170, pp. 291–3.
[132] *Ibid.*, p. 293.
[133] *Ibid.*, no. 170, p. 291; no. 171, pp. 293–4.
[134] *PSRL*, vol. 14, p. 105, para. 249.

for a tactical withdrawal to Astrakhan', and sent an aide to that city to inform his loyal subjects that Tsar Dimitry and Tsaritsa Marina intended to honour them by setting up court there.[135] According to Żółkiewski, Dimitry planned to establish his new headquarters at Voronezh, and had that town fortified and provisioned to serve as a refuge if he were pressed hard at Kaluga by Sapieha's forces.[136]

By the end of the year, however, Dimitry had greater cause for optimism. The Polish occupation of Moscow was leading to disaffection in the northern towns; and there was evidence of sympathy for the pretender even in the ranks of the boyars. In October 1610 a priest was arrested and put to the torture in Moscow, accused of acting as an intermediary between Dimitry at Kaluga and the Princes Golitsyn, Vorotynskii and Zhirovoi-Zasekin. It is not clear whether there was any real basis for the accusation; the entire affair was skilfully manipulated by Gosiewski in order to tighten his control over the capital, and to suppress opposition to Sigismund's candidacy for the throne.[137] Certainly there are signs that Dimitry's confidence had revived by the autumn of 1610; in a proclamation to Pskov he stated his intention of marching again on Moscow to regain his throne.[138] Before he could implement any such plan, however, the pretender was murdered at Kaluga.

The Khan of Kasimov, a Tatar prince who had been in Russian service since the reign of Ivan the Terrible, had recently come to Dimitry's camp at Kaluga, to join his wife and son. His son, however, denounced the khan as a traitor, and the pretender had him killed. The Tatar prince Peter Urusov resolved to seek revenge, and on 11 December, when the pretender was out driving with his jester, Peter Koshelev, Urusov shot Dimitry and cut off his head. Urusov and his followers fled to the Crimea; and when Koshelev returned to Kaluga and raised the alarm, the Tatars who remained in the town were massacred by the Russians. The pretender's body was brought back to Kaluga, and given an honourable burial in the local cathedral.[139]

The death of the Second False Dimitry did not however eradicate the phenomenon of pretence. Shortly after the murder of her husband, Marina gave birth to a son, who was named Ivan in honour of his putative grandfather. The child was baptised into the Orthodox faith, and the people of Kaluga swore allegiance to him as the true heir to the throne.[140] Most commentators accept that this infant was indeed Marina's son by the pretender;

---

[135] Bussov, *Moskovskaya khronika*, pp. 177–9.

[136] Zholkevskii, *Zapiski*, p. 110.

[137] *Ibid.*, pp. 109–10; *RIB*, vol. 1, pp. 690–3; Skrynnikov, *The Time of Troubles*, pp. 109–11.

[138] *AI*, vol. 2, no. 305, pp. 359–60.

[139] *Ibid.*, no. 307, pp. 364–5; Zholkevskii, *Zapiski*, pp. 111–13; Bussov, *Moskovskaya khronika*, pp. 177–9; *PSRL*, vol. 14, pp. 104–5, para. 248.

[140] Bussov, *Moskovskaya khronika*, p. 179; *PSRL*, vol. 14, p. 105, para. 248; Zholkevskii, *Zapiski*, p. 113.

the sceptical nineteenth-century historian Karamzin, however, suggested that the suspiciously well-timed birth might have been feigned by the tsaritsa in order to retain some political influence: 'Marina, in her despair losing neither her wits nor her ambition, immediately declared herself pregnant and soon gave birth ... to a son who was solemnly christened and called Tsarevich Ioann, to the lively delight of the people. A new deception had been prepared.'[141]

[141] Karamzin, *Istoriya*, vol. 3, t. XII, col. 161.

Ivan Zarutskii and the national liberation movement

After the death of the Second False Dimitry at Kaluga, the cossack *ataman* Ivan Zarutskii became the protector of Marina and her infant son. The Russian boyars in Moscow sent an envoy to Kaluga to persuade the inhabitants to swear allegiance to Władysław, and Zarutskii fled from the town with Marina and her child.[1] At this time Prokopii Lyapunov, the governor of Ryazan', was attempting to organise an army to liberate Moscow from the Poles, and Zarutskii offered his services to Lyapunov. It must be assumed that even at this early stage Zarutskii hoped that the Russians might accept Marina's son as tsar; and there is some evidence that he was encouraged in this belief by Lyapunov,[2] although the official programme of the liberation army was to serve 'whomever the Lord God grants to us in the Muscovite state'.[3] In March 1611 the various detachments marched on Moscow from the towns where they had mustered.[4] Lyapunov brought servicemen from Ryazan', and Zarutskii led his Don cossacks from Tula, having installed Marina and her son in the town of Kolomna.[5] Kaluga too sent troops. After Zarutskii's departure the townspeople had refused to acknowledge Władysław, and the boyars' representative had to flee back to Moscow.[6] The contingent of men from Kaluga was headed by Prince Dimitry Trubetskoi, the most senior of the Second False Dimitry's boyars.[7]

As the liberation army approached Moscow, the inhabitants of the capital staged an unsuccessful uprising against the Poles on 19 March 1611. The occupiers withdrew into the Kremlin, burning the outlying parts of the city as they retreated. The liberators arrived to find smoking ruins and hordes of

---

[1] The sequence of events in Kaluga following the pretender's death is somewhat confused. For a useful review of the sources, see the editor's introduction to Bussov, *Moskovskaya khronika*, pp. 28–30.

[2] Solov'ev, *Istoriya Rossii*, vol. 4, p. 625; Girshberg, *Marina Mnishek*, pp. 269, 337.

[3] *AAE*, vol. 2, no. 179.ii, p. 308.

[4] Platonov, *Ocherki*, pp. 376–8.

[5] *PSRL*, vol. 14, p. 112, para. 270.

[6] *Ibid.*, p. 105, para. 251.

[7] *Ibid.*, para. 250; Palitsyn, *Skazanie*, p. 215.

homeless Muscovites. They set up camp outside the capital and took an oath to elect a tsar. But the forces besieging Moscow were very heterogeneous in their composition, and were riven with disputes and disagreements. They could not even agree on the choice of a single leader, creating instead a triumvirate of Lyapunov, Trubetskoi and Zarutskii.[8] On 30 June an agreement was signed by the triumvirs and by representatives of the troops, which attempted to resolve conflicts over land allocations to the servicemen.[9] New disputes soon broke out, however, over their preferred candidate for the throne. Lyapunov favoured a Swedish prince, one of the sons of Charles IX. This choice was dictated by pragmatism: Smolensk had been captured by King Sigismund at the beginning of June, and Lyapunov hoped for military assistance from the Swedes against the Poles. But instead of coming to the aid of the Russian forces at Moscow, the Swedish commander De La Gardie occupied Novgorod on 16 July, and the citizens swore allegiance to Gustav Adolph or Charles Philip of Sweden. Zarutskii, however, still cherished hopes for the succession of Marina's son, Tsarevich Ivan Dmitrievich, subsequently to be known as the *vorenok* ('little rogue').[10] The two leaders' support for rival candidates for the throne contributed to a conflict which was to lead to Lyapunov's murder by the cossacks on 22 July.[11]

The death of Lyapunov freed Zarutskii's hands *vis-à-vis* Marina. At Kolomna, the widow of the two False Dimitrys had set up a royal court for herself and her son, with an entire hierarchy of boyars and other nobles and a host of high-born ladies-in-waiting, including the mother of Prince Dimitry Trubetskoi. In letters to her boyars and *voevody* – the *Piskarev Chronicle* notes indignantly – Marina still signed herself 'tsaritsa'.[12] The same chronicle, noting that Zarutskii dispatched his wife to a convent and sent his son to Kolomna as one of Marina's table-attendants, adds that the *ataman* himself 'wanted to marry her and sit on the Muscovite throne and be tsar and grand prince'.[13] It is unlikely that Zarutskii aimed so high, but as Marina's protector (and presumed lover) he could realistically have expected to be *de facto* regent for the infant Tsarevich Ivan. It is not clear whether Zarutskii openly avowed his support for Ivan's candidature at this time: his enemies, however,

---

[8] *PSRL*, vol. 14, pp. 108–9, paras. 258–9.

[9] For discussion of the agreement, see Platonov, *Ocherki*, pp. 381–90.

[10] The term *vorenok*, the diminutive of *vor* (scoundrel, rogue), is used to designate Marina's son in the *New Chronicle*: *PSRL*, vol. 14, p. 112, para. 270; p. 123, para. 306; p. 134, para. 343. *Vorenok* is rendered by Hugh Graham as 'Tiny Thief' in his translation of R. G. Skrynnikov's *The Time of Troubles*; and, even more alliteratively, as 'Baby Brigand' by Robert Crummey in *The Formation of Muscovy*.

[11] There are conflicting accounts of the background to Lyapunov's murder. See, for example: *PSRL*, vol. 14, pp. 112–13, paras. 270–1; Maskevich, 'Dnevnik', pp. 77–8; Marchocki, *Historya*, pp. 123–4.

[12] *PSRL*, vol. 34, p. 216.

[13] *Ibid.*, p. 217.

were quick to allege that the cossacks planned to put the pretender's son on the throne.[14] In August 1611 Patriarch Germogen, who was then a prisoner of the Poles in the Kremlin, managed to smuggle out a letter in which he called on the 'boyars and the cossack host' not to recognise 'the accursed son of Panna (Lady) Marinka', adding that the child had been declared anathema both by the Holy Synod and by the patriarch himself.[15] Germogen's letter was taken to Nizhnii Novgorod, and then forwarded to Kazan', where the inhabitants resolved

not to want the accursed son of Panna Marinka on the throne; and if the cossacks decide to choose that son of Marinka's, or anyone else, for the Muscovite throne, by their own arbitrary will, without consulting with all the land, then we shall not accept that Sovereign on the Muscovite throne, and we shall stand against him unanimously, as the entire state of Kazan'; and we shall elect as Sovereign for the Muscovite state, having consulted with all the land, whomever the Lord God grants.[16]

The receipt of Patriarch Germogen's letter in Nizhnii Novgorod, in August 1611, served as an impulse for the organisation of a new liberation army.[17] The collection of resources was undertaken by a local butcher and elected representative of the townspeople, Koz'ma Minin; and the command of the troops was entrusted to Prince Dimitry Pozharskii. At the beginning of December 1611 Pozharskii and his colleagues in Nizhnii Novgorod sent proclamations to the northern towns of Vologda and Sol' Vychegodsk, calling for support.[18] These appeals, which presented an apocalyptic picture of Russia's current woes, contained strongly worded denunciations of pretenders as 'false Christs' and 'precursors of the Antichrist' who planned to implement the will of 'their father, Satan'.[19] The equation of pretenders, as 'false tsars', with the 'false Christs' who were expected to appear before the last days,[20] partly reflects the Russian identification of the tsar with Christ; the recent fall of Moscow to the 'heretical' Poles seemed to confirm to pious Orthodox Christians that the end of the world was imminent. The specific brunt of Prince Dimitry's attack, however, was directed against the supporters of Marina and her son, whom he described as illegitimate (*zakonoprestupnym*).[21]

---

[14] Platonov, *Ocherki*, pp. 395–7; Dolinin, *Podmoskovnye polki*, pp. 54–5.

[15] *AAE*, vol. 2, no. 194.ii, pp. 333–4.

[16] *Ibid.*, no. 194.i, pp. 332–3.

[17] Zabelin, *Minin i Pozharskii*, pp. 74–81; Platonov, *Ocherki*, pp. 400–1; Lyubomirov, *Ocherk*, pp. 47–52, 336–40.

[18] *AAE*, vol. 2, no. 201, pp. 338–41; Lyubomirov, *Ocherk*, pp. 233–7. For a discussion of the dating and content of these proclamations, see *ibid.*, pp. 73–7.

[19] *AAE*, vol. 2, no. 201, pp. 338–9; Lyubomirov, *Ocherk*, pp. 233–4. In a later proclamation to Vychegda, Pozharskii referred to Grisha Otrep'ev as a 'precursor of the Antichrist who wars against God' (*predotecha bogobornogo Antikhrista*): *AAE*, vol. 2, no. 203, p. 344.

[20] Matthew 24.5, 24.11, 24.23–4.

[21] *AAE*, vol. 2, no. 201, p. 339; Lyubomirov, *Ocherk*, p. 234. The assertion that Marina's son was illegitimate, which was frequently repeated by contemporaries, may simply refer to the

Kolomna had become a centre of agitation by Marina on behalf of herself and Tsarevich Ivan. Pozharskii reported that Marina had sent a messenger from Kolomna to Astrakhan' with 'subversive letters' (*smutnymi gramotami*), and also that she had written similar letters to the Shah, entrusting them to a Persian envoy, who had however been arrested in Kazan'.[22] There is little evidence to indicate how effective or how widespread the distribution of Marina's proclamations was. They may have influenced events in the town of Arzamas, where in early February 1612 the *strel'tsy* rose against the nobility, killing, robbing, torturing and burning in the name of Marina and her son.[23] And Marina's correspondence with Astrakhan' may not have been unconnected with the rumoured appearance there, at the beginning of 1612, of a pretender claiming to be Tsar Dimitry, in the company of 'Prince Peter Urusov, who killed the rogue of Kaluga'.[24] No more is known about this pretender, who appears to have vanished from the scene by the time of Zarutskii's arrival in Astrakhan' with Marina and her son towards the end of 1613. The existence in the Astrakhan' provincial archive of two documents which refer to Tsar Dimitry Ivanovich, Tsaritsa Marina Yur'evna and Tsarevich Ivan Dimitrievich,[25] led the historian Kostomarov to speculate that they might refer to this pretender of 1612, but it is more likely that they derive from the later period when Zarutskii was present in the city.[26] Writing in December 1611, Pozharskii did not appear to have heard of the Astrakhan' pretender, but linked Marina's name instead with 'the rogue who is standing near to Pskov'.[27] This was the Third False Dimitry, who had been active in the north-west of Russia since the spring of 1611.

The Third False Dimitry

The Third False Dimitry had appeared in Novgorod at the beginning of 1611, but he failed to gain much support there, and went to Ivangorod with some of his followers.[28] He arrived there on Easter Saturday (23 March) 1611, and was greeted with great enthusiasm by the town's inhabitants.[29] Very little is

allegation that she was never legally married to the Second False Dimitry. The author of the *Piskarevskii Chronicle*, however, openly states that the child's father was unknown, because of Marina's promiscuity ('*mnogie s neyu vorovali*'): *PSRL*, vol. 34, pp. 216, 219. Contemporary documents frequently referred to the child as 'the bastard' (*vybledok, vyblyadok*): e.g. *AI*, vol. 3, no. 15, p. 114; no. 282, p. 447.

22 *AAE*, vol. 2, no. 201, p. 340; Lyubomirov, *Ocherk*, p. 236.
23 Dolinin, *Podmoskovnye polki*, p. 103.
24 *SGGiD*, vol. 2, no. 277, p. 585.
25 *AI*, vol. 3, nos. 263–4, pp. 429–30. One of these documents is a decree on fishing rights, the other a petition from an imprisoned *strelets*.
26 Kostomarov, *Smutnoe vremya*, p. 628, n. 2. See p. 221 below.
27 *AAE*, vol. 2, no. 201, p. 340; Lyubomirov, *Ocherk*, p. 236.
28 Petrei, *Istoriya*, p. 297; Widekind, *Historia*, pp. 229–30.
29 *PL*, vol. 1, p. 139; vol. 2, p. 275; Widekind, *Historia*, p. 230.

known about the origins of this pretender. The *New Chronicle* says that he was Matyushka, a deacon from the district beyond the River Yauza in Moscow; but it entitles this paragraph, 'On Sidorka, the rogue of Pskov', and refers to him elsewhere as Sidorka.[30] Petrei states that the pretender had been a simple secretary in Moscow, and adds that he was a cunning fellow with a clever tongue.[31] The Swedish historian Widekind says that some people believed the new Tsar Dimitry to be the illegitimate son of Chodkiew-icz, the Lithuanian hetman; but Widekind himself asserts that he was a common market trader in knives, who had been recognised as such in Novgorod.[32] There is no evidence that any individual or group acted as backers for this pretender; he appears to have assumed the role of Tsar Dimitry on his own initiative, modelling himself on previous pretenders.[33] We do not know how he attempted to justify his claim to be Dimitry, nor whether his appearance was preceded by rumours concerning yet another miraculous escape from death. The Pskov chronicler notes simply that although the rogue of Tushino had been killed at Kaluga by Peter Urusov, it was now said that he had not been killed, but had gone to Ivangorod.[34] According to Widekind, when the pretender arrived in Ivangorod he provided a long and eloquent account of his three successive escapes from death in Uglich, Moscow and Kaluga.[35] He was soon able to attract a following, not only in Ivangorod, but also in the neighbouring towns of Yam, Kopor'e and Gdov.[36] Some cossacks also came from Novgorod to join him – 'abandoning Novgorod to the Germans [Swedes]', in the words of the chronicler – and some *strel'tsy* arrived from Pskov.[37]

While he was at Ivangorod, the pretender sent envoys to Philip Scheding, the Swedish governor of Narva, asking for military assistance from Charles IX to help him to regain his throne. The king dispatched the diplomat Petr Petrei to Ivangorod to check the identity of the pretender, but the latter, aware that Petrei had seen the First False Dimitry in Poland and in Moscow, made various excuses to avoid meeting him. The Swedish envoy did have an audi-

---

[30] *PSRL*, vol. 14, p. 115, para. 279; p. 118, para. 289. The 'Karamzin chronograph' also calls him Matyushka, a former deacon from beyond the Yauza: Popov, ed., *Izbornik*, p. 354. The Pskov chronicler describes him as Matyushka, a former deacon who had fled from Moscow: *PL*, vol. 1, p. 139. A Novgorod chronicle describes him as Matyushka, a deacon from Kaluga: *Novgorodskie letopisi*, p. 474. Pozharskii, in a proclamation of 7 April 1612 from Yaroslavl' to Sol' Vychegodsk, refers to the Pskov pretender as Sidorka: *AAE*, vol. 2, no. 203, p. 346.

[31] Petrei, *Istoriya*, p. 297.

[32] Widekind, *Historia*, p. 355.

[33] Zabelin suggests that the Third False Dimitry was set up by Zarutskii and Trubetskoi, but provides no evidence for this: Zabelin, *Minin i Pozharskii*, p. 73.

[34] *PL*, vol. 1, p. 139.

[35] Widekind, *Historia*, p. 230.

[36] Petrei, *Istoriya*, p. 298; *Novgorodskie letopisi*, p. 474.

[37] *PL*, vol. 1, p. 139.

ence with the pretender's advisers, who promised to send ambassadors to negotiate an agreement with the king concerning an alliance. But the embassy never materialised, and the Swedes subsequently denounced the new Tsar Dimitry as an impostor.[38] Charles IX may at first have believed that the new pretender was indeed 'Tsar Dimitry',[39] but when he was assured that he was an impostor, the Swedish king instructed Scheding to break off relations with him.[40]

On 24 June 1611 the pretender left Ivangorod for Pskov.[41] Although Pskov had been one of the most loyal bases of support for the Second False Dimitry, its citizens were not at first eager to acknowledge this new pretender. The troops from Pskov who came to join him at Ivangorod had had to leave the town clandestinely: one local chronicler states that 'on 15 April the Pskov cossacks said they were going against Lisowski, but went to the rogue at Ivangorod'.[42] When the pretender showered the town with his proclamations, in which he claimed to be the tsar, the Pskovans denounced him as a godless apostate. Having failed to win the town by propaganda, the pretender marched against Pskov with heavy artillery – cannon, battering rams and throwing engines. But before he could force the town's submission, the pretender learned that Swedish troops were advancing against him, and on 23 August he retreated to Ivangorod, abandoning his cannon to the Pskovans, and losing many of his men in a skirmish with the Swedes at Gdov.[43]

With the Swedish occupation of Novgorod in July 1611, the Russian inhabitants of the city had accepted the candidacy of one of the sons of Charles IX for the Russian throne. From this point onwards, the Swedes' relations with the Third False Dimitry became overtly hostile, although they did not abandon peaceful negotiations. On 17 October the king ordered his agent at Narva, Arved Peterson, to demand that the pretender surrender Ivangorod, Yam, Kopor'e and Gdov; Dimitry himself was to entrust himself to Swedish protection and would be granted a refuge in Sweden.[44] The pretender, however, rejected these overtures, and encouraged his cossacks to attack Swedish territory.[45]

[38] Petrei, *Istoriya*, pp. 298–9.
[39] His first letter to the Third False Dimitry was dated 27 February 1611, when the pretender was still at Novgorod; his second letter, of 1 May, was sent to him at Ivangorod: Pirling, *Istoricheskie stat'i i zametki*, p. 170; Forsten, 'Politika Shvetsii', p. 348.
[40] Widekind, *Historia*, p. 232.
[41] Petrei, *Istoriya*, p. 299.
[42] *PL*, vol. 2, p. 276.
[43] *PL*, vol. 1, pp. 139–40; vol. 2, p. 276; Petrei, *Istoriya*, p. 299.
[44] Forsten, 'Politika Shvetsii', pp. 348–9.
[45] Petrei, *Istoriya*, pp. 307–8. As late as April 1612, however, peace negotiations were still being conducted between Dimitry's commanders and the Swedes at Novgorod: *AI*, vol. 2, no. 235, p. 401.

Soon after this, the Pskovans invited the pretender to enter Pskov, and voluntarily acknowledged him as tsar. The sources do not adequately explain this *volte-face* on the part of the townspeople, which undoubtedly reflected some shift in the complex and turbulent internal political history of the town, as well as their need for defence against the growing Swedish threat. According to one of the local chroniclers,

The inhabitants of Pskov did not know what to do nor whom to support, and could not hope for any help, since there were Lithuanians in Moscow and Germans [Swedes] in Novgorod. Surrounded on all sides, they decided to invite the false tsar. What utter madness! At first they had sworn not to listen to the false tsar, and not to submit to him, but now they themselves sent representatives of all social groups to bow down to him and beg his pardon.[46]

And Petrei comments that 'the Pskovans imagined that if they had some Sovereign or Grand Prince, even if he were not of true princely origin, no-one would dare trouble them and besiege the town of Pskov: they dispatched envoys to Ivangorod and invited the pretender to come and be their Grand Prince'.[47] If the people of Pskov hoped that the presence of 'Tsar Dimitry' in their town would protect them against foreign enemies, the pretender in his turn believed that his invitation to Pskov would save him from harrassment by the Swedes. 'The accursed one rejoiced with great joy that he had been freed from German encirclement, from which he would have perished, and came quickly to Pskov,' says the chronicler.[48] He made his way to the town 'through the Germans', arriving on 4 December 1611,[49] and was greeted with great honour.[50]

There is conflicting evidence on when and how contacts were established between the pretender at Pskov and the liberation army encamped outside Moscow. In a proclamation to Yaroslavl', dated 26 January 1612, the Russian boyars who were besieged in the Kremlin alleged that Zarutskii and his companions were electing fellow cossacks as tsars: not only had they recognised the son of the Second False Dimitry, but they had also sent a delegation headed by Kazarin Begichev and Nekhoroshko Lopukhin to the pretender at Pskov.[51] The *New Chronicle*, however, indicates that it was the pretender

---

[46] *PL*, vol. 1, p. 140.
[47] Petrei, *Istoriya*, p. 299.
[48] *PL*, vol. 1, p. 140.
[49] *PL*, vol. 2, p. 277.
[50] *PL*, vol. 1, p. 140.
[51] *SGGiD*, vol. 2, no. 277, p. 585. The *New Chronicle* also refers to a mission by Kazarin Begichev to Pskov, but names his companion as Ivan Pleshcheev and implies that their journey took place after the cossacks at Moscow had taken the oath to the pretender: *PSRL*, vol. 14, p. 115, para. 279; p. 118, para. 289; see also *Novgorodskie letopisi*, p. 474. The 'Karamzin

who initiated contacts, sending a delegation from Pskov to Zarutskii's camp at Moscow, headed by the cossack *ataman* Gerasim Popov. Popov bore a proclamation from 'Tsar Dimitry', assuring his subjects that he was alive and living in Pskov.[52] This caused great tumult and division in the camp. Many of the cossacks were eager to swear allegiance to the new tsar, but the nobles were very wary of this revival of pretence, and some chose to flee the encampment rather than take the oath to the new 'rogue'.[53] The role of Zarutskii and Trubetskoi is unclear. Budzilo claims that the Don cossacks forced both Zarutskii and Trubetskoi to swear to the Third False Dimitry, which they did on 15 March (N.S.) 1612.[54] In a missive of April 1612 to Prince Dimitry Pozharskii, however, Archimandrite Dionisii and Cellarer Avraamii Palitsyn of the Monastery of the Trinity and St Sergius stated that on 2 March Ivan Pleshcheev – whom they described as a 'villain and heretic' – and the cossacks had forced Prince Trubetskoi and the nobles and servicemen to take the oath against their will to 'the rogue who calls himself Tsar Dimitry in Pskov'. Zarutskii's name is not mentioned at all in this document, although it implies that he was amongst the cossacks who had taken the oath voluntarily.[55]

Some historians have assumed that it was Zarutskii who masterminded the swearing of allegiance to the Third False Dimitry by the cossacks at Moscow. P. G. Lyubomirov, the author of a detailed study of the events of 1611–13, states that by organising the oath-taking to 'Tsar Dimitry', Zarutskii hoped to revive his own flagging authority, and to persuade the new liberation army of Minin and Pozharskii also to recognise the pretender of Pskov.[56] R. G. Skrynnikov, however, argues that the cossacks in the camps outside Moscow themselves accepted the Pskov pretender as Dimitry, and compelled not only Trubetskoi but also Zarutskii to acknowledge him. Initially, Skrynnikov suggests, Zarutskii may have been willing to accept the new pretender, since the resurrection of 'Tsar Dimitry' would have enhanced Marina's status. Subsequently, however – Skrynnikov argues – the Third False Dimitry came to represent a dangerous rival in Zarutskii's eyes. The imminent arrival of Marina's lawful husband at Moscow threatened the *ataman*'s own influence

Chronograph' refers to a visit to Pskov by Kazarin Begichev and the *d'yak* Ivan Shevyrev, after the camps had taken the oath, but before the visit by Ivan Pleshcheev: Popov, ed., *Izbornik*, p. 354. In general, however, the chronology in this source is rather confused.

[52] *PSRL*, vol. 14, p. 115, para. 279. There is a similar account in the Novgorod chronicle: *Novgorodskie letopisi*, p. 474.

[53] *PSRL*, vol. 14, p. 115, para. 279.

[54] *RIB*, vol. 1, col. 287.

[55] *AAE*, vol. 2, no. 202, p. 342. See also Palitsyn, *Skazanie*, p. 219. The *New Chronicler* describes Ivan Pleshcheev and Kazarin Begichev as the main authors of the oath taking (*nachal'nykh vorovstvu zavotchikov*): *PSRL*, vol. 14, p. 115, para. 279.

[56] Lyubomirov, *Ocherk*, p. 101.

over the widow of Kolomna, and Zarutskii planned to have him eliminated from the scene.[57]

If Zarutskii did engineer the swearing of allegiance to the Third False Dimitry in order to bolster his own prestige, he miscalculated badly.[58] The oath-taking drove many of his former supporters into the rival camp of Minin and Pozharskii.[59] And it created an unbridgeable gulf between the encampment outside Moscow and the new liberation army. Pozharskii had left Nizhnii Novgorod at the beginning of March, heading for Yaroslavl'.[60] En route, he was informed that the encampments around Moscow had sworn allegiance to the Third False Dimitry.[61] When he reached Yaroslavl', Pozharskii received a letter from Zarutskii and Trubetskoi, advising him directly of their oath to 'Tsar Dimitry'.[62] Pozharskii immediately despatched proclamations to various towns, condemning Zarutskii and Trubetskoi and their cossacks for recognising the Pskov pretender, and calling on all true Christians to renounce the Third False Dimitry and Marina and her son.[63]

Within a few days of their recognition of 'Dimitry', Zarutskii and Trubetskoi appear to have had second thoughts.[64] Not only had the oath-taking proved divisive within the encampments, but most of the towns around Moscow had refused to swear allegiance to the new pretender.[65] A mere handful of towns in the south and east – Arzamas and Alatyr', Zaraisk, Vorotynsk, Tarusa, Bolkhov and Kurmysh – acknowledged 'Dimitry', although he appears to have had more success in the *ukraina* towns.[66] Trubetskoi attempted to dissociate himself from the decision to acknowledge the Pskov pretender. He sent envoys to the Trinity monastery on 28 March to ask the authorities there to intercede on his behalf with Pozharskii, to persuade him that he had recognised the pretender only under duress, and to ask him to send him military assistance as soon as possible.[67]

In March, too, Ivan Pleshcheev was sent from the cossack encampments to Pskov to determine whether the pretender really was Tsar Dimitry.[68] Plesh-

---

[57] Skrynnikov, *The Time of Troubles*, pp. 180–2, 224–5.

[58] Lyubomirov, *Ocherk*, p. 101.

[59] Popov, ed., *Izbornik*, p. 354.

[60] Lyubomirov, *Ocherk*, pp. 90–1.

[61] *PSRL*, vol. 14, p. 118, para. 289.

[62] *SGGiD*, vol. 2, no. 281, p. 595.

[63] *AAE*, vol. 2, no. 203, p. 346; cf. no. 208, pp. 353–4.

[64] On 9 and 13 March Trubetskoi and Zarutskii issued proclamations in the name of Tsar Dimitry, but Dimitry's name was absent from a proclamation dated 17 March: Zabelin, *Minin i Pozharskii*, prilozheniya, nos. V–VI, pp. 300–3; Veselovskii, ed., *Akty*, nos. 66–9, pp. 80–3.

[65] *AAE*, vol. 2, no. 202, p. 343.

[66] *SGGiD*, vol. 2, no. 281, p. 595; Popov, ed., *Izbornik*, p. 354; Lyubomirov, *Ocherk*, p. 101. Arzamas had earlier taken the oath to Marina and her son (see above, p. 211).

[67] *AAE*, vol. 2, no. 202, p. 342; Palitsyn, *Skazanie*, p. 220.

[68] The date of Pleshcheev's mission to Pskov can be established from the April letter from the Trinity Monastery to Yaroslavl', stating that they had heard on 28 March that Pleshcheev had

cheev was chosen for this mission, according to one contemporary source, because he 'had been close to the rogue of Kaluga'.[69] The *Novgorod Chronicle* states that Pleshcheev was sent by those nobles who had been forced to take the oath against their will, to denounce the new Dimitry as an impostor.[70] R. G. Skrynnikov argues that Ivan Pleshcheev was Zarutskii's agent, and that he was sent to Pskov on Zarutskii's orders, to arrest the pretender and bring him to Moscow as a prisoner.[71] It is not impossible, however, that Pleshcheev was acting on his own initiative. When he reached Pskov, Pleshcheev did not dare to expose the pretender immediately. He recognised him as Tsar Dimitry, and became one of his most intimate courtiers, while plotting his overthrow.[72]

The Third False Dimitry had quickly made himself unpopular in Pskov. He ruled by terror, giving his cossack supporters free rein to extort money and property from the citizens, and himself seducing their wives and daughters.[73] Pleshcheev was able to take advantage of this discontent in order to engineer a coup against the pretender. He gained the support of the governor, Prince I. F. Khovanskii, and of the 'best people in Pskov, the merchants and the traders', for his plan to arrest Dimitry and take him to Moscow as a prisoner. The occasion presented itself when the Swedes approached the town. The cossacks were sent to intercept them on 10 May, and in their absence the conspirators acted against the pretender. On 18 May Dimitry fled from Pskov, but was pursued and forced to return as a captive on 20 May. On 1 July he was taken to Moscow under a strong escort.[74] According to Petrei, 'he was kept for a considerable time at the gates of the Kremlin, for public abuse and humiliation, until the Russians elected the present Sovereign, Mikhail Feodorovich Romanov, as tsar, and took the oath to him. He ordered him to be hanged in the most piteous manner.[75]

On receiving the news of the pretender's arrest, Trubetskoi and Zarutskii sent a delegation to Pozharskii at Yaroslavl' with a letter in which they humbly admitted their error in having acknowledged the new Tsar Dimitry. Their investigations had shown, they said, that he was 'a real rogue, not the one who was at Tushino and Kaluga'. Now they had sworn to renounce all pretenders, including Marina and her son, and to join with Minin and Pozharskii in liberating Moscow from the Poles and in electing a new tsar by

been refused entry to Tver': *AAE*, vol. 2, no. 202, p. 343. He arrived in Pskov on 11 April: *PL*, vol. 2, p. 276.

[69] Popov, ed., *Izbornik*, p. 354.
[70] *Novgorodskie letopisi*, p. 474.
[71] Skrynnikov, *The Time of Troubles*, p. 225.
[72] Popov, ed., *Izbornik*, p. 354.
[73] *PL*, vol. 1, p. 140; Popov, ed., *Izbornik*, p. 354; Petrei, *Istoriya*, p. 299.
[74] *PL*, vol. 1, p. 140; *PL*, vol. 2, p. 277; Popov, ed., *Izbornik*, p. 355; Petrei, *Istoriya*, p. 300.
[75] Petrei, *Istoriya*, p. 300. See also *RIB*, vol. 1, cols. 287–8; *Novgorodskie letopisi*, p. 475.

common agreement.[76] Pozharskii reacted somewhat coldly to these expressions of penitence, and displayed no haste in coming to the aid of his rivals.[77] He wrote to Putivl' calling on its inhabitants, and those of the *ukraina* towns, to reject the Third False Dimitry, and also Marina and her son.[78]

Zarutskii's last stand

The overthrow of the Third False Dimitry marked a major defeat for Zarutskii within the encampments, since he was obliged to renounce the claim not only of the Pskov pretender, but also of Marina and Tsarevich Ivan Dimitrievich. According to one chronicler, Zarutskii was so embittered against Pozharskii that he tried to harm him by witchcraft, and succeeded in making him ill.[79] On another occasion, Zarutskii sent cossacks to Yaroslavl' to hire an assassin to kill Prince Dimitry, but the attempt failed, and under torture the culprits implicated Zarutskii.[80] On 27 July 1612, Minin and Pozharskii finally left Yaroslavl'. On the following day Zarutskii fled from his camp outside Moscow, apparently fearing that he would be deposed from his command by the leaders of the new liberation army. Polish sources additionally suggest that Zarutskii had established contact with the Lithuanian hetman, Jan Karol Chodkiewicz, who was marching towards Moscow to relieve the Polish garrison, and the *ataman* fled when his treason was revealed to Prince Trubetskoi. Zarutskii was accompanied by about half of the army, probably about 2,500 men.[81] He headed for Kolomna, where he collected Marina and her son. After looting Kolomna, they rode with their cossacks to the Ryazan' district, raiding as they went, and set up their headquarters in the town of Mikhailov.[82]

Pozharskii's army arrived outside Moscow in mid-August 1612, just in time to play a major part in the rout of Chodkiewicz's Polish forces, which were advancing on the capital from the west. Zarutskii's flight had removed an important obstacle to the creation of a single army of liberation, and at the end of September Trubetskoi and Pozharskii agreed to form a united command. A month later, the occupants of the Kremlin surrendered, and Moscow was liberated at last. But the danger was not yet over. With the defeat of Chodkiewicz, King Sigismund decided to march on Russia again to obtain the throne for his son Władysław. The Polish army advanced rapidly, and a detachment headed by Adam Żółkiewski reached the outskirts of Moscow by mid-November. But military failures and the onset of winter

[76] *SGGiD*, vol. 2, no. 281, p. 597; *PSRL*, vol. 14, p. 118, para. 289.
[77] Lyubomirov, *Ocherk*, pp. 103–4.
[78] *SGGiD*, vol. 2, no. 281, pp. 593–7.
[79] *PSRL*, vol. 34, pp. 219–20. Pozharskii apparently suffered from epilepsy.
[80] *Ibid.*, p. 220. For a detailed account of this episode, see *PSRL*, vol. 14, pp. 121–2, para. 300.
[81] Lyubomirov, *Ocherk*, pp. 147–8; Stanislavskii, *Grazhdanskaya voina*, pp. 47–51.
[82] *PSRL*, vol. 14, p. 123, para. 306; Stanislavskii, *Grazhdanskaya voina*, pp. 52–8.

obliged the Poles to retreat. In December 1612 an assembly of the land finally met to elect a new tsar.

In spite of the rebuff he had received in the summer of 1612, Zarutskii had still not abandoned hope of having Marina's son chosen as tsar. Taking advantage of the Polish incursion into Russia in the autumn, he left Mikhailov in order to try to take the town of Ryazan', no doubt planning to return from there to Moscow. But the governor of Ryazan' defeated him outside the town, and Zarutskii withdrew with Marina and his remaining men to the *ukraina* towns, again raiding and looting as they went.[83] According to Isaac Massa, Zarutskii crossed the country 'like an enemy, devastating everything in his path'.[84] By the end of 1612 he had attracted the support of many bondslaves and peasants from the Ryazan' district, and in the spring and summer of 1613 Tsar Michael's government was deluged with petitions from local land-owners, complaining of attacks on their estates, the looting of property and executions of nobles.[85] In the territory which he occupied in the winter of 1612–13, Zarutskii made the inhabitants swear loyalty to the infant tsarevich Ivan Dimitrievich; some sources suggest that the oath may also have included Marina.[86]

The candidature of Tsarevich Ivan had been supported by some of the cossacks who had remained at Moscow during the election campaign. Ivan Filosofov, a *syn boyarskii* from Smolensk who was taken prisoner by the Poles in November 1612, told his captors that the cossacks' favoured candidates for the Russian throne were 'the son of Filaret and [the son] of the rogue of Kaluga'.[87] One of the first decisions of the assembly of the land, however, was to reject any foreign candidates for the throne, a decision which was directed not only against the Polish and Swedish kings and princes, but also against 'Marinka and her son'.[88] This left three main Russian contenders: Prince Ivan Golitsyn, Prince Dimitry Trubetskoi and Michael Romanov, the sixteen-year-old son of Filaret. Of these, the cossacks supported the latter two, because of their connections with Tushino. The young Romanov also enjoyed broad support from other sections of the population, and he was the eventual choice of the electoral assembly in February 1613. The Romanovs' connection by marriage with the old dynasty undoubtedly helped Michael's election, and his supporters revived the story that Michael's father, Fedor

---

[83] *PSRL*, vol. 14, p. 128, para. 327; Lyubomirov, *Ocherk*, p. 163; Stanislavskii, *Grazhdanskaya voina*, p. 64.

[84] Massa, *A Short History*, p. 184.

[85] Zimin, 'Nekotorye voprosy', p. 104. For a detailed account of Zarutskii's activities in 1612/13, which offers a more cautious assessment of the elements of class struggle involved, see Stanislavskii, *Grazhdanskaya voina*, pp. 46–79.

[86] Stanislavskii, *Grazhdanskaya voina*, pp. 55, 72.

[87] Hirschberg, ed., *Polska a Moskwa*, p. 363.

[88] *SGGiD*, vol. 3, nos. 2–6, pp. 5–22; *Dvortsovye razryady*, vol. 1, cols. 13, 14, 20, 27, 35, etc.

Nikitich Romanov, had been Tsar Fedor's personal choice for the succession in 1598.[89]

One of the first actions of Tsar Michael's government was to send troops in pursuit of Zarutskii. In June 1613 Prince I. N. Odoevskii caught up with him at Voronezh, and after a battle Zarutskii crossed overland from the Don to the Volga, heading for Astrakhan'.[90] Perhaps only a few hundred men remained with him, since many of his cossacks had deserted him on the way, and had returned to Moscow to swear allegiance to Tsar Michael.[91] There were disagreements about their future plans. Defectors reported in the spring of 1613 that Zarutskii aimed to go to Persia, but Marina wanted them to go to Poland;[92] another source says that both Zarutskii and Marina planned to go to Poland, but that their cossack followers would not agree to this.[93]

According to Budzilo, Zarutskii went to Astrakhan' because the inhabitants had sent for 'the son of the tsaritsa, whom she had by the Second Dimitry'.[94] This is not at all improbable. As we have seen, Astrakhan' had been a hotbed of pretence since the summer of 1606, and a new False Dimitry had been reported there as recently as January 1612. The Second False Dimitry had planned, shortly before his death, to move his court from Kaluga to Astrakhan'; and Marina had sent 'subversive letters' to the city at the end of 1611. Astrakhan' offered a number of advantages for Zarutskii and his mistress. It was a convenient centre of communications with the cossack hosts of the rivers Don, Volga, Terek and Yaik; it had links with the indigenous nomadic peoples of the Volga basin, whose loyalty to Moscow was often uncertain; and it was well placed for contacts with both Persia and Turkey, whose rulers might prove no less willing than the Polish and Swedish kings to support Russian pretenders. As we have already noted, Marina attempted to send letters to the Shah from Kolomna; and Zarutskii himself allegedly planned to flee to Persia in the spring of 1613.[95] Because of its remoteness, moreover, Astrakhan' had not suffered from the depredations of the Polish supporters of the Second False Dimitry, whose activities had tended to discredit Dimitry's name in the central parts of Russia.

---

[89] Lyubomirov, *Ocherk*, pp. 208–22; Stanislavskii and Morozov, eds., 'Povest' o zemskom sobore'; Stanislavskii, *Grazhdanskaya voina*, pp. 85–92.

[90] The sources are contradictory concerning the date and outcome of the battle at Voronezh. See Stanislavskii, *Grazhdanskaya voina*, pp. 73–4.

[91] *AAE*, vol. 3, no. 23, p. 39; *PSRL*, vol. 14, p. 130, para. 334; p. 132, para. 340. Stanislavskii (*Grazhdanskaya voina*, pp. 75–6) suggests that many cossacks defected from Zarutskii because they suspected him of having secret contacts with the Poles.

[92] *Dvortsovye razryady*, vol. 1, prilozheniya no. 27, col. 1109.

[93] *AAE*, vol. 3, no. 23, p. 38.

[94] *RIB*, vol. 1, col. 317.

[95] For a good discussion of the reasons why Zarutskii may have chosen to go to Astrakhan', see Tkhorzhevskii, *Narodnye volneniya*, pp. 48–50.

Zarutskii arrived in Astrakhan' in the autumn of 1613. He was pursued to the Volga by the tsar's generals Prince I. N. Odoevskii and S.V. Golovin, but they halted at Kazan' and wintered there, reluctant to commence hostilities before the spring.[96] According to the *Piskarev Chronicle*, Zarutskii was welcomed to Astrakhan' with great honour, as if he were royalty (*po tsarskomu obychayu*) and was given a mansion in which he and his entourage held court in regal fashion (*po tsarskomu chinu*).[97] It is not clear whether Zarutskii called himself 'Tsar Dimitry' in Astrakhan'. As mentioned earlier, there are two documents in the Astrakhan' provincial archive in the name of Tsar Dimitry Ivanovich, Tsaritsa Marina Yur'evna and Tsarevich Ivan Dimitrievich, which the editors of the collection of Historical Acts date '1614, before 12 May'.[98] The nineteenth-century historian Solov'ev regarded these as evidence that Zarutskii gave himself out to be Dimitry.[99] Kostomarov was less sure, noting that Zarutskii was such a well-known figure in his own right that it would have been difficult for him to carry out a convincing pretence.[100] There is also evidence, as Kostomarov points out, to the effect that Astrakhan' acknowledged Ivan Dimitrievich as its tsar.[101] In May 1614 the Nogai Tatar prince Ishterek told Tsar Michael's commanders that, after he had sworn allegiance to Michael, 'the people of Astrakhan' and the entire Tatar horde began to oppress us, saying, "Serve the son of the true tsar. All the Christian people have agreed to declare the son of Tsar Dimitry to be the Sovereign ..."'[102] The Soviet historian Stanislavskii saw the existence of petitions in the name of Dimitry, Marina and Tsarevich Ivan as evidence that Zarutskii might have revived 'the legend about the miraculous escape of "Tsar Dimitry"', and he noted that rumours that Dimitry was alive and in Persia were circulating on the Don in September 1613.[103] Tsar Michael's government itself did not accuse Zarutskii of being a pretender on his own account, but only of encouraging the 'simple people' of Astrakhan' to rebellion by calling 'the son of the Rogue the son of a Sovereign'.[104] It seems most probable that Zarutskii claimed that 'Tsar Dimitry' was still alive, and

---

[96] *PSRL*, vol. 14, p. 134, para. 343.

[97] *PSRL*, vol. 34, p. 219.

[98] *AI*, vol. 3, nos. 263–4, pp. 429–30. Zarutskii fled from Astrakhan' with Marina and her son on 12 May 1614.

[99] Solov'ev, *Istoriya Rossii*, vol. 5, pp. 24–5.

[100] Kostomarov, *Smutnoe vremya*, p. 628, n. 2. Kostomarov suggests that these two petitions may relate to the period of activity of the False Dimitry whose presence in Astrakhan' was reported in January 1612. The reference in one of these petitions to the Terek cossacks as traitors to Tsar Dimitry, however, indicates that it should be dated to the spring of 1614, after the defection of Terek from Zarutskii: *AI*, vol. 3, no. 264, p. 430.

[101] Kostomarov, *Smutnoe vremya*, pp. 628–9.

[102] *AI*, vol. 3, no. 277, p. 444.

[103] Stanislavskii, *Grazhdanskaya voina*, p. 78.

[104] *AAE*, vol. 3, no. 28, p. 64.

issued proclamations in Dimitry's name as well as those of Marina and her son, without himself attempting to play the role of Dimitry.

Zarutskii had been warmly welcomed to Astrakhan', but the honeymoon period did not last long. Within a few weeks there were signs that he was suffering from an acute sense of insecurity. Tsar Michael's commanders learned from their spies that before Christmas 1613 Zarutskii had sent a cossack round the town with a document which he made everyone sign without allowing them to read it; and Marina, who feared an uprising, had forbidden the ringing of church bells in the mornings, saying that the sound disturbed her son.[105] During the winter of 1613–14 Zarutskii initiated a reign of terror in Astrakhan'. The governor, Prince Khvorostinin, who at first had apparently cooperated with Zarutskii, as he had earlier with Tsarevich Ivan Augustus, was one of the victims.[106] Tsar Michael's letter to the Don cossacks, of 18 March 1614, asserted that Zarutskii had killed Khvorostinin and 'many of the best people' because they had opposed his wicked policies, including his alleged plan to surrender Astrakhan' to the Shah.[107] Other sources suggest that Khvorostinin had made secret attempts to obtain assistance from the governor of Terek and from the Shah in order to overthrow Zarutskii.[108] The Carmelite missionary Father John Thaddeus indicates that Khvorostinin was killed in the course of a popular uprising. Father John, who on his return from Persia in 1611 had been imprisoned by Khvorostinin as a spy, describes a revolt that subsequently broke out in the city. The governor was dragged through the streets by the populace to the main square, where he was ignominiously put to death[109] – presumably in a manner befitting a 'traitor-boyar'.

Other victims included a captain of musketeers (*golova streletskii*), Semen Churkin. The Karamzin Chronograph states that in addition to executing Khvorostinin, Zarutskii drowned Churkin and killed many *murzy* and 'best people'.[110] The governor of Samara reported on 30 March that Zarutskii had tortured Semen Churkin and 'many good people' at night, by fire and by immersion in water, and that his daily executions had caused much blood to be shed.[111] Another source reports that Zarutskii had executed not only Semen Churkin and many 'good people', but also priests and monks, throwing their

[105] *AI*, vol. 3, no. 248, p. 412.
[106] *AAE*, vol. 3, no. 19, p. 24; *PSRL*, vol. 14, p. 134, para. 343; *PSRL*, vol. 34, p. 219.
[107] *AAE*, vol. 3, no. 22, p. 33.
[108] *Dvortsovye razryady*, vol. 1, cols. 136–7; Veselovskii, ed., *Pamyatniki*, vol. 3, pp. 18, 24. Tkhorzhevskii plausibly suggests that Zarutskii had Khvorostinin killed when he learned of his secret relations with the Shah: Tkhorzhevskii, *Narodnye volneniya*, p. 56.
[109] Florencio, *En Persia*, p. 79; *A Chronicle of the Carmelites*, vol. 1, p. 197.
[110] Popov, ed., *Izbornik*, p. 361. On the killing of the 'best people' by Zarutskii, see also *PSRL*, vol. 34, p. 219.
[111] *AI*, vol. 3, no. 248, p. 412.

bodies into the river and looting their property. He had also committed the blasphemous act of taking a silver censer from the Trinity monastery and having it made into a pair of stirrups for himself.[112] Some evidence suggests that Zarutskii was able to take advantage of social antagonisms within Astrakhan'. A letter from the Holy Synod to the Don cossacks, of March 1614, asserts that Zarutskii 'led the simple people into tumult'.[113] The sources frequently describe his victims as the 'good' or 'best' people; and he was said to have confiscated the property of the rich merchants in order to pay his servicemen.[114]

Soon after his arrival in Astrakhan', Zarutskii established contacts with Shah Abbas.[115] The *ataman*'s envoys, Ivan Khokhlov and Yakov Glyadkov, were sent to Persia in the company of a Persian merchant, Murtaza. Murtaza subsequently reported to Tsar Michael's officials that Yakov Glyadkov had been privately instructed by Marina to request money and grain from the Shah. Glyadkov told Abbas that Russia was still under Polish occupation, and that the rightful heir, the son of Tsar Dimitry, had taken refuge in Astrakhan'. On Marina's behalf, he besought the Shah to provide aid to put Tsarevich Ivan on the throne and to liberate Russia from the Poles.[116] The Shah at first believed Glyadkov's story, and decided to offer assistance to Zarutskii, but Murtaza and Ivan Khokhlov provided Abbas with a correct account of the situation, and Murtaza handed him a secret letter from Prince Khvorostinin, written in the name of Tsar Michael.[117] Faced with these two contradictory accounts of the political situation in Russia, the Shah decided to delay action.[118] The envoys sent an optimistic message to Astrakhan'. 'God will grant your desire,' Khokhlov reported to Marina from Baku, whereupon Zarutskii stepped up his preparations for war.[119] But the Shah was playing a double game and kept his options open. He eventually sent Glyadkov back

---

[112] *SGGiD*, vol. 3, no. 20, p. 97.

[113] *AAE*, vol. 3, no. 23, p. 39. A. A. Zimin sees this as evidence of the 'class war' character of his movement: Zimin, 'Nekotorye voprosy', pp. 104–5.

[114] *AI*, vol. 3, no. 27, p. 26.

[115] *Ibid.*, no. 248, pp. 411–12.

[116] Veselovskii, ed., *Pamyatniki*, vol. 3, p. 1. Tsar Michael's government received intelligence that Zarutskii was offering to surrender Astrakhan' to the shah in return for military assistance, but there is little evidence to support this allegation, other than rumours of a conspiracy between Zarutskii and the shah to kill the inhabitants of Astrakhan': *ibid.*, vol. 2, pp. 222, 351–2; cf. *AAE*, vol. 3, no. 19, p. 24; no. 23, p. 39.

[117] Veselovskii, ed., *Pamyatniki*, vol. 3, pp. 2, 18, 24, 56–7. Murtaza's sympathies were clearly with Tsar Michael throughout. As early as March 1614 the governor of Samara learned that the Persian merchant had assured the 'good people' of Astrakhan' that the shah would not send men or money to Zarutskii, for he favoured good relations with Moscow: *AI*, vol. 3, no. 248, p. 412.

[118] Veselovskii, ed., *Pamyatniki*, vol. 3, p. 3.

[119] *Ibid.*, vol. 2, p. 222.

to Astrakhan' with gifts for Zarutskii and Marina, but also entrusted Murtaza with presents for Tsar Michael.[120]

Shah Abbas's response was made too late to help Zarutskii's cause. At Derbent the envoys learned that Zarutskii and Marina had fled from Astrakhan'. Murtaza continued on his journey up the Volga to Moscow, but Khokhlov and Glyadkov returned to Persia.[121] The Russian sources thus imply that Zarutskii received no aid whatever from Persia. According to Father John Thaddeus, however, Marina did obtain some assistance from the Shah. The missionary reported that out of gratitude for her role in securing his release from prison Abbas gave her the cargo of a Persian vessel moored at Astrakhan', which was sufficiently valuable to pay for the upkeep of 600 soldiers for six months.[122]

There is some evidence that in addition to his negotiations with Persia Zarutskii attempted to gain support from the Turkish Sultan. According to Isaac Massa, 'Zarutsky proposed to cede the realm of Astrakhan to the sultan if he would order the Crimean Tatars to come to the aid of the young Tsar Ivan Dmitrievich, help him conquer the kingdom of Kazan, and, after that, the empire of Muscovy.'[123] In April it had been reported to Tsar Michael's generals that the vanguard of an army of 20,000 men that the Sultan was sending to assist Zarutskii was already at Azov, in the Crimea, preparing to come to Astrakhan' overland across the steppe.[124] Tsar Michael had sent an embassy to Constantinople to try to preserve peace with the Sultan, and begged the Don cossacks not to attack Azov until the envoys returned.[125] The Turks were anxious to establish good relations with the new Russian government, and Zarutskii's plans for a spring campaign against Samara and Kazan' went ahead without any realistic hopes of help from either Persia or Turkey.

Zarutskii did however manage to obtain some support from the Volga Tatars. Tsar Michael's officials learned that the *ataman* was constantly surrounded by an escort of 500 or 600 Nogai Tatars, who lived in his palace and accompanied him whenever he ventured out of town.[126] Zarutskii had gained the backing of the Nogai by highly unscrupulous means. Soon after his arrival in Astrakhan' he released the Tatar prince Yanaraslan Urusov from prison, and used him against his rival, Ishterek, who had already acknowledged Tsar Michael. Yanaraslan took Ishterek's sons hostage, and thereby

[120] *Ibid.*, vol. 3, pp. 3–4, 18.
[121] *Ibid.*, vol. 3, pp. 3–4, 18; vol. 2, p. 293.
[122] *A Chronicle of the Carmelites*, vol. 1, p. 197; Florencio, *En Persia*, pp. 79–80.
[123] Massa, *A Short History*, p. 184.
[124] *AI*, vol. 3, no. 258, p. 425.
[125] *AAE*, vol. 3, no. 21, pp. 28–9.
[126] *AI*, vol. 3, no. 248, p. 412.

obtained Ishterek's promise to participate in the campaign which Zarutskii was planning for the spring against Samara and Kazan'.[127]

Zarutskii also tried to secure the support of the Don cossacks, but they refused to help him, and swore allegiance to Michael Romanov. The Volga cossacks were divided in their loyalties. Only *ataman* Verziga, from the lower Volga, was willing to support Zarutskii: the *ataman*s on the upper Volga joined with the Don cossacks in opposing him, although some of the younger cossacks agreed to join the campaign against Samara. Other Volga cossacks planned to go to Zarutskii in Astrakhan', with the aim of obtaining money from him under false pretences. Instead of following him to Samara, they intended to go to the Caspian Sea to rob the supply ships which the shah was supposedly sending him.[128]

There is evidence that if Zarutskii had launched his campaign in the spring, he could have hoped for support from various roving cossack bands from the north of Russia, some of whom were intercepted by Tsar Michael's commanders on the upper Volga in April 1614, *en route* for Astrakhan'.[129] But even though reinforcements were flocking towards him from the north, Zarutskii had already begun to lose support in the south by the spring of 1614. The town of Terek, which had at first given its backing to Zarutskii,[130] defected from him when the inhabitants learned the details of his reign of terror in Astrakhan'.[131] They swore allegiance to Tsar Michael, news of whose election had reached them very belatedly,[132] and the governor of Terek, Peter Golovin, sent the musketeer captain Vasilii Khokhlov against Astrakhan' with a detachment of several hundred musketeers and cossacks.[133] The defection of Terek had a demoralising effect on Zarutskii's supporters in Astrakhan'. Before Easter, six musketeers from Terek who had arrived in Astrakhan' had been drowned, on Zarutskii's orders, to prevent them from spreading information about what had happened in Terek. In spite of Zarutskii's efforts, however, a musketeer officer (*pyatidesyatnik*) from Terek, Zhdanko Chermnyi, was able secretly to spread the news in Astrakhan' that the people of Terek had renounced Zarutskii and sworn allegiance to Tsar Michael.[134]

Thus by the spring of 1614 Zarutskii's support in Astrakhan' had already begun to falter, when Tsar Michael's generals, Prince I. N. Odoevskii and

---

[127] *AAE*, vol. 3, no. 20, pp. 26–7; *AI*, vol. 3, no. 248, pp. 411–13; no. 277, p. 444.

[128] *AI*, vol. 3, no. 248, pp. 412–13; no. 257, pp. 424–5.

[129] *Ibid.*, nos. 13–14, pp. 13–14; no. 255, p. 422; no. 258, pp. 425–6.

[130] *Ibid.*, no. 248, p. 411.

[131] *Ibid.*, no. 257, p. 424; *SGGiD*, vol. 3, no. 20, p. 97; Popov, ed., *Izbornik*, p. 361.

[132] *AI*, vol. 3, no. 15, p. 14; *PSRL*, vol. 34, p. 219; Stanislavskii, *Grazhdanskaya voina*, p. 255, n. 72.

[133] *AI*, vol. 3, no. 15, p. 14; no. 18, p. 17; *SGGiD*, vol. 3, no. 20, p. 97; *PSRL*, vol. 14, p. 134, para. 343; Popov, ed., *Izbornik*, p. 361.

[134] *AI*, vol. 3, no. 269, p. 436.

S. V. Golovin, instigated an intensive propaganda campaign against him, in advance of the launching of military operations on the lower Volga. In proclamations to the Don and Volga cossacks, and to the citizens of Astrakhan', they depicted Zarutskii and Marina as agents of the Polish king and of the Pope, and accused them of planning to surrender Astrakhan' to the Shah.[135] They promised a pardon to the inhabitants of Astrakhan' if they surrendered, but threatened them with dire consequences if they held out.[136] The dissemination of these proclamations, and the inhabitants' awareness of the imminence of a military campaign against the city, undoubtedly influenced the subsequent course of events in Astrakhan'.

In Palm Week a band of 560 Volga cossacks arrived in Astrakhan' to join Zarutskii. The rumour quickly spread throughout the city that these cossacks planned to attack the musketeers and residents (*zhiletskie lyudi*) of Astrakhan' on Easter Day.[137] According to the most detailed account of this episode, Zarutskii allegedly planned to send a thousand servicemen out of the city on various pretexts, and to kill the remainder during the Easter morning service, and loot their property. The dissemination of this rumour led to a split between the cossacks and the townspeople, and on the Wednesday before Easter fighting took place. Zarutskii was obliged to withdraw into the kremlin with 800 supporters, including the Volga cossacks, while his opponents, numbering 3,000 servicemen, besieged them from the town.[138]

Meanwhile, the musketeers who had been dispatched from Terek by Peter Golovin were approaching Astrakhan'. Hearing of Khokhlov's imminent arrival, Zarutskii decided to flee. On 12 May he made his escape from the citadel with Marina and her son and a detachment of Volga cossacks and other devoted followers. At first they headed upriver, but then changed their plans and turned back towards the Caspian Sea. Khokhlov meanwhile had entered Astrakhan', where he was warmly welcomed by the inhabitants and administered the oath of loyalty to Tsar Michael. When Zarutskii returned to the mouth of the Volga, Khokhlov was waiting for him. Khokhlov's troops attacked Zarutskii's men, and defeated them, but Zarutskii himself escaped to sea with Marina and her child and a handful of followers. Two weeks were to pass before the fugitives were sighted again, rowing up the River Arychan, to the east of Astrakhan', and Khokhlov dispatched a detachment of soldiers to retrieve them.[139]

---

[135] For the texts of these proclamations, dated 12 and 18 March 1614, and variously issued in the names of the *voevody*, of the tsar and of the holy synod, see *AAE*, vol. 3, nos. 18–29, pp. 21–68; and *RIB*, vol. 18, nos. 11–29, cols. 42–200. For a discussion of the accusations made against Zarutskii by Tsar Michael's government, see Dolinin, 'K razboru'.

[136] *AAE*, vol. 3, no. 19, pp. 25–6.

[137] *AI*, vol. 3, no. 265, pp. 430–1; no. 267, pp. 432–3.

[138] *Ibid.*, no. 269, pp. 435–6.

[139] *Ibid.*, no. 15, pp. 14–15; no. 282, p. 447.

The first contingent of government troops reached Astrakhan' on 27 May, and were greeted with the ringing of church bells.[140] On 1 June Prince Odoev-skii himself made his belated entry into Astrakhan', to a triumphal welcome which he had instructed Khokhlov – the real victor over Zarutskii – to prepare for him.[141] Odoevskii sent the musketeer captains Gordei Pal'chikov and Sev-ast'yan Onuchin to the River Yaik in search of Zarutskii,[142] and despatched Khokhlov to Moscow to report to the tsar.[143] Pal'chikov and Onuchin were soon able to report that they had found traces of the fugitives on the Yaik.[144] After travelling upriver for two weeks, the musketeers caught up with Zaruts-kii and his companions on Medvezh'ii Ostrov (Bear Island), where after a skirmish they besieged them in an improvised fort which the fugitives had constructed. On the next day, 25 June, the cossacks, realising that their situation was hopeless, surrendered and handed over Zarutskii, Marina and her son.[145] According to two Nogai Tatars captured on the Volga by Odoevskii's troops, Zarutskii's camp on Medvezh'ii Ostrov consisted of 600 cossacks, many of whom were wounded. Their real leader was the *ataman* Trenya Us, who held Zarutskii and Marina as virtual prisoners, and exerted control over 'Marina's bastard'.[146] On 6 July Zarutskii, Marina and Ivan were brought into Astrakhan', whence they were quickly despatched upriver to Kazan' under a strong escort.[147] Mopping-up operations against Zarutskii's cossack sup-porters on the Yaik and Volga continued for some time, and Trenya Us was still at liberty at the end of August.[148]

When the captives reached Moscow, Zarutskii was impaled, and the three-year-old 'Tsarevich' Ivan was hanged. Marina died soon afterwards.[149] There is conflicting evidence about the circumstances of her death, the Poles alleg-ing that she was murdered, while the Russians claimed that she died of natural causes.[150]

Russian historians have provided somewhat contradictory assessments of Zarutskii's significance in the Time of Troubles. Pre-revolutionary scholars regarded him as yet another representative of cossack rebelliousness, whose actions in Astrakhan' delayed the restoration of order by Tsar Michael's government.[151] In the early Soviet period, however, he was reassessed as a

---

[140] *Ibid.*, no. 279, p. 445.
[141] *Ibid.*, no. 17, p. 16; nos. 280–1, pp. 446–7.
[142] *Ibid.*, no. 19, pp. 19–20; no. 283, p. 448.
[143] *Ibid.*, no. 29, p. 27.
[144] *Ibid.*, no. 23, p. 23. On the role of Pal'chikov, see also Koretskii, ed., 'Novoe', p. 103.
[145] *AI*, vol. 3, no. 32, p. 32.
[146] *Ibid.*, no. 26, pp. 25–6.
[147] *Ibid.*, no. 33, p. 33; no. 35, p. 34; no. 36, p. 34.
[148] *Ibid.*, no. 42, pp. 38–9.
[149] *PSRL*, vol. 14, p. 134, para. 343; *PSRL*, vol. 34, p. 219.
[150] Kostomarov, *Smutnoe vremya*, p. 635.
[151] See, for example, Solov'ev, *Istoriya Rossii*, vol. 5, pp. 19–27; Kostomarov, *Smutnoe vremya*, pp. 627–36.

revolutionary figure, comparable to Bolotnikov, who paved the way for the later cossack rebels Razin and Pugachev.[152] But by the late 1930s this was regarded as a heresy typical of the discredited 'Pokrovskii school' of historiography. Pokrovskii had regarded Minin and Pozharskii as the leaders of a feudal restoration supported by the merchant class, while Zarutskii and the poorer cossacks represented a revolutionary democratic force in society.[153] In the climate of Russian nationalism which prevailed under Stalin, however, Minin and Pozharskii became patriotic heroes, while Zarutskii was depicted as an adventurer and opportunist, the traitorous tool of foreign interventionists.[154] In the debate about the 'first peasant war' in the immediate post-Stalin period, A. A. Zimin argued that Zarutskii's movement involved anti-feudal class struggle, and this view met with some support from other Soviet historians.[155] A later study by A. L. Stanislavskii, however, stressed that Zarutskii's support was drawn predominantly from the cossacks. Although there was some evidence of 'anti-noble' sentiments on the cossacks' part, the sources did not permit any firm conclusions about Zarutskii's 'social programme'.[156] The interests of the cossacks, in Stanislavskii's view, were different from those of the peasants, and often conflicted with them; and the events of the Time of Troubles could not be regarded as a 'peasant war' simply because of the part played in it by cossacks who were originally recruited from the ranks of the peasantry.[157]

Zarutskii's rebellion, according to Stanislavskii, was 'the last serious attempt to put a pretender on the Muscovite throne' during the Time of Troubles.[158] Ivan Dimitrievich was not a pretender in the conventional sense, being, in Chistov's words, 'an involuntary *samozvanets* by birth',[159] but it is nevertheless true that the campaign which Zarutskii organised on his behalf had much in common with earlier cossack support for such pretenders as Peter-Ileika and the Third False Dimitry.

---

[152] Tkhorzhevskii, *Narodnye volneniya*, pp. 44–76.
[153] Pokrovskii, *Izbrannye proizvedeniya*, vol. 3, pp. 71–4.
[154] Bernadskii, 'Konets Zarutskogo'. These simplistic evaluations still persist in the popularising works of Skrynnikov: see his *Minin i Pozharskii* and *The Time of Troubles*.
[155] Zimin, 'Nekotorye voprosy', pp. 104–5; Ovchinnikov, 'Nekotorye voprosy', p. 83; 'O krest'yanskoi voine', p. 119; Dolinin, 'K razboru', pp. 143–4; Figarovskii, 'Krest'yanskoe vosstanie', pp. 200–1; Shepelev, 'Mesto i kharakter', p. 238; Makovskii, *Pervaya krest'yanskaya voina*, pp. 445–50, 457–62.
[156] Stanislavskii, *Grazhdanskaya voina*, pp. 62, 64.
[157] *Ibid.*, p. 247.
[158] *Ibid.*, p. 77.
[159] Chistov, *Russkie narodnye*, p. 66.

Epilogue After the Troubles: pretence in the later
seventeenth century

The execution of Zarutskii and the *vorenok* Ivan Dimitrievich effectively
marked the end of the Time of Troubles, although sporadic social unrest
continued for some years.[1] Peace was concluded with Sweden in 1617, when
Novgorod was returned to Russia as a result of the Treaty of Stolbovo. Hostilities with Poland continued, however, and Chodkiewicz invaded Russia
again in 1617 in a further attempt to place Prince Władysław on the throne.
The Poles were obliged to retreat, but in the Treaty of Deulino, signed in
December 1618, Russia ceded Smolensk and a number of border fortresses
to King Sigismund. The Poles, moreover, refused to drop Władysław's claim
to the Russian throne. In accordance with the terms of the treaty Patriarch
Filaret was released from captivity, and he returned to Russia in 1619 to
become *de facto* ruler of the country. In 1632, on the death of King Sigismund, Tsar Michael's government went on to the offensive against Poland,
in a bid to recapture Smolensk. In this main aim they were unsuccessful, but
in the 'perpetual' Peace of Polyanovka, of 1634, Władysław – who had been
elected king of Poland in succession to his father – formally renounced his
claim to the Russian throne.

The continuation of tense relations between Russia and Poland after the
accession of Michael Romanov encouraged new intrigues concerning pretenders. In 1643, Russian envoys to Poland raised the case of a man aged
about thirty, with a 'royal' emblem (*gerb*) on his back, who claimed to be
Tsarevich Ivan Dimitrievich. He had, they alleged, been kept for more than
fifteen years by the king in a Jesuit monastery at Brest-Litovsk. The Poles
summoned the pretender to Warsaw and allowed the Russians to interrogate
him. He turned out to be Ivan Dimitrievich Luba, the son of a petty Polish
noble from Podlasie who had taken him to Russia as a small child during
the Time of Troubles. When his father was killed, the boy was adopted by
a Pole named Belinski, who took him back to Poland and brought him up
to believe that he was the son of Marina Mniszech and the Second False
Dimitry, who had supposedly escaped execution in 1614. When the boy was

[1] See, for example, Figarovskii, 'Krest'yanskoe vosstanie'; Stanislavskii, *Grazhdanskaya voina*.

older, Belinski informed King Sigismund and the *Sejm* of his existence. They entrusted him to the care of Leo Sapieha, allocating the sum of 6,000 zlotys for his maintenance, and Sapieha sent him to the Semenovskii monastery at Brest-Litovsk to study Russian, Polish and Latin. He had remained there for seven years, but when peace was concluded between Poland and Russia, his stipend was reduced and he was completely forgotten.[2] Belinski had subsequently told Luba the true story of his origins. When the real Ivan Dimitrievich was sentenced to death the Pole had hoped to save him by substituting his ward for Marina's son. But he had not been able to do so, and had instead decided to call Luba the tsarevich, 'for any eventuality'. The Polish chancellor Ossoliński confirmed Luba's story in the presence of the Russian envoys, assuring them that no-one now claimed that he was Tsarevich Ivan, and that the youth's only desire was to take holy orders and become a priest.[3]

The Russians were not however convinced that Luba's case was quite as innocent as the Poles made out. They claimed that when they had passed through Brest-Litovsk some members of their embassy had seen the pretender, who was still calling himself a Russian tsarevich, and they insisted that they had obtained letters which he had signed as tsarevich. In Craców, moreover – the envoys added – Polish nobles had threatened that if the Russians did not reach agreement with the *Sejm* on matters of state, then 'we have a Dimitrievich ready to go to war along with the Zaporozhian cossacks'.[4] Eventually the Poles agreed to send Luba to Russia for questioning, on the understanding that he would subsequently be returned to Poland. In November 1644 the 'tsarevich' was brought to Moscow by the Polish ambassador Gavrila Stempkovski, but the Russians were reluctant to allow him to return.[5] The issue was still unresolved at the time of Tsar Michael's death in 1645, but the new tsar, Aleksei, agreed to allow Luba's departure as a gesture of goodwill to the Poles. Stempkovski promised that on his return to Poland the pretender would be imprisoned in a strong fortress and would never be allowed to leave the *Rzeczpospolita*. The Russians subsequently complained that the Poles were not keeping to their agreement; but they were offered new assurances, and Luba played no further part in Russo-Polish relations.

---

[2] Solov'ev, *Istoriya Rossii*, vol. 5, pp. 248–51. Assuming that Luba was the same age as the real Ivan Dimitrievich, he would have been about 24 years old at the time of the conclusion of the Peace of Polyanovka in 1634. The Russians stated that he was 'about 30' in 1643: *ibid.*, p. 249. If he had spent seven years in the monastery at Brest before the Treaty of 1634 (and more than fifteen years before 1643), he must have come to the monastery at the age of about 17. Luba was probably the 'son of Dimitry' whose name appeared on a list of pupils of the Jesuit college in Vilnius in 1626; Bercé, *Le roi caché*, p. 129.

[3] Solov'ev, *Istoriya Rossii*, vol. 5, pp. 250–1.

[4] *Ibid.*, pp. 250–2.

[5] *Ibid.*, pp. 253–4.

According to some accounts, he was killed by the Crimean Tatars at the battle of Pilyavtsy in 1648, during Bogdan Khmel'nitskii's rebellion.[6]

The willingness of the Polish government to be conciliatory to the Russians in the case of Luba suggests that after the Peace of Polyanovka, at least, they were reluctant to become involved with pretence. Earlier, however, they had been only too anxious to threaten the Russians with new pretenders. In 1618, during the negotiations at Deulino, the Polish diplomat Alexander Gosiewski had said, 'Even though we are leaving your territory on the conclusion of peace, your own cossacks will acquire a new rogue, and then our rogues will support him, so they will have another Dimitry even without our prince [Władysław].'[7] In the following year the Poles warned the Russians that pretenders were ready to cause trouble:

You yourselves know that several of your Russian people, calling themselves tsars' sons, are again issuing proclamations and summoning free military men to join them. They are in contact with the Zaporozhian and Don cossacks and they plan to wage war against the Muscovite state, modelling themselves upon Dimitry. This has caused great turmoil in your *ukraina*, but the king has issued a firm order that none of his people should dare go.[8]

In October 1620 Polish envoys to Moscow reported that proclamations in the name of Tsarevich Ivan Dimitrievich had been circulating among Polish troops at Orsha. These proclamations stated that the tsarevich was alive, 'and beseeched the troops that they, remembering his father's generosity towards them, march on the land of Muscovy and help him to gain his inheritance, the state of Muscovy, and he promised them a fine reward'. The Polish officers had tried to dissuade the troops from lending any credence to these appeals (the envoys said), but some cossacks and servicemen had gone off to the Zaporozhian cossacks, 'in order to join them in accompanying this Ivan to the Muscovite land'. The king, however, had immediately sent decrees to Ukraine to the Zaporozhians, ordering them to stay away from the Russian border.[9] As K. V. Chistov has observed, it is difficult to judge whether there were any real facts behind the information which the Poles passed on to the Russians in 1619–20: 'whether they were linked with Luba or another false "Ivan Dimitrievich", or elicited by the desire of the Polish government to ascribe to itself non-existent services'.[10] It certainly seems unlikely that Luba's patron Belinski had kept quiet about him before he was sent to com-

---

[6] *Ibid.*, pp. 460–2, 470, 541.
[7] *Ibid.*, p. 115; Stanislavskii, *Grazhdanskaya voina*, p. 193.
[8] Solov'ev, *Istoriya Rossii*, vol. 5, p. 156.
[9] *Ibid.*, pp. 156–7.
[10] Chistov, *Russkie narodnye*, pp. 67–8.

plete his education at the king's expense in Brest-Litovsk in about 1627; so
these rumours may well refer to Luba.

Another false Ivan Dimitrievich appeared around 1640, in the Crimea. He
was Ivan Vergun or Vergunenok, the son of a cossack from the town of
Lubny in Ukraine. Vergun had lived with the Zaporozhian and Don cossacks
before being captured on the steppe by the Tatars, who sold him as a slave
to a Jew in Kaffa. There Vergun decided to call himself the son of a Russian
tsar, in order to impress his master. He paid a Russian woman to brand him
between the shoulders with a half-moon and stars, and persuaded his fellow
captives that these marks were a sign of his royal origin. When the Crimean
khan heard of the presence of this supposed 'tsarevich' in Kaffa, he summoned him to his court, where he kept him under guard.[11] In 1644 Vergun
succeeded in sending a letter to the Turkish sultan in Constantinople, offering
him half of Muscovy if he helped him to regain his rightful realm.[12] Subsequently the Khan sent Vergun to Constantinople, where the Vizier was at
first inclined to give credence to his claim to be Tsarevich Ivan Dimitrievich.
Soon, however, he was imprisoned by the sultan because of his drunken and
quarrelsome behaviour.[13]

At around the same time two pretenders appeared calling themselves sons
of Tsar Vasilii Shuiskii, who had died in captivity in Poland in 1612. In 1643
the Russian envoys to Poland who had raised the case of Luba complained
that the Poles were also harbouring a false Tsarevich Semen Shuiskii.
According to the envoys' information, this man had appeared in the Sambor
region in 1639, where a priest for whom he worked had noticed a special
'emblem' on his back. The priest took him to the Polish treasurer Daniłowicz,
and under questioning the man admitted to being a son of Tsar Vasilii. He
said that he had been captured by the *cherkasy* (Ukrainian cossacks) while
accompanying his father into imprisonment in Poland, and had lived among
the cossacks ever since. Daniłowicz had obtained a state allowance for his
protégé, and had sent him to study Russian in a monastery. The Poles at first
denied any knowledge of this pretender, but promised to investigate the case.
They eventually admitted that an impostor had approached Daniłowicz, but
claimed that he had been beaten by him and sent away.[14] This was probably
the same 'Semen Shuiskii' who turned up in Moldavia in July 1639. He
showed the Moldavian ruler a star and cross on his back, and the words 'son
of Shuiskii' as conclusive proof of his identity. The ruler handed him over
to the Russian envoy B. M. Dubrovskii, who promised to take him to Tsar
Michael, but killed him *en route* and sent his head and skin to Moscow.[15]

[11] Solov′ev, *Istoriya Rossii*, vol. 5, pp. 463–4.
[12] *Ibid.*, p. 248.
[13] *Ibid.*, pp. 464–6.
[14] *Ibid.*, pp. 249–50.

A better documented False Shuiskii is the notorious Timofei (Timoshka) Akundinov, a former official (*pod'yachii*) from Moscow, who made various claims to royal identity in Lithuania and Moldavia. The Moldavian ruler sent him to Constantinople, where he arrived in 1646. Here Akundinov called himself the son of Tsar Vasilii Shuiskii and promised to hand over Astrakhan' to the sultan in return for military assistance. The Turks were not interested, and after several years' further wandering around the capitals of Europe Akundinov was arrested in Holstein and returned to Russia, where he was executed and quartered in December 1653.[16]

None of these pretenders had any support within Russia. They all made their claims to royal identity outside Muscovy, and their attempts to obtain military assistance from foreign rulers seem to have been made as the result of individual initiatives, unconnected with Russian internal affairs. Because of this, the Soviet scholar S. M. Troitskii classified them as 'political adventurers' rather than leaders of anti-feudal popular movements.[17] K. V. Chistov, however, saw the appearance of these false Ivan Dimitrieviches and false Shuiskiis as evidence of the continued existence of 'popular socio-utopian legends' in the second quarter of the seventeenth century.[18] But for this period – as for the Time of Troubles itself – the fictional 'biographies' of the pretenders constitute the only evidence that Chistov can adduce for the existence of such 'legends'.

Within Russia, the authorities' investigation of alleged cases of 'sovereign's word and deed' (political offences) in the first years of the new dynasty showed that there was widespread discontent with Michael Romanov's government, that found expression in criticism and abuse of the tsar and his family.[19] There is also evidence of nostalgia for 'Tsar Dimitry'. In 1614, for example, a certain retired guide (*otstavnoi vozh*) was accused of refusing to drink to the health of Tsar Michael, calling instead for a toast to 'Tsar Dimitry'.[20] Some people even believed that Dimitry was not dead. In 1622 a peasant was denounced for saying that Tsar Michael should not marry, because 'the rogue of Tushino, who called himself Tsarevich Dimitry' was still alive. Another peasant had allegedly told him that there would be a great war,

---

[15] Chistov, *Russkie narodnye*, p. 71, n. 123; cf. Solov'ev, *Istoriya Rossii*, vol. 5, pp. 465–6. According to other sources, the pretender who appeared in Moldavia and was handed over to Dubrovskii called himself Tsar Dimitry: *ibid.*, pp. 249, 566, 571.

[16] On Akundinov, see *ibid.*, pp. 464–7, 564–71, 607–11; Moshin, 'Iz istorii snoshenii'; Chistov, *Russkie narodnye*, pp. 70–7; Longworth, 'Timoshka Ankidinov'.

[17] Troitskii, 'Samozvantsy', pp. 144–5.

[18] Chistov, *Russkie narodnye*, pp. 66–78.

[19] See, for example, Novombergskii, ed., *Slovo i delo gosudarevy*, vol. 1, nos. 4–6, pp. 4–7; no. 12, pp. 10–11; no. 19, pp. 16–17; no. 24, pp. 25–6; no. 30, pp. 36–40.

[20] *Ibid.*, no. 1, pp. 1–2. Similar cases were reported in 1624 and 1631: no. 10, p. 10; no. 21, p. 18; no. 54, pp. 66–9.

because Tsarevich Dimitry was alive.[21] In the same year a *cherkashenin* (Ukrainian cossack) had said, 'Tsar Dimitry is alive; he declared himself in Zaporozh'e, and from Zaporozh'e [*ataman*] Sagadachnoi has sent him to the king.'[22]

Not everyone remembered the Time of Troubles with nostalgia, however. In 1625 a priest who was attacked by a cossack said to him, 'You son of a bitch, it's not the old days when you manufactured tsars and raided, beating up decent folks like me'; and he added that it was likely that because of cossack banditry, 'a tsar will appear again in *ukraina*'.[23] Also in 1625 the post official (*yamskoi prikazchik*) Vas'ka Igolkin recalled how, 'when the rogue was at Kaluga' the peasants of Shatskii district had assembled and had said, 'Let us get together and elect ourselves a tsar.' In response to this, the courier (*yamshchik*) Kuz'ka Antonov retorted, 'It was because of those damned tsars whom we peasants elected for ourselves during the internecine war that the land was laid waste.'[24] These comments are revealing, suggesting as they do that pretenders were widely acknowledged to have been 'manufactured' or 'elected' by their supporters.

There are no clear cases of pretence within Russia itself in the period between 1614 and the death of Michael Romanov in 1645. Tsar Michael's government, however, was pathologically fearful of the appearance of new pretenders, and assiduously investigated many seemingly innocent people who were suspected of *lèse-majesté*. In 1625, for example, a musketeer was beaten and imprisoned for saying when drunk that he had ridden in a borrowed sledge 'like a Grand Prince'.[25] In 1629 an investigation was held into the case of a prison guard who was accused by one of his prisoners of saying, 'I have a beard like the tsar's.'[26] The cases in which individuals were accused of calling themselves tsars or tsareviches seem to have been equally trivial. A certain Bogdashko Rezanov was accused of calling himself a tsar's son,[27] and on another occasion the inn-keeper (*kabatskii otkupshchik*) Ivashka Perfil'ev allegedly called himself the sovereign's brother.[28] In November 1624 a peasant was investigated on the basis of claims that he had said, 'When I was living in the village of Mishneva in Serpeiskii district, I was a tsar in those days.'[29] In October 1629 the prisoner Savinko Vasil'ev was accused by a fellow prisoner of having said, 'Now I am living in poverty in prison,

[21] *Ibid.*, no. 22, pp. 19–22.
[22] *Ibid.*, no. 236, p. 428.
[23] *Ibid.*, no. 20, pp. 17–18.
[24] *Ibid.*, no. 325, pp. 583–6.
[25] *Ibid.*, no. 18, pp. 15–16.
[26] *Ibid.*, no. 43, pp. 49–50.
[27] *Ibid.*, no. 32, pp. 41–2.
[28] *Ibid.*, no. 68, pp. 124–6.
[29] *Ibid.*, no. 26, pp. 27–8.

but when I get out of jail, I shall be tsar over you peasants.'[30] And the monk Seliverst Romanov was accused in January 1630 of calling himself tsar of the monks and peasants.[31] When interrogated by the authorities, these 'pretenders' usually denied making any claims to royal status, or maintained that they had been drunk at the time and could not remember what they had said.[32]

The reign of Tsar Michael's son, Aleksei, provides an interesting example of 'pretenders' who were allegedly elected by their fellow peasants. In March 1666 the Tver' landowner N. B. Pushkin accused the peasants of two of his villages of having committed high treason ('sovereign's word and deed'). Pushkin alleged that on the Saturday of Shrove Week the peasants had chosen one of their number as their leader, and had created a disturbance by marching about with banners and drums and rifles. Witnesses for the prosecution claimed that the peasants had given their chosen leader, Mit'ka Demidov, the title of 'tsar', and had carried him through the village of Vasil'evskoe on a litter, with a funnel on his head. In the neighbouring village of Mikhailovskoe, Mit'ka's place had been taken by a certain Pershka Yakovlev. Pershka had ordered another peasant to be birched, whereupon the intended victim had begged to be spared, crying out, 'Have mercy, Sire.' The official investigation showed that the suspicious incident was little more than a variant of the traditional Shrovetide procession. The festive symbol, a sheaf of straw tied to a pole, was carried at the front of the procession, together with the special fermented boiled milk (varenets) which was part of the ritual Shrovetide fare. The banners turned out to be old clothes tied to poles; and their weapons – the peasants claimed – were merely sticks. The villagers admitted that they had called Mit'ka their ataman and Pershka their voevoda, but they denied that they had called either of them 'tsar' or 'sire'. Everyone had been drinking, the peasants explained, and they had had to carry Mit'ka and Pershka aloft, because they had been too drunk to walk unaided. The case went all the way to the boyar duma in Moscow, which found the main charges unproven. But the peasants were found guilty of causing an affray. Mit'ka and Pershka were mutilated, each losing two fingers from his right hand; they were also sentenced to be flogged with the knout and exiled to Siberia with their families, as were those who had carried them aloft; and the other villagers who had participated in the procession were birched.[33]

[30] *Ibid.*, no. 52, pp. 63–6.
[31] *Ibid.*, no. 203, pp. 354–9.
[32] *Ibid.*, no. 26, pp. 27–8; no. 32, pp. 41–2; no. 52, pp. 63–6; no. 68, pp. 124–6; no. 203, pp. 354–9. L. V. Cherepnin regarded these cases as genuine examples of pretence (Cherepnin, ' "Smuta" ', p. 104); A. M. Panchenko views them, more realistically, as 'curiosities' (Panchenko, *Russkaya kul'tura*, pp. 21–2).
[33] Polosin, ' "Igra v tsarya" ', pp. 59–62.

Scholars have disagreed in their interpretation of this incident. The historian Ivan Polosin, who first drew attention to the case, concluded that although no treason was involved, the behaviour of the Tver' peasants was not entirely innocent politically: they were 'playing at tsar', in a drunken game based on the 'manufacture' of tsars by peasants and cossacks during the Time of Troubles.[34] Later scholars, however, have claimed that the episode represents a Russian example of the Western European practice of electing 'carnival kings' at Shrovetide.[35] There is, however, no evidence that the election of mock tsars was part of an indigenous Russian Shrovetide tradition. But in so far as 'carnivalesque' elements (mummery, travesty and play-acting) were inherent both in Shrovetide rituals and in pretence, it was highly appropriate that *samozvanchestvo* should be recalled at this particular time of year.

A similar case, to which Polosin also drew attention, had occurred earlier in the century in a very different social milieu. In 1620 four princes from the Shakhovskoi family were sentenced to death for an incident in which one of their number, Prince Matvei Fedorovich Shakhovskoi, was addressed by his brothers as 'tsar', and Prince Matvei in turn referred to them as 'boyars'. The death sentences were commuted to thirteen years imprisonment; but even this was a gross over-reaction by the government to what was clearly a drunken prank, albeit one which may have contained a consciously parodic reference to the Time of Troubles.[36]

By the time of the death of Michael Romanov in 1645, the new dynasty appeared to have acquired a degree of legitimacy and acceptance. Certainly popular unrest in the reign of Aleksei Mikhailovich assumed the form primarily of 'rebellions in the name of the tsar'; that is, discontent with government policies was directed against his advisers rather than against the tsar himself. In the 'salt riots' and other urban revolts of 1648–50, the insurgents petitioned Tsar Aleksei to remove corrupt boyars and officials.[37] The 'copper riot' in Moscow on 25 July 1662 was also directed against the 'traitor boyars', who were accused of dealings with the Polish king as well as corruption and debasement of the coinage.[38]

Even the most significant popular uprising of the later seventeenth century, the Razin revolt of 1669–71, assumed the form of a 'rebellion in the name of the tsar'. In March 1670 Razin called on his cossack followers to 'go from

[34] *Ibid.*, pp. 62–3.
[35] Belkin, *Russkie skomorokhi*, p. 157; Uspenskii, 'Tsar' i samozvanets', pp. 207–9; Likhachev, Panchenko and Ponyrko, *Smekh v drevnei Rusi*, p. 196.
[36] *RIB*, vol. 9, pp. 529, 550–1; Polosin, ' "Igra v tsarya" ', pp. 62–3; Uspenskii, 'Tsar' i samozvanets', pp. 207–8.
[37] Chistov, *Russkie narodnye*, pp. 70–8; Chistyakova, *Gorodskie vosstaniya*; Pokrovskii, *Tomsk, 1648–1649 gg.*
[38] Buganov, *Moskovskoe vosstanie 1662 g.*

the Don to the Volga, and from the Volga go to Russia against the sovereign's enemies and traitors, to remove from the Muscovite state the traitor boyars and the counsellors and governors and officials in the towns'.[39] Later in the year, however, it was claimed that the rebels were accompanied by the Tsarevich Aleksei Alekseevich, Tsar Aleksei's eldest son, who had died in January 1670 at the age of 16. The disgraced patriarch Nikon was also said to be with the cossacks, and the tsarevich and the patriarch supposedly travelled incognito on barges covered with red and black velvet respectively. It is not clear whether there really were pretenders in Razin's camp who played the roles of Aleksei Alekseevich and Nikon. Some have suggested that the 'tsarevich' was a young Kabardinian, Prince Andrei Cherkasskii, who had been taken prisoner by the rebels; others have speculated that he was Maksim Osipov, one of Razin's cossack *atamans*. At first Razin asserted that the tsarevich was accompanying them on the orders of the tsar; but later the rebels were said to have sworn an oath of loyalty to Tsarevich Aleksei. But it seems unlikely that Razin planned to put 'Tsarevich Aleksei' on the throne to replace his father; the pretender's role was simply to help the cossacks to rescue the tsar from the clutches of the 'traitor boyars'.[40]

In 1671, after the suppression of the cossack revolt and the execution of Razin, a young man claiming to be Tsarevich Aleksei was arrested in Toropets, in north-west Russia. He turned out to be Ivan Alekseevich Kleopin, the adopted son of a nobleman from Novgorod. In spite of evidence that he was mentally deranged, Kleopin was tortured and hanged.[41] Two years later, a youth aged about fifteen appeared in Zaporozh'e, in the company of Ivan Miyuska, one of Razin's *atamans*. The lad claimed to be Tsarevich Simeon, another son of Tsar Aleksei, who had died in 1669 at the age of three (the real Simeon would therefore have been only seven years old in 1673). As proof of his royal origin he displayed 'signs' on his body: red birthmarks on his shoulder in the form of a royal crown, a double-headed eagle, and a moon and a star. The pretender's cossack patrons claimed that Tsarevich Simeon had fled from Moscow after a quarrel with his maternal grandfather, the boyar Il'ya Danilovich Miloslavskii. Miloslavskii had boxed the boy's ears, whereupon Simeon had run to his mother to complain, angrily declaring that if he ever became tsar he would kill all the boyars, starting with Miloslavskii. The tsaritsa had been furious with her son, and ordered an official to poison him. This man, however, had a choirboy poisoned in his stead, and organised the tsarevich's escape. Simeon wandered far and wide, and even participated

---

[39] *Krest'yanskaya voina pod predvoditel'stvom Stepana Razina*, vol. 1, p. 235.
[40] Chistov, *Russkie narodnye*, pp. 78–85; Indova, Preobrazhenskii and Tikhonov, 'Lozungi i trebovaniya', p. 245.
[41] Chistov, *Russkie narodnye*, p. 85.

incognito in the Razin revolt, before fleeing to Zaporozh'e with *ataman* Miyuska.[42]

The Zaporozhian cossacks eventually agreed to send the pretender to Moscow, where he was interrogated before the boyar duma. He turned out to be a Pole, Simeon Ivanovich Andreev or Vorob'ev, whose father claimed kinship with the Vishnevetskiis. He had been sold into slavery, but had escaped and joined the Don cossacks. There he had met Miyuska, who had taken him to Zaporozh'e and persuaded him to call himself Tsarevich Simeon. Under torture, the pretender admitted that the cossacks' aim had been to gather troops to invade Muscovy and kill the boyars. As soon as he had made his confession, Vorob'ev was executed on Red Square. This pretender, like Razin's Tsarevich Aleksei, does not seem to have planned to overthrow the tsar, but simply wanted to attack the boyars: he even sent a letter from Zaporozh'e to his 'father', Tsar Aleksei, in which he begged to be allowed to fall at his feet, and assured him of the loyalty of the cossack host.[43]

After the execution of Tsarevich Simeon in 1674, no further pretenders were reported in Russia until the early eighteenth century, when a series of *samozvantsy* claimed to be Tsarevich Aleksei Petrovich, the eldest son of Peter the Great. After Peter's death in 1725 the complex struggles for the succession created a conducive climate for pretence, and Philip Longworth has counted 'no fewer than forty-four' pretenders in eighteenth-century Russia. The great majority of these were of lower-class origin; but although Longworth suggests that most of them were would-be leaders of peasant revolts, few succeeded in achieving much popular support. The greatest concentration of pretenders – twenty-six, in Longworth's estimation – occurred in the reign of Catherine II ('the Great'). Of these, no less than sixteen claimed to be Catherine's murdered husband, Peter III.[44] The most successful False Peter was the Don cossack, Emel'yan Pugachev, who headed the vast cossack-peasant rebellion of 1773–4.

[42] Solov'ev, *Istoriya Rossii*, vol. 6, pp. 457–64.
[43] *Ibid.*, pp. 471–3; Chistov, *Russkie narodnye*, pp. 85–7.
[44] Longworth, 'The Pretender Phenomenon'.

Conclusion

The pretenders of the Time of Troubles: a comparative analysis

The Russian pretenders of the Time of Troubles appeared at a time of dynastic crisis. The death of Tsar Fedor in 1598 created a fertile soil for pretence, and the series of false Dimitrys challenged rulers whose legitimacy was questionable: Boris Godunov and his son Fedor; Vasilii Shuiskii; and the Polish prince Władysław. By asserting claims to belong to the old dynasty, the pretenders appealed to the traditional principle of hereditary succession, in contrast to the various types of election that had brought their opponents to the throne.

Elsewhere in fifteenth- and sixteenth-century Europe, too, pretenders appeared against the background of dynastic crisis and the dubious legitimacy of the current ruler. Lambert Simnel and Perkin Warbeck challenged the Tudor King Henry VII's right to the throne by claiming to be legitimist princes of the house of York. The Moldavian pretenders Ivan Podkova and Alexander maintained that they were the brothers of Ivan Voda, who had led a national uprising against the Turks in 1574; they opposed Peter the Lame, the Turkish nominee who had replaced Ivan Voda on the throne. The false Don Sebastians challenged the succession of Philip II of Spain to the Portuguese throne.[1] Other sixteenth-century pretenders opposed rulers of a different religious persuasion: William Featherstone, the false Edward VI, appeared in the reign of the Catholic Mary Tudor; François de La Ramée, who claimed to be the son of Charles IX of France, was a 'true' Catholic rival to the recently converted Henri IV.[2]

Dynastic crisis in itself, however, was not a sufficient cause for the appearance of a pretender. The availability of an appropriate 'prototype' was also relevant. If he had survived, Tsarevich Dimitry of Uglich would have been fifteen years old at the time of Tsar Fedor's death, and in spite of his technical illegitimacy he would have had the strongest claim to the throne. If an impos-

---

[1] For references to studies of these pretenders, see Introduction.
[2] Bercé, *Le roi caché*, pp. 144–85, 365–7.

tor were to take advantage of the crisis of political legitimacy created by the accession of Boris Godunov, the identity of Dimitry of Uglich was the obvious one for him to choose. In England, 'legitimist' prototypes for pretence had been available at the time of Henry VII's accession to the throne: Edward, Earl of Warwick, was ten years old in 1485, and Richard of York, had he lived, would have been twelve. Lambert Simnel and Perkin Warbeck respectively were to take the names of these two princes.

Of all the identities adopted by the pretenders of the Time of Troubles, that of Dimitry of Uglich was the most popular and the most persistent. Tsarevich Dimitry served as the prototype for the First, Second and Third False Dimitrys of 1603–6, 1607–10 and 1611–12 respectively, as well as for Michael Molchanov's half-hearted pretence in 1606–7. The other *samozvantsy* of the early seventeenth century also claimed to be scions of the old dynasty. But there were no real historical prototypes for any of these pretenders, who adopted the identities of fictional descendants of Ivan the Terrible rather than those of Ivan's two real sons who reached adulthood. Ivan Ivanovich and Fedor Ivanovich, who had died at the ages of twenty-seven and forty-one respectively, would both have been around fifty at the time of Vasilii Shuiskii's accession. But it was Dimitry of Uglich – a tsarevich supposedly hidden in childhood – who provided the model on which the later pretenders apparently based their choice of identity. It was obviously easier for a pretender to claim to be a tsarevich concealed at birth than to provide a convincing impersonation of a familiar historical figure. But the age of the prototype appears to have been an important consideration in its own right. The pretenders who challenged the right of Philip of Spain to the Portuguese throne chose to claim the identity of Don Sebastian, who had died at the age of 24, rather than that of his elderly uncle and immediate successor, Cardinal Henrique. Yves-Marie Bercé notes that pretenders must be young, to embody innocence and hope for the future; and, at a more mundane level, youthful pretenders are probably more malleable by their backers than older men.[3]

The circumstances of the prototype's death might also be pertinent. The mysterious deaths of the princes in the Tower, and the rumoured murder of Edward of Warwick, led to wishful thinking about their escape, which may have influenced the appearance of pretenders. The body of Don Sebastian could not at first be found on the battlefield of Alcazarquivir, and doubts about the identity of the corpse that was buried as his gave rise to the belief that he had not died. Similarly, the obscure circumstances of Tsarevich Dimitry's death at Uglich provided a basis for the pretender's tale of a substitute victim. And after the murder of the First False Dimitry in May 1606, rumours

---

[3] *Ibid.*, pp. 341–2; cf. p. 127.

that he had escaped death were encouraged by suspicions about the body that was publicly displayed.

The Russian pretenders sought to justify their claims in various ways. According to the story that the First False Dimitry told Prince Adam Vishnevetskii in Lithuania, another boy had been put in Dimitry's bed by his tutor, and was killed in the tsarevich's place; the real Dimitry escaped and was brought up in secrecy by a nobleman, before fleeing to Poland. The Second False Dimitry, in his proclamation to Smolensk of April 1608, claimed that a German had been killed in his stead, while he himself had escaped to Lithuania. Tsarevich Peter-Ileika was said to have been replaced at birth by a baby girl who became Tsarevna Feodosiya.

According to K. V. Chistov, these tales, with their recurring motifs of the substitution and concealment of royal victims, were derived from the 'popular socio-utopian legends about returning tsar(evich)-deliverers' that he regards as a distinctive genre of folklore. But, as Chistov himself recognises, such motifs are not unique to folklore: rumours about the switching and hiding of heirs are a common part of the dynastic politics of any hereditary monarchy or aristocracy.[4] Outside Russia, too, the motif of the concealment of the true heir was employed by pretenders in order to justify their claims. Perkin Warbeck, the false Richard of York, told his patron, Isabella of Castile, that after the murder of his elder brother he 'had been delivered to a gentleman who had received orders to destroy him, but who, taking pity on his innocence, had preserved his life and . . . sent him away under the care of two persons, who were at once his jailors and governors'.[5]

Far from constituting evidence of 'socio-utopian legends', the pretenders' stories represented attempts to provide rational or scientific explanations of how the true heir had escaped death. As such, they were generally crude and unconvincing, but they demonstrate that the pretenders found it necessary to try to persuade their prospective subjects (and their foreign patrons) of their royal identity. 'Recognition' of the pretenders by people who claimed to have known the prototype also served this purpose: the First False Dimitry was recognised in Lithuania by men who allegedly knew Dimitry of Uglich, and the Second False Dimitry was recognised at Starodub by Zarutskii. The acknowledgement of the First False Dimitry by Marfa Nagaya, the mother of Dimitry of Uglich, played an important part in establishing his credibility, as did Marina Mniszech's acceptance of the Second False Dimitry as her husband.

Successful pretence, of course, requires the availability of a willing actor. It is difficult, however, to make any comments about the psychology of the

[4] Chistov, *Russkie narodnye*, p. 229.
[5] Pollard, ed., *The Reign of Henry VII*, vol. 1, no. 68, p. 95.

pretenders of the Time of Troubles, since the true identities of the great majority of them are either unknown or are the subject of conflicting evidence and continuing controversy. Yves-Marie Bercé suggests that pretenders are often young men who have suffered an identity crisis, perhaps because they were bastards or foundlings; and that some may suffer from a type of paranoid delirium.[6] Given the deficiencies of the sources, it is virtually impossible to reach any conclusions about the personalities and motives of the Russian pretenders. Those who made their false claims to royal identity on their own initiative may well have been psychologically disturbed; but in other cases, where they were groomed for their role by political conspirators, no particular personality type need be expected.

The sources do, however, contain some information about the social origins of the *samozvantsy*. The most convincing explanation of the identity of the First False Dimitry is the 'traditional' view that he was Grisha Otrep'ev, a young monk of petty noble origin who had served as a scribe at the Patriarch's court. The background of the Second False Dimitry probably lay in the lower clergy; and the Third False Dimitry was apparently of similar background. Thus all three of these pretenders were literate, and all had experience of clerical life. Since they had all subsequently defected from the Church, we may reasonably attribute to them a degree of disaffection with Orthodox Christianity that might have predisposed them to the blasphemous act of falsely claiming the sacred status of a tsar. Contemporaries condemned pretenders for their heterodox beliefs. The First False Dimitry was accused of being a heretic and a necromancer; the Second False Dimitry was said to be a secret Jew; and Michael Molchanov, the reluctant pretender of 1606–7, allegedly shared the First False Dimitry's interest in black magic.

If the False Dimitrys were recruited from the petty nobility or from the clerical estate, all of the other pretenders of the Time of Troubles belonged to the lower classes of Russian society. The confession of Tsarevich Peter-Ileika provides us with the fullest biographical details of any pretender: the illegitimate son of a tradesman's wife, orphaned at an early age, he led an itinerant life before becoming a service cossack. Peter-the-Bear's background was similar (if we assume that his fictional biography contains some genuine elements of autobiography). Biographical details of the other minor pretenders are more sparse. The Astrakhan' tsareviches were said to include a 'boyar's man' and a 'ploughing peasant', and the pretenders from the *pol'skie yurty* were probably all cossacks. Since most cossacks were fugitives who had abandoned their former family and neighbourhood ties on fleeing to the

---

[6] Bercé, *Le roi caché*, pp. 339–45.

steppe, the assumption of a false identity may have been psychologically and practically easier for them than for members of more settled communities.

Most pretenders appeared either on the periphery of Muscovy, or beyond its frontiers. The First False Dimitry, having been unsuccessful in his initial attempts to gain credibility for his claims in Russia, travelled to Poland–Lithuania, obtained military backing there, and launched his campaign for the throne through the Seversk lands, the south-west borderland of Russia. Michael Molchanov fled from Moscow to Sambor, in Poland, where he remained in hiding. The Second False Dimitry first appeared in Lithuanian Belorussia, before crossing the Russian frontier and recruiting military support in Starodub, in the Seversk district. The geographical base of the Third False Dimitry lay in the north-west, especially in the towns of Ivangorod and Pskov.

The cossack tsareviches, of course, came from the river basins of the southern steppe. Tsarevich Peter-Ileika appeared first among the Terek cossacks, and gained additional support from the Volga cossacks on his journey upriver towards Moscow. Astrakhan' produced Tsareviches Ivan Augustus, Lavrentii and Osinovik, as well as the rumoured false Dimitry of 1612. It also provided the main base of support for Zarutskii and the infant Tsarevich Ivan Dimitrievich in 1613–14. The sources consistently associate Tsarevich Fedor Fedorovich with the Don cossacks; and the Second False Dimitry asserted that Tsareviches Klementii, Savelii, Semion, Vasilii, Eroshka, Gavrilka and Martinka – as well as Peter and Fedor – came from the *pol'skie yurty*, the cossack settlements on the steppe.

The appearance of cossack pretenders on the periphery of Russia is not surprising, since cossacks more or less by definition were inhabitants of the southern frontiers. The other pretenders may have chosen their spots from tactical considerations: border towns were furthest from the centre of power; and such towns, especially those that had only recently been incorporated into Russia, might be regarded as having a shaky loyalty towards Moscow. Frontier regions also provided convenient points from which to recruit military assistance from abroad; and several pretenders, of course, actually began their campaigns from beyond the Russian border. The first two False Dimitrys obtained military support from Poland–Lithuania; and the Third False Dimitry attempted to acquire assistance from Charles IX of Sweden. Zarutskii tried to obtain aid from Persia for Tsarevich Ivan Dimitrievich, and also made a bid for support from the Turkish sultan. Pretence thus provided a pretext for the intervention of foreign powers in Russian affairs. A similar pattern can be found elsewhere. Lambert Simnel rallied support in Ireland before crossing to England; and Perkin Warbeck acquired backing in Ireland, France, Flanders and Scotland. The false Don Sebastian of 1594 appeared in

Madrigal, in Spain; the Sebastian of 1598 staked his claim in Venice. Some of the Moldavian pretenders – who provide the closest parallel to the cossack 'tsareviches' in Russia – obtained support in Ukraine from the Zaporozhian cossacks.

The backing they received from abroad often served to discredit the pretenders in the eyes of their opponents. Patriarch Iov condemned the First False Dimitry as the tool of King Sigismund, who planned to replace Orthodoxy in Russia with Roman Catholicism. The pretender's choice of a Polish wife – who was 'inherited' by subsequent False Dimitrys – further damaged the image of 'Tsar Dimitry' as a Russian national hero, and Shuiskii found it easy to condemn the Second False Dimitry as a Polish creation. When it suited them, however, the pretenders did not hesitate to pose as Russian patriots and as defenders of Orthodoxy against 'heretical' foreign invaders. On more than one occasion after his flight from Tushino the Second False Dimitry attempted to rally opposition to the Catholic Poles; and when the Third False Dimitry was invited to Pskov, he was apparently regarded as a symbol of the town's resistance to the Swedish army of intervention.

The circumstances in which pretenders appear can vary considerably. Sometimes they are groomed by representatives of vested political interests, as seems to have been the case with Lambert Simnel and Perkin Warbeck. Grisha Otrep'ev, however, initially acted independently, and acquired influential patrons only after his flight to the *Rzeczpospolita*. Within Russia he gained his initial support from the population of the south-west frontier, where disaffection with Moscow was strong. The boyars did not come over to his side until after Tsar Boris's sudden death in April 1605, when they decided that the pretender was preferable to the young Fedor Godunov.

This interpretation of events has implications for our broader understanding of the causes and nature of the Time of Troubles. In S. F. Platonov's classic analysis, the First False Dimitry was the creation of the boyars from the outset, their chosen weapon in the struggle against Boris Godunov for the succession. In the view of some other historians, the pretence was set up by the Poles, and the origins of the Troubles lay in the external relations of Muscovy with the *Rzeczpospolita*. But since there are no grounds to suppose that the First False Dimitry was prepared for his role by any powerful faction in either Russia or Poland, we must conclude that Otrep'ev's own actions were crucial to the development of the Troubles. If it had not been for his individual initiative, it is unlikely that the diffuse dissatisfaction with Boris Godunov within Russia would have assumed the form of open armed opposition. The phenomenon of pretence, therefore, played a major part in the outbreak of the civil war; and it continued to influence its course and character.

If the First False Dimitry acted at first on his own initiative, many of the subsequent pretenders of the Time of Troubles had backers from the outset.

The Second False Dimitry was probably part of an organised conspiracy at the time of his first appearance in Belorussia. And Ileika Muromets was 'chosen' as Tsarevich Peter by his fellow cossacks. The success of the First False Dimitry had demonstrated the effectiveness of pretence as a political device, and there was clearly a 'copy-cat' element in the claims of the later impostors. Elsewhere, too, pretenders tended to occur in clusters. Lambert Simnel's adventure of 1486–7 was followed by that of Perkin Warbeck in 1491–7. At least six separate pretenders appeared in Moldavia in 1577–83; and there were four Don Sebastians of Portugal between 1584 and 1603.

Pretenders, even in Russia, did not always attract mass support. When they did so, it usually reflected the depth not only of the crisis of political legitimacy, but also of a broader social and economic crisis. In early seventeenth-century Russia, the end of the old dynasty was followed by an unprecedented natural catastrophe that exacerbated existing social and political tensions. Such a situation had much in common with the preconditions for millenarian and messianic movements in medieval Europe. Yves-Marie Bercé has suggested that pretenders were often able to take advantage of a mood of popular expectation of the return of a 'hidden king', which he characterises as a type of secular messianism.[7] These expectations were influenced by existing political myths concerning monarchs. One common motif was that of the ruler who voluntarily surrendered his power in order to live in obscurity, doing penance for his own sins, or expiating those of his people. The abdication of the Emperor Charles V provided a historical example of the 'saintly prince in the monastery'; and the image of the 'sacrificial king' undoubtedly influenced the expectations of the return of Don Sebastian that preceded the appearance of the first Portuguese pretender. In its later manifestations, Sebastianism was influenced by another myth, that of the 'sleeping king', such as Arthur or Charlemagne, who would return to save his people in their hour of need.[8]

Russian tradition, however, did not know legends of this kind. In so far, however, as all such myths about returning rulers appear to have been based on analogies with Christ and his resurrection and Second Coming,[9] the sacralisation of the monarchy in sixteenth-century Russia facilitated a messianic image of the 'true tsar'. Boris Godunov's innocent child victim, later to be canonised as a *strastoterpets* – a martyr or 'passion-sufferer' in the imitation of Christ – was an appropriate candidate for the role of royal saviour. The popular belief that Tsarevich Dimitry had been miraculously resurrected from

[7] *Ibid.*, p. 312.
[8] *Ibid.*, p. 264 and *passim*.
[9] *Ibid.*, pp. 228–9, 313–17. The Christian myth, in its turn, was of course based on pagan concepts of rulers sacrificed and reborn in fertility cults.

the grave appears to reflect a view of the monarch as a Christ-like figure, the 'sun of righteousness' who would rise again. The notion of the charismatic nature of the tsar may have contributed to the popular enthusiasm aroused by the appearance of pretenders. There certainly seem to have been elements of millenarianism or messianism in the euphoric welcome provided by their earliest supporters for the first two False Dimitrys; and the fanaticism of many of their adherents, who were apparently willing to undergo horrific deaths by torture rather than renounce their belief in the 'true tsar', is also more reminiscent of a religious mentality than of a purely secular political allegiance.

For some Russians, the quasi-religious notions associated with the monarchy may have been more important than any 'scientific' evidence in determining the credibility or otherwise of the pretenders. But for the majority, one suspects, 'proofs' of any kind were relatively unimportant in themselves; they were significant only in so far as they enabled people to rationalise and justify their acceptance of a pretender. Many of their followers must have known perfectly well that the pretenders were not descendants of Ivan the Terrible. Russians of all classes supported the first two False Dimitrys because they thought it in their interest to do so; and the main attraction of pretence lay in its capacity to legitimise opposition to unpopular rulers and their policies. In the latter stages of the Time of Troubles, in particular – from the Tushino period onwards – cynical motives of self-interest appear to have predominated over the genuine faith and idealism that were often present earlier.

Examples of the phenomenon of pretence can, as we have seen, be found in many countries other than Russia in the early modern period. But it was only in Russia, during the Time of Troubles, that pretenders succeeded in obtaining such widespread support from all sectors of society. The First False Dimitry achieved an unparalleled success in obtaining the throne and occupying it for nearly a year; and during the Tushino period the Second False Dimitry was almost as successful. It is very striking that Russians at this time were apparently unable to legitimise revolt except through the ideology of hereditary monarchy. Religious and moral values, which were commonly invoked in the West as a standard against which the actions of rulers should be judged, played no significant part in Russian risings. The subordination of the Orthodox Church to the state in the sixteenth century, and its counterpart, the sacralisation of the monarchy, had deprived Muscovites of any source of legitimacy other than the tsar. In this intellectual and cultural context, 'rebellion in the name of the tsar' was virtually the only possible form of revolt; and at a time of uncertainty about the succession, pretence was a very convenient device for the justification of rebellion.

Pretence and popular monarchism

Some Soviet scholars depicted pretenders as 'peasant tsars' and as leaders of anti-feudal uprisings. But the evidence suggests that this was true only to a limited extent in the Time of Troubles. One of the strengths of pretence as a political weapon was its capacity to mobilise members of all social groups under the banner of the 'true tsar'; and support for 'Tsar Dimitry' was always socially heterogeneous. The First False Dimitry, in particular, made no special attempt to attract the lower classes of Russian society, and – contrary to K. V. Chistov's hypothesis concerning Tsarevich Dimitry as the reformer-hero of a 'popular socio-utopian legend' – there is no evidence that peasants and bondsmen supported him in the expectation that he would abolish serfdom and slavery.

Like members of other social groups, however, the peasants and slaves doubtless hoped for some kind of reward for the loyalty that they displayed towards the 'true tsar'. But when he came to the throne the First False Dimitry did little to satisfy the aspirations of his lower-class supporters. Their response was governed by the 'popular monarchist' notions that had developed in the sixteenth century. Dimitry's disappointed followers did not criticise the tsar himself, but concluded that he had become a hostage of the boyars. The complaint of the Terek cossacks that 'the tsar wanted to reward us, but the wicked boyars intercepted our reward' is a classic statement of the belief, characteristic of later 'rebels in the name of the tsar', that it is only the undue influence of his noble advisers that prevents the benevolent ruler from favouring his humble subjects.

Tsarevich Peter's pretence appears to have been devised by the cossacks in order to impart status to their bid to persuade Dimitry to grant them the reward they felt that they deserved. Later in the century, Sten'ka Razin's cossacks were to claim that they were accompanied by Tsarevich Aleksei Alekseevich in their campaign to free the tsar from the clutches of his wicked boyars. The relationship of Razin's 'Tsarevich Aleksei' to Tsar Aleksei was analogous in many ways to that of 'Tsarevich Peter' to Tsar Dimitry. (The fact that Aleksei was a real tsar, while 'Tsar Dimitry' was himself an impostor; and that Tsarevich Aleksei had a historical prototype while Tsarevich Peter did not, should not obscure the parallel.) In both cases, the rebels equipped themselves with pretender-tsareviches whose role was to help rescue the reigning tsar from the pernicious influence of his boyars.

Similarly, within the broad movement 'in the name of Tsar Dimitry' in 1606–8, there appeared a multitude of petty cossack pretenders whose actions were apparently modelled on those of Tsarevich Peter. All of these pretenders seem to have acted in the name of Tsar Dimitry, and they all claimed, as he did, to belong to the old dynasty. Their pretence served to provide legitimacy for the actions of the various bands of cossacks who supported Dimitry's cause against Vasilii Shuiskii, and to bolster their prestige: the cossacks hoped to be rewarded by Tsar Dimitry for the services they had rendered to his long-lost relatives who had supposedly sought refuge in their midst. It seems unlikely that their followers believed that these pretenders really were scions of the old dynasty; indeed, the humble origin of the false tsareviches may have constituted part of their appeal to the cossacks, whose political ideal combined the concept of the 'good tsar' with allegiance to an *ataman* elected from their own ranks.

For the devotees of popular monarchism, the overthrow of the First False Dimitry in May 1606 served to confirm his reputation as a victim of the 'evil boyars', and hence, by implication, as a champion of the common people. The 'rebels in the name of Tsar Dimitry' of 1606–7 included a disproportion-ate number of members of the lower classes – peasants, cossacks and slaves. Their claim that Dimitry was still alive enabled the insurgents not only to depict Tsar Vasilii as a usurper but also to condemn Shuiskii's noble sup-porters as traitors to the true tsar. The absence of a False Dimitry in Russia in 1606–7 meant that the rebels were free to act in accordance with their own notions of Tsar Dimitry's wishes and intentions, and their actions were very revealing of what 'popular monarchism' meant in practice. Bolotnikov appealed to the slaves in Moscow to kill their masters and appropriate their property, calling on them as loyal subjects to punish traitors to the tsar; Tsare-vich Peter ordered cruel public executions of Shuiskii's commanders at Putivl'; and Tsarevich Ivan Augustus executed high-born traitors to Tsar Dimitry on the lower Volga. Within the framework of the broader movement to restore 'Tsar Dimitry' to the throne, the rhetoric of a campaign against treason served to legitimise attacks by the poor and the dispossessed on the rich and the privileged. The agents of the absent Dimitry sanctioned the pun-ishment of 'traitor-boyars', and promised to reward the ordinary people for their loyalty to the true tsar by permitting them to expropriate the traitors and to share in the redistribution of their property.

The actions of the 'rebels in the name of Tsar Dimitry' in 1606–7 suggest that their perception of Dimitry had much in common with the popular image of his supposed father, Ivan the Terrible, whose persecution of his noble opponents had helped to reinforce popular notions of the 'good tsar'. Russian folklore described Ivan's cruel executions of boyars who had not only plotted against him, but were also exploiters and oppressors of the people; the rebel-lion in Dimitry's name enabled the insurgents to brand their social antagonists as 'traitor-boyars' and put them to death. Even the forms assumed by these executions were similar to those of Ivan's reign of terror: the victims were publicly humiliated and subjected to rituals of mockery and abuse.

But even at this stage of the Time of Troubles, with its acute social con-flicts, there was no evidence of a radical 'anti-feudal' programme on the part of the insurgents. Individual peasants and slaves may have acquired their freedom by joining Dimitry's armies as cossacks, but serfdom and slavery were not abolished. Individual boyars and officials were put to death and expropriated, but others were promoted in their stead, and the hierarchy of ranks and titles was preserved. Even the cossack tsareviches Peter-Ileika and Ivan Augustus had their titled courtiers, Prince Grigorii Shakhovskoi and Prince Ivan Khvorostinin. And the institution of the monarchy itself remained, of course, though 'Tsar Dimitry' at this time was little more than a phantom. The aims and aspirations of the ordinary people in the Time of Troubles seem to have involved not the anti-feudal revolution envisaged by Soviet historians, but rather the notion – very typical of the popular culture of early modern Europe – of a 'world turned upside down', in which the system itself did not change, but only the relative places of individuals within it.[10]

Soviet scholars characterised popular hopes in the 'good tsar' as 'monarchist illusions' that reflected the naivety of the peasantry. But the people were not prepared to believe against all common-sense evidence that 'Tsar Dimitry' was their benefactor. The short reign of the First False Dimitry, and the absence of a pretender in Russia during the Bolotnikov revolt, enabled 'naive monarchism' to persist for some time. But the reality of life under the Second False Dimitry and his successors led eventually to disillusionment.

To the extent that he inherited many of the supporters of Bolotnikov and Tsarevich Peter, the Second False Dimitry was obliged initially to live up to their image of 'Tsar Dimitry' as the scourge of the 'traitor-boyars'. In the winter of 1607–8 he made a bid for popular support by confiscating the lands of noble 'traitors' and reallocating them to their slaves who entered his service. Soon, however, as he attempted to broaden his social base, he modified his image, denouncing the cossack pretenders as impostors, and condemning the violence that had been employed by Tsarevich Peter. For a time, the Second False Dimitry succeeded in attracting support from the same broad spectrum of society that had backed the First False Dimitry in 1605. But the Tushino boyars never really trusted him, and they were quick to transfer their allegiance to Władysław when the opportunity arose. Although the 'little people' of Pskov remained loyal to the Second False Dimitry, elsewhere the rapacious activities of his cossacks and his Polish mercenaries cost the pretender the support not only of the nobility, but also of many of the peasants and townspeople who had earlier rallied to his cause.

Even after the death of the Second False Dimitry at Kaluga, the name of Tsar Dimitry was still able to mobilise some support. The Third False Dimitry

---

[10] Burke, *Popular Culture*, p. 176.

was initially welcomed by the townspeople of Pskov as their protector against the Swedes, but the activities of his cossacks soon led to dissatisfaction. Zarutskii, too, was at first received with enthusiasm in Astrakhan', but the citizens became rapidly disillusioned with his brutal rule. In the end, the indiscriminate looting and killing committed by their cossack followers served to discredit pretenders in the eyes of most ordinary people. Many of the rebel leaders of the Time of Troubles were deposed by their former supporters. The people of Pskov overthrew the Third False Dimitry, and the inhabitants of Astrakhan' revolted against Zarutskii.

By the end of the Time of Troubles, even the cossacks had abandoned the device of pretence. The Romanovs' claim to the throne (based as it was on their connection by marriage with the old dynasty) was little stronger than Boris Godunov's had been; but Michael's election achieved widespread acceptance largely as a result of the exhaustion of all sectors of society by a decade of civil strife and foreign intervention. After the Time of Troubles, pretence as a political weapon was eschewed by the elites of Russian society, who recalled the social upheaval of 1606–7 with fear and revulsion. The popular monarchist notion of a tsar who shared their hatred of the boyars persisted among the ordinary people, but the Romanov dynasty was soon recognised as legitimate, and the ideal of the 'good tsar' was again embodied in the reigning monarch. Pretenders recurred sporadically, but they failed to obtain mass support, and 'rebellion in the name of the tsar' remained the predominant form of popular revolt in the seventeenth and eighteenth centuries. Pretence played only a minor part in the Razin rebellion of 1669–71, and no pretender appeared in the Bulavin rising of 1707–8. It was only in the reign of Catherine the Great – a blatant usurper who, like Boris Godunov, was widely considered to be responsible for the death of the legitimate ruler – that popular protest was again to be associated with pretence, in the great Pugachev rising.

Bibliography

Afanas'ev, A. N., comp., *Narodnye russkie skazki*, 3 vols., Moscow, 1957.

Akty Istoricheskie, sobrannye i izdavaemye Arkheograficheskoyu Kommissieyu, vols. 1–3, St Petersburg, 1841.

Akty, sobrannye v bibliotekakh i arkhivakh Rossiiskoi imperii Arkheograficheskoyu ekspeditsieyu Imperatorskoi Akademii nauk, vols. 2–3, St Petersburg, 1836.

Aleksandrenko, V. N., comp., 'Materialy po Smutnomu vremeni na Rusi XVIIv.', *Starina i Novizna*, kn. 14, Moscow, 1911, pp. 185–453, 524–45.

Alexander, M. *The First of the Tudors: a Study of Henry VII and his Reign*, London: Croom Helm, 1981.

Bakhtin, Mikhail, *Rabelais and his World*, trans. H. Iswolsky, Cambridge, MA: MIT Press, 1968.

Barbour, Philip L. *Dimitry, Called the Pretender, Tsar and Great Prince of All Russia, 1605–1606*, London: Macmillan, 1967.

Baretstsi, Baretstso [Barezzo Barezzi], 'Povestvovanie o Dimitrii Samozvantse', in Obolenskii, comp., *Inostrannye sochineniya*, vol. 4.

Belkin, A. A. *Russkie skomorokhi*, Moscow, 1975.

Belokurov, S. A., ed., *Razryadnye zapisi za Smutnoe vremya (7113–7121 gg.)*, in *ChIOIDR*, vol. 221, 1907, kn. 2, otd. I, pp. 1–80.

Bercé, Yves-Marie, *Le roi caché. Sauveurs et imposteurs. Mythes politiques populaires dans l'Europe moderne*, Paris: Fayard, 1990.

Bernadskii, V. N. 'Konets Zarutskogo', *Uchenye zapiski Leningradskogo Gosudarstvennogo Pedagogicheskogo Instituta*, vol. 19, 1939, pp. 83–130.

Berry, L. E. and Crummey, R. O., eds., *Rude and Barbarous Kingdom: Russia in the Accounts of Sixteenth-Century English Voyagers*, Madison, WI: University of Wisconsin Press, 1968.

Berthold-Ignace de Sainte-Anne, Révérend Père, *Histoire de l'Etablissement de la Mission de Perse par les Pères Carmes-Déchaussés (de l'année 1604 à 1612)*, Brussels, 1885.

Bestuzhev-Ryumin, K. N. 'Obzor sobytii ot smerti Tsarya Ioanna Vasil'evicha do izbraniya na prestol Mikhaila Feodorovicha Romanova', *ZhMNP*, chast' 252, otd. 2 (July–Aug. 1887), pp. 49–112.

Pis'ma K.N. Bestuzheva-Ryumina o smutnom vremeni. Pod red. A. O. Kruglova, St Petersburg, 1898.

Bitsyn, N. 'Pravda o Lzhedimitriii', *Den'*, no. 51/2, 19 Dec. 1864, pp. 9–21.

Bodyanskii, O. 'O poiskakh moikh v Poznanskoi Publichnoi Biblioteke', *ChIOIDR*, 1846, no. 1. otd. 1, pp. 1–45.

Bond, E. A., ed., *Russia at the Close of the Sixteenth Century*, London: Hakluyt Society, 1856.

Brody, Ervin C. *The Demetrius Legend and its Literary Treatment in the Age of the Baroque*, Rutherford, NJ: Fairleigh Dickenson University Press, 1972.

Brooks, Mary E. *A King for Portugal: the Madrigal Conspiracy, 1594–5*, Madison, WI: University of Wisconsin Press, 1964.

Buganov, V. I. *Moskovskoe vosstanie 1662 g.*, Moscow, 1964.

Burke, Peter, *Popular Culture in Early Modern Europe*, London: Temple Smith, 1978.

Bushkovitch, Paul, *Religion and Society in Russia: the Sixteenth and Seventeenth Centuries*, New York: Oxford University Press, 1992.

Bussov [Bussow], Konrad, *Moskovskaya khronika, 1584–1613*, Moscow, 1961.

Buturlin, D. *Istoriya smutnogo vremeni v Rossii v nachale XVII veka*, 3 vols., St Petersburg, 1839–46.

The Cambridge History of Poland, from the Origins to Sobieski (to 1696), eds. W. F. Reddaway, J. H. Penson, O. Halecki, R. Dyboski, Cambridge: Cambridge University Press, 1950.

Cherepnin, L.V. ' "Smuta" i istoriografiya XVII v.', *Istoricheskie Zapiski*, vol. 14, 1945, pp. 81–128.

Cherniavsky, Michael, *Tsar and People; Studies in Russian Myths*, New York: Yale University Press, 1961.

Chistov, K. V. *Russkie narodnye sotsial'no-utopicheskie legendy XVII–XIX vv.*, Moscow, 1967.

Chistyakova, E. V. *Gorodskie vosstaniya v Rossii v pervoi polovine XVII veka (30–40-e gody)*, Voronezh, 1975.

A Chronicle of the Carmelites in Persia, and the Papal Mission of the XVIIth and XVIIIth Centuries, 2 vols., London: Eyre and Spottiswoode, 1939.

Cohn, Norman, *The Pursuit of the Millennium. Revolutionary Millenarians and Mystical Anarchists of the Middle Ages*, London: Secker and Warburg, 1957.

Crummey, Robert, *The Formation of Muscovy, 1304–1613*, London: Longman, 1987.

D'Antas, M. M. *Les faux Don Sébastien*, Paris: 1866.

Davies, Norman, *God's Playground. A History of Poland*, vol. 1, *The Origins to 1795*, Oxford: Clarendon Press, 1981.

Davis, Natalie Zemon, *The Return of Martin Guerre*, Harmondsworth: Penguin Books, 1985.

De-Tu, Yakov [Jacques De Thou], 'Skazaniya De-Tu o Dimitrii Samozvantse', in Ustryalov, ed., *Skazaniya sovremennikov*, part 1, pp. 319–53.

'Dnevnik Mariny Mnishek i Pol'skikh poslov s 1605 goda po 1608', in Ustryalov, ed., *Skazaniya sovremennikov*, part 2, pp. 125–262.

Dobrotvorskii, A. 'Kto byl pervyi Lzhedmitrii?', *Vestnik Zapadnoi Rossii*, vol. ii, kn. 6, ii, pp. 93–105; vol. iii, kn. 7, ii, pp. 1–14. Vil'na, 1866.

'Svedenie o knige Vasiliya Velikogo, prinadlezhashchei nyne Zagorovskomu Monastyryu i sokhranivsheisya na nei nadpisi', *Zapiski Imperatorskogo Arkheologicheskogo Obshchestva*, vol. VIII, St Petersburg: 1856. Perechen' zasedanii ... za 1853 i 1854 gg., pp. 56–73.

Dolinin, N. P. 'K izucheniyu inostrannykh istochnikov o krest'yanskom vosstanii pod rukovodstvom I. I. Bolotnikova, 1606–1607 gg.', in *Mezhdunarodnye svyazi*, pp. 462–90.

'K razboru versii pravitel'stva Mikhaila Romanova o I. M. Zarutskom', *Arkheograficheskii ezhegodnik za 1962 g.*, Moscow, 1962, pp. 138–46.

Podmoskovnye polki (kazatskie 'tabory') v natsional'no-osvoboditel'nom dvizhenii 1611–1612 gg., Khar'kov, 1958.

Dunning, Chester S.L. 'R. G. Skrynnikov, the Time of Troubles, and the "First Peasant War" in Russia', *Russian Review*, vol. 50, Jan. 1991, pp. 71–81.

Dvortsovye razryady, vol. 1, St Petersburg, 1850.

Dyamentowski, W., 'Dyariusz Waclawa Dyamentowskiego (1605–1609)', in Hirschberg, ed., *Polska a Moskwa*.

Elliott, J. H. *Europe Divided, 1559–1598*, Glasgow: Fontana, 1968.

Emerson, Caryl, *Boris Godunov; Transpositions of a Russian Theme*, Bloomington: Indiana University Press, 1986.

Field, Daniel, *Rebels in the Name of the Tsar*, Boston: Houghton Mifflin, 1976.

Figarovskii, V. A. 'Krest'yanskoe vosstanie 1614–1615 gg.', *Istoricheskie Zapiski*, vol. 73, 1963, pp. 194–218.

Fletcher, Giles, *Of the Russe Commonwealth*, London, 1591. Facsimile edn, with introduction by Richard Pipes, Cambridge, MA: Harvard University Press, 1966.

Florencio del Niño Jesus, P. Fr. *A Persia (1604–1609)* (Biblioteca Carmelitano-Teresiana de Misiones, Tomo II), Pamplona, 1929.

En Persia (1608–1624) (Biblioteca Carmelitano-Teresiana de Misiones, Tomo III), Pamplona, 1930.

Forsten, G. V. 'Politika Shvetsii v Smutnoe vremya', *ZhMNP*, part 261, Feb. 1889, pp. 325–49; part 265, Oct. 1889, pp. 185–213; part 266, Nov. 1889, pp. 17–65.

Frantsev, V. A., ed. 'Istoricheskie i pravdivoe povestvovanie o tom, kak moskovskii knyaz' Dimitrii Ioannovich dostig otsovskogo prestola', *Starina i Novizna*, kn. XV, St Petersburg, 1911.

Gairdner, James, *Henry the Seventh*, London: Macmillan, 1899.

History of the Life and Reign of Richard the Third, to which is added the Story of Perkin Warbeck from Original Documents, Cambridge: Cambridge University Press, 1898. Reprinted Bath: Cedric Chivers, 1975.

Gerkman [Herckman], E. 'Istoricheskoe povestvovanie o vazhneishikh smutakh v gosudarstve Russkom, vinovnikom kotorykh byl tsarevich knyaz' Dimitrii Ivanovich, nespravedlivo nazyvaemyi samozvantsem', in *Skazaniya Massy i Gerkmana*.

Girshberg [Hirschberg], A. *Marina Mnishek*, Moscow, 1908.

Gnevushev, A. M., ed. 'Akty vremeni pravleniya Tsarya Vasiliya Shuiskogo (1606g. 19 maya–17 iyuliya 1610 g.)' (Smutnoe vremya Moskovskogo gosudarstva 1604–1613, vyp. 2), in *ChIOIDR*, 1915, kn. 2 (vol. 253), Moscow, 1915.

Golobutskii, V. A. *Zaporozhskoe kazachestvo*, Kiev, 1957.

Golubtsov, I. A. ' "Izmena" smol'nyan pri B. Godunove i "izvet" Varlaama', *Uchenye zapiski Instituta istorii RANION*, kn. 5, Moscow, 1928, pp. 218–51.

Graham, Hugh F. 'A Note on the Identity of False Dmitrii I', *Canadian Slavonic Papers*, vol. 30, no. 3, Sept. 1988, pp. 357–62.

Grey, Ian, *Boris Godunov, the Tragic Tsar*, London: Hodder and Stoughton, 1973.

Hakluyt, Richard, *Voyages*, vols. 1–2, London: Dent, Everyman's Library Edition, 1967–73.

Hamel, J. *England and Russia*, London: R. Bentley, 1854. Reprinted London: Frank Cass & Co. Ltd., 1968.

Hellie, Richard, *Enserfment and Military Change in Muscovy*, Chicago: University of Chicago Press, 1971.

Slavery in Russia, 1450–1725, Chicago: University of Chicago Press, 1982.

Hirschberg, A. *Dymitr Samozwaniec*, Lwów, 1898.

Hirschberg, A., ed., *Polska a Moskwa w pierwszej polowie wieku XVII*, Lwów, 1901.

Howe, Sonia E., ed., *The False Dmitri. A Russian Romance and Tragedy Described by British Eye-Witnesses, 1604–1612*, London: Williams and Norgate, 1916. Reprinted Cambridge: Oriental Research Partners, 1972.

Ikonnikov, V. S. 'Kto byl pervyi samozvanets?', *Kievskie Universitetskie Izvestiya*, Kiev, 1865, no. 2, ii, pp. 22–56; no. 3, ii, pp. 1–12.

Ilovaiskii, D. *Smutnoe vremya moskovskogo gosudarstva*, Moscow, 1894. Reprinted The Hague: Mouton, 1970.

Indova, E. I., Preobrazhenskii, A. A. and Tikhonov, Yu. A., 'Lozungi i trebovaniya uchastnikov krest'yanskikh voin v Rossii XVII–XVIII vv.', in *Krest'yanskie voiny v Rossii*, pp. 239–69.

Istoricheskie pesni XIII–XVI vekov, eds. B. N. Putilov and B. M. Dobrovol'skii, Moscow, 1960.

Istoricheskie pesni XVII veka, eds. O. B. Alekseeva et al., Moscow, 1966.

Istoricheskie svyazi narodov SSSR i Rumynii v XV – nachale XVIII v.: dokumenty i materialy v trekh tomakh, vol. 1, *1408–1632*, Moscow, 1965.

'Iz L'vovskogo arkhiva knyazya Sapegi', *Russkii Arkhiv*, 1910, no. 11, pp. 338–52.

Kaiser, Daniel H. 'Symbol and Ritual in the Marriages of Ivan IV', in R. Hellie, ed., *Ivan the Terrible; a Quarcentenary Celebration of his Death, Russian History/ Histoire Russe*, vol. 14, nos. 1–4, 1987, pp. 247–62.

Karamzin, N. M. *Istoriya Gosudarstva Rossiiskogo*, 5th edn, vol. 3 (tt. IX–XII), St Petersburg, 1843. Reprinted Moscow, 1989.

Keenan, Edward L. 'Muscovite Political Folkways', *Russian Review*, vol. 45, 1986, pp. 115–81.

Khvalibog [Chwalibog], Pan, 'Donesenie G. Khvaliboga o lozhnoi smerti Lzhedimitriya', *Vremennik Imperatorskogo Moskovskogo Obshchestva Istorii i Drevnostei Rossiiskikh*, kn. 23, Moscow, 1855, iii (smes'), pp. 3–5.

Klein, V., ed., *Delo rozysknoe 1591 godu pro ubivstvo tsarevicha Dimitriya Ivanovicha na Ugliche*, Moscow, 1913.

Klier, John D. *Russia Gathers her Jews: the Origins of the Jewish Question in Russia, 1772–1825*, DeKalb, IL: Illinois University Press, 1986.

Klyuchevskii, V. O. *Sochineniya*, vol. 3 (Kurs russkoi istorii, ch. 3), Moscow, 1957.

Kognowicki, K. *Życia Sapiehów y listy od monarchów*, 3 vols., Vilno and Warsaw, 1790–91.

Kollmann, Nancy Shields, *Kinship and Politics. The Making of the Muscovite Political System, 1345–1547*, Stanford, CA: Stanford University Press, 1987.

Koretskii, V. I. 'Aktovye i letopisnye materialy o vosstanii Bolotnikova', *Sovetskie Arkhivy*, no. 5, 1976, pp. 45–58.

Formirovanie krepostnogo prava i pervaya krest'yanskaya voina v Rossii, Moscow, 1975.

'Iz istorii krest'yanskoi voiny v Rossii nachala XVII veka', *Voprosy Istorii*, no. 3, 1959, pp. 118–37.

'O formirovanii I.I. Bolotnikova kak vozhdya krest'yanskogo vosstaniya', in *Krest'yanskie voiny v Rossii*, pp. 122–47.

Zakreposhchenie krest'yan i klassovaya bor'ba v Rossii vo vtoroi polovine XVI v., Moscow, 1970.

Koretskii, V. I., ed. 'Novoe ob I. I. Bolotnikove', *Sovetskie Arkhivy*, no. 4, 1967, pp. 100–3.

Koretskii, V. I., Solov'eva, T. B. and Stanislavskii, A. L., eds. 'Dokumenty pervoi krest'yanskoi voiny v Rossii', *Sovetskie Arkhivy*, no. 1, 1982, pp. 34–41.

Kostomarov, N. I. *Kto byl pervyi Lzhedimitrii? Istoricheskoe issledovanie*, St Petersburg, 1864.

Kostomarov, N. *Smutnoe vremya Moskovskogo gosudarstva*, St Petersburg, 1904.

Krest'yanskaya voina pod predvoditel'stvom Stepana Razina. Sbornik dokumentov, 4 vols. (in 5), Moscow, 1954–76.

Krest'yanskie voiny v Rossii XVII–XVIII vekov; problemy, poiski, resheniya, Moscow, 1974.

Kusheva, E. 'Iz istorii publitsistiki Smutnogo vremeni XVII v.', *Uchenye Zapiski Saratovskogo gosudarstvennogo universiteta*, vol. 5, Saratov, 1926, pp. 21–97.

Likhachev, D. S., ed., *Puteshestviya russkikh poslov XVI–XVII vv. Stateinye spiski*, Moscow, 1954.

Likhachev, D. S., Panchenko, A. M. and Ponyrko, N. V. *Smekh v drevnei Rusi*, Leningrad, 1984.

Longworth, Philip, *The Cossacks*, London: Sphere Books, 1971.

'The Pretender Phenomenon in Eighteenth-Century Russia', *Past and Present*, no. 66, February 1975, pp. 61–83.

'Timoshka Ankidinov', in *The Modern Encyclopedia of Russian and Soviet History*, ed. Joseph L. Wiecynski, vol. 2, Gulf Breeze, FL: Academic International Press, 1976, pp. 2–4.

Lyubavskii, M. 'Litovskii Kantsler Lev Sapega o sobytiyakh Smutnogo Vremeni', *ChIOIDR*, 1901, kn. 2 (vol. 197), pp. 1–16.

Lyubomirov, P. G. *Ocherk istorii nizhegorodskogo opolcheniya 1611–1613 gg.* Revised edn, Moscow, 1939.

Lyubomirov, P. G., ed., 'Novye materialy dlya istorii Smutnogo vremeni', *Uchenye Zapiski Saratovskogo gosudarstvennogo universiteta*, vol. 5, Saratov, 1926, pp. 102–5.

Makovskii, D. P. *Pervaya krest'yanskaya voina v Rossii*, Smolensk, 1967.

Mal'tsev, S., ed., 'Barkulabovskaya letopis'', in *Arkheograficheskii Ezhegodnik za 1960 god*, Moscow, 1962, pp. 291–320.

Marchocki, M. *Historya wojny moskiewskiej*, Poznań, 1841.

Margeret, Jacques, *The Russian Empire and Grand Duchy of Muscovy*. Trans. and ed. Chester S. L. Dunning, Pittsburgh: University of Pittsburgh Press, 1983.

Maskevich [Maskiewicz], S. 'Dnevnik Maskevicha, 1594–1621', in Ustryalov, ed., *Skazaniya sovremennikov*, part 2, pp. 1–124.

Massa, I. 'Kratkoe povestvovanie o nachale i proiskhozhdenii sovremennykh voin i smut v Moskovii', in *Skazaniya Massy i Gerkmana*.

A Short History of the Beginnings and Origins of These Present Wars in Moscow under the Reign of Various Sovereigns down to the year 1610, translated and with an introduction by G. Edward Orchard, Toronto: University of Toronto Press, 1983.

Mérimée, Prosper, *Episode de l'histoire de Russie; les faux Démétrius*, 2nd edn, Paris: Calman-Levy, 1889.

Mezhdunarodnye svyazi Rossii do XVII v. Sbornik statei, Moscow, 1961.

Mokhov, N. A. *Ocherki istorii moldavsko-russko-ukrainskikh svyazei (s drevneishikh vremen do nachala XIX veka)*, Kishinev, 1961.

Morozov, B. N. 'Vazhnyi dokument po istorii vosstaniya Bolotnikova', *Istoriya SSSR*, no. 2, 1985, pp. 162–8.

Moshin, V. A. 'Iz istorii snoshenii Rimskoi kurii, Rossii i yuzhnykh slavyan', in *Mezhdunarodnye svyazi*, pp. 491–511.

Moskovskaya tragediya, ili razskaz o zhizni i smerti Dimitriya. Perevod s latinskogo A. Braudo i I. Rostsiusa, St Petersburg, 1901.

Nazarov, V. D. 'K istorii nachal'nogo perioda pervoi Krest'yanskoi voiny v Rossii', in *Genezis i razvitie feodalizma v Rossii*, Leningrad, 1985, pp. 184–200.

'K nachal'noi istorii vosstaniya pod predvoditel'stvom I. I. Bolotnikova', in *Gorod i gorozhane Rossii v XVII – pervoi polovine XIX v. Sbornik statei*, Moscow, 1991, pp. 148–67.

Nazarov, V. D. and Florya, B. N. 'Krest'yanskoe vosstanie pod predvoditel'stvom I. I. Bolotnikova i Rech' Pospolitaya', in *Krest'yanskie voiny v Rossii*, pp. 326–52.

Nemoevskii [Niemojewski], S. 'Zapiski Stanislava Nemoevskogo (1606–1608)', in A. A. Titov, ed., *Rukopisi slavyanskie i russkie, prinadlezhashchie I. A. Vakhromeevu*, vyp. 6, Moscow, 1907.

Novgorodskie letopisi. Izdanie Arkheograficheskoi Kommissii, St Petersburg, 1879.

Novombergskii, N., ed., *Slovo i delo gosudarevy. (Protsessy do izdaniya Ulozheniya Alekseya Mikhailovicha 1649 goda)*, vol. 1, Moscow, 1911.

Novyi letopisets, sostavlennyi v tsarstvovanie Mikhaila Feodorovicha, izdan po spisku knyazya Obolenskogo, Moscow, 1853.

Nowakowski, F. K., ed., *Źródła do dziejów Polski*, 2 vols., Berlin, 1841.

Oakley, Stewart P. *War and Peace in the Baltic, 1560–1790*, London: Routledge, 1992.

Obolenskii, K. M., comp. *Inostrannye sochineniya i akty, otnosyashchiesya do Rossii*, 4 vols., Moscow, 1847–8.

'O krest'yanskoi voine v Russkom gosudarstve v nachale XVII veka. (Obzor diskussii)', *Voprosy Istorii*, no. 5, 1961, pp. 102–20.

'O nekotorykh spornykh voprosakh klassovoi bor'by v Russkom gosudarstve XVII veka', *Voprosy Istorii*, no. 12, 1958, pp. 204–8.

Ovchinnikov, R. V. 'Nekotorye voprosy krest'yanskoi voiny nachala XVII veka v Rossii', *Voprosy Istorii*, no. 7, 1959, pp. 69–83.

'O nachal'nom periode vosstaniya I. Bolotnikova', *Voprosy Istorii*, no. 1, 1955, pp. 116–200.

Paerle [Peyerle], G. 'Zapiski Paerle, o puteshestvii iz Krakova v Moskvu i obratno, s 19 marta 1606 goda po 15 dekabrya 1608', in Ustryalov, ed., *Skazaniya sovremennikov*, part 1, pp. 153–234.

Palitsyn, A. *Skazanie Avraamiya Palitsyna*, Moscow, 1955.

Pamyatniki literatury Drevnei Rusi: konets XVI – nachalo XVII vekov, comp. L. A. Dmitriev and D. S. Likhachev, Moscow, 1987.

Panchenko, A. M. *Russkaya kul'tura v kanun petrovskikh reform*, Leningrad, 1984.

Panchenko, A. M. and Uspenskii, B. A. 'Ivan Groznyi i Petr Velikii: kontseptsii pervogo monarkha. Stat'ya pervaya', *Trudy Otdela Drevne-Russkoi Literatury*, vol. 37, Leningrad, 1983, pp. 54–78.

Paneyakh, V. M. *Kholopstvo v XVI – nachale XVII v.*, Leningrad, 1975.

Parker, Geoffrey, *Europe in Crisis, 1598–1648*, Glasgow: Fontana, 1979.

Pavlov, A. P. *Gosudarev dvor i politicheskaya bor′ba pri Borise Godunove (1584–1605 gg.)*, St Petersburg, 1992.

Perrie, Maureen, 'Female Rule, Popular Monarchism and Pretence in Tsarist Russia', unpublished paper presented to the Conference on Women in the History of the Russian Empire, Ohio, US, August 1988.

The Image of Ivan the Terrible in Russian Folklore, Cambridge: Cambridge University Press, 1987.

'Jerome Horsey's Account of the Events of May 1591', *Oxford Slavonic Papers*, new series, vol. 13, 1980, pp. 28–49.

'The Popular Image of Ivan the Terrible', *Slavonic and East European Review*, vol. 56, 1978, pp. 275–86.

' "Popular Socio-Utopian Legends" in the Time of Troubles', *Slavonic and East European Review*, vol. 60, 1982, pp. 223–43.

Petrei de Erlezunda, Petr [Peer Persson], *Istoriya o Velikom Knyazhestve Moskovskom*, Moscow, 1867.

Petrei, Petr [Peer Persson], *Relyatsiya Petra Petreya o Rossii nachala XVII v.*, Moscow, 1976.

Pierling, P. *Rome et Démétrius*, Paris, 1878.

La Russie et le Saint-Siège; Etudes Diplomatiques, vol. 3, Paris: Plon-Nourrit, 1910. Reprinted The Hague: Europe Printing, 1967.

Pirling [Pierling], P. *Istoricheskie stat′i i zametki*, St Petersburg, 1913.

Iz smutnogo vremeni; stat′i i zametki, St Petersburg, 1902.

'Nazvannyi Dimitrii i Adam Vishnevetskii', *Russkaya Starina*, Jan. 1904, pp. 123–8.

Platonov, S. F. *Boris Godunov, Tsar of Russia*, trans. L. Rex Pyles, with an introductory essay by J. T. Alexander, Gulf Breeze, FL: Academic International Press, 1972.

Drevnerusskie skazaniya i povesti o smutnom vremeni XVII veka, kak istoricheskii istochnik, 2nd edn, St Petersburg, 1913.

Ocherki po istorii smuty v Moskovskom gosudarstve XVI–XVII vv. (Pereizdanie), Moscow, 1937.

The Time of Troubles, trans. J. T. Alexander, Lawrence, KS: University of Kansas Press, 1970.

Pokrovskii, M. N. *Izbrannye proizvedeniya*, vols. 1–3, Moscow, 1966–7.

Pokrovskii, N. N. *Tomsk, 1648–1649 gg. Voevodskaya vlast′ i zemskie miry*, Novosibirsk, 1989.

Pollard, A. F., ed., *The Reign of Henry VII from Contemporary Sources*, 3 vols., London: University of London Historical Series, 1913–14.

Polnoe sobranie russkikh letopisei, vol. 4, St Petersburg, 1848; vol. 5, St Petersburg, 1851; vol. 14, St Petersburg, 1910, reprinted Moscow, 1965; vol. 32, Moscow, 1975; vol. 34, Moscow, 1978.

Polosin, I. I. ' "Igra v tsarya." (Otgoloski smuty v moskovskom bytu XVII v.)', *Izvestiya Tverskogo pedagogicheskogo instituta*, vyp. 1, Tver′, 1926, pp. 59–63.

Popov, A., ed., *Izbornik slavyanskikh i russkikh sochinenii i statei, vnesennykh v khronografy russkoi redaktsii*, Moscow, 1869.

Prochaska, A., ed., *Archiwum domu Sapiehów*, vol. 1, *Listy z lat 1575–1606*, Lwów, 1892.

Pskovskie letopisi, vol. 1, ed. A. Nasonov, Moscow, 1941. Reprinted The Hague: Slavica, 1967, vol. 2, ed. A. N. Nasonov, Moscow, 1955.

Ptashitskii, S. L. 'Despoty Zenovichi v kontse XVI i nachale XVII vekov', *Russkaya Starina*, vol. 21 (1878), pp. 125–38; vol. 22 (1878), pp. 503–11.

'Perepiska litovskogo kantslera L'va Ivanovicha Sapegi', *ZhMNP*, part 285, Jan. 1893, pp. 194–223.

Purchas, Samuel, *Purchas his Pilgrimage*, London, 1626.

Pyasetskii [Piasecki], P. *Materialy dlya epokhi smutnogo vremeni, izvlechennye iz raznykh avtorov*. *Khronika Pyasetskogo*, Warsaw, 1909.

Rosovetskii, S. K. 'Ustnaya proza XVI–XVII vv. ob Ivane Groznom – pravitele', *Russkii Fol'klor*, vol. 20, 1981, pp. 71–95.

Rowland, Daniel, 'Did Muscovite Literary Ideology Place Limits on the Power of the Tsar (1540s–1660s)?', *Russian Review*, vol. 49, 1990, pp. 125–55.

Russkaya Istoricheskaya Biblioteka, izdavaemaya Imperatorskoyu Arkheograficheskoyu Kommissieyu, vol. 1, 1872; vol. 9, 1884; vol. 13, 1892; vol. 16, 1897; vol. 18, 1898, St Petersburg.

Ryan, W. F. 'Aristotle and Pseudo-Aristotle in Kievan and Muscovite Russia', in Jill Kraye, W. F. Ryan and C. B. Schmitt, eds. *Pseudo-Aristotle in the Middle Ages*, London: Warburg Institute Surveys and Texts, vol. XI, 1986, pp. 97–109.

'The *Secreta Secretorum* and the Muscovite Autocracy', in W. F. Ryan and C. B. Schmitt, eds. *Pseudo-Aristotle, the 'Secret of Secrets': Sources and Influences*, London: Warburg Institute Surveys, vol. IX, 1982, pp. 114–23.

Sbornik Imperatorskogo Russkogo Istoricheskogo Obshchestva, vol. 137, Moscow, 1912.

Shaum, M. 'Tragoedia Demetrio-Moscovitica', in Obolenskii, comp., *Inostrannye sochineniya*, vol. 1.

[Shcherbatov, M. M.] *Kratkaya povest' o byvshikh v Rossii samozvantsakh*, St Petersburg, 1774.

Shepelev, I. S. 'Mesto i kharakter dvizheniya I. M. Zarutskogo v period krest'yanskoi voiny i pol'sko-shvedskoi interventsii (do ukhoda ego iz-pod Moskvy) 1606–1612 gg.', *Trudy Leningradskogo Otdeleniya Instituta Istorii AN SSSR*, vyp. 9, 1967, pp. 223–38.

Osvoboditel'naya i klassovaya bor'ba v Russkom gosudarstve v 1608–1610 gg., Pyatigorsk, 1957.

'Skazanie i povest', ezhe sodeyasya v Tsarstvuyushchem Grade, Moskve, i o Rastrige Grishke Otrep'eve, i o pokhozhdenii ego', *ChIOIDR*, 1847, no. 9, ii.

Skazaniya Massy i Gerkmana o smutnom vremeni v Rossii, St Petersburg, 1874.

Sklyar, I. M. 'O nachal'nom etape pervoi krest'yanskoi voiny v Rossii', *Voprosy Istorii*, 1960, no. 6, pp. 90–101.

Skrynnikov, R. G. *Boris Godunov*, Moscow, 1978.

Boris Godunov, ed. and trans. Hugh F. Graham, Gulf Breeze, FL: Academic International Press, 1982.

'Boris Godunov i tsarevich Dmitrii', in *Issledovaniya po sotsial'no-politicheskoi istorii Rossii* (Trudy Leningradskogo Otdeleniya Instituta Istorii SSSR AN SSSR, vyp. 12), 1971, pp. 182–97.

'The Civil War in Russia at the Beginning of the Seventeenth Century (1603–1607): its Character and Motive Forces', in L. Hughes, ed., *New Perspectives on Muscovite History*, London: Macmillan, 1993, pp. 61–79.

Ivan Groznyi, Moscow, 1975.

Minin i Pozharskii; khronika smutnogo vremeni, Moscow, 1981.

Rossiya nakanune 'smutnogo vremeni', 2nd edn, Moscow, 1985.

Rossiya posle oprichniny: ocherki politicheskoi i sotsial'noi istorii, Leningrad, 1975.

Rossiya v nachale XVII v. 'Smuta', Moscow, 1988.

Samozvantsy v Rossii v nachale XVII veka: Grigorii Otrep'ev, Novosibirsk, 1987.

Sibirskaya ekspeditsiya Ermaka, 2nd edn, Novosibirsk, 1986.

Smuta v Rossii v nachale XVII v. Ivan Bolotnikov, Leningrad, 1988.

Sotsial'no-politicheskaya bor'ba v russkom gosudarstve v nachale XVII veka, Leningrad, 1985.

'Spornye problemy vosstaniya Bolotnikova', *Istoriya SSSR*, 1989, no. 5, pp. 92–110.

The Time of Troubles: Russia in Crisis, 1604–1618, ed. and trans. Hugh F. Graham, Gulf Breeze, FL: Academic International Press, 1988.

Tsarstvo terrora, St Petersburg, 1992.

'V to smutnoe vremya . . .', *Nauka i religiya*, no. 1, 1988, pp. 44–8.

Smirnov, I. I. 'Kogda byl kaznen Ileika Muromets? (Neskol'ko khronologicheskikh sopostavlenii)', *Istoriya SSSR*, no. 4, 1968, pp. 108–19.

'K kharakteristike vnutrennei politiki Lzhedimitriya I', *Uchenye Zapiski Leningradskogo Gosudarstvennogo Universiteta*, Seriya Istoricheskikh Nauk, no. 19, 1938, pp. 186–207.

'O nekotorykh voprosakh bor'by klassov v russkom gosudarstve nachala XVII veka', *Voprosy Istorii*, no. 12, 1958, pp. 116–31.

Vosstanie Bolotnikova 1606–1607, 2nd edn, Leningrad, 1951.

Smith, R. E. F. *The Enserfment of the Russian Peasantry*, Cambridge: Cambridge University Press, 1968.

Smith, Sir Thomas, *Sir Thomas Smithes Voiage and Entertainment in Rushia*, London, 1605.

Sobieski, W. *Szkice Historyczne*, Warsaw, 1904.

Sobranie Gosudarstvennykh Gramot i Dogovorov, khranyashchikhsya v Gosudarstvennoi Kollegii Inostrannykh Del, vols. 2–3, Moscow, 1819–22.

Solov'ev, S. M. *Istoriya Rossii s drevneishikh vremen*, vols. 4–6, Moscow, 1960–1.

'Zametki o samozvantsakh v Rossii', *Russkii Arkhiv*, god shestoi, Moscow, 1868, cols. 265–81.

Soloviev, S. M. *History of Russia*, vols. 14–15, ed. and trans. G. Edward Orchard. Gulf Breeze, FL: Academic International Press, 1988–9.

Stadnitskii [Stadnicki], M. 'Dnevnik Martyna Stadnitskogo', *Russkii Arkhiv*, 1906, kn. 6, vyp. 2, pp. 129–74, 177–222.

Stalin, I. V. 'Beseda s nemetskim pisatelem Emilem Lyudvigom, 13 dekabrya 1931 g.', in his *Sochineniya*, vol. 13, Moscow, 1951, pp. 104–23.

Stanislavskii, A. L. *Grazhdanskaya voina v Rossii XVIIv. Kazachestvo na perelome istorii*, Moscow, 1990.

Stanislavskii, A. L., ed. 'Novye dokumenty o vosstanii Bolotnikova', *Voprosy Istorii*, no. 7, 1981, pp. 74–83.

Stanislavskii, A. L. and Morozov, B. N., eds. 'Povest' o zemskom sobore 1613 goda', *Voprosy Istorii*, no. 5, 1985, pp. 89–96.

Suvorin, A. S. *O Dimitrii Samozvantse. Kriticheskie ocherki*, St Petersburg, 1906.

Tatishchev, V.N. *Istoriya Rossiiskaya*, vol. 6, Moscow, 1960.

Tikhomirov, M. N. 'Samozvanshchina', *Nedelya*, no. 1, 1964, pp. 20–21.

'Samozvanshchina', *Nauka i zhizn'*, no. 1, 1969, pp. 116–21.

Tikhomirov, M. N., ed. 'Novyi istochnik po istorii vosstaniya Bolotnikova', *Istoricheskii Arkhiv*, kn. VI, Moscow, 1951, pp. 81–130.

Tkhorzhevskii, S. I. *Narodnye volneniya pri pervykh Romanovykh*, Petrograd, 1924.

Troitskii, S. M. 'Samozvantsy v Rossii 17–18 vekov', *Voprosy Istorii*, no. 3, 1969, pp. 134–46.

Tyumenev, A. I. 'Peresmotr izvestii o smerti Tsarevicha Dimitriya', *ZhMNP*, new series, vol. 15, 1908, pp. 93–135, 323–59.

Uspenskii, B. A. 'Tsar' i samozvanets: samozvanchestvo v Rossii kak kul'turno-istoricheskii fenomen', in *Khudozhestvennyi yazyk srednevekov'ya*, Moscow, 1982, pp. 201–35.

Uspenskij, B. A. 'Tsar and Pretender; *samozvančestvo* or Royal Imposture in Russia as a Cultural-Historical Phenomenon', in Ju. M. Lotman and B. A. Uspenskij, *The Semiotics of Russian Culture*, ed. Ann Shukman, Ann Arbor: Michigan Slavic Contributions, 1984, pp. 259–92.

Ustryalov, N. G., ed. *Skazaniya sovremennikov o Dimitrii Samozvantse*, 3rd edn, St Petersburg, 1859.

'Utverzhdennaya gramota ob izbranii na Moskovskoe gosudarstvo Mikhaila Fedorovicha Romanova', *ChIOIDR*, vol. 218, 1906, otd. 1, pp. 1–110.

Veselovskii, N. I., ed. *Pamyatniki diplomaticheskikh i torgovykh snoshenii Moskovskoi Rusi s Persiei*, 3 vols., 1890–98 (*Trudy Vostochnogo Otdeleniya Imperatorskogo Russkogo Arkheologicheskogo Obshchestva*, vols. XX–XXII).

Veselovskii, S. B., ed. *Akty podmoskovnykh opolchenii i Zemskogo Sobora 1611–1613 gg.* (Smutnoe vremya Moskovskogo gosudarstva 1604–1613, vyp. 5), Moscow, 1911.

Vosstanie I. Bolotnikova; dokumenty i materialy, comp. A. I. Kopanev and A. G. Man'kov, Moscow, 1959.

Waliszewski, K. *La crise révolutionnaire, 1584–1614*, Paris, 1906.

Widekind, J. *Historia belli Sveco-Moscovitici decennalis*, Stockholm, 1672.

Worsley, Peter, *The Trumpet Shall Sound: a Study of 'Cargo' Cults in Melanesia*, London: Paladin, 1970.

Yakovleva, O. A. 'K istorii moskovskikh volnenii 1584 g.', *Zapiski NII pri Sovete Ministrov Mordovskoi ASSR (istoriya i arkheologiya)*, no. 9, Saransk, 1947, pp. 200–217.

Zabelin, I. *Minin i Pozharskii. Pryamye i krivye v Smutnoe Vremya*, Moscow, 1883.

Zakonodatel'nye akty russkogo gosudarstva vtoroi poloviny XVI – pervoi poloviny XVII veka, ed. N. E. Nosov, Leningrad, 1986.

Zguta, Russell *Russian Minstrels; a History of the 'Skomorokhi'*, Oxford: Clarendon Press, 1978.

Zhivov, V. M. and Uspenskii, B. A. 'Tsar' i bog. Semioticheskie aspekty sakralizatsii monarkha v Rossii', in *Yazyk kul'tury i problemy perevodimosti*, Moscow, 1987.

Zholkevskii [Żółkiewski], S. *Zapiski getmana Zholkevskogo o Moskovskoi voine*, 2nd edn, St Petersburg, 1871.

Zimin, A. A. 'I. I. Bolotnikov i padenie Tuly v 1607 g.', in *Krest'yanskie voiny v Rossii*, pp. 52–64.

'Nekotorye voprosy istorii krest'yanskoi voiny v Rossii v nachale XVII veka', *Voprosy Istorii*, no. 3, 1958, pp. 97–113.

'Smert' tsarevicha Dimitriya i Boris Godunov', *Voprosy Istorii*, no. 9, 1978, pp. 92–111.

V kanun groznykh potryasenii: predposylki pervoi krest'yanskoi voiny v Rossii, Moscow, 1986.

Index